HW

THE ROMANOVS

THE
ROMANOVS

The Rise and Fall of a Russian Dynasty

by IAN GREY

DAVID & CHARLES : *NEWTON ABBOT*

ISBN 0 7153 5371 3
First published 1970 in the United States of America
by Doubleday & Company Inc
First published 1971 in Great Britain
by David & Charles (Publishers) Limited
© 1970 by Ian Grey

Printed in Great Britain by
Redwood Press Limited Trowbridge and London
for David & Charles (Publishers) Limited
South Devon House   Newton Abbot
Devon

To my father

Preface

Of the dynasties which have ruled in past centuries, the Romanov dynasty is of outstanding interest and importance. It provides a fascinating variety of individual Autocrats, ranging from the great to the cruel and contemptible. It affords the contrast between Peter the Great and the puny Peter III, between the massive masculine sadist, Anna, and Elizabeth, the gay beauty who was a pleasure-loving libertine and yet possessed integrity. The reign of Catherine the Great, who was an even greater libertine, presented a splendor which rivaled that of Louis XIV of France. In Alexander I, whom Napoleon called "the Sphinx" and "the cunning Byzantine," the dynasty produced an enigma, who contrasts with his brother, the oppressive despot, Nicholas I.

The Romanov dynasty was, moreover, unique in that several of its Autocrats in their piety, and notwithstanding their faults, might be called good men. Tsars Mikhail, Alexei, Fedor, and Nicholas II belong to this group. All were deeply imbued with the teaching of the Orthodox Church, especially its precept of humility.

The personal characters of these gentle Autocrats are the more striking because they ruled over a country more barbaric in its customs and savage in its punishments than other countries of Europe. It is, indeed, a matter of surprise that their personal example and influence did not ameliorate the harshness of Russian life. One reason was that, apart from Tsar Alexei Mikhailovich, they were weak, self-effacing men, who belonged to the monastic world, and only an Autocrat cast in the heroic mold of Peter the Great could make an impact on the vast and troubled expanse of Russia.

The Romanovs are of exceptional importance because, enshrined by a profound and enduring mystique of autocratic power and dynastic continuity and commanding the loyalty and obedience of their people, they played the dominant role in Russia's history throughout the three centuries of their rule. For all Russians the Tsar-autocrat was the nation; it could not exist without him. They looked to him to rule and defend the nation and, since he was appointed by God, they expected of him both magnificence and magic. They retained until the twentieth century this exalted conception of the position and power of their Autocrats.

The Romanov Autocrats thus played a far more dominant role in the internal and external affairs of the Russian nation than their Western contemporaries played in their countries. Indeed, the extreme centralization of government and administration, as developed in Russia, concentrated the formulation and execution of policy in the hands of the Tsar. A further notable feature of Russia's history, distinguishing it from the experience of all other European nations, except perhaps Spain, was that every significant change and reform resulted from the initiative and power of the Autocrat. The history of Russia in the seventeenth, eighteenth, and nineteenth centuries is, in fact, inseparable from the history of the Romanov dynasty.

By the twentieth century the tsarist regime had become an anachronism. It had endured because Russians could envisage no other system that would ensure their unity and their defense against the aggression of neighboring powers. Defense was a matter of special importance to the Russian people. In every century they have experienced invasion and calamity on a vast scale; indeed, no country has a history more crowded with catastrophe and suffering. Against the background of this common experience the Russians have found strength and security in the rule of an Autocrat rather than of an oligarchy or more democratic systems. The regime might have evolved, nevertheless, as a constitutional monarchy. The First World War, the inadequacy of the last Tsar, and other factors combined to prevent this development, and the regime collapsed.

The fashion, current at present, of regarding Nicholas II as the epitome of the Romanovs and, because of his failure and personal tragedy, of referring to them as ill-fated mediocrities—"The Tragic Dynasty"—distorts history. Although a man of some noble qualities, Nicholas II was pathetic and inadequate as Autocrat and cannot be taken to represent a dynasty which included Alexei Mihailovich, Peter Alexeevich, Elizabeth Petrovna, and others who ruled positively.

In this study my purpose has been to portray each Autocrat as a person and to describe succinctly the policies and achievements of the reign. I recognize that it was bold to attempt so much in one volume. I hope, however, that I may have succeeded in conveying something of the striking variety of the dynasty and its importance.

Notes to each chapter, some giving sources of materials and of quotations, and others explanatory, will be found at the end of the volume.

vi

The notes and the short bibliography together set out the main sources and the studies consulted.

None of the systems of transliteration of the Cyrillic alphabet is entirely satisfactory. I have, however, followed with slight modification, the system adopted by the British Academy. Also, except where it would lead to confusion, I have retained the Russian forms of Christian names. I prefer Mikhail, Ivan, and Alexei to Michael, John, and Alexis, but since to use Pyotr in place of Peter or Ekaterina instead of Catherine would confuse many readers, I have used the Western form of these names.

The Russian or Julian calendar has been used throughout except where the date is followed by the letters N.S. (new style) indicating that the date is according to the Western or Gregorian calendar. The Russian calendar was ten days behind the Western calendar in the seventeenth century, eleven days in the eighteenth, twelve days in the nineteenth and thirteen days behind in the twentieth century.

To Mrs. Jakki Becker, who has typed so much of this book, and to Miss Helen Roy who made the index, I express my thanks. To my dear wife, Winsome, I am as always indebted for unwavering cooperation and support.

Contents

ix

CONTENTS

THE ROMANOVS

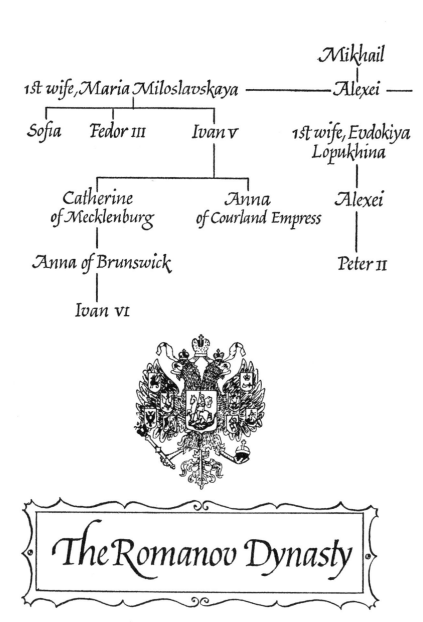

Mikhail
|
1st wife, Maria Miloslavskaya ———————— Alexei ———
| |
Sofia   Fedor III   Ivan V   1st wife, Evdokiya
| Lopukhina
| |
Catherine   Anna   Alexei
of Mecklenburg   of Courland Empress
| |
Anna of Brunswick   Peter II
|
Ivan VI

The Romanov Dynasty

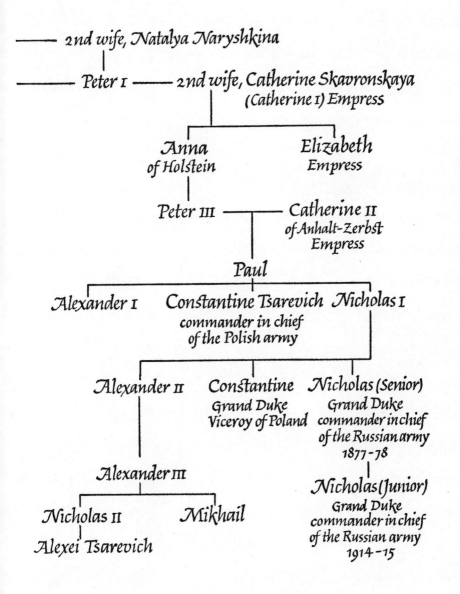

—— 2nd wife, Natalya Naryshkina

—— Peter I —— 2nd wife, Catherine Skavronskaya
(Catherine I) Empress

Anna
of Holstein

Elizabeth
Empress

Peter III —— Catherine II
of Anhalt-Zerbst
Empress

Paul

Alexander I   Constantine Tsarevich   Nicholas I
commander in chief
of the Polish army

Alexander II   Constantine   Nicholas (Senior)
Grand Duke   Grand Duke
Viceroy of Poland   commander in chief
of the Russian army
1877-78

Alexander III   Nicholas (Junior)
Grand Duke
commander in chief
of the Russian army
1914-15

Nicholas II   Mikhail

Alexei Tsarevich

Prologue

Early in 1613 chosen representatives of the Russian people began to arrive in Moscow by sledge and on horseback. All had faced severe hardships and dangers. Travel was an ordeal in the cold of midwinter. The great dangers were the bands of Cossacks, Tatars, Russian brigands, Poles, and Lithuanians, who ravaged the land, burning down villages, murdering, and plundering at will. The chosen men had nevertheless hastened to attend the Assembly of the Land (*Zemsky Sobor*). The meeting was of exceptional importance, for it had to elect a new Tsar.

This Assembly was the most representative that had yet met. Its members came not only from the great boyar families, the gentry and provincial nobility, but also from the townsmen and even the village peasantry. For three days they fasted and prayed, and then they proceeded to their momentous task. The first question was whether to elect a Tsar from among the contending foreign princes or to limit their choice to a Russian. The decision was prompt and unanimous that "the Lithuanian and Swedish Kings and their children, and others of foreign faith, and foreign powers occupying Muscovite territory, shall not be chosen . . ."[1]

All unanimity vanished, however, when they came to discuss who among the Russians should be Tsar. No man had emerged from the Time of Troubles as a national leader. The boyars who claimed position and power had contributed little to the national revival or to the defeat of the Poles and Swedes. Prince Pozharsky had led the second national militia, but was of mediocre ability and modest origins. The nation had been saved by the church, the gentry, the townsmen, and the Cossacks. But it was unthinkable that a Tsar could be chosen from those classes.

The Assembly split into rival factions, each intriguing in support of its own candidate, and agreement seemed remote. But then the representatives of the gentry, the townsmen, and the Cossacks began demanding Mikhail Romanov. A member of the gentry from Galich presented a paper in which he stated that Mikhail Romanov was closest by birth to the old dynasty and so should be elected Tsar. In the midst of the angry disputes, aroused by this proposal, the Ataman of the Don Cossacks advanced from the crowd and placed a written note on the table.

"What is this writing you have submitted, Ataman?" asked Prince Pozharsky.

"It is about the natural Tsar—Mikhail Fedorovich," replied the Ataman.[2]

Suddenly the Assembly had reached agreement. Without further debate Mikhail Fedorovich Romanov was elected Tsar. The decision then had to be confirmed by the people at large. Trusted envoys were dispatched to all towns. It is not known how they collected voices, but within a few days they began returning to Moscow and all reported the popular demand that Mikhail should be Tsar.

A sixteen-year-old boy, weak in health and showing no special abilities, Mikhail had not been chosen for any personal qualities. The powerful boyar families saw in his youth and weakness a guarantee that their privileges and power would be secure from attack by the Autocrat. But Mikhail's strongest claim to the throne was his link with the previous dynasty. His grandfather, Nikita Romanov, had been the brother of Anastasia, the first wife of Ivan the Terrible, and uncle of Tsar Fedor I, the last of the Rurik line. In Mikhail they saw a continuation of the old dynasty.

The Romanov family was not among the most ancient of the noble Muscovite families. It had originated from Lithuania or "the Prussian lands" whence its earliest members had arrived in Moscow in the fourteenth century. It had been the one untitled boyar family that had remained prominent in the following century when the titled provincial nobles had crowded to the court of Ivan III. But the Romanovs had won goodwill at court and among the people. Nikita Romanov was renowned for his efforts to moderate the severity of Ivan the Terrible. His six sons were also popular and in exiling them to distant parts of the country Boris Godunov had enhanced their popularity and made them appear as martyrs.

The Assembly of the Land, having proclaimed Mikhail, appointed a mission, headed by an archbishop, to petition him to accept the throne. No one knew where he was and only after a search was he found, taking refuge in the walled Ipateev Monastery at Kostroma. The mission hastened there and, on March 14 (1613), bearing ikons and chanting prayers, processed into the monastery to be received by Mikhail and his mother. But when they related the purpose of their visit, Mikhail rebuffed them "with great wrath and tears."[3] He stated heatedly that he did not want to be Tsar. His mother added that she would not give her blessing to the elevation of her son to the throne. Mother and son even refused to go with the mission into the chapel so that they could all pray together, and were persuaded to do so with difficulty.

For six hours the mission from the Assembly argued and pleaded with Mikhail "to go to his Tsar's throne in Moscow and by his noble presence to grant us relief from all our present misfortunes and humiliations; for when you, Sovereign, are on our Tsar's throne in Moscow, then hearing of your arrival the Lithuanian people and all the enemies of the state will be in terror and all the people of Muscovy will rejoice."[4] But Mikhail and his mother rejected these blandishments, pointing out that previous Tsars, like Boris Godunov, had been betrayed, although all had sworn allegiance to them. Martha said that her son was too young and inexperienced for such dangerous office, and that he could not accept without the blessing of his father, who was a prisoner in Polish hands.

The archbishop and other members of the mission grew desperate. They threatened that, if Mikhail continued to refuse the throne, God would hold him responsible for the final destruction of the Tsardom. The threats of these venerable bearded churchmen and the persuasions that all brought to bear wore down the resistance of the young Mikhail. He would have been content to lead the prayerful life of the monastery, but he could not withstand such pressures and, declaring himself to be in God's hands, he assented to be Tsar. He allowed each member of the mission to kiss his hands in allegiance and promised to go to Moscow without delay.

With his acceptance of the throne the Time of Troubles ended. A new era began under the rule of the Romanov dynasty which was to endure for three hundred years.

I

Russia in the Seventeenth Century

By the beginning of the seventeenth century the broad pattern of Russian society was already determined. The Tsar was absolute and ruled a nation divided into the landowning nobility and gentry, owing the Tsar service, the church, which was wealthy and upheld the Tsar's authority, and the peasantry who were burdened with taxes and shackled by the bonds of serfdom to the land and the landowners. The Tsar was of paramount importance in this pattern and when toward the end of the sixteenth century the ruling dynasty of Rurik died out, the nation came near to collapse. But other factors, rooted in geography and history, contributed to the calamities of this period.

The immensity of the Russian plain had been a major influence in the development of the nation. Rolling eastward to the low-lying Ural Mountains, the plain provided no natural frontiers for defense or to foster a sense of unity. At the same time the network of magnificent rivers encouraged the mobility of the people.

In their early history the Russians had been concentrated mainly in the Dnieper Valley. They were then primarily traders, engaged in the rich commerce between the Turkish and Byzantine empires and northern

4

Europe. Kiev, their great commercial center, grew to be a wealthy and splendid city. But the steppeland was like a vast sea across which merchant caravans passed and Asiatic hordes swept in destructive waves. Concerned wholly with commerce and defense, the Russians were slow to move toward nationhood in this period.

The Grand Princes of Kiev tried to unite them and in the tenth and eleventh centuries Kievan Rus became a powerful state, extending across the steppelands and into the dense forests to the north. But Kievan Rus was never more than a loose federation. Conflicts over the succession to the Grand Princes and rivalry over trade undermined the unity of the people. Pounded by Asiatic invasions and then by the Mongols who in 1240 razed Kiev to the ground, this first political union of the Russian people disintegrated.

Already in the previous century, however, the Russians had begun to move from the Dnieper Valley. Some went into Galicia and White Russia and were to come under the rule of Poland-Lithuania. The main flow was from the exposed steppelands to the northeast into the dark forests of the upper Volga region. Here the Russians were still disunited. In Kievan Rus they had been traders, centered on the towns; now they worked the land and were divided among principalities, each ruled by an independent prince. Moreover, they were still a people on the move. They spread over the Russian plain to the south and east, settling the lands watered by the Don and Volga rivers. Soon they were pressing beyond the Ural Mountains and colonizing Siberia. But the lands between the Volga and Oka rivers remained the heart of what was already emerging as the new Russian nation.

No chapter in Russia's history is more fascinating than the rise of Moscow during the 250 years of the Mongol-Tatar occupation. The Mongol empire had split into several Khanates after the death of Chingiz Khan. The Golden Horde with its capital at Sarai (now part of Volgograd) had exercised suzerainty over the Russians. The Khans found that the Grand Princes of Moscow were useful agents in collecting tribute and representing the Horde among the other Russian principalities. Taking full advantage of their position, the Muscovite Grand Princes had gradually extended their authority over the Russian lands.

From a small insignificant town Moscow became in the sixteenth and seventeen centuries the matrix and capital of the nation formed by the union of the Great Russian people under the rule of the Muscovite sovereign. Wealthier and more powerful neighbors, such as Tver and Ryazan, seemed stronger claimants to the leadership. But Moscow had certain advantages. The city stood at the center of river and land communications, and her inner position afforded some protection from invading enemies. But no factor was more important in the rise of Moscow than the character and ability of her rulers.

The early Muscovite Grand Princes do not emerge from the past as individuals. Materials that have survived are too scanty. Even Ivan III, the Great, who in the fifteenth century was the chief architect of the unification of Muscovy, is hardly known as a man. Tsar Ivan IV, the Terrible, is the first Muscovite ruler to come to life in the pages of Russian history. But from their policies and the events of their reigns, all from Ivan Kalita, the Purser, down to Ivan III had certain characteristics in common. They were ambitious, unscrupulous, and tenacious. All were concerned to strengthen their principality. All contributed to its growth not by stirring victories and dramatic leadership, but by astute management and by quietly and relentlessly extending their authority over other principalities.

The unification of the Russian lands had nevertheless progressed slowly under the early Grand Princes. They were cautious men who did not overreach themselves. By the mid-fifteenth century Muscovy was still only a comparatively small region between the upper Volga and Oka rivers. The three city states of Pskov, Vyatka, and, most important of all, Lord Novgorod the Great remained independent. Novgorod had escaped destruction at the hands of the Mongols and during the Mongol-Tatar occupation, when the Khans had guaranteed its political and trading privileges, the city's trade with the Baltic countries and down the Volga to the Caspian Sea had flourished. Novgorod had prided itself on its freedom and its republican constitution and on its empire which stretched northward to the White Sea. But Novgorod, like Pskov and Vyatka, stood as an obstacle to the Muscovite policy of uniting all the Russian people and their lands under the rule of Moscow.

The process of unification had quickened in the second half of the fifteenth century. Ivan III (1462–1505) brought Novgorod and its empire under his rule and also the lands to the south and southwest of Tula, nearly to Kiev. Vasily III, his son, had continued this policy, but his reign had been taken up mainly with repelling assaults by the Khanates of Kazan and the Crimea, allied with Poland-Lithuania.

The unification of Muscovy as a strong centralized state was finally achieved by Ivan IV. In 1552 he conquered the Khanate of Kazan, thus freeing Muscovy from the most immediate Tatar menace. Soon afterward he seized the Khanate of Astrakhan. His authority then extended over the whole of the mighty Volga and the Don region. Before the end of his reign the Russians were advancing into Siberia and colonizing its great expanse. But it was the conquest of Kazan, inspiring legends and awakening in the Russians a sense of unity and nationhood, which may be said to have brought the nation to birth.

In the west Ivan IV sought to conquer Livonia and to secure a permanent foothold on the Baltic Sea which would enable him to revive trade with Western Europe. But this policy brought him into conflict with the Poles, Lithuanians, Swedes, and Teutonic Knights. At first his armies were successful, but defeats followed which strained the resources of the young nation.

In just over one hundred years (1462–1584) Muscovy had had three strong rulers in succession—Ivan III, Vasily III, and Ivan IV. Their reigns had been periods of rapid expansion and constant war. The nation now needed a Tsar who would consolidate these gains. Tsarevich Ivan Ivanovich, son of Ivan IV by his first wife, Anastasia Romanovna, gave promise of being an able Autocrat who would rule wisely and continue his father's work. But on November 15, 1581, in one of the most gruesome and tragic scenes in Russian history, the Tsar, giving way to an outburst of anger, killed this son. Ivan IV's second surviving son, Tsarevich Fedor, was feeble minded and weak in health, and not expected to live long. A further son, Tsarevich Dmitri, survived, but he was in swaddling clothes at the time of the Tsar's death.

During the last years of Ivan the Terrible's reign all Russians brooded anxiously over the succession. The nation had suffered constant upheavals in the process of unification under Moscow's rule. The lives of the people had been disrupted and discontent was widespread. The one element of stability was the Tsar on whom they believed their security and national survival depended. They dreaded the anarchy that would result if the throne was vacant and the great boyar factions began struggling for power. This had happened during the minority of Ivan and all had suffered. Internicine struggles would also be the signal for Poles, Lithuanians, Germans, Swedes, Tatars, and Cossacks to invade and plunder. The Russians were, however, to experience all their worst fears during the fifteen years, known as the Time of Troubles.

Fedor succeeded on his father's death in 1584 and occupied the throne for fourteen years. He was, however, incapable of ruling and his brother-in-law, Boris Godunov, who had been one of Ivan IV's trusted favorites, wielded the supreme power throughout his reign. When in 1598 Fedor died, leaving no children, the Rurikid dynasty was extinguished in Russia, and the Patriarch offered the crown to Boris Godunov. He demanded that the Assembly of the Land should be convened to decide the matter, especially since this was the first time that the Tsar had been elected. The Assembly decided unanimously to offer the crown to Boris and after a brief show of reluctance he ascended the throne.

Boris was, however, uneasy as Tsar. He at once disposed of all rivals. Fedor Nikitch Romanov, an able man of strong personality, was forced to become a monk under the name of Filaret and incarcerated in a distant monastery. His infant son, Mikhail, was sent to Beloozero, more than 150 miles to the north of Moscow, and the rest of the Romanov family was scattered. Boris, who had exercised a moderating influence on Tsar Ivan and had been a humane man, now became a jealous suspicious monarch, dealing ruthlessly with all boyars who aroused his mistrust. But he was careful to show concern for the welfare of the people and to foster his popularity. The tide of events was, however, flowing against him. Social conditions deteriorated and the terrible famine of the years 1601 to 1603 brought new suffering to the people. Peasants fled in thousands from the land to seek food and freedom to the south and east. Many joined the large bands of brigands who plundered and murdered at will. Tsar Boris found himself powerless to check the mounting disorder and discontent.

At this time a pretender to the Russian throne, calling himself Tsarevich Dmitri, suddenly appeared in Poland. Tsar Ivan IV's seventh wife, Maria Nagoi, had borne him a son, named Dmitri, who had been sent to live in Uglich soon after Ivan's death. In May 1591 Dmitri died, it was said as a result of an accident when playing with a knife and overtaken by a fit of epilepsy. The Nagoi and the people of Uglich were convinced, however, that agents, sent from Moscow by Boris Godunov, had murdered him. Boris certainly had a motive for killing the Tsarevich, but his guilt cannot be established. Evidently he was exonerated by the Russian people at the time, for he remained popular and was in 1598 elected to the throne.

The identity of the pretender who now appeared was also a mystery. In Moscow it was officially stated that he was Grigori Otrepev, a serf from one of the Romanov estates who had become a monk but had been unfrocked. Whatever his true identity, he was a remarkable young man who knew Polish and Latin, was a swordsman and an accomplished courtier. The Poles readily accepted him as the true Tsarevich and, without giving him official support, allowed him to prepare on Polish soil for his march on Moscow. They found in him a useful means of weakening the government of their traditional enemy and also, since the false Dmitri had embraced Roman Catholicism, the powerful church element in Poland saw in him an instrument to unite the Eastern and Western churches. Moreover, within Russian the many enemies of Tsar Boris, including the Romanovs, may well have connived in the plans of the false Dmitri.

Discontent mounted and the popularity of Boris declined. Rumors gained strength among the Russians that Tsarevich Dmitri had not died in Uglich and was about to claim his throne. In October 1604 the false Dmitri with a small army of Poles and runaway serfs began his march on Moscow. In the Ukraine the people and the Cossacks rallied to his banner and, although he met with defeats at the hands of troops sent by Boris, his advance continued. As he approached the capital, Tsar Boris suddenly died. His son, Fedor Godunov, ascended the throne, but was soon afterward brutally murdered with his mother. The enemies of the Godunovs were quick to kill all who had supported the former regime.

On June 20, 1605, the false Dmitri entered Moscow and received an enthusiastic welcome from all classes. But his popularity was shortlived. He was not the man to resolve the acute problems or to reconcile the conflicting interests of classes or factions. Moreover, his large entourage of Poles and Jesuits and his disregard for Orthodox ritual and Russian custom deeply offended the Muscovites. Popular uprisings took place, promoted by the boyars, and on May 17, 1606, less than a year after his triumphal entry into the city, he was besieged in the Kremlin and murdered. Two days later Vasily Ivanovich Shuisky, a member of a branch of the Rurik dynasty, was proclaimed Tsar.

Shuisky ascended the throne without reference to the Assembly of the Land. He was in effect appointed by the nobility and boyars and accepted by the people of Moscow who feared nothing so much as that the throne might be left vacant. Shuisky was, however, incapable of giving either unity or leadership to the nation. His own supporters struggled among themselves for greater power and rewards. The Muscovites remained dangerously unruly. The peoples of the southern provinces, and especially the Cossacks, refused to accept him as Tsar. Rumors circulated afresh that the true Tsarevich Dmitri was still alive. Among the Cossacks, Ivan Bolotnikov emerged as leader of a mass movement. Claiming that he would restore Dmitri to the throne and preaching revolution in which the peasants and runaway serfs would take over the lands and wealth of the landowners, he quickly massed a large army which in October 1606 advanced on Moscow. The boyars and the gentry, many of whom had at first supported the rebels, united to resist this dangerous challenge to the established regime and their own interests. In December 1606 Shuisky defeated Bolotnikov's forces, and the government armies swept through the southern provinces during 1607, killing all who had been connected with the rebellion. Shuisky pursued policies of ruthless repression not only in putting down rebels but also in enforcing order and preventing flight among the peasantry.

In June 1607 a second pretender emerged, claiming to be Tsarevich Dmitri. He, too, used Poland as his base and he had more active Polish support. Trained Polish and Lithuanian troops formed the core of his army. In spring 1608 the pretender crossed the frontier and advanced to Tushino, not far from Moscow, where he established his headquarters. Shuisky managed to repel the first attempt to take Moscow, but his position was desperate. Maintaining a blockade of Moscow, the invading force advanced through the northern provinces, expecting plentiful booty. They met with stubborn resistance from the people, however, and were gradually forced to retreat. Meanwhile Shuisky had negotiated an agreement with Sweden whereby he ceded Russian territories on the Gulf of Finland in return for Swedish military help. With reinforcements of 15,000 Swedish, English, Scottish, and French mercenaries, Prince Mikhail Skopin-Shuisky, commanding the Muscovite army, forced the pretender to abandon Tushino and to flee to Kaluga.

In September 1609, however, Sigismund, King of Poland, using the pretext that Russia was now allied with Poland's enemy, Sweden, invaded Russia and laid siege to Smolensk. The town was stoutly defended and did not fall. But in June 1610 the Poles defeated the Russian armies at Klushino, and advanced on Moscow. The threat to the capital, far from uniting the Muscovites, brought into the open the bitter rivalries among the boyars and gentry, and discontent among the people also erupted. One result was that Shuisky was compelled to abdicate and to become a monk. The Boyar Council with Prince Fedor Mstislavsky as its leader now provided a provisional government, but it was ineffective. With the Polish army at the gates of Moscow, elements of the Assembly of the Land, hastily convened, elected the Polish Prince, Vladislav, then only fifteen years of age, to the Russian throne. This would, it was hoped in Moscow, unite Poland and Russia in the way that Poland and Lithuania had originally been united. The Poles thought otherwise, regarding Russia as conquered territory. They established a military government in Moscow and treated the Russians as a subject people. Resentment of arrogant foreign rule spread rapidly among the Russians. A national militia (*opolchenie*) was formed and, supported by the Cossacks, advanced to Moscow in spring 1611, forcing the Polish garrison to withdraw into the Kremlin.

The leaders of the militia and of the Cossacks, massed around Moscow, now tried to form a national government. But again the conflicts of interests between boyars, gentry, Cossacks, and peasantry led to internicine struggles. Forgetful of its mission to save the nation, the militia dissolved, leaving Russia defenseless. The Poles had now captured Smolensk and Sigismund in a jubilant mood celebrated in Warsaw, even parading as his prisoner the deposed Tsar, Vasily Shuisky.

By 1612 Russia was near to disintegration and national morale had sunk to its lowest ebb. At this time Kuzma Minin, a butcher who was mayor (*starosta*) of Nizhni-Novgorod and a man of remarkable ability, aroused the people of the upper Volga region to action. He was the organizing force behind the second national militia. The military leadership was provided by Prince Dmitri Pozharsky, a provincial noble. The movement grew, becoming truly national. Led by Minin and Pozharsky, the second national militia cleared Russia of foreign troops, reached a working arrangement with the Cossacks, and then prepared for the most important task of all—the election of the Tsar.

The election of a Tsar who would establish a strong dynasty was of special significance to the Russians. The Tsar was the national sovereign to whom they looked for the government of the country and its defense against enemies. But he was also their lord upon whose presence Muscovite, society was wholly centered. The Tsardom was his *votchina*, the inalienable hereditary estate of the dynasty. The people could conceive of no rights or interests apart from those of the Tsar. They themselves existed merely to serve him and his realm. Without him the nation could not exist. Olearius observed that "No people in the world have a greater veneration for their Prince than the Muscovites . . ." They took servile pride in being his subjects; "No Muscovite, what quality soever he be of, but makes it his brag to be the Great Duke's *kholop* or slave."[1]

The office and person of the Tsar had, moreover, been exalted. A church council defined the position in 1504, stating that "by nature the Tsar is like any other man, but in power and office he is like the highest God."[2] This was a fairly recent development. Relations between ruler and people had been marked by a simple frankness until the fifteenth century. Ivan III had begun the transformation in the status of the throne. He had in 1472 married Sofia Palaeologa, niece of the last Byzantine Emperor, and this union had given support to the legend that the Grand Princes of Moscow were descended directly from the Byzantine Emperors.

The main legend was that Vladimir, Grand Prince of Kiev, after his coronation in Kiev, sent troops against Emperor Constantine Monomachus (1042–54). But Constantine responded by sending the Greek Metropolitan to Kiev with gifts and his imperial crown to propose peace so that all orthodoxy might dwell in harmony "under the combined power of our Tsardom and your mighty autocracy, 'Great Rus'."[3] Vladimir was crowned with Constantine's crown and took the name of Monomakh, divinely ordained ruler of Great Rus. Thereafter the *Shapka Monomakhus* was always used for the coronation of the Tsars of Russia.

After 1480, when 250 years of Tatar suzerainty over Muscovy came to an end, Ivan III began using more resounding titles. Ceremonial at his court became grandiose as it followed Byzantine ritual. He was "Tsar of All Russia" in his diplomatic relations with Western courts. On occasions "Samoderzhets," the Russian equivalent of the Byzantine title of "Autocrat," was added. In his use of Tsar and Autocrat, Ivan III was at first proclaiming, not that he was an absolute sovereign, but that he was independent and not ruling as the vassal of the Khan or other power. But soon both titles were carrying the full significance of Autocrat. He was "Ivan by the Grace of God, Sovereign of All Russia" and his seal incorporated the double-headed eagle of the Byzantine Emperors.

The new titles also reflected the religious source of the Tsar's authority. The Emperors of Byzantium had been absolute in both temporal and spiritual spheres. The Russian Orthodox Church had consistently supported the Grand Princes of Moscow in uniting the Russian peoples under their rule. It now endorsed the conception of the Tsar's power as God-given and the Tsar himself was the sole defender of the true faith.

Ivan IV, the Terrible, had elevated the prestige and power of the throne still further. At the age of sixteen he had announced that he would "assume the titles of our ancestors . . . and of our kinsmen, Grand Prince Vladimir Vsevolodovich Monomakh."[4] Following Byzantine precedents and using the regalia received five centuries earlier from Emperor Constantine, he was crowned Tsar of All Russia on January 16, 1547, the first Russian sovereign to be crowned Tsar. He at once demonstrated that for him the title meant more than independent ruler: the Tsar was absolute and answerable only to God. Ivan IV had both presence and personality to uphold this conception. He was tall, strongly built, and with an impressive aquiline face. He overawed all who came before him. Intellectually he was without equal among his people. He wielded power naturally, as of right. Even though they suffered from his excesses, the people drew comfort and strength from his presence on the throne.

The Tsar was the chief pillar of the nation, but in the early centuries the Orthodox Chruch was scarcely less important. The Russians were converted to Christianity in the tenth century. According to the legend, Vladimir, Grand Prince of Kiev, considered various faiths and sent his envoys abroad to witness their worship. They reported to him that in Constantinople they had been so impressed by the Orthodox services that in the Cathedral of St. Sofia, "We knew not whether we were in heaven or on earth." Influenced by the fact that his grandmother, Olga, had been baptized in 955, he accepted the report on the Greek church and embraced Orthodox Christianity.[5] On his baptism in 988 he had forbidden all forms of pagan worship and had directed that his people should be baptized. At about the same time Christianity had spread northward into Hungary, Poland, and Scandinavia, but they had embraced the Church of Rome, while the Russians adopted the Orthodox faith from Constantinople. This religious difference was to divide the Slavs and to engender hatreds and wars.

The Russians followed the Church of Constantinople closely in worship and organization. The Metropolitan of Kiev, primate of the Russian church, was appointed by the Patriarch of Constantinople and was at first usually a Greek. The local bishops, nominated by the princes and consecrated by the Metropolitan, were usually Russians. Again following Greek practice, the church hierarchy was appointed from the black clergy, the monks who were celibate; the pastoral or secular clergy, known as the white clergy, were required to marry and, far from enjoying the advantages and security of the numerous great monasteries, they were illiterate and merged with the peasantry.

Eastern Christianity at once struck deep roots among the Russian people. They looked to Byzantium as the source of authority in matters of faith and also in art, writing, and architecture. The Mongol invasion in the thirteenth century, which destroyed all in its path, had not brought the suppression of the church. Indeed, the Khans were sympathetic toward Christianity and at one time seriously considered embracing it as the religion of the Horde. Even when toward the end of the thirteenth century they were adopting Islam, they continued to favor the Russian Church by granting it exemption from payment of taxes and by allowing it considerable autonomy in managing its affairs.

During the Mongol-Tatar occupation the Russian church grew rich and powerful and its influence over Russian life deepened. Moreover, isolated from the rest of Christendom, it developed its own distinctive forms of worship and religious life, and evolved a rich spiritual tradition. The greatest manifestation of this religious resurgence was the monastic movement which arose in the fourteenth century. No fewer than 150 new monasteries were founded between 1340 and 1440. Nearly all of them were in the forests to the north and in the wilderness beyond. Usually the monks were pioneers in these lands, leading the way for the peasants who were moving out to colonize the virgin lands.

The new monasteries grew out of communities of monks, gathered around a leader of exceptional sanctity and strength. At this time the Russian church produced a number of such men. The chief initiator of the movement, however, was the humble monk, St. Sergius of Radonezh, one of the most venerated saints of Russia. He resembled St. Francis of Assisi in many ways, but he was too humble to presume to preach or to found a monastic order. His influence flowed wholly from example. His followers founded a chain of monasteries in the northern forests, dedicated to his ideals.

Other outstanding leaders of monasticism in the fifteenth century were St. Stephen of Perm, St. Nilus of Sora, St. Joseph of Volok, and St. Cyril of Beloozero. Each was a distinctive individual, but the faith and daily lives of all were dedicated to the "loving communion of souls," to humility and brotherly compassion for suffering and poverty.[6] Another feature of Russian religious life was the *yurodivie* or "Fools for Christ's sake." They were often simpletons or idiots, but were respected and allowed licence to speak their minds, because they were "wise in Christ."[7]

In the example of such men as St. Sergius, St. Alexei, and St. Stephen, and in its teaching of humility, compassion, and communion of souls, the church actively pursued the ideals of Christianity. At its best, Russian spirituality possessed a gentle charity which is deeply moving. Religion was an intimate part of the daily lives of all Russians; indeed, religion has rarely entered so fully into the thoughts and customs of a people. But the influence of the church was often negative. It fostered an attitude of submission and fortitude. The church in pursuit of its mission to preserve Orthodoxy unchanged also promoted a stultifying conservatism. The simple people, guided by a largely illiterate clergy, observed every detail of their faith, and especially their ritual, with superstitious awe. The worship of ikons was carried to extremes. In every church numerous ikons, often of great beauty and believed to have miracle-working powers, attracted worshipers. In every house and hovel at least one ikon hung on the wall with a tallow candle burning before it. Everyone on entering the house prayed before the ikon. They were promiscuous, but no man would think of intercourse with a woman without first covering the ikon. A robber, planning a crime, would first pray before the ikon of his saint for protection. This faith in the powers of the ikon was part of the childlike simplicity and superstition which were as characteristic of the Russians and their church as their conservatism.

Moscow around which the nation had been united was for Russians their capital and the white-walled city of the Tsar. But it also had for them a far greater significance than London or Paris had for contemporary English or Frenchmen. Moscow was the center of the Orthodox Church. The Metropolitan of "Kiev and All Russia," the Primate of the Russian Church, had resided in Moscow since about 1300, and indeed the presence of the primates and their consistent support for the Grand Princes of Moscow had contributed to the rise of the city.

In the fifteenth century two major events were to lead to Moscow being vested with divine majesty as the "third Rome." The first event was the Council of Florence which in 1439 sought to reunite the Eastern and Western churches under the papacy. Isidore, the Metropolitan of Kiev, agreed to the reunion. On his return to Russia, however, he met with such hostility from the Grand Prince, the Russian clergy, and people that he had to flee for his life. The second event was the capture of Constantinople by the Turks in 1453. The city which Russians had accepted as the center of Orthodoxy was now in the hands of the infidel. The Russian Church was prompt to assert its independence and it became increasingly nationalistic, especially after the Tatar yoke had been discarded about 1480. The Metropolitan was Russian in future and there was no longer any question of his appointment by the Patriarch in Constantinople.

Soon Russians were proclaiming Moscow as the center of Orthodox

Christianity, the successor to Constantinople, and the "third Rome." In a letter to Vasily III, the son and successor of Ivan III, Philotheus, a monk in a monastery in Pskov, expressed the new elevated conception of Moscow.

"I wish," he wrote, "to add a few words on the present Orthodox Empire of our ruler; he is on earth the sole Emperor [Tsar] of the Christians, the leader of the Apostolic Church which stands no longer in Rome or in Constantinople, but in the blessed city of Moscow. She alone shines in the whole world brighter than the sun . . . All Christian Empires are fallen and in their stead stands alone the Empire of our ruler in accordance with the prophetical books. Two Romes have fallen, but the third stands, and a fourth there will not be."[8]

Already in the seventeenth century Moscow was "one of the greatest cities in Europe," according to Adam Olearius, who was secretary to the Holstein embassy to the Tsar in 1633–39.[9] John Perry, an English engineer, wrote that "The numerous churches, the monasteries, and noblemen's and gentlemen's houses, the steeples, cupolas, and crosses at the tops of the church, which are gilded and painted over, make the city look to be one of the most rich and beautiful in the world, as indeed it appeared to me at first sight coming from the Novgorod road."[10]

The Kremlin or Citadel, standing on a slight hill on the bank of the Moskva River, was the heart of the city and the administrative center of state and church. It contained the Tsar's palace, the *prikazi* or government ministries, the Patriarch's palace, and the most magnificent and venerated cathedrals in the land. In the twelveth century it had been merely a country seat, built of timber and surrounded by a palisade of logs, which belonged to Yuri Dolgoruky, Prince of Rostov. It had grown into a city during the Mongol-Tatar occupation and especially in the fourteenth century when the Grand Princes of Moscow began asserting their authority over the other Russian principalities. But it was Ivan III who transformed the Kremlin and Moscow into the capital city.

Ivan considered the crowded and insignificant timber buildings, which included his own palace, unworthy of the now powerful Grand Prince. He embarked on the reconstruction of the Kremlin in stone and the task was almost completed within his reign. In 1472 he ordered a new cathedral to take the place of the Uspensky Cathedral, built over a century earlier of timber and now collapsing. The Russians were not accustomed to working with stone, and the two Russian masters, entrusted with erecting the new cathedral, had to be dismissed because the walls fell down. Meanwhile Ivan, probably influenced by his wife, Sofia, who had been educated in Rome, was sending his agents through

Europe to engage foreign artists and craftsmen to work in Moscow. They had most success in Italy and among the masters hired there a cetain Aristotle Fioraventi proved an architect and builder of genius. He began work on the Uspensky Cathedral in 1475 and completed it in four years. It was a mighty and spacious building with five cupolas. Its pillars, ceiling, and walls were richly decorated with murals and brooding ikons, the finest that could be found. Here the Tsars were anointed and crowned, their baptisms and marriages were celebrated, and the Patriarchs were entombed.

Next Ivan instructed two Italians, Solario and Ruffo, to build him a palace of stone. In 1491 the Granovitaya or Faceted Palace was completed. With its magnificent exterior staircase and vaulted audience chamber, it reflected the new majesty and power of the Grand Prince. In the following year two Russian masters from Pskov finished the new Blagoveshchensky Cathedral. Toward the end of his reign Ivan gave orders for rebuilding the old Arkhangelsky Cathedral. His successors carried on the work of transformation. The bell tower, Ivan Veliky, the tallest building in Moscow, was completed by Boris Godunov in 1600. The Terem Palace, richly adorned inside and outside, was built in 1635–36 to house the women of the Tsar's family and their attendants.

The Italian masters, responsible for most of the new monumental buildings in the Kremlin, did not, however, impose a foreign style. Their influence was apparent, but they worked from Russian models and their buildings were overwhelmingly Russian in character. Moreover, the Russian builders learned quickly from the foreigners. Nowhere was this more remarkable than in the great cathedral, built on the Red Square, by Ivan the Terrible to commemorate the conquest of Kazan and Astrakhan. The two master builders, Postnik and Barma, entrusted with this task, created in their cathedral one of the triumphs of Russian architecture.

Beyond the Kremlin walls and the Red Square, Moscow sprawled in untidy squalor. The buildings with rare exceptions were of timber and the roads and outer walls, surrounding the city, were of logs. In winter snow and slush and in summer filth and stench were inescapable. Fires were commonplace. Primitive stoves burned in every house in winter and in the heat of summer the timber was tinder dry, so that fires started readily. In 1633, shortly before the arrival of Adam Olearius in Moscow, fires destroyed a third of the city. The Muscovites, skillful in the use of timber, rebuilt with great speed. Ready-made houses could be bought in sections in the market and erected at once on the old sites. Houses were thus expendable and fires were taken for granted as the will of God.[11]

In its magnificence Moscow reflected the power and prestige of the

Tsar and the grandeur of the Orthodox Church. But the widespread squalor of the city revealed the poverty and oppression of the great majority of the people. Moscow was, in fact, a city of contrasts and in this, as in all else, it was the epitome of the nation. Cathedrals, palaces, and mansions were surrounded by squalid huts. Paupers swarmed at the doors of every church.

The Tsar stood apart, isolated by his absolute power and surrounded by ponderous but magnificent Byzantine ceremonial. Church dignitaries belonged to the social hierarchy and in wealth and well-being they contrasted with the simple priests who were poor and merged with the masses. The princes and great boyars also stood apart. Wearing long-sleeved coats of velvet or brocaded cloth, which reached to the ground, they rode on horseback or on sledges through the streets, escorted by suites of retainers. They were usually fat and full of pride in their bulk which, like the profusion of their attendants, signified wealth and station. They moved against a background of peasant-serfs, ragged holymen, beggars, and peddlers. In fact, the population divided under the Tsar into two distinct categories: the landowning nobility, embracing the princes, boyars, and the gentry, who owed the Tsar service, and the traders, artisans, and townsmen and the peasantry who were the *tyaglie lyudi,* or taxpaying people.

The princes and boyars were relics of the time when Russia was divided into principalities. They had then been free to serve the Grand Prince of their choice. But now they owed their allegiance and service to the Grand Prince of Moscow who had absorbed the other principalities. They had proved unable to unite as a class to resist the growing absolutism of the Muscovite Tsars. Many nevertheless continued to cherish ideas of independence and voluntary service; when the Tsar was weak they scrambled for power, but a strong Tsar kept them in check, and as a class they never recovered from the savage assaults of Ivan the Terrible.

The serving gentry, or *dvorianstvo,* began to expand rapidly as a class in the sixteenth century, as the military needs of the Grand Prince became more pressing. The gentry received grants of land on condition of military service. Such lands, known as *pomestie,* were at first distinct from the hereditary estates of the princes and boyars, but soon this distinction was lost and all estates became hereditary. The gentry themselves merged with the nobility.

Of the taxpaying people, the traders, artisans, and townsmen were never numerous and they failed to develop into the strong middle class which played a leading part in the development of the countries of Western Europe. The peasants were numerous, making up the vast majority of the population. They worked the lands of the Tsar and the landowners and, subject to their paying the prescribed taxes, they were free, at least in theory, to move to the lands of other owners after the harvest had been gathered each year. In practice the peasants were burdened not only by the weight of taxes but also by dues to their landowners, paid in labor or in money, and often they were heavily in debt to their landowners.

Working under harsh conditions and crippled by debt, the peasants' only escape lay in flight. Some fled eastward to the Urals and beyond; others moved south to settle in the regions of the lower Volga and the Don rivers. The central provinces began to suffer severely from shortage of labor. Powerful landowners and monasteries offered rewards to lure peasant labor from the smaller estates. The government was compelled, however, to intervene to stop this poaching. The smaller estates belonged to the serving gentry upon whom the defenses of the country depended. The Tsar was concerned to ensure that they had labor to work their lands, so that they were economically secure and able to provide men and their own services for the army.

Runaway peasants remained a problem. Landowners had a limited right to reclaim their peasants when found, and this right was extended so that a peasant could be recovered within five years. Soon the period was extended further. Inexorably the peasant was being tied to the land, becoming the serf of the landowner, attached to his land and to him as his chattel.

By the beginning of the seventeenth century the social and economic inequalities between the small landowning class and the vast mass of the people were already sharply developed. They pointed to the problems at the root of Russian society which were to remain unresolved and were to give rise to unrest and rebellion throughout the three centuries of the Romanov dynasty's rule.

At all levels Russian life was marked by brutishness and degradation. Drunkenness was the national vice. To be drunk was accepted by all classes as part of normal living. Tsar Mikhail, who was, like his son, Tsar Alexei, sober and moderate in his habits, hated drunkenness, but was unable to stop it. The humble people could escape their misery only in intoxication. Women were as addicted as men. "They are often the first to become raving mad with immoderate drafts of brandy and are to be seen half-naked and shameless in almost all the streets," Dr Samuel Collins observed.[12]

Olearius remarked on the amount that the women drank. He described an evening "in the house where I lodged, whither many Muscovian women came one day to their husbands, sat down with them, and took off their cups as smartly as they did. The men, being got drunk, would have gone home, but the women thought it not yet time to draw off, though invited thereto by a good number of boxes o' th' ear, and got their husbands to sit down again, and to drink roundly as before, till such time as that the men being fall'n down asleep upon the ground, the women sate upon them, as upon benches, and drunk on until they also were forc'd to lye down by them."[13]

The church, far from combating this evil, condoned and encouraged it. Drunkenness was common among the priesthood. For all classes the times of greatest indulgence were the church festivals. Dr Collins wrote that "In the carnival before Lent they give themselves to all manner of debauchery and luxury and in the last week they drink as if they were never to drink more . . . Some of those going home drunk, if they are not attended by a sober companion, fall asleep upon the snow, a sad, cold bed, and there they are frozen to death . . . 'Tis a sad sight to see a dozen people brought upright in a sledge, frozen to death; some have their arms eaten off by dogs, others their faces, and others have nothing left but bones. Two or three hundred have been brought in after this manner in time of Lent."[14]

Heavy drinking went hand in hand with debauchery. Olearius considered that they were "wholly given up to all licentiousness, even to sins against nature, not only with men, but also with beasts . . ." The postures of their dancing and the insolence of their women are infallible marks of their bad inclinations. We have seen at Moscow both men and women come out of the publick brothel-houses stark naked and incite some young people of our retinue to naughtiness by filthy and lascivious expressions."[15]

The Russian attitude toward women was a contributory factor in the barbarity of their lives. The code of chivalry had influenced manners and raised standards of social behaviour in Western Europe. But Russia, under the Mongol-Tatar yoke, had known nothing of chivalry and social life had become increasingly brutalized. Women were no more than chattels or, among the peasantry, beasts of burden. In the upper classes they had the sole function of childbearing. Surrounded by serfs they had no household or other duties. They lived segregated in the *terem* or women's quarter, prey to boredom, drink, and fear.

Many women lived in dread of their husbands. Marriages were arranged. Bride and groom set eyes on each other for the first time only after the wedding ceremony. Wives often found themselves at the mercy of cruel husbands. Olearius and Collins both observed that Russian men treated their wives harshly. "Some of these barbarians will tie up their wives by the hair of their head and whip them stark naked," Dr Collins wrote. But Olearius considered this something "not to be much wondered at," since the women "have lewd tongues, are given to wine, and will not let slip the opportunity to pleasure a friend."[16] A husband who had whipped his wife to death went unpunished, since it was presumed to have happened in the course of correction. Women who were driven to desperation by cruel usage and murdered their husbands were punished severely. The guilty wife was buried alive with only her head above the ground and left to die. This terrible fate evidently failed to deter many women, for Western travelers usually witnessed unfortunate creatures undergoing this sentence of death.

In a society so degraded, in which many people lived in dire poverty and order was barely maintained, crime was widespread. The Time of Troubles had bred countless robber bands which lived by violence and plunder. The dense forests of the Volga-Oka region provided cover and on the roads leading to Moscow the dangers of being robbed and murdered were so great that those who had to travel moved in armed groups. In Moscow itself violence and crime were commonplace. Olearius noted that it was unsafe to go out at night without an armed escort. Murder was a nightly occurrence and at festivals when drinking was at its height the number of dead rose sharply. On St. Martin's Eve he counted fifteen corpses in the courtyard where bodies were taken to be claimed by kindred and friends. Unclaimed bodies were dragged to a common ditch and left there to rot.[17]

Punishments were savage. Men found guilty of treason or rebellion were executed by being seated on sharpened and greased stakes which probed upward into their entrails and they died a lingering death. Olearius describes the execution of a certain Timoshka who was guilty of fraud and imposture. He had been examined several times under torture and then condemned to death. The executioner cut off "with an axe first his right arm below the elbow, then the left leg below the knee, and afterwards the left arm and right leg, and last of all the head."[18]

The common punishments were beating with *batogi*, which were rods the thickness of a man's finger, and, more severe, with the knout, a thick leather thong of some three and a half feet in length. *Batogi* were used indiscriminately for minor offenses, although they sometimes caused death. The offender lay with his back bare, his arms and legs extended, while two men, one kneeling on his legs and the other on his arms, beat him with the rods.

The knout was a dreaded punishment. For less serious crimes the offender was lifted on the back of another man and the knoutmaster skillfully laid on the number of strokes ordered, each stroke falling in a different place and flaying the flesh to the bone. For more serious crimes the offender's arms were tied behind his back and he was lifted from the ground by a rope tied to his wrists. To make sure that his arms were pulled out of joint, the knoutmaster usually fixed a weight to his feet. He then laid on his back the number of strokes ordered or continued until told to stop by the official present. The knoutmaster then took the offender down and pulled his arms into joint again. In extreme cases the victim on being taken down was tied to a pole and his flayed back was slowly roasted over a fire, while he was examined further and called on to confess. Women were also subjected to the ordeal of the knout, and the fact that so many survived the punishment was an indication of the incredible toughness of the Russians.[19]

The seventeenth century was a time of cruel punishments and barbarous customs throughout Europe, but Western travelers were invariably shocked by the extreme degradation and barbarity of the Russian people. They lived like animals, fighting, murdering, and cheating to survive. The Orthodox Church which they embraced wholeheartedly served to comfort them in their misery, but not to teach and guide them by establishing standards by which they could live. Western travelers nevertheless described the nation at a time when it was suffering from the aftermath of invasion and the breakdown of order and when it was only beginning its struggle to develop. They noted the backwardness and barbarity and understandably saw no further. But Manstein, a German soldier in the Tsar's service, considered them to be certainly as intelligent as people in the West.[20] Others noted that the people were ingenious, possessed of great stamina and fortitude.[21]

Russia was, in fact, a country of unlimited natural wealth, inhabited by a people of great ability and strength. History and geography had combined to retard their development. But at the time of the accession of the new dynasty the Russian nation was beginning to develop. It was not a measured advance but happened in violent spasms, alternating with periods of lethargy. But within a few decades the nation was to become a European power.

II

Mikhail Fedorovich

1613–1645

Tsar Mikhail, the mild inexperienced youth who became the first of the Romanov dynasty, found himself faced with conditions that would have daunted the strongest Autocrat. The past fifteen years had reduced the country to chaos and economic collapse. Fields lay untilled; trade had ceased; hunger stalked the land. Villages were burnt ruins, their inhabitants scattered or murdered. Moscow, the venerated capital, was scarred by war and much of the city had been destroyed by fires. The nation had only survived because the Russian people, chastened by these calamities, were now desperately concerned to maintain the throne and the tsardom.

On March 19, 1613, Mikhail had set out from Kostroma for Moscow. Crowds of people of all ranks gathered at Yaroslavl, Rostov, and other halts to swear loyalty to him. But he traveled anxiously. He had no money to equip and mount his own attendants and went in fear of brigands.[1] The devastation and butchery which marked every village through which he passed distressed him deeply. At the Troitsa Monastery he halted and threatened to go no farther until, in accordance with the oath of loyalty and obedience which the nation had sworn to him, the lawlessness and bloodshed ceased.[2] But he was persuaded to continue his journey and on May 2, escorted by the whole population of the city who had come to greet him, he entered Moscow.

On July 11, Mikhail was crowned in the Uspensky Cathedral, but the celebrations that followed were modest. The treasury was empty and he could not even pay or provision the nucleus of troops needed to guard the capital and maintain order. He was forced to write to his subjects the Stroganovs, the merchant family which had prospered by colonization in Siberia and by astute commercial enterprise. In his letter to the head of the Stroganovs, Mikhail requested "for Christian peace and order loans of money, grain, fish, salt, cloth, and other goods for the troops."[3] Supporting the Tsar's appeal a letter was sent in the name of the church to the Stroganovs and a special appeal was made to all towns for loans of money and goods.

Mikhail's first concern was to put down the brigands and marauders who laid waste the country and prevented cultivation of the land. The Cossack, Zarutsky, who called himself Tsar Dmitri, posed a special danger. He had set himself up in Astrakhan with Marina Mnishek, the Polish widow of the first false Dmitri. He sought to establish a personal kingdom at the mouth of the Volga under the protection of the Shah of Persia and to add Kazan and Samara to his empire. But he and the Nogai Tatars who provided his bodyguard behaved so barbarously that the local people rebelled and besieged him in Astrakhan. On the night of May 13, 1614, however, he escaped with Marina to the Yaik River. There the Muscovite governor captured him and in June he was spitted on a stake in Moscow.

The first six years of Mikhail's reign were, in fact, as troubled as the years of the interregnum. Constant war was waged against the Tatar, Cossack, and other robber bands. The levies of money, food, and men, made for the purpose, were collected with difficulty. The Tsar's agents had to be escorted by troops. Often the church had to intervene with threats of excommunication before the decreed contributions were forthcoming. But although beset with such difficulties the restoration of order slowly progressed.

The next important task facing the young Tsar was to deal with Sweden and Poland who between them occupied nearly half the tsardom. Mikhail had neither the military strength nor the money to fight either country. He had no choice but to negotiate the best terms possible so as to gain time in which Russia could restore her economy and build up her army.

In 1611-12, while Russia was in a state of turmoil, the Swedes had taken Novgorod and the towns on the Gulf of Finland which gave Russians access to the Baltic Sea. The new Swedish King, Gustavus Adolphus, was determined to capture Pskov. In the summer of 1615 he laid siege to the town, but was repelled by the garrison. Impressed by the defense of Pskov and concerned with developments in Germany where a long war threatened, Gustavus Adolphus decided to come to terms with the Tsar.

Meanwhile Mikhail's government had turned to England to mediate between Russia and Sweden. King James I had received the Russian envoy with every courtesy and, keeping in mind the privileged position enjoyed by his merchants in Russia, he promised help. He appointed as his special envoy an English merchant, John Merrick, who was knighted for the occasion. He set out at once for Moscow, bearing handsome gifts for the Tsar. He was to work assiduously to gain the best terms possible for Russia, and returning from the Gulf of Finland in triumph, he was richly rewarded by the Tsar before returning to England. By the Treaty of Stolbovo, signed on March 10, 1617, Russia recovered Novgorod and the Swedes recognized Mikhail as Tsar. But the price was the surrender of all the Russian towns on the Gulf of Finland, which meant the loss of direct access to the Baltic Sea. The terms, especially the recovery of Novgorod, were accepted with some jubilation in Moscow, but only as a temporary arrangement, for the Russians could never rest until the Baltic Sea was open to them and they could trade freely by this ancient route.

Russia's greatest and most hated enemy was the Rech Pospolitaya, the Kingdom of Poland-Lithuania. All Russians had been humiliated by Polish arrogance; they could never forget that the Poles had burnt down part of their capital and had occupied and defiled the Kremlin. Moreover, the youthful Vladislas, who had been proclaimed Tsar and who was heir to Sigismund as King of Poland-Lithuania, was actively preparing for war. He still insisted on his claim to the Russian throne, refusing to recognize Mikhail. Meanwhile Russia and Poland were still formally at war. A conference, opened in September 1615 in Smolensk, led only to bitter recriminations. Early in 1618 Vladislas marched from Smolensk and quickly captured Vyazma and Dorogobuzh. In the autumn of 1618, joined by Zaporozksky Cossacks from the south, he advanced on Moscow. But Mikhail, supported by the Assembly of the Land and the people of Moscow, stoutly defended the capital and the Polish expedition failed.

Vladislas, his troops ill equipped and supplied and fearing the onset of winter, now offered to discuss terms. Negotiations took place in the village of Deulino, near the Troitsa Monastery, and a truce for fourteen and a half years was agreed. Vladislas recognized Mikhail as Tsar and abandoned his own claims to the Russian throne. But Mikhail had to surrender vast territories to Poland, while confirming Polish possession of the ancient Russian lands on the Dnieper and in the north. Moreover, with their new territorial acquisitions, the Poles were well placed for further attacks on Russia. The truce of Deulino was, however, to prove the farthest eastward expansion that the Poles achieved. Agreement was also reached at Deulino for an exchange of prisoners. This resulted in the return of the Tsar's father, Filaret, Metropolitan of Rostov, from his long captivity in Poland.

On June 24, 1619, the Tsar, his boyars, and great crowds met him five miles from Moscow. Ten days later he was enthroned as Patriarch with the title "Great Autocrat" (*Veliki Gosudar*). He ruled jointly with his son until his death in 1633. Filaret was sixty-six years old on his return from captivity, but neither age nor the hardships of his life had diminished his physical and mental vitality, and he brought a new vigor and purpose to his son's rule. He was respected and loved by the Russians, except for the powerful boyar families who feared that he would reduce their influence. Indeed, it was widely believed among the people that Tsar Fedor I, the last of the old dynasty, had made his cousin, then Fedor Romanov and now Filaret, his successor. But Filaret was now able to exercise the supreme power and his rule was directed to uniting the nation and strengthening the dynasty, the throne, and the church.

Many among the boyars had been anxious to limit the absolute power of the Tsar. But, so far as is known, no attempt was made to impose restraints or conditions on the powers of Mikhail at the time of his election or later. Probably it was felt that this mild-tempered youth would be incapable of ruling as Ivan the Terrible had ruled. It was therefore unnecessary to impose restraints on his power. Indeed most of the boyars had supported his election, because he was so unlikely to challenge their privileged position. But on his return to Russia Filaret was clearly concerned to entrench the absolute power of the Tsar so that it was beyond challenge or limitation.

On his election, however, while Filaret was a prisoner in Poland, Mikhail's immaturity and the critical state of the country had compelled him to rely on the guidance of the Council of Boyars and, in matters of major importance, on the Assembly of the Land, which included both the Council of Boyars and the Church Council. The Assembly was in almost continuous session during the early years of his reign. As he became more secure on the throne, and especially after the return of Filaret, it was summoned less frequently. The Council of Boyars and the *prikazi* or government ministries, which shared legislative and executive power with the Tsar, underwent major changes at Filaret's direction. The composition of the Council was broadened and its scope of activity was narrowed, so that in effect its importance was severely reduced. Disputes over land and the serfs were removed from its jurisdiction and it was excluded from secret diplomatic matters. Soon it was only meeting to consider business specially referred to it by the Tsar or the Patriarch. A

Privy Council (*Blizhnyaya Soviet*) of four boyars became responsible for the machinery of government. At the same time, as part of his policy of strengthening the autocracy, Filaret gave increased powers to the *prikazi*.

At the beginning of Tsar Mikhail's reign the Assembly of the Land and his practice of referring to it and heeding its views contained the seeds of parliamentary government. The Assembly was then representative of all classes except the peasantry and, although its function was consultative and advisory, its voice was often decisive. But, as the dynasty became more secure and the threats of economic collapse receded, the need for such a representative body weakened. It had functioned at a time of crisis when the people had rallied to shore up the throne and to avert the collapse of the nation. Once this danger had passed, the Russians were content that power should vest absolutely in the hands of the Autocrat.

The Orthodox Church had played a distinctive role in uniting the nation. It now upheld the authority of the throne and its support was a major factor in establishing the new dynasty. Filaret, as Patriarch and joint ruler with his son who deferred to him in all things, strengthened the position of the church. By special deed, signed by the Tsar, he extended his authority over the priesthood and monastery serfs, except in major criminal proceedings. As Patriarch he also took wider powers over church finance and administration. He established his patriarchal court with a magnificence and ceremonial as imposing as the court of the Tsar himself. The Russian Church was, in fact, in a position to rival the monarchy as happened in the West. But this rivalry did not develop in Russia. Filaret and his successors not only refrained from challenging the authority of the Tsar but, obedient to their Byzantine heritage, exalted his power and majesty.

With the gradual return of order, agriculture revived. Fields, untended for years, especially around Moscow, were plowed and sown. The area under cultivation increased rapidly as from the 1620s. But the peasantry still could not produce enough to feed the growing towns and the armed forces. Food shortage was aggravated by the government's policy of exporting grain, primarily to purchase much-needed armaments, and in exporting grain it paid too little heed to domestic food requirements. Yields were small and when crops failed the villagers went hungry. Peasants continued to flee in growing numbers from the burdens of taxation and the demands of their landlords. They settled the frontier lands to the south of the Oka River, in the mid-Volga region, and in western Siberia. Generally the runaway peasants managed to settle peacefully among the Turkish tribes (Tatars, Chuvash, Morvin, and others) in these vast regions where land was plentiful.

The continued movement of peasants from the central regions

alarmed the government, the great boyar landowners, and the serving gentry or *dvorianstvo*. Mikhail's government paid special attention to the needs of the gentry. The country stood in desperate need of their military service not only against the Ottoman Porte, Poland, and Sweden, but also against the marauding Tatars and others. In the spring the gentry assembled in Tula with their troops to repel invaders from the south. In 1639 this frontier force comprised 2089 musketeers and 13,634 men. The southern defenses had to be manned on this scale every year. The interests of this class were for this reason a matter of government priority. But the peasants suffered.

The restraints imposed on the movement of peasants to prevent flight and also to put an end to the practice of enticing or abducting peasant labor to serve on the estates of the great landlords had developed into serfdom in the previous century. Boris Godunov's decrees in the 1590s had introduced a system of registers by means of which a peasant who had been abducted or had fled from a service estate could be legally recovered within five years. But the government had to deal also with evasion of taxes and obligations to the state on the part of free peasants and townsmen. The practice had grown whereby they voluntarily gave up their freedom and became the household dependents of the monastery or landowner, who was not liable to pay taxes. By means of the voluntary surrender of freedom both free peasants and townsmen could also gain exemption.

Filaret and the government of Tsar Mikhail took vigorous action to put an end to this tax evasion and also to check the flight of peasants. A census of lands and population was decreed. Work began on it in 1619, and in spite of obstruction and delays it was completed in 1628. This register, listing landowners, estates, and peasants of the whole country, effectively tied the peasant to the estate on which he worked. In 1642 the period within which the runaway could be recovered was extended to ten years and soon the time-limit was to be abolished. Peasants were then completely shackled as serfs. But still they fled in large numbers to the expanses of free land to the east and the south. Many joined the Cossacks. Among those who could not escape the hardships of serfdom fed their resentment and in the decades to come gave rise to savage peasant rebellions.

The revival of the Russian economy was not limited to agriculture. Manufactures recovered, especially in the northern lands. Linen and cloth weaving were of special importance. Rope-making became a major industry, developed primarily by English merchants to supply the King's ships. The two centers of rope-making in the sixteenth century had been Kholmogory and Vologda, but now a new and far bigger rope-making industry was established in Archangel. Military needs gave impetus to the expansion of foundries, producing guns and other weapons. The government gave every encouragement to the iron industry and to prospecting for iron ore. In the 1620s metal works were set up in the region of Tomsk and in the Urals, and workers were sent from Moscow to man them. More successful was the metal industry established in the Tula region by the Dutch merchant, Andrei Vinius. He had found rich deposits of iron ore there. On February 29, 1632 he had been granted a monopoly for ten years to work these deposits and had developed a profitable foundry.

Foreign trade revived notably during Mikhail's reign. England and Holland were the principal countries engaged in trade with Russia and the rivalry between them was keen. Both used the flourishing port of Archangel on the White Sea. English merchants continued to enjoy the privilege of duty-free trading, first granted to them by Ivan the Terrible. The Tsar was under constant pressure from his own merchants to withdraw these privileges. Fearing that he might act, the English Muscovy Company sent a mission to Moscow in 1618, but for some reason it failed to obtain the confirmation sought. In 1620 a new mission, this time led by Sir John Merrick, whom the Russian's knew and trusted, arrived in Moscow, bearing rich gifts for the Tsar and Filaret. Merrick obtained confirmation of the exemptions, enjoyed by the English traders. Dutch merchants paid half-duty, but benefited by importing a wider range of goods.

At the beginning of June each year the ships began to arrive in the White Sea and a busy traffic continued until the autumn when ice closed the port for the winter. The chief imports were iron, copper, tin, and articles manufactured from these metals, cloth, paper, dyes, chemicals, sugar, wine, and glass. The main exports were leather, canvas, linen, bristles, tallow, fur pelts, linseed, hemp, and large quantities of fish, especially salmon.

The English merchants maintained permanent trade representatives in Russia. Dutch, Swedish, and Danish merchants followed their example. They competed keenly for a larger share of the Russian market. Russian merchants, virtually excluded from the rich trade with the West, continued to petition the Tsar to revoke the special rights of the English and Dutch merchants. But Mikhail's government acted cautiously, reluctant to do anything which might damage the mounting trade with the West, and in particular the import of armaments. Finally, in July 1646, after Mikhail's death, the exemptions so long enjoyed by the English and Dutch, were abolished.

The need to build up Russian military strength was a matter of priority. In equipment, training, and morale the serving gentry had proved inadequate. They had come to enjoy a quiet life on the estates granted to them in return for military services and answered the Tsar's summons only with reluctance. Both cavalry and infantry were armed with cumbersome, old-fashioned weapons, which put them at a serious disadvantage against the well-mounted and fast-moving Tatars and Cossacks and against the disciplined formations of Western troops. The *streltsi* or musketeers had also been undermined by easy living and privileges. They were regular troops quartered on the outskirts of Moscow and certain other cities, who received pay and special allowances. Their most treasured privilege was the right to engage in trade free of taxes, when not required by the army. But their zeal for military service had diminished as they became more and more involved in trade. Moreover, the *streltsi* had become an hereditary military caste, for in practice recruiting was limited to the sons of serving *streltsi*. Mikhail's government took steps to halt evasion of service obligations. Filaret introduced severe regulations requiring all serving men and *streltsi* to justify their estates and salaries by giving real service.

Early in Mikhail's reign and increasingly after Filaret had taken up the reins of government, foreign mercenaries were enlisted to serve in the Tsar's forces. They were needed to train the Russians in the latest Western formations and weapons. They were also intended to provide a strong nucleus in battle which would hold the Russian forces from flight. Scots, like Leslie, Matthison, and Keith; Englishmen, such as Fox and Sanderson; and Germans, such as Scharl, Fuchs, and Samuel, were prominent among the officers training and commanding Russian troops.

As war against Poland became more imminent, Filaret stepped up his efforts to forge a strong army. He sent officers to the West to recruit experienced mercenaries in greater numbers. The only restriction was that they should not be Roman Catholics. Colonel Leslie, the Scot, on proceeding to the West was instructed "To engage soldiers in Sweden and other countries, except for Frenchmen and others of the Roman faith who must not be engaged on any account."[4] Many of the foreign officers received estates on the same basis as the serving gentry; others received money for their services and were well paid.[5] But once engaged all were expected to remain permanently in the Tsar's service and leave of absence to visit their homelands was rarely granted.

The new arms and equipment, imported from abroad or manufactured in Russian foundries, the reorganization and training of the Russian forces, and the recruiting of experienced mercenaries were transforming the armies of Tsar Mikhail. But time was needed to make these measures fully effective. War interrupted the process too soon and the Russian armies again failed.

The Treaty of Stolbovo with Sweden and the Truce of Deulino with the Poles were regarded by all parties as merely temporary agreements. In Moscow they had been justified as providing a respite while Russia recovered her strength and developed her armed forces before dealing with both of these Western enemies.

Filaret had returned from being a prisoner in the hands of Sigismund obsessed with the policy of forming a coalition against Poland-Lithuania. Events seemed at first to favor him. In 1620 war broke out between the Swedes and Poles over the Baltic lands. Gustavus Adolphus appealed to the Tsar to join him against the Catholic Poles, the enemies of Orthodox and Lutheran alike. Then in August 1621 the Turkish Sultan, Osman II, sent Foma Cantacuzene as his special ambassador to Moscow with proposals for alliance and joint action against the Poles. Filaret saw his opportunity to destroy Russia's most dangerous enemy. He summoned the Assembly of the Land which in October 1621 endorsed his coalition policy with enthusiasm. But the massive army of the Ottoman Porte was defeated by a gallant Polish force and, so great was the humiliation of the Turks, the Sultan was murdered by his own janissaries on returning to his capital. The next disappointment for Filaret was that Gustavus Adolphus, having captured Riga, agreed to an armistice with Poland.

During the ten years that passed before Russia was again ready to embark on war against Poland, Filaret made frantic efforts to build up a coalition, based on alliance with Sweden and the Ottoman Porte. He proposed that Gustavus Adolphus should occupy the Polish throne on the death of Sigismund who was now old and ailing. At the beginning of 1631 the Tsar informed the Kings of Sweden, England, Denmark, and the government of the Netherlands that he was prepared to march against Poland and thus to participate in the Thirty Years' War against the Catholic powers, led by the Habsburgs. In May 1631 the Swedes proposed plans for a joint Russo-Swedish attack on Poland. The Russians agreed to engage a large force of Swedish troops for the campaign. Spirits rose further in Moscow when Gustavus Adolphus won a brilliant victory against Catholic forces near Leipzig.

Russian plans for marching on Poland-Lithuania were nevertheless delayed several times during 1631–32. Filaret was anxious to ensure that the Russian army was fully prepared. Imports of military materials and the output of Russian foundries were increased. A chain of fortresses and defense points along the western frontier, begun in 1630, was hurried toward completion. The finance for the campaign was raised by special taxes and duties, levied on merchants, townspeople, and the peasants. A further reason for delay was that negotiations with both Swedes and Turks dragged on without agreement on coordinated action.

In April 1632 Sigismund III died. Polish and Lithuanian nobles at once became involved in disputes over the succession. In Moscow it was clear that the time for attack had come. In June the Assembly of the Land met and approved immediate military action. Still the Russian government delayed. Crimean Tatars had launched attacks from the south and the Russians lands there were undefended, all troops being concentrated to march westward. The Tatars advanced so far north that they even threatened Moscow before they were forced to retreat.

In August the Swedish plan of campaign was received and the Russian armies, commanded by Boyar M. B. Shein who had distinguished himself in the defense of Smolensk in 1609–11, advanced to the frontier. In October Shein captured Dorogobuzh and other towns. He then laid siege to Smolensk, the stronghold which was the key to the advance westward. In November, however, Gustavus Adolphus, after winning a brilliant victory at Lutzen, was killed. A few days later Vladislas was elected King of Poland. He hurriedly mustered an army and marched to the relief of Smolensk.

Shein with his army of thirty thousand men had held Smolensk under siege for eight months. The Polish garrison was small, but it made fullest use of the almost impregnable fortifications of the town. Constant bombardment and assaults nevertheless brought the Poles near to surrender. Meanwhile in the three Russian camps from which Shein had surrounded the town morale had fallen dangerously. The serving gentry and the Cossacks were not accustomed to long grim operations like this siege. They were pressing to go home before the winter started.

Toward the end of August 1633 Vladislas reached Smolensk with fifteen thousand troops. He captured two of the Russian camps and laid siege to Shein's camp for four months. A Russian army, advancing to relieve Shein, was defeated at Dorogobuzh by a Polish detachment. This last defeat and the news of the death of Filaret in Moscow made Shein's position seem hopeless and in January 1634 he readily accepted Polish proposals to negotiate an armistice.

Vladislas imposed harsh terms. The Russians had to surrender all artillery and other weapons. All foreign mercenaries were to be free to transfer to the Poles and at Smolensk, on February 19, 1634, there were 8056 foreign officers and men under Shein's command who went over to Vladislas. The final humiliation was that Shein and his senior officers were required to make humble obeisance before the Polish king. On his return to Moscow, Shein and Izmailov, his second in command, were arraigned and beheaded.[6]

Encouraged by his victory at Smolensk, Vladislas went on to besiege the small fortress of Belaya, held by a Russian garrison of only a thousand men. But despite bombardment and numerous assaults Belaya did not surrender. As the weeks passed Vladislas became worried, for he had received reports that the Turkish Sultan was about to lead a vast army against Poland. He entered into negotiations with the Russians and in June 1634 signed the treaty of Polyanovsky. This treaty confirmed Polish possession of all the towns and territories, tentatively conceded under the Deulino armistice. The Tsar surrendered all claims to Livonia, Esthonia, and Courland and paid a war indemnity of twenty thousand rubles. But Vladislas finally renounced his claims to the Russian throne, acknowledging Mikhail as Tsar, but not "Tsar of All Russia."

Throughout these years Russia was suffering severe damage and loss of men from raids by the Crimean and Nogai Tatars. Every year the Tsar sent gifts of money and furs to the Khan in the hope that he would refrain from sending his Tatars on their plundering expeditions. But the Tatars continued their raids. Their main purpose was to take prisoners whom they sold into slavery. In the first half of the seventeenth century alone some two hundred thousand Russians were captured, and the fair Russian slaves fetched high prices in the markets of the East.

The dispatch of troops to the southern frontiers of the tsardom in the spring of each year was costly in men and equipment, which were needed in the West. In 1635 Mikhail's government began constructing a massive defense line along this frontier. Twenty-nine new towns were established and settled with selected people. By 1650 the Belgorod defense line, stretching from the Vorskla River through Belgorod and Voronezh to Tambov and farther eastward had been completed. It gave the central provinces greater security from Tatar attack and from these positions the Russians began pressing southward.

Beyond the Tatars, however, lay the powerful Ottoman Empire which the Tsars had always treated with special respect, anxious to give the Sultan no cause to march on Russia. The danger was that the Cossacks of the Don might provoke the Turks into declaring war. Their numbers constantly swollen by runaway peasants and townsmen from the north, the Don Cossacks were a formidable force. Tsar Mikhail's election to the throne in 1613 had owed much to their support. He acknowledged their existence as a political unit and annually sent envoys to the Don with gifts of money, cloth, grain, and weapons. The Don Cossacks for their part swore loyalty to the Tsar and were invaluable as a frontier force, always ready to attack the Tatars and even the Ottoman Porte itself. But they could be unreliable and unpredictable. The Tsar constantly warned and ordered them to refrain from attacking the Turks who might reply in force against him as their overlord. In the period from 1620 to 1640 numerous embassies departed from Moscow for Istanbul, bearing rich gifts of sables and other furs for the Sultan and seeking his support against the Poles or his pardon for raids by the Don Cossacks. But in 1637 the Don Cossacks staggered Istanbul, Moscow, Warsaw, and Bakhchisarai by their impudent daring in capturing the important and, it was believed, impregnable Turkish stronghold of Azov.

Commanding the mouth of the Don River, Azov contained three stone-walled towns, all surrounded by a strong outer wall and a deep trench. The Turkish garrison of four thousand troops with two hundred guns mounted in eleven towers, did not take the Cossack force with its four cannon seriously when it began its siege preparations. But after eight weeks the Cossacks managed to mine part of the outer wall and stormed the fortress. Fighting raged for three days before the Turks capitulated.

The Sultan had been occupied with the Persian War, but concluding it in 1639 he announced a campaign to recover Azov. In June of the following year a Turkish army of more than two hundred thousand men and the latest equipment began what was expected to be a brief siege of the Cossacks in Azov. But, although only five thousand strong, the Cossacks repelled no less than twenty-four Turkish assaults. In September, the Turks raised the siege and retired. But the Cossacks had suffered heavy losses and it was clear that they would not be able to hold out again in the following year. In October 1641 their leaders proposed to Tsar Mikhail that he should annex Azov and defend it with a strong garrison.

The initial alarm in Moscow over the Cossack exploit had passed as the small garrison held out against the massive Turkish forces. The Tsar and the Boyar Council now gave serious consideration to the Cossack proposal. Possession of Azov would be a considerable compensation for the failure to take Smolensk. But it was clear that a force of a thousand troops would be needed to man the fortress and the danger of a Turkish invasion of Russia in retaliation was a strong deterrent. In January 1642 the question was referred to the Assembly of the Land, summoned for the purpose. The Assembly was divided; all agreed that Azov should be held, but long arguments took place about the way in which money should be raised to repair and defend the fortress. Finally on April 30, 1642, the Tsar ordered the Don Cossacks to evacuate Azov. They obeyed, but only after reducing the fortress to ruins.

The concern of all Russians, once Mikhail was secure on the throne, was that he should take a wife and through his children ensure the succession. Only three years after his accession a bride had been chosen. She was Maria Ivanovna Khlopova, and was treated as Tsaritsa in anticipation of her marriage. But then it was reported that she suffered from an incurable illness, and the unfortunate maiden and her family were at once exiled to Tobolsk.

Filaret resolved to find a bride for his son from a foreign ruling family. This would both enhance the dignity of the new dynasty and also further his policy of forging a coalition against Poland. His envoys were, however, rebuffed in Denmark and in Sweden. He then began seeking a Russian bride. He had long suspected the truth about the alleged illness of Maria Khlopova. On investigation now it was found that she was perfectly healthy and that the vomiting, which had led to the exile of her and her family, had been caused by emetics deliberately administered by Mikhail Saltykov who had quarreled with the Khlopov family. The Saltykovs were found guilty of "interruption to the Tsar's pleasure and wedding"; their estates were confiscated and they were exiled to Siberia, but recalled after Filaret's death.

Tsar Mikhail had decided by this time, however, that he no longer wanted Maria as his bride. He married Maria Dolgorukaya, but she died within a few months. He then chose Evdokiya Streshnevaya, daughter of a minor member of the gentry, and she bore him the son who was to carry on the dynasty.

Like his father, Mikhail was anxious to forge links with royal families in the West. In April 1642 he sent an embassy to King Christian of Denmark, proposing the marriage of his daughter, Irina, with the Danish prince, Waldemar. This mission failed because the envoys told the King that his son would have to embrace the Orthodox faith before he could marry the Tsarevna. In December the Dane, Peter Marselis, who had long been resident in Russia and was highly regarded by the Tsar, arrived in Copenhagen to renew proposals for this marriage. He expressed regret on behalf of the Tsar that the earlier envoys had misinformed him. He gave formal assurances that the Tsar would not insist on the prince embracing Orthodoxy in order to marry the Tsarevna.

Prince Waldemar arrived in Moscow with a considerable retinue in January 1644. The King had made it an express condition of his traveling to Russia that he should enjoy complete freedom of worship and should be accorded all the respects and precedence due to his royal position. No sooner had Waldemar arrived in Moscow, however, than the Patriarch began urging him to embrace Orthodoxy. Next the Tsar himself tried to persuade him to be rebaptized in the true faith. Waldemar heatedly reminded the Tsar of his promise not to put pressure on him to change his faith. The Tsar replied that he had undertaken not to use force or to put pressure on the prince, but that this did not mean that he could not seek to persuade him. Waldemar next demanded that he should be allowed to return to Copenhagen. The Tsar refused permission and doubled the guards posted at Waldemar's house. For months the dispute raged. Every argument and device was brought to bear on the unfortunate prince, who was now a prisoner, to allow himself to be rebaptized. He stubbornly refused and his complaints about his treatment became more furious. He even tried with his retinue to break out of Moscow by force, hoping to make his way to the frontier. In the struggle one Russian guard was killed and others were wounded, but the prince and his companions were held, now under even closer guard.

In November 1644 letters reached Moscow from the Danish King, demanding the immediate release of his son. The Tsar protested that Waldemar was like a son to him and that he could not let him go. Mikhail's obstinacy in holding the Danish prince is difficult to understand. An extremely devout man, he probably thought that with time Waldemar would inevitably recognize in Orthodox Christianity the true faith, and that he would thus save a soul. But the obstinacy of the captive prince and the bitter disputes with him, his retinue, and with the King in Copenhagen deeply distressed him. He had never been robust in health. He was now forty-eight years old and, except for the fourteen years when Filaret had wielded power, his reign had been burdensome. Early in 1645 he suffered a double bereavement in the deaths of his two eldest sons, Ivan and Vasily, within a few weeks of each other. This tragedy, coming after the long months of dispute with Waldemar, affected him deeply. His doctors declared that his incessant weeping had chilled his blood.[7]

On July 12, 1645, while attending divine service, he suddenly collapsed. He was carried to his suite. It was clear that he was near to death. He regained consciousness and summoned Tsarevich Alexei, his surviving son. In the presence of the Patriarch, the Tsaritsa, and of Boyar Boris Ivanovich Morozov, he declared Alexei to be his successor, and begged Morozov to watch over and guide him. Soon afterward he died.

Pious and gentle, Tsar Mikhail had carried out his duties conscientiously. But he was a sickly man and because of a weakness in his legs he had seldom ventured beyond the Kremlin. He made no impact through personality or ability, but by his presence on the throne he gave the nation the focal point which it needed and held it from disintegrating. His reign then became a time of recovery from all the evils of the Time of Troubles and a time of national revival, and through his son he ensured the continuity of the new dynasty.

III

Alexei Mikhailovich

1645–1676

Alexei, the second Tsar of the dynasty, was sixteen years old when he ascended the throne. He was a gentle, exceedingly pious boy, who seemed at first to resemble his father closely. But he developed strongly in intelligence and character and, far from being weak and insipid, he soon revealed a robust personality.

Dr. Samuel Collins, his English physician, was to write of him as "a goodly person, about six foot high, well set, inclined to fat, of a clear complexion, lightish hair, somewhat low forehead, of a stern countenance, severe in his chastisements, but very careful of his subjects' love."[1]

As a child Alexei had lived in the special apartment in the Kremlin, set aside for the Tsarevich. A suite of noble ladies cared for him. When he was old enough a group of playmates, known as *komnatnie stolniki*, shared in his games. At the age of six he had begun lessons with an alphabet book especially ordered for him by his grandfather, Patriarch Filaret, which contained simple prayers and a shortened catechism. As soon as he could read he was given the psalter, a book of hours, and other religious works. By the time he was ten he had had intensive instruction in the minutiae of Orthodox ritual.

At this point the education of the Tsarevich, exclusively religious in character, usually ended. Alexei was to benefit from the Western customs which were already spreading within the Kremlin. Patriarch Filaret, influenced by his period of Polish captivity, had been more tolerant of Western fashions and ideas than his predecessors. He and other relatives as well as some members of the court gave the young Alexei toys of Western manufacture. But the most important influence in the boy's life was his tutor, Boyar Boris Morozov, who was among the first and most ardent Westernizers in Russia. Learned and intelligent he might have been a leading statesman, but he was too greedy for money and power to be able to subordinate his own interests to those of the Tsar and the nation. But his influence over Alexei was evidently not harmful, especially after 1645, the year in which both his mother and father died and Morozov took their place. Alexei rewarded him with his friendship, which did not waver even when popular feeling against Morozov erupted dangerously.

Certainly one of the most attractive of Romanovs, Alexei has been known in Russian history as *tishaishy Tsar*, the quietest or gentlest Tsar. He was, in fact, given to violent outbursts of anger when he personally chastised the offending subject, no matter how highly placed. He could not stand arrogance or incompetence. In 1660, when the Russian armies had suffered disastrous defeat by the Poles, he summoned the Council of Boyars to consider what should be done. Miloslavsky, his own father-in-law, inexperienced in military matters, suddenly boasted that, given the army command, he would readily defeat the Poles and capture the King of Poland himself. This idle boast infuriated Alexei. He leaped from his throne, boxed Miloslavsky's ears and, physically dragging him to the door, threw him out of the audience chamber.[2]

In church, when the priest made mistakes in the ritual, Alexei halted the service, cursed him for his incompetence and made him repeat the service until he performed it correctly. He did not hesitate to admonish the Patriarch himself.[3] But his outbursts of anger were at once followed by lenience or pardon. Indeed, if he saw that he had been in the wrong, he would ask forgiveness, and for the Tsar to apologize to one of his subjects was in itself remarkable.

In a deeper sense the description of Alexei as *tishaishy Tsar* was merited. He embodied in his outlook and his daily living the humility, devoutness, and spiritual striving which were of the essence of Orthodox teaching. He combined these qualities with a strong sense of duty to his people and country. Moreover, he had a gift for choosing able advisers to whom he gave his trust and friendship and certain of whom in their own characters reflected something of the goodness in Alexei himself.

In the nineteenth century the Slavophiles who believed fervently in the unique culture and institutions of Orthodox Russia, as they had been before Peter the Great's Westernizing onslaught, looked back to Alexei's reign as a golden age. As Tsar he seemed to justify the legend of old Muscovy with its firm but just and kindly paternalism and its magnificence, order, and piety.

Alexei cultivated the pomp and ceremony of his court. He always appeared before his people splendidly robed and attended by a numerous suite. When visiting a monastery outside Moscow, he was accompanied by a thousand horsemen and longer journeys required an escort of five to ten thousand men. At Easter and other great festivals and when receiving foreign ambassadors his robes were even more magnificent.[4] Foreigners who visited the Kremlin Palace were awed by the splendor. Guy Miege, secretary to the embassy sent by Charles II of England to the Tsar in 1664, reported that, passing into the audience chamber

... we were like those who, coming suddenly out of the dark, are dazzled with the brightness of the sun; the splendour of their jewels, seeming to contend for priority with that of the day, so that we were lost, as it were, in this confusion of glory. The Tsar, like a sparkling sun (to speak in the Russian dialect), darted forth most sumptuous rays, being most magnificently placed upon his throne, with his sceptre in his hand, and having his crown upon his head. His throne was of massy silver gilt, wrought curiously on the top with several works and pyramids, and being seven or eight steps higher then the floor it rendered the person of the Prince transcendently majestic. His crown (which he wore upon a cap lined with black sables) was covered quite over with precious stones; it terminated towards the top in the form of a pyramid, with a golden cross on the spire. The sceptre glistened also all over with jewels; his vest was set with the like from the top to the bottom down the opening before, and his collar was answerable to the same. By his side he had four of the tallest of his lords, standing below his throne, each of them with his battle-axe upon his shoulder, and with a profound gravity casting their eyes now and then upon their Tsar, inviting us to an admiration of his grandeur. Their habits were no less remarkable than their countenances, being all ᵤur of them, from the top of their head to the sole of their foot, clothed in white vests of ermine, and having great chains of gold, and their caps of that large sort which they use in the ceremonies, but whereas others were of black fox, these were of ermine, as well as their vests; their very boots also were covered with the same. But that which was further admirable was the glorious equipage of the Boyars present at this audience, who were as so many beams of the sun elevated in his triumphal car, and seemed to have no lustre but to do homage withal to their great monarch. They were about two hundred, clothed all with vests of cloth of gold, cloth of silver or velvet set with jewels, all placed in order upon benches covered with tapestry about by the wall; the floor being raised there three or four steps higher and about the breadth of a good walk. At the entrance into the hall there was a great number also of his *goses* (gosti) which are his merchants or factors, whom he furnishes with rich robes to appear at such ceremonies. This was the splendour we found this great prince in, with a countenance perfectly majestic, as having not only the advantage of a handsome proportion, but of a lively and vigorous age, for this was but his four and thirtieth year.[5]

Alexei was also a man of great piety. The routine of his day began at 4 A.M. with prayers in his private chapel. He then joined the Tsaritsa and with her attended matins. He also took part in a late morning service, lasting some two hours. In the great Easter celebrations he would stand for five or six hours without relief, and make as many as 1500 prostrations to the ground. Moreover, he observed strictly the fasts in Lent, dining only three times during the week and on other days eating a piece of black bread and a salted mushroom. In general his habits were moderate; he ate simple dishes and drank sparingly.[6]

Such arduous devotions and aesthetic living befitted a monk rather than the Autocrat, ruling a vast and troubled country. Alexei nevertheless found time for public business. Early every morning his boyars and councilors assembled at the palace or in the appointed church. Anyone absent or late without good reason incurred his anger and might even be flung into prison.[7]

On first seeing "the bright eyes of the Tsar," whether in the audience chamber or in church, all bowed low to the ground, sometimes, if seeking special favor, making as many as thirty obeisances.[8] In church at convenient times during the service the Tsar listened to reports and gave instructions, but he never failed to observe every detail of the ritual. At midday he withdrew to dine, often by himself. He then slept until about 3 P.M. when he attended vespers. If business was pressing, he followed an afternoon routine like that of the morning, but usually he relaxed with his family or conversed with those close to him or with the old men who enjoyed favor because of their age and piety, and were housed in quarters near the palace.

In his way of life Alexei came close to the Muscovite ideal. His conception of his power and position as Tsar also belonged to the Muscovite heritage. He believed implicitly, as Ivan the Terrible had believed, that he was divinely appointed to rule as absolute monarch and defender of the Orthodox faith. But in his humility and love for his people he wielded power more moderately than Tsar Ivan. Moreover, contrary to the Muscovite legend, he was far from being an archconservative, who regarded all change as wicked. He reflected the two currents in the Russia of his time and later, one driving the country toward equality and kinship with Western Europe, the other holding her unchanged and inviolate as the stronghold of Orthodox Christianity.

The mass of the people, working the soil, were staunchly conservative and the church fortified their opposition to change. Among the nobles and gentry, however, were certain individuals who recognized that Russia would stagnate if she turned her back on the ideas and developments of Western Europe. Alexei was naturally conservative, but his was not a closed mind. He listened to the men at his court who spoke of education and reforms.

The thirty years of his reign, far from being a time of stability and kindly paternalism were, in fact, a time of tremendous change. Every aspect of Russian life was affected by the new legal code, by the Schism in the church, by the influx of Western ideas, and by developments in foreign relations. It was also a time of widespread discontent, rebellion, and mounting crisis. Indeed his reign was one of the most turbulent in Russia's history, but its importance has been obscured by the even more dramatic reign of his son, Peter.

The general unrest had carried over from the Time of Troubles. Russia had recovered from the chaos of that period and the economy had revived. The recovery was, however, superficial and the nation had further been strained by the Smolensk war in the 1630s. The great social problems remained and had even been exacerbated by the hasty expedients adopted in the reign of Tsar Mikhail. His government had been concerned to exact higher taxes and to strengthen the armies needed to impose order internally and to defend the tsardom against enemies on its frontiers. But the Russian people were growing more and more restive. They endured increasing burdens as authority was further centralized in the hands of an arbitrary and corrupt bureaucracy.

During the reign of Alexei popular discontent erupted in a series of violent rebellions. In 1646–47 outbreaks took place on the lower Don, in the extreme north, and in Siberia where peasants and townsmen refused to pay increased taxes. But the first serious revolt was in Moscow in 1648, just three years after Alexei had come to the throne. In the capital as in other parts of the country the taxes were borne by as few as one third of the population. The people who were exempt belonged to the vast estates of the nobles and the church. Petitions were addressed from the provinces and from Moscow to the Tsar who probably never saw them. The officials of the *prikazi*, wielding almost unlimited power, ignored complaints, while adding to the burdens of the people by their own peculations.

Boris Morozov whom Alexei trusted and who virtually ruled the country in the first years of the young Tsar's reign condoned the widespread

—corruption in the bureaucracy. He himself became the wealthiest man of his time. He had during 1646–47 changed the chief officials in many *prikazi*. Two of his appointees, L. S. Pleshcheev and P. T. Trakhaniotov, had carried their corruption and arbitrary rule to new extremes.

As the discontent of the Muscovites mounted, their anger was directed primarily at Morozov. He had, moreover, been responsible for the new salt tax introduced in February 1646 and for subsequent tax changes which imposed impossible burdens on the people.

Thwarted in their efforts to petition the Tsar for justice, a group of Muscovities planned to deliver their petition directly into his hands. The opportunity offered on June 1, 1648, when the Tsar and Tsaritsa were returning from prayers at the Troitsa Monastery. But the bodyguard scattered them before they could get near him, and some of them were arrested. On the following day the Tsar rode to the Sretensky Monastery outside Moscow. This time, as the petitioners were pushed aside, the crowd began shouting for Pleshcheev to be handed over to them and for the release of the men arrested the previous day. The people were now angry. As the Tsar returned to Moscow, the crowd, now several thousand strong, pressed forward. The *streltsi*, posted by Morozov to guard the entrances to the Kremlin, refused to fire on them. The uproar mounted. Alexei himself, holding an ikon in his hands, finally came before the people and called on them to cease their unruly behavior. His appeal had little effect. The crowd went on to destroy the palaces of Morozov, Pleshcheev, Trakhaniotov, and others against whom their anger was directed.

On June 3 fire broke out in the city. It spread rapidly, destroying thousands of houses as well as the city's grain supplies. It was widely rumored that servants of Morozov had started the fire. The people gathered on the Red Square and laid siege to the Kremlin palace, noisily demanding the immediate punishment of Morozov, Pleshcheev, and Trakhaniotov.

Alexei, aged only nineteen, faced a crisis. The people were in a dangerous mood. But he could not surrender Morozov whom he regarded as a father and on whom he depended. On his own decision or on the advice of Morozov, he had Pleshcheev given up to the crowd who dragged him to the Red Square and tore him to pieces. But the death of one hated official was not enough to placate the people. On the following day (June 4) the crowd again gathered at the Kremlin Palace and noisily demanded Morozov and Trakhaniotov. Alexei had tried to save Trakhaniotov by sending him to a distant province. The people had become so threatening, however, that he recalled him. Trakhaniotov then was surrendered and promptly killed at the execution place (Lobnoe Mesto) on the Red Square.

The turbulence continued. It seemed that only the execution of Morozov would satisfy the Muscovites. Alexei himself appeared before the people. He begged them with tears in his eyes to spare Morozov, promising to remove him from office and to send him far from Moscow. Popular anger was in no way directed at the Tsar himself and his plea was heard. Morozov went unscathed, remaining for a time in the Kirillov-Belozersky Monastery, where the Tsar had sent him for his safety. Later he returned to Moscow, but he was never again to hold the same power and position as in the first years of Alexei's reign.

The rebellions in Moscow and all over the country had alarmed the Tsar and his government. He took steps to ensure the loyalty of the serving gentry and the *streltsi* on whom the security of the regime depended. Special payments were made to the *streltsi* and on the Tsar's personal instruction they were presented with wine and honey. Many among the serving gentry received new grants of land and increased payments. Officials in the *prikazi* whose conduct had so incensed the people, were replaced by men held in higher respect. Moreover, Alexei immediately agreed to summon the Assembly of the Land in response to the demands of servingmen, merchants, and townsmen in Moscow and the provinces. This Assembly resolved that a further Assembly should be summoned to consider a new code of laws (*ulozhenie*), the drafting of which was entrusted to a special commission under the chairmanship of Prince N. I. Odoevsky.

The Assembly which met in September 1648 remained in session for six and a half months. The deputies, some 350 in number, represented all classes, except the peasantry. The gentry or *dvoriane*, who held their lands in service tenure, were the dominant group. The Assembly divided itself into a lower house, comprising the deputies from towns and provinces, and the upper house of the Tsar, the Patriarch, the Council of Boyars, and the Church Council.

The Code which resulted enacted the principle of the primacy of the state and recognized the people only as a source of taxes, of grain, and of manpower for the armed forces. The population was divided into classes to facilitate the collection of taxes. Several forms of tax evasion were stamped out. The serving gentry and townsmen in particular were forbidden to assign themselves to great landowners, thereby escaping tax liability. Townsmen were required to live in the towns in which they were registered. The duty of the gentry to serve in the army was confirmed. The church which owned extensive lands was forbidden to expand its estate further. Serfdom was enacted in its final form by the abolition of the time-limit within which landowners could recover runaway serfs. The peasant became permanently tied not only to the estate but also directly to the landowner.

The Code thus gave legal form to the rigidly centralized autocratic regime. It regimented the people, subordinating them wholly to the financial and military needs of the state. It entrenched a system which crippled Russia as she struggled to develop in the following centuries. But the Code, endorsed by the leading classes as represented in the Assembly of the Land, also reflected the requirements of the young nation at this time. Its vast expanse, the need to restore order and at the same time to defend itself against the enemies on its frontiers required a strong centralized power as well as a dependable revenue and an adequate army. The tragedy was that on attaining internal stability and secure frontiers early in the eighteenth century, the Code was not revised to give a more liberal system in which individual citizens and society as a whole could develop freely and strongly.

In approving the new Code, Alexei was merely responding to the immediate needs of the nation and to his belief in his own role as Autocrat. He was to show later in his reign, especially in his choice of such advisers as Ordin-Nashchokin and Rtishchev, that he could be mindful of the welfare of his subjects as individuals, and he took some steps to ameliorate hardships. But he was himself so imprisoned in the autocratic system that he was incapable of modifying it for the benefit of the mass of the people.

Meanwhile unrest continued. The summer of 1650 was a time of major uprisings in Pskov and Novgorod, and Moscow itself seemed threatened. Rebellion erupted in Pskov in February when townsmen, artisans, and *streltsi* stationed there objected forcibly to the passage of grain to Sweden. The Pskov region was suffering at the time from a food shortage. The people were in no mood to understand that the grain was being sent to Sweden under the terms of the Treaty of Stolbovo. They rebelled against the governor and refused to allow the grain to be moved. In March the people of Novgorod rose against their governor and the local nobility and the *streltsi* supported them. From Moscow Prince Khovansky was sent with troops to restore order. He succeeded within a month in Novgorod. But the collapse of the Novgorod rebellion made the Pskovtsi more determined to resist. In May, Alexei sent a punitive force, again commanded by Khovansky, to put down the revolt in Pskov. In the course of three months Khovansky lost many men before the rebels finally came to terms.

The 1650s were a time of mounting crisis for Alexei's government. War against Poland-Lithuania was exhausting the financial and manpower resources of the country. In 1654 plague broke out, causing countless deaths and so aggravating the manpower shortage that the grain harvest suffered. But the first concern of the government was to raise revenues to finance the war. Wealthy monasteries and prominent merchants had to make special loans and contributions to the treasury. But this was not enough.

The government had in 1654 debased the coinage by halving the amount of silver in coins while holding their nominal value. In 1656 Alexei adopted the drastic policy of minting copper coins which would have the same value as the silver coinage. At first the treasury drew tremendous profits from the exchange of copper for silver. But popoular confidence in the new coinage was shortlived. Soon one silver coin could buy fifteen copper coins of the same nominal value. Counterfeiters began to multiply. Rumors circulated that Miloslavsky, the Tsar's father-in-law, and others at court were buying copper and minting their own coins. The prices of food and goods soared. In increasing numbers people became destitute and desperate from hunger.

Toward the end of July 1662 thousands of people began moving from Moscow on the road to Kolomenskoe, the country palace to which Alexei retreated with his family whenever he could get away from the pressures of ceremonial and business in the Kremlin. The crowd was raging about certain boyars who were alleged to be traitors in communication with the King of Poland; at the same time they were the boyars believed to be responsible for the copper coinage and all the suffering that had resulted from it.

Alexei was at prayers when the crowd reached Kolomenskoe. The Tsaritsa and her children waited in the women's quarters in a state of terror as they heard the roar of the approaching mob. Alexei left the church to face his subjects. He heard their demands and quietly told them to return to their homes. He did not call upon his bodyguard when two of the leaders came closer and gave him a petition or when others grasped the buttons of his robes, demanding his assurance that he would see that they received justice. He swore before God that he would order a thorough investigation. The crowd then dispersed and made its way back to the capital.

Meanwhile in Moscow the people who had remained were enraged by the escape of two of the wealthiest merchants, rumored to have counterfeited copper money. Suddenly in a mass these people decided to see the Tsar in Kolomenskoe. They were on the road when they met the first mob returning. The latter, readily inflamed afresh, turned about and it seemed that the whole population of Moscow was on the road to Kolomenskoe and in an excited savage mood.

By this time, however, the *streltsi* regiments had been ordered to the defense of the Tsar. They arrived as Alexei was facing the vast angry mob, which had started to shout threats and abuse at him. Learning of the arrival of the *streltsi* Alexei ordered them to put down the rebellion. They at once fired into the crowd and then proceeded to cut them down. A massacre developed in which some seven thousand people were killed, hunted into the Moscow River and drowned, or rounded up for interrogation and punishment. Hundreds of innocent people among them perished.

Unrest increased as the bondage of serfdom settled more heavily upon the mass of the people. The peasants reacted to the Code of 1649, which made them the slaves of their landowners, by rebellion, outbreaks of arson, murder and destruction, and above all by flight to the east into Siberia, but mainly to the south to the lands of the Don and the Volga. Here they could find freedom, joining the Cossacks of the Don, the Yaik, and the Kuban. They formed a great brotherhood of runaway serfs, deserters, and the nomadic peoples. While acknowledging the suzerainty of the Tsar, the Cossacks continued to pursue their own interests as freebooters, hunters, and robbers, raiding and plundering where they saw profit. The Tsar sent gifts, exhortations, and occasionally punitive expeditions, but they did not seriously interfere with the Cossacks' way of life, which provided the ideal of all who were enslaved and desperate.

The flood of runaway serfs to the south was growing seriously despite all government efforts to halt it. Instead of seeking the causes of the discontent more repressive measures were applied and still peasants braved the savage punishments and escaped. From this southern region of the Don and Volga arose a challenge which threatened the tsardom. Its leader was a Cossack named Stenka Razin, a man of great energy and enterprise. In the spring of 1661 the Don Cossack leaders had sent him on a mission to persuade the Kalmyks to join with them against the Crimean Tatars. Stenka visited Moscow later the same year and then went on a pilgrimage to the Solovetsky Monastery in the White Sea. His movements during the next five years are not known. But in 1667 Alexei sent warning to his commanders on the Volga that a great Cossack horde was preparing to plunder the towns and traffic along the Volga and to occupy Tsaritsyn. The Ataman or leader of this Cossack horde was Stenka Razin.

Starting his campaign by moving north along the Don, Stenka Razin took Tsaritsyn. He then proceeded down the Volga to occupy Astrakhan. In 1669 he fitted out a flotilla which plundered vessels, trading on the Caspian Sea, engaged and defeated a Persian naval squadron, and even invaded northern Persia. On his return the people of Astrakhan greeted him as a hero.

Alexei was alarmed by these exploits. Stenka Razin might easily involve Moscow in war with the Persians or, more serious, with the Ottoman Porte. Also he was disrupting trade on the Volga, challenging and setting aside the Tsar's authority, and rallying the poor, the oppressed, and the mass of the people in the south to his banner. Alexei sent an offer of full pardon to him on condition that he gave up the ships, the Tsar's commanders, and officials and other prisoners he had taken and committed no further acts of plunder and piracy. This offer evidently failed to deflect Stenka Razin from his plans.

In 1670 he advanced up the Volga, taking Saratov and Samara. His advance detachments moved as far west as Tambov and Nizhni-Novgorod. The whole character of his campaigning had now changed. He had started as a typical Cossack, leading his men in search of action and booty. He now launched a class war, calling on peasants to kill their landowners, to rebel against all authority, and to follow him. A born leader whose exploits and generosity were already legendary among the Russians, he rallied thousands to his banner. He was soon posing a grave threat to the Tsar and the whole regime.

At Simbirsk, in October 1670, however, Stenka Razin met with strong resistance by the garrison and townsmen. The Tsar's army, commanded by Prince Baryatinsky, routed his forces. He himself was wounded and had to flee by night to Samara. But there, where he had so recently been hailed as a liberator, he was refused admission and also at Saratov. He made his way south to the Don where he began raising forces to renew his campaign. But on April 14, 1672, the Ataman of the Don Cossacks seized him. Under strong escort he was taken to Moscow and on June 6 he was executed on the Red Square. But he had made an indelible impression on the Russian people. He became part of a strong and living popular tradition as the savior of the oppressed, the great rebel against autocracy, and the champion of the free.

Against this background of unrest, a change in the relations of Russia with Western Europe was taking place. The influx of Western ideas into Muscovy had begun in the late fifteenth century. In the reign of Tsar Mikhail the need for the reform and modernization of Russia had come to be recognized. The process gathered real momentum under Tsar Alexei. In the reign of Peter the Great it became a dynamic movement.

In the sixteenth and seventeenth centuries the peoples of Western Europe, freed from the shackles of feudalism, had entered on a period of intensive activity in trades industry, military science, and intellectual life. Russia stood outside the stream of these developments. In the fifteenth and sixteenth centuries the unification of the state under the rule of Moscow and defense against neighboring enemies had absorbed the energies of all Russians. They had, moreover, retained since the fifteenth century a sense of self-sufficiency. The Orthodox Church, and especially the idea of Moscow as the heir of Constantinople, the third and perfect Rome, had bred in them a mood of arrogance and complacency. Suddenly in the seventeenth century the Tsar and leading men at court awoke to the fact that Russia had fallen far behind the rest of Europe and that, unless they were prepared to learn from the West, the nation would continue to lag behind and would remain vulnerable.

Late in the fifteenth century Ivan III had engaged architects and artists from Italy. Ivan IV, the Terrible, had sought without much success to engage foreign engineers and artisans, especially those skilled in the manufacture and use of the latest military equipment. The first real influx of Western influence happened in the reign of Tsar Mikhail. He began enlisting foreign mercenaries, for it was in the field of defense that Russia felt her backwardness most acutely.

Western military and industrial techniques were accepted, although with reluctance, by conservative Orthodox Russians as not affecting the spiritual life of the nation. But with these innovations was inevitably introduced a broader Western influence which was soon permeating the daily life of the capital. An important channel of this influence was the Foreign Quarter or *Nemetskaya Sloboda*.

In the previous century the foreign officers and soldiers, doctors, merchants, and artisans in Russia had established this Foreign Quarter on the banks of the Yauza River outside Moscow. They were scattered and their Quarter destroyed during the Time of Troubles. But they had returned and their numbers had begun to increase in the reign of Tsar Mikhail. They settled now in Moscow and even built Protestant churches within the city. But Orthodox churchmen and xenophobic Muscovites took offense at this invasion of their city by foreign heretics. An ukaz, issued by Tsar Mikhail, forbade the purchase of houses and building of churches by foreigners in Moscow. A further ukaz in 1652 resettled all foreigners on the banks of the Yauza River beyond the city limits, and on the site of the old the new Foreign Quarter arose.

The Quarter had a population of some 1500 at the beginning of Alexei's reign, but it grew rapidly until it was soon about one-fifth the size of Moscow. Scots, English, Dutch, and Germans were the most numerous inhabitants, and all apparently lived in harmony. They made full use of the artisans among them and built a pleasant town with broad avenues and attractive timbered houses with gardens. It included two Lutheran churches and two schools. The Quarter provided a strong contrast to Muscovite towns and villages which were unplanned and unkempt and the houses of which stood unrepaired until they fell or were burned to the ground.

Within their Quarter the foreigners enjoyed freedom to pursue their own way of life. Their community, which included a high proportion of cultured and learned men, was a civilized society. Many of them managed to keep in touch with the cultural and scientific developments of their own countries. General Patrick Gordon, a Scot greatly respected by the Russians, regularly received reports of the proceedings of the Royal Society in London. The diplomatic missions of England, Holland, Sweden, and other countries, which were in the Quarter, received mail regularly from their capitals. The foreigners in Russia were, in fact, better informed about developments of every kind in Western Europe than the Tsar's embassies.

Already in Alexei's reign the Foreign Quarter had begun to make a deep impact on Russian life in the capital. Russians lived in primitive conditions without comfort or grace and they had no social life as it was understood in the West. Forbidden to travel abroad, except on the Tsar's commissions, they had no conception of other ways of living. From returning missions and contact with the Poles earlier in the century, the Tsar and members of his court learned something of the elegance of other capitals. But the Foreign Quarter served as a visible example of Western standards of living.

Certain men at Alexei's court, and especially Boris Morozov, Nikita Romanov, Fedor Rtishchev, Afanasy Ordin-Nashchokin, and Artamon Matveev, were strongly attracted not only by the comfort, but also by the culture and learning of the West. They recognized that Russian society was coarse and illiterate. They were eager to adopt Western standards, to study and to encourage education in Russia. But it was the elegance and comfort of Western life that first attracted them.

Prestige was another reason for this growing eagerness to learn from the West. Russians were always sensitive about comparisons with other countries, and it was a matter of honor that the Tsar's court should not appear inferior to the courts of other monarchs. Alexei's ambassadors on proceeding abroad had instructions to report on the arrangements and entertainments of other courts. Thus Likhachev, who went in 1659 on a mission to Tuscany and was invited to a ball and a theater in Florence, described the occasion in the closest detail. Similar reports by other envoys were studied carefully in Moscow.[9]

Western theatrical and musical entertainments were of special interest, for they were unknown in the Kremlin. Indeed, even the simple folk dances and music of the Russian peasants were condemned as ungodly pastimes. Early in his reign Alexei himself had issued an ukaz, forbidding his subjects "to dance, play games, or watch them; at wedding feasts either to sing or to play on instruments; to give over one's soul to perdition in such pernicious and lawless practices as word-play, farces and magic."[10]

It was a measure of the transformation in Alexei's outlook that a few years later he was listening to music and sending instructions to his ambassadors abroad to engage good trumpet players. Even more significant was his sudden interest in the theater which had always been sternly forbidden in Russia. He had consulted earnestly with his spiritual advisers and they had finally agreed that such performances were permissible since the Byzantine Emperors had attended them. Alexei at once ordered the erection of a theater at Preobrazhenskoe, another of his country residences. A Lutheran pastor, Johann Gregory, was found in the Foreign Quarter and ordered to produce a play. He got together a cast mainly among the Quarter's older children and produced a play called *Esther*. Alexei was enthralled. According to a contemporary account he was so impressed that he "watched for ten hours without once moving from his seat." Fittingly he had ordered the performance to celebrate the birth of his son, Peter.[11]

The theater became one of Alexei's regular entertainments. Music was, however, his great passion. Banquets at his court were occasions for music and at dinner "a foreigner played the organ, trumpeters trumpeted, and kettledrums beat."[12] Soon the palace and boyars' mansions were graced with Western elegance. Paintings, clocks and mirrors, velvet hangings and upholstery appeared in chambers which had been bare but for ikons. The craze for elegance led to extremes. As a wedding present Alexei gave Boris Morozov a carriage covered with gold brocade, lined with sables and with silver instead of iron even for the axles.[13]

While seizing on the trappings of Western life, however, Alexei and those close to him recognized that they must also embrace the intellectual life of the West. They had to put an end to the general ignorance and illiteracy at least among the boyars and gentry by introducing education. Schools were nonexistent in Russia. Such education as was provided was private and limited to a few boyar families and to certain monasteries. But, whereas they had turned directly to the West for military and other skills and for artistic innovations, they turned to the Ukraine and Poland in the field of education and learning.

Southwestern Russia had long been under Roman Catholic Polish rule, but except for the Polish landowning nobility the population was Orthodox Russian. While stubbornly defending their faith against Jesuit persecution, the Orthodox had studied Latin, adopted Jesuit methods, and absorbed elements of Western culture. The struggle for survival had in fact stimulated them so that in intellectual activity they were far ahead of their fellow believers in Moscow. In 1633 the Metropolitan of Kiev, Peter Mogila, established an academy which quickly became the center of Orthodox learning, but it was Orthodox learning revitalized and in part transformed by Latin culture.

Moscow's approach to Kiev happened in 1649-50 when three learned monks—Slavinetsky, Satanovsky, and Ptitsky—were engaged from the academy. Their task was to produce a Slav version of the Bible, for it had suddenly been realized that for six centuries only the Greek text had been available, and few in Russia understood Greek. The learned monks from Kiev also translated into Russian, at the request of the Tsar and others, a number of nonreligious books. Many at court eagerly read the new books. Their intellectual curiosity was aroused and they made further demands for education.

In 1665 Simeon Polotsky, from the Kiev academy, started a small school in a building especially erected in the Spassky Monastery in Moscow. Alexei also engaged him as tutor to his elder sons and to his daughter, Sofia. He taught them Latin and Polish and how to write verse.

A gentle, dedicated scholar, Polotsky earned wide respect. Others at court followed the Tsar's example. Ordin-Nashchokin, the outstanding Russian statesman of the day, surrounded his son with Polish prisoners of war so that he would learn Polish and imbibe Western culture.

Foremost in encouraging education in the reign of Alexei was Fedor Mikhailovich Rtishchev, a saint, scholar, and an active official, who was one of the most remarkable men of his time. He had built the Andreevsky Monastery outside Moscow at his own expense and in 1649 he engaged from the Ukraine some thirty learned monks who lived there. They had the tasks of translating foreign books into Russian and teaching all who wished to learn Greek, Latin, Slavonic languages, philosophy, and other subjects. He himself studied at the school, going every night to learn from the monks.

The great moral authority which he gave to the promotion of education in Russia was as important as his school. A selfless man, dedicated to serving his fellows and his country, Rtishchev was loved and repected. Alexei turned to him increasingly as a friend and wise counselor. He promoted him and gave him many responsibilities, but Rtishchev declined the rank of boyar and other rewards. He gave away his own money and estates, and freed his serfs. In 1654, when traveling with Alexei to the Polish campaign, he filled his carriage with poor and sick people whom he saw by the road. Soon there was no room for him and he had to continue on horseback, although in pain from an injured leg. He later made provision for these people to be cared for. In Moscow he had the sick and the drunk collected from the streets and given shelter until they had recovered. For the aged and the incurable he built almshouses where they were maintained at his expense. His example as a social reformer produced wider results. In 1681 Alexei proposed to the Patriarch and church council that such shelters and almshouses be erected throughout the city for the needy, and the church undertook this responsibility.

The spread of Western influence and the intellectual awakening, represented by Peter Mogila's Kievan academy, and in particular the study of Greek, led to the reform of the church books and ritual and then to the *Raskol*, the great Schism within the Church, an event of dramatic importance not only for the Russian Church but for the whole nation.

The Russian Church, turning from the ideal of the universal church, had become intensely nationalistic since the fifteenth century and, fired by an arrogant belief in its mission and its infallibility, it interpreted Orthodoxy to mean the preservation of the faith in pristine purity. Change of any kind was abhorrent. Not only dogma, but the smallest details of ritual were divinely ordained and immutable. Russians refused to acknowledge that errors had come into the liturgical texts in the course of copying them by hand over the years, and that the introduction of printing in 1552 had multiplied these errors, spreading them throughout Russia. Visiting Greek prelates had repeatedly pointed to the need for correction of the books. But the Russians held the Greeks in contempt; they had failed in their mission as guardians of the faith; Greek churchmen had come begging, often indulging in sharp practices, and they had lost the respect of the Russians. They were merely foreigners of dubious faith and certainly in no position to advise the Holy Russian Church.

In turning to Kiev for instruction in Greek, Latin, and other subjects, Alexei and those close to him awakened many to the fact that the Russian Church had become petrified in its adherence to the customs of the past. Alexei himself had not only invited Satanovsky and Slavenitsky to Moscow to make a Russian translation of the Bible, but had encouraged 'Greek clerics to visit the tsardom to discuss church matters. He also gave his support to Rtishchev and others in their efforts to stimulate learning and especially to the study of the Greek texts.

A movement toward reform within the church had thus begun. It would probably have dragged on for decades. It was accelerated and brought to a climax by Patriarch Nikon, a man of great energy and ability, who was also brutal and imperious in his methods.

Nikon was born the son of a peasant in 1605 when the country was enduring the worst horrors of the Time of Troubles. He lost his mother when only a little child and was so ill-treated by his stepmother that he himself came near to death several times. Somehow he learned to read and write, the one road to advancement for the son of a peasant. He read avidly and was drawn to monastic life, but left it to marry. He retained his vocation, however, and as a member of the white clergy he became a parish priest at the age of twenty. He had three children, but all died in infancy. Feeling thwarted by parish life, he persuaded his wife to be shorn as a nun, while he entered a White Sea hermitage. Here, however, he quarreled with the brothers and moved on to a monastery where he found acceptance and outlets for his restless energy and ambition. In 1643 the monks chose him as their *igumen* or superior. His fame spread and when he visited Moscow on monastery affairs in 1646 he was summoned to court.

Tsar Alexei, then only seventeen, was always eager to meet and talk with outstanding churchmen. He at once came under the spell of this forceful monk. Nikon was soon settled in Moscow as archimandrite of the Novospassky Monastery. Every Friday he took matins in the palace church and then conversed with the Tsar. In 1648 he was consecrated Metropolitan of Novgorod and during the rebellion there two years later he anathematized the rebels and apparently intended to burn down the cathedral in protest against their godlessness. Alexei sent urgent instructions, forbidding such drastic action. Nikon was offended by this order and wrote at great length to justify the stand he had taken.[14]

On his return to Moscow in 1651, however, Nikon was able to restore his ascendancy over the Tsar. When in the following year the Patriarch Iosif died, the Church Council, obedient to the Tsar's wishes, elected Nikon in his place. At first he would not accept the office and only on July 22, 1652, after the Tsar had publicly prostrated himself at his feet in the Uspensky Cathedral and had begged him in tears not to refuse, did he agree. Three days later he was consecrated.

Nikon at once took action to support the movement, already gaining ground in the church hierarchy, for bringing the Russian and Greek churches closer together and eventually for establishing a "universal" Orthodox Church. The first step was to purge the Russian Church of the errors which had become part of its worship. In 1653 Nikon without reference to the church council ordered the use of three fingers, not two, in making the Sign of the Cross. Genuflections were reduced from twelve to four at certain points in the service. He next declared that all ikons, departing from the Byzantine model and polluted by Roman influence, must be destroyed. His priests entered homes to examine the ikons. He himself took part in the inspections and in the public burning of corrupted ikons.

The changes provoked an outcry among parish clergy and the people. Their ikons were an intimate part of their daily existence. They prayed before them frequently and in the misery of their lives the ikons were a source of solace. To change details of their worship and to burn their ikons struck at the heart of every man and woman. But Nikon who had launched his reforms with such unnecessary violence would brook no opposition. All who dared to protest were promptly punished.

In 1654 learned Greek and Kievan monks began correcting the liturgical texts. The revised *sluzhebnik* or missal was issued in 1655. Again changes of detail—writing "Iisus" in place of "Isus" and similar points —distressed the great mass of the Russian Orthodox. The fact that the new manual had been revised from a Greek text, published in Venice in 1602, confirmed their belief that the changes amounted to sacrilege. Opposition to the reforms mounted in a great wave which swept over the country.

Early in this period of church reform Nikon had come into conflict with Alexei. He was eager not only to cleanse the church of corruptions, but also to assert the authority of the spiritual over the temporal power. He bitterly resented the Muscovite adoption of the Byzantine practices with their implication of imperial authority, as when the Tsar summoned the church councils, stated the matters to be considered, and made their decisions law. In his overweening ambition he saw himself as "Lord Sovereign," wielding power in the same way as Patriarch Filaret had wielded power in the reign of Mikhail. He had always been able to establish his ascendancy over Tsar Alexei, and he was carried away into believing that he could assert the primacy of the Patriarch over the Tsar. In preparation he created a patriarchal court which rivaled the Tsar's court in magnificence. He used regal titles, normally applied only to the Autocrat. His name was soon appearing immediately after that of the Tsar in all official documents. But he underestimated Alexei.

In his piety Alexei had shown every deference to the Patriarch. But, like all who had contact with Nikon, he evidently found intolerable his increasing arrogance and interference in matters of no concern to the church. Moreover, as Autocrat, owing his position to God, he was affronted by Nikon's obvious ambition.

Nikon's fall came about suddenly in 1658. He had taken violent umbrage over a slight, alleged to have been suffered at court by a member of his retinue. He hurriedly set out for the Voskresensky Monastery, declaring that he was no longer Patriarch. He clearly expected Alexei to come after him with humble requests to return to Moscow. Alexei made no move and sent no message. Nikon next declared that he was still Russian Patriarch, but not in Moscow. Alexei and Nikon became deadlocked in a conflict that was to drag on for eight years, causing confusion within the church and among the Orthodox faithful. The bitterness between the two men sharpened and Nikon became more and more vindictive.

Toward the end of 1666 the Patriarchs of Antioch and Alexandria arrived in Moscow on the invitation of Alexei himself. He consulted earnestly with them about Nikon's misconduct. He then summoned a council, including the church hierarchy, the boyars, and many state counselors, to try him, and the two Greek Patriarchs attended. The Archbishop of Pskov was sent to the Voskresensky Monastery to summon Nikon. He refused to come. Alexei sent a firm order to him to appear in Moscow by a certain time. But Nikon had already changed his mind, for the envoy bearing the second summons met him on the road to Moscow.

On December 1 Nikon made a ceremonial appearance before the council. The proceedings quickly turned into a heated dispute. Asked why he had renounced the patriarchate and had gone away, leaving the church and the faithful without their pastor, Nikon said that the reason was the Tsar's anger and his refusal to attend church. Further charges and countercharges were exchanged, but Nikon, always the outspoken accuser of others, now found himself accused by the whole council and his arrogant conduct had left him without a friend among them. He was found guilty of deserting his high office for eight years, of abusing two archbishops, of accusing the Tsar of heresy and other serious misconduct. The sentence was that he should be dismissed from the patriarchate, reduced to the status of an ordinary monk, and detained in the Ferapont Belozersky Monastery. But when the simple cowl of a monk was placed over his head, the archbishop's crozier and mantle were not taken from him, apparently at the request of Alexei himself who was anxious not to humiliate him more than necessary.[15]

Alexei had lost his temper several times during the council sessions. He had been infuriated by Nikon's arrogance, his insulting behavior toward the two visiting Patriarchs, and toward himself. But his anger passed and his first thought then was to forgive. Moreover, toward Nikon, a man of great ability, strong personality and deep faith, he felt a special deference. The council's decision to dismiss Nikon and exile him to the monastery in the icy waste to the north had no sooner been announced than Alexei sent a message to Nikon proposing that they should as Christians forgive each other; the message was rejected. When Nikon left Moscow by sledge under close escort, the Tsar sent him money and furs for his comfort on the long journey; he refused to accept them. Alexei asked for his blessing, but Nikon, a righteous, unwielding man who did not forgive, merely sent an admonition that he should await God's judgment.

By the end of the year, however, Nikon was weary of exile; he sent his blessing and himself asked pardon. Now it was Alexei's turn to withhold his reply for a year, reluctant to allow him to return to Moscow where he would cause trouble. Further messages passed between them and only in 1672 were they reconciled. Nikon did not return to Moscow, but he became increasingly querulous, complaining especially about the provision made for him, which was, in fact, generous. But Alexei now treated his complaints with patience and forebearance.

The council which had judged Nikon had also endorsed his reforms. It went further and excommunicated all who rejected the revised liturgy and sacred books. The mass of the people, including those at court and in the church hierarchy, accepted the reforms endorsed by the Tsar, but their sympathies were with the large numbers of Old Believers who stood firmly by the old books and under their leaders, especially the Archpriest Avvakum, a remarkable man of great dedication and humanity, they prepared for martyrdom.

The Russian Church was riven by the *Raskol* or Schism. The Raskolniki (Schismatics) or Old Believers, who rejected the changes, were persecuted and expelled from the church as heretics. Their leaders, including Avvakum, were burnt at the stake. The monks of the Solovetsky Monastery on the islands in the White Sea condemned the reforms as blasphemy. They closed their gates and in 1668 on the approach of a detachment of *streltsi* sent from Moscow, they opened fire with cannon. Entrenched behind the strong walls of their monastery, the monks were under siege for nine years before they were induced to surrender.

The Old Believers formed strongholds, particularly in the northern forests. A wave of mass-suicide spread among them. In a spirit of martyrdom they crowded together in their wooden churches and, on the approach of agents from Moscow, set them alight. Singing the old liturgies men, women, and children were burnt to death. Thirty-seven of these mass suicides took place between 1672 and 1691, and more than twenty thousand Old Believers met their end in this way. The fact that Patriarch Nikon had launched the reforms and that the church hierarchy and the state had enforced them convinced many Russians that the reign of the Antichrist had begun. Some even identified Alexei himself as the Antichrist.

Conversion to Christianity had been one of the strongest bonds uniting the Russians. But the influx of Western influence had opened a gulf between the Autocrat and landowning nobility on the one hand and the church and people on the other. Now the Schism had broadened this gulf and at the same time had divided the church hierarchy from the lower clergy who sympathized with the people in their dislike of the reform of the liturgy and church books. Moreover the authority of the church and its ability to oppose the mounting wave of Western influence had been gravely weakened.

The reign of Alexei was also a time of momentous development in Russia's relations with neighboring powers. The traditional objective of Russian policy remained unchanged: it was to bring under Moscow's rule the Russian lands still in foreign possession. Under Tsar Mikhail the primary concern had been to recover the Smolensk and Seversk regions of western Russia and to re-establish direct access to the Baltic Sea. At the end of Mikhail's reign, however, Sweden still barred the way to the Baltic and the Poles still held the western regions. Moreover, after the Polish war of 1632–34 Russia was exhausted and desperately needed time for recovery. But shortly after Alexei had ascended the throne a new factor erupted. It had the effect of expanding and complicating the field in which Russia, despite her reluctance, was compelled to take action. The new factor was the rebellion of Little Russia or the Ukraine against Polish rule.

Lying at the center of the triangle between the powerful Ottoman Porte in the south and Poland and Russia in the north, the Ukraine was a vast fertile steppeland. Lithuania had conquered the western and southwestern parts of Russia in the thirteenth century. In 1386 Lithuania and Poland had taken the first step toward union. The Orthodox people of the Ukraine then came under the pressure of Roman Catholic propaganda and their resentment quickly mounted. In 1569 Poland and

Lithuania welded themselves into a single political unit, the Rech Pospolitaya, and in the rearrangement of territories the Ukraine was brought under direct Polish rule.

The Orthodox inhabitants of the Ukraine now found themselves harried by Polish landlords and by Jesuits. Revolts against Polish authority broke out as early as 1591. Roman Catholic propaganda began to prove effective among Orthodox bishops and nobles. In 1596 at the Council of Brest they agreed to create the Uniat Church, which amounted to a union of the two churches under the authority of the Pope.

The mass of the Orthodox clergy and the peasants, however, were staunchly opposed to the Uniats and the Roman Catholic Poles. They joined forces with the Cossacks, united by religious and national fervor. During the first half of the seventeenth century anti-Polish uprisings were frequent, but the Poles suppressed them ruthlessly. They even attempted to eradicate the Cossacks, except for the "registered Cossacks" whom they sought to train as a frontier force. Neither the Cossacks nor the peasantry were to be suppressed so easily and in 1648 they arose in a massive rebellion.

The leader of this rebellion was Bogdan Khmelnitsky, a resourceful Cossack of great energy and ability who had been educated in Kiev and Lvov. He had been imprisoned by the Poles and had escaped at the end of 1647 to the south. He had proposed an uprising against the Poles to the Zaporozhskaya Sech, the ancient center of authority of the Dnieper Hetman.

In May, supported by Crimean Tatars, Khmelnitsky defeated the main Polish forces. He realized, however, that he could not for long stand alone against the Poles. He sent a letter on June 8, 1648, to Tsar Alexei, asking him to take the Ukraine under his protection. Moscow hesitated, remembering the defeats suffered by the Russian armies at Polish hands in the 1630s. The Tsar sent grain to the Ukraine, where the harvest had failed in 1648, as well as other goods. But he stopped short of the provocative action of proclaiming Russia's sovereignty. Meanwhile Khmelnitsky in subsequent action against the Poles had suffered defeat and Polish troops were devastating the Ukraine.

In Moscow, where Khmelnitsky's threats that, if he did not receive the Tsar's support he would turn to the Turkish Sultan, made a strong impression, it was gradually recognized that Russia had no alternative but to support the Ukrainian rebellion against Poland. The dangers and the economic stress that would arise from war with Poland were preferable to having the Mohammedan Turks on Russia's southern frontiers. In February 1651 the Assembly of the Land met in Moscow and gave support to the decision to declare the Tsar's sovereignty over the Ukraine. In January 1654 the Cossacks, gathered in Pereyaslavl, swore allegiance to the Tsar. Under the "Articles of Agreement" signed in

Moscow in March 1654, the right of the Cossacks to self-government and the maintenance of their existing social and legal system were guaranteed. For the Ukrainian peasantry there could be no hope of improvement in their conditions, but they would be freed at least from their Polish landlords and from the incessant pressure of the Jesuits.

In 1654 Alexei declared war against Poland. Charles X of Sweden also marched against the Poles. The Russian armies swept over White Russia and other regions of Lithuania. The Swedes occupied vast areas of Poland. Only rivalry between Swedes and Russians saved the country. Sweden wanted Lithuania, occupied then by Russian troops. Tsar Alexei had designs on the Polish throne. In 1656 the Treaty of Vilna was signed between Russia and Poland whereby the whole of White Russia and Little Russia were ceded to Moscow. War was then declared against Sweden in the hope of recovering access to the Baltic Sea. But now Alexei found his fortunes reversed. The war against Sweden ended with the Treaty of Kardis (1661) which confirmed the Treaty of Stolbovo, shutting Russia off from the Baltic Sea and the Gulf of Finland.

Khmelnitsky, fearing now a Russo-Polish coalition, began secret negotiations with Charles X of Sweden, with the Crimean Khan, and with others who might ensure Cossack independence of Moscow. He died in 1657 and two years later his successor, Hetman Vygovsky, went over to the Poles and with Tatar support defeated the Russian army at Konotop. The Cossacks then elected Bogdan's son, Yury Khmelnitsky, to be Hetman. He revived their allegiance to Moscow, but almost immediately turned back to Poland.

The Ukraine was now divided in its allegiances. On the right or west bank of the Dnieper, the Ukraine, under Yury Khmelnitsky's leadership, adhered to Poland. On the left or east bank the Ukraine elected a new Hetman, Bryukhovetsky, who was loyal to the Tsar. Meanwhile the Russians suffered defeat in the new war against Poland and lost all that they had gained under the Treaty of Vilna. But by this time both Poland and Russia were exhausted and their peoples were in a rebellious mood. Both countries feared, moreover, that the Turkish Sultan might take advantage of their exhaustion to extend his power northward into the Ukraine. Under the shadow of this threat they came to terms.

By the Treaty of Andrussovo, signed in 1667, Russia secured the Seversk province and the whole of left-bank Ukraine, as well as Kiev and a small surrounding enclave on the right bank. Kiev was to be returned to Poland after two years, but when the time came Alexei could not bring himself to honor this undertaking. Poland retained right-bank Ukraine.

The Treaty of Andrussovo, marking a reorientation of Russian policy, was the work of Afanasy Ordin-Nashchokin, one of the most remarkable men close to Alexei. Born a member of the provincial nobility of the

Pskov region, he had had an advanced education, embracing subjects considered heretical by the Muscovites. Bordering on the Baltic states, Pskov had always enjoyed close contact with Western Europe, and Ordin-Nashchokin grew up in conditions free from the xenophobia and conservatism of Moscow. He was strongly attracted to the West and became a bitter and outspoken critic of Muscovy, its medieval methods, and bigoted complacent outlook.

To the service of the Tsar he brought a brilliant and original mind, vision, and humanity. He first attracted attention in the reign of Tsar Mikhail and he was soon recognized by all who had dealings with him as the most able Russian of his time. Dr. Collins wrote of him, that he was one "who will not be corrupted . . . a very sober, abstemious man, indefatigable in business, a great politician and a very grave and wise minister of state, not inferior to anyone in Europe."[16]

Ordin-Nashchokin's greatest achievement was the Treaty of Andrussovo which ended thirty years of war between Russia and Poland. It opened a new era in Russian foreign policy and formed part of his great plan of uniting Russia and Poland and eventually all the Slav peoples under their leadership. The treaty won him national acclaim because its advantageous terms included the return of Kiev, the mother of Russian cities, to the Tsar's rule. Beset by more immediate problems, the Russians were not at this stage interested in his broad vision of the future.

It was during this period, when head of the Possolsky Prikaz or Foreign Office and the Tsar's chief minister, that he reviewed the whole machinery of government. Diplomacy was his first concern, but he recognized that diplomatic and military success depended on efficient administration and a sound economy. He stormed against the indolence, corruption, nepotism, and bureaucracy of Muscovite officials. He drew up a series of projects providing a plan of reform of the whole government. He gave special attention to the reorganization of the administration, the selection and training of officials, and fairer allocation of tax liability, which would increase the national revenue without adding to the burden on the people.

The development of trade and industry were of special concern to him. In his native Pskov he organized the merchants in an association which enabled them to compete with foreign merchants. He tried to open up trade with Central Asia, Persia, and the Far East. His proposals included reorganization of the army, creation of fleets in the Baltic and Caspian seas, a regular postal service, the improvement of towns by laying out gardens. Ideas and practical plans poured from his fertile brain and if only a fraction had been implemented the country would have been transformed. But many of his ideas were soon to be introduced.

Ordin-Nashchokin was, however, a difficult man, extremely outspoken, tempestuous, and umbrageous. His enemies were numerous. He remained in office only because Tsar Alexei supported him and, recognizing his ability and devotion, would not tolerate attempts to remove him. Indeed in his relations with Ordin-Nashchokin, Alexei showed the capacity for sympathy and understanding for the feelings of others which were among his most attractive qualities. When Ordin-Nashchokin's son, as a result of his Western education and the influence of his Polish tutors, fled to the West, he refused to return, fearing his father's anger and even more the penalty for flight abroad which was death. Enemies made full play of the incident, calling the son a traitor and an apostate like his father. Expecting exile or some other punishment for his son's crime, Ordin-Nashchokin at once petitioned to be allowed to retire into a monastery. But Alexei would not accept his petition. Breaking with custom and overruling the law he even defended the son. "You ask me to allow you to resign," he wrote. "But why do you make such a request? It must be because of your great sadness. But what is so remarkable about your son's foolish behavior? He has acted stupidly. He is a young man and he wishes to see God's world and all its wonders. Like a bird which flies here and there and, when weary, flies back to its own nest, so your son will remember his home and his holy bonds with it and he will return to you."[17]

Between Alexei and Ordin-Nashchokin, and also Rtishchev who was the close friend of both, the special bonds uniting them were their piety and their sense of humanity. Ordin-Nashchokin in particular maintained that the state existed to serve the well-being of the people and in all his plans this was the basic principle. It was an attitude well in advance of the ideas of the seventeenth-century Russia and of Western Europe. In his personal life, too, he was a kind man. Tsar Alexei in the citation elevating him to the rank of boyar in 1658 described him as one who "feeds the hungry, gives drink to the thirsty, clothes the naked, is considerate to humble people, and gives no quarter to the wrongdoer."[18] But in diplomacy as in other fields he was also a man of high principle. This finally brought him into conflict with Tsar Alexei who refused to return Kiev to Poland under the terms of the Treaty of Andrussovo. Ordin-Nashchokin petitioned to be released from office and this time Alexei reluctantly agreed. He retreated into a monastery, took holy orders, and died in 1680.

The reign of Alexei was a time of hardships and near-calamities, both internally and in Russia's relations with her neighbors. Fortunately they did not happen at the same time and Russia, although unstable and economically weak, was able to gather enough strength to meet each new crisis. But for the Tsar and his government the thirty-one years were a period of strain and anxiety.

In his family life, too, Alexei knew anxiety and grief. Maria Miloslavskaya, his first wife, bore him six daughters and five sons. The daughters were healthy, but without exception the sons were weaklings. Three sons died in childhood and in March 1669 the Tsaritsa herself died. The hope at court and throughout the country was that the Tsar would marry again. All Russians feared nothing so much as a return of the horrors of the Time of Troubles which had followed the extinction of the previous dynasty. Of Alexei's two surviving sons, Ivan was cretinous and Fedor was ailing and not expected to live long. The announcement in February 1670 that the Tsar intended to marry again was heard with general rejoicing.

Alexei met his second wife at the house of Artamon Matveev, who had succeeded Ordin-Nashchokin as chief minister, and was imbued with his ideas. He had married a daughter of the Scots family of Hamilton which had entered the Russian service at the turn of the century. So far as was possible in Moscow, he lived as a Western European. Alexei, strongly attracted to the Western way of life, sometimes went informally to Matveev's house, although it was almost unprecedented for the Tsar to visit the home of a subject. There he met Natalya Naryshkina, the young and vivacious daughter of an impoverished landlord of Tatar origin, entrusted to Matveev's care. He fell in love on sight and, on January 22, 1671, married her.

Alexei was devoted to his young wife. She was used to Western customs, not to the seclusion of the Muscovite *terem*, and she encouraged him in his Western tastes. The birth of a son, Peter, in the Kremlin Palace on May 30, 1672, completed Alexei's happiness, especially as the son from birth gave every sign of robust health. But he was not to enjoy this new happiness for long. Alexei had always been strong and energetic. He was forty-seven years old and, when he caught a chill, it did not seem serious. Suddenly his condition deteriorated and on January 29, 1676, he died.

As Tsar, Alexei had been far more effective than his father, the first of the Romanovs. He had not dominated the government and country as his son was to dominate, but he had embodied in his person the ideal of the Autocrat and had ruled in a way that commanded the respect and affection of his people. His strength was that he had recognized the able men among his subjects and that he had not lacked the courage to break from the past and to support their policies. Often the immediate results were of a kind to distress a man of his character. The Schism in the church, followed by the excommunication and persecution of the Old Believers, must have saddened one so devout as he was. But he did not waver in his support for the revision of the liturgy and the church books. Again he was devoted to the Orthodox Muscovite heritage, but unlike the vast majority of Russians he did not close his eyes or his mind to the need for reforms and modernization. He listened to Rtishchev, Ordin-Nashchokin, Matveev, and others, and he encouraged and supported them. He was able to achieve very little improvement in the conditions of his people. But with the acquisition of Kiev and eastern Ukraine he added to the power and prestige of the nation. His greatest achievements, however, were that he opened the gates to Western ideas and reform more widely and that he left to Russia as a successor his son, Peter.

IV

Fedor Alexeevich

1676–1682

Fedor succeeded to the throne without dispute. On September 1, 1674, the Russian Orthodox New Year's Day, his father had presented him as his heir to the people and the representatives of foreign rulers, summoned for the purpose to the Red Square. It had been an impressive occasion when the great crowd had heard the Tsar formally proclaim his eldest son as their next Tsar. But few had expected the Tsarevich to ascend the throne. Then a thirteen-year-old boy of poor physique and suffering from scurvy, he had seemed unlikely to live long and certainly not to outlive his robust father. But fate had ruled otherwise and the sickly boy was now Tsar of Russia.

The court was immediately torn by savage rivalries, which had been suppressed but had smoldered beneath the order established by Tsar Alexei. The family of the Tsaritsa had always enjoyed prominence and power at court. The Miloslavsky after some twenty years had been displaced by the Naryshkini, the family of Tsar Alexei's second wife. The daughters of Maria Miloslavskaya, and Tsarevna Sofia in particular, had resented the change. It was a setback to their hopes of escaping the usual fate of the Tsarevni which was to be isolated in the *terem* and, when they were older, to be shorn as nuns and to pass their lives in religious seclusion. No subject could be considered worthy of the hand of a daughter of the Tsar, and attempts to arrange marriages with ruling families in the West had all failed. But now Western influence, spreading through the Kremlin, was moderating some of the harsh conventions of Muscovite life, and raising the hopes of the Tsar's daughters that they might take part at least in court life.

Tsarevna Sofia, a young woman of energy, strong will, and intelligence, had grasped the new opportunities. She had shared Fedor's tutor, Simeon Polotsky, and had been educated to a degree exceptional for a woman in seventeenth-century Russia. She had also had contact with her brothers and leading men at court and had been especially close to her father. Suddenly Alexei's second marriage had threatened her new position and her ambition to break free from the *terem*. The hatred which she felt for her stepmother, who was about her age, was sharpened by Natalya's influence over Alexei and by the fact that she refused to accept her stepdaughters. Despite her own Western upbringing, Natalya as Tsaritsa was concerned only to push them back into the *terem*. But now with Fedor on the throne and the Miloslavsky once more prominent at court, Sofia was in a strong position. Natalya and her children, Peter and Natalya, born in August 1673, were without influence. Artamon Matveev, Alexei's chief minister, although a consummate man of affairs, had not anticipated the sudden death of the Tsar and, like Natalya, he now found himself exposed to the hostility of the Miloslavsky.[1]

With the aid of two of Matveev's enemies at court, Bogdan Khitrovo and Vasily Volynsky, the Miloslavsky planned his downfall. First he was told that the Tsar had appointed him to be *voevod* or governor of the Verkhoture region beyond the Urals. This was honorable exile, but he had hardly set out from Moscow when he was halted and faced with numerous charges. The main accusation was that he had failed to taste the Tsar's medicine before and after giving it to him, the standard precaution against attempts to poison the Autocrat, and so by implication was responsible for his death. Matveev was stripped of the rank of boyar and of his estates and exiled with his son to Pustozersk, a primitive settlement within the Arctic Circle.

Tsar Fedor approved or at least condoned this treatment of his father's minister. But he was soon to show that he was no mere tool in the hands of the Miloslavsky and their faction. Although so young and ailing, he did not lack character and a certain independence of mind. While they disposed of Matveev and other rivals and while the Patriarch, Ioakim, dealt with his personal enemies in the church, whom Alexei had protected, Tsar Fedor chose his own favorites. Confined most of the time by illness to his own chamber, he found the men he trusted in his personal court. Chief among them were Ivan Yazykov, whom he was to advance to the rank of boyar, and Alexei Likhachev.

Allied with them was the young boyar, Prince Vasily Vasilievich Golitsyn, who was to become for a time the most powerful man in the land. Golitsyn belonged to one of the oldest and most respected Muscovite noble families. He himself was young, handsome, and extremely able. He was highly educated and cultured in his tastes and, like Ordin-Nashchokin, an enthusiastic Westernizer. His palace in Moscow, considered by many foreigners to be among the most magnificent in Europe, was furnished in Western style. The walls were hung with mirrors, portraits, maps, and fine carpets; on the ceilings was painted the planetary system as then known; clocks and instruments of the best European workmanship were in every room. His library contained a valuable collection of manuscripts and printed books in Latin, Russian, Polish, and Greek, all of which languages he knew fluently. He entertained lavishly and kept open house for foreigners of learning. But Golitsyn was also an able man of affairs. He shared the ideas and policies of Ordin-Nashchokin and, on gaining a position of power, he developed them further. His plans for internal reform, for instance, went so far as to include the freeing of the peasants from serfdom and grants of land to them together with a system of direct taxation which would increase the Tsar's revenues.

On Fedor's accession a matter of immediate concern to all who were close to him was his marriage. The Miloslavsky, in particular, were anxious that he should marry someone of their choosing who would ensure their position at court both at present and, through heirs to the throne, in the future. No time could be lost in finding Fedor a wife, if they were to prevent the succession of Peter and the return of the Naryshkini.

Fedor, however, made his own decision. During the procession of the cross at Easter he caught sight of a maiden who pleased him. He sent Yazykov to enquire about her and, on learning that she was Agrafya Semenovna Grushetskaya, the daughter of a *Dumny Dyak* (Clerk to the Council), he gave orders that she was not to marry without his approval. Meanwhile Ivan Miloslavsky, learning of Yazykov's enquiries about the maiden and her family, made his own investigations and, evidently not approving the match, did everything to blacken the reputation of the family. Fedor was displeased. He married Agrafya in July 1680 and ordered the expulsion of Ivan Miloslavsky from court. The young Tsaritsa interceded on his behalf, but Fedor mistrusted his uncle so deeply that he excluded him from positions of influence.

During Alexei's reign the movement for change and reform had gathered momentum and Fedor, although young and enfeebled and destined to reign so briefly, made his own contributions. Probably encouraged by Golitsyn he tried to modify the savagery of Russian life. The usual punishments for theft, for instance, were to cut off two or more of the offender's fingers, a hand or a foot, depending on the gravity of the crime. In 1679–80 Fedor issued ukasi, forbidding such punishments and directing that offenders should in future be sent to work the land in Siberia with their wives and any children over three years old. Instructions were also sent to all towns in 1680 that people accused of crimes were not to be held in prison for lengthy periods awaiting trial, but must be dealt with promptly. Fedor also sought to ease the intolerable position of women. In 1677 a peasant woman who had cut off her husband's head with a scythe and who had survived burial for several days was released by Fedor on condition that she entered a monastery. Two other guilty wives were also pardoned on the same condition. In 1679 the rights of women to their own patrimonies were protected. Moreover, husbands and wives were forbidden to dissolve their marriages unilaterally by entering a monastery with the result that the other spouse could not remarry and might be destitute. The regulation benefited women who were often deserted by their husbands in this way. But a society so sternly patriarchal was not prepared to concede extensive rights to its women and they continued to suffer inhuman burdens and cruelties.

The persecution of Old Believers continued. They were found in small groups in the Ukraine, in Siberia and in the northern forests, worshiping according to the old rites, and ready to suffer as martyrs. But the church itself, shaken by the fury of the Schism, now turned its attention to reform. A church council, summoned in 1681, considered a series of propositions from the Tsar. The reforms that resulted affected the appointment of archbishops, eliminated laxity in the domestic arrangements of monasteries, and included a ban on alcohol in religious establishments as a step to counteract the widespread drunkenness among priests and monks.

Ambitious projects were prepared for the reform of the national financial system, for the division of the landowning nobility and gentry into those rendering civil and those providing military service to the state, and to establish a college or academy. The three projects were probably the work of Golitsyn. Fedor gave them his approval and support, but did not live to introduce them. An important achievement, however, was his abolition of *mestnichestvo* as a preliminary to further reform of the army. Vasily Golitsyn was also responsible for this reform and as one of the great nobles of the day he alone was in a position to promote it. *Mestnichestvo* was the crippling system under which no member of a boyar family would accept an appointment in the Tsar's service which was inferior to an appointment held by a forebear. Experience and ability counted for nothing; the position of the family and its members in the hierarchy was the deciding factor. Records of appointments (*razryadny knigi*) were carefully maintained'and referred to in all disputes. In most of the major campaigns in the reigns of Mikhail and Alexei *mestnichestvo* had been set aside by general agreement only to be revived by jealous boyars as soon as the campaign was over.

On January 12, 1682, at a formal session of the Council of Boyars, Tsar Fedor, followed by the Patriarch, spoke forcefully against this pernicious system and threatened punishment by the state and excommunication by the church for any boyar who again invoked it. Surprisingly the boyars concurred and without delay the records were taken out to the forecourt of the palace and burnt.[2] Abolition of *mestnichestvo* not only cleared the way for reform of the army, but it also broke down the entrenched position of the nobles; they served now on terms of equality with the gentry with whom in time they were to merge.

Defense made pressing demands during Fedor's brief reign. As the Russians colonized new lands to the south, north, and east, the local peoples became unsettled. Moscow received reports of disputes between Don Cossacks and Kalmyks, of unrest along the Yaik (Ural) River, among the Tatars and Bashkirs, the Kirgiz, and even the Samoeds in the north and the Yakuts and Tungus in the east. In response to each report officials and small detachments of troops had to be sent.

These incidents at vast distances from the capital provided the background to the three main problems of Fedor's reign. They were, first, the Ukraine and in particular the question of Hetman Doroshenko's loyalty to the Tsar; second, the Polish demand that the terms of the treaty of Andrussovo should be honored and that Kiev and the right-bank enclave should be surrendered; third, and by far the most serious threat, was war with Turkey.

In the summer of 1677 Turkish and Tatar forces invaded the Ukraine and for the first time in history Russia and Turkey were at war. The Russo-Ukrainian army, commanded by Prince Romodanovsky and Hetman Samoilovich, comprised some sixty thousand men, but the invading army had double this strength. Fedor ordered Don Cossacks and Russian reinforcements to move up in support. In Moscow there was acute anxiety over the outcome of this campaign. The Ottoman Porte was a formidable power with far greater resources than Russia.

The Turks planned to take Chigirin, then the political center of the Ukraine, and from there to conquer the whole steppeland. They began their assault in August 1677 expecting easy victory, but the small garrison held out for three weeks until the relief armies arrived. On August 28 Russians and Turks joined in battle which ended with the rout of the Sultan's forces. It was a severe blow to Turkish prestige and in the summer of the following year the Sultan sent an army of two hundred thousand men to take Chigirin. The defending forces again resisted bravely and Chigirin was reduced to ruins before it was taken. But the Turks, having suffered heavy losses, now retired to the Bug River.[3]

Fearing a new campaign by the Turks, the Russians urgently reinforced their positions and at the same time sought allies. Austria and Poland were both threatened by Turkey. But Austria refused to join Russia in an alliance against Turkey, and Poland made the return of Kiev the condition of her participation. Left to face Turkey alone, the Tsar made proposals for peace and the Sultan, anxious to concentrate his forces against Austria, readily agreed.

The treaty, negotiated at Bakhchisarai in the Crimea and ratified by the Sultan in May 1681, gave Russians real grounds for satisfaction. The Turks agreed a twenty-year armistice and acknowledged Russian sovereignty over both left-bank Ukraine and Kiev and its right-bank enclave. Moreover the treaty gave Russia a new sense of security, especially in her relations with Austria and Poland. Both countries had often sought to deflect Turkish aggression from themselves against Russia and this threat had always disturbed Moscow. But the Treaty of Bakhchisarai now exposed them rather than Russia to attack by the Ottoman Porte.

In the midst of these stirring events, the succession to the throne continued to arouse anxiety at court and among the people. There was general rejoicing when on July 11, 1681, Tsaritsa Agrafya gave birth to a son, Tsarevich Ilya. But within six days mother and son were dead. At once the remarriage of the young Tsar was actively discussed. Ivan Yazykov, who was closest to Fedor, proposed Marfa Matveevna Apraksina, who was related to him and was also a goddaughter of Artamon Matveev, and on February 14, 1682, Fedor married her. Soon afterwards, aged twenty-one years, he died.

V

The Regency of Sofia Alexeevna

1682–1689

On April 27, 1682, shortly after 4 P.M., the bell of the Ivan Veliky tower in the Kremlin tolled three times, and the people of Moscow knew that Tsar Fedor was dead. The body was at once laid out and in the presence of the Patriarch and other church dignitaries, the boyars and gentry filed past the bier, taking leave of their Tsar. It was customary then to kiss the hand of the Tsar's successor as a token of loyalty. On this occasion they kissed the hands of both Peter and Ivan, who were equal in title to the throne. Fedor had not left an heir and had not named a successor, and it was not clear who should be Tsar. Tsarevich Ivan, Alexei's surviving son by his first marriage, was the elder, but he was physically and mentally backward. Peter was alert, energetic, and with a fine physique for his age. The general preference was that he should mount the throne.

After the ceremony of leave-taking the Patriarch, church hierarchy, and members of the Council of Boyars gathered in the palace antechamber to consider the succession. They agreed at once that only the Assembly of the Land could make the decision. Most of the representatives, entitled to attend the Assembly, were already in Moscow.

Many from the provinces had come some days earlier to consider certain taxation proposals and others were more or less permanently in the capital. Thus the Assembly which gathered in the Kremlin was fairly representative. The Patriarch addressed the Assembly on the problem for decision and the response with few exceptions was to demand Peter. The Patriarch then proclaimed him and, returning to the palace, blessed him as Tsar.[1]

The succession was not, however, to be resolved so simply and was to lead to violence. Of the three factions directly interested, Yazykov and Likhachev, the favorites of Fedor, had joined with the Naryshkini in promoting Peter's accession. They had strong support from the Dolgoruky family and from Princes Boris and Ivan Golitsyn, cousins of Vasily Golitsyn. All were united in their anxiety to prevent the return of the Miloslavsky to power, as would inevitably happen if Tsarevich Ivan became Tsar. Moreover, since Peter was a minor, his mother, Natalya, would be regent and her rule under the guidance of Artamon Matveev was generally acceptable. The Patriarch, Ioakim, favored Peter because he was clearly the more fitted to be Tsar. But he was also influenced by the fact that the Miloslavsky in the persons of their leaders, Sofia and Vasily Golitsyn, were for him dangerous innovators and Westernizers. A staunch conservative he believed that Peter and the Naryshkini would uphold Orthodoxy.

At once, on the accession of her son, Natalya recalled Artamon Matveev from exile. She had been living at Preobrazhenskoe, out of touch with the court during Fedor's reign and her new responsibilities as regent frightened her. She was a nervous woman, unfitted to rule. The Naryshkini, her father and brothers, were greedy for the spoils of office and lacked both the political sense and ability to help her in her task. She waited desperately for Matveev's return, but he did not reach Moscow until the evening of May 12 and by then Sofia had laid her plans.

Although only twenty-five years old and faced with the strong prejudice of a society which relegated the daughters of the Tsar to the *terem*, never allowing them to be seen in public, Sofia managed to dominate during these days.[2] She had fought stubbornly against being locked away in some monastery. But with the accession of Peter and the elevation of her hated stepmother to the position of regent, she faced defeat. She now fought desperately and she showed that she was capable of complete ruthlessness. Her first aim was to displace Peter, Natalya, and the Naryshkini. To do this she had to gain the support of public opinion and to remove Matveev who was already on the road to Moscow.

By a bold stroke Sofia contrived to appeal to the people and to unsettle public opinion throughout the city. At the funeral of Fedor the two widowed Tsaritsi, Natalya and Marfa, Fedor's second wife, and Peter were present in accordance with custom. It was unheard of that any of the Tsarevni should be present and seen in public. But Sofia entered the Arkhangelsky Cathedral alone and took up a prominent position near the coffin where all could see her. Natalya was so incensed by this brazen disregard for decorum and the affront to her that she hurriedly left the cathedral, taking Peter with her, before the end of the funeral service. Her brusque departure aroused disapproval as an act of disrespect. Sofia's display of grief for her dead brother, whom she had nursed so solicitously, was observed with approval and sympathy. Walking from the cathedral to the palace she turned to the crowds, crying out that enemies had poisoned her brother. "Have mercy on us, orphans," she cried, "or let us depart into the care of a Christian king of a foreign land!" Her appeal made a deep impression on the Muscovites.[3]

Natalya, alone and afraid, waited in the Kremlin for Matveev to arrive. She could not understand how Sofia and the Miloslavsky were managing to rally public opinion more and more in their support. But most troubling of all was the rebellious mood of the *streltsi* in the face of which she felt powerless.

During the reign of Fedor, discontent among the *streltsi* had mounted. One regiment had presented a petition, shortly before his death, alleging that their colonel had withheld their pay and had ordered them to work on his estate during Holy Week. Prince Yuri Dolgoruky, commanding the *streltsi* jointly with his son, had dismissed the petition as an act of insubordination. He ordered that the *streltsi* who had presented it should be severely knouted. But his comrades had attacked his guard and had released him. This incident brought the *streltsi* closer to mutiny. Seventeen regiments combined to demand the punishment of their colonels for disregarding their privileges. The death of the Tsar delayed their plans, but on the day after the funeral they presented their petitions. Natalya and the Naryshkini took fright. Without investigation she ordered that the colonels should be deprived of their rank and beaten with *batogi*. The mutinous *streltsi* took charge and beat their officers savagely.

Discipline broke down and the *streltsi* were soon in a dangerous mood. The one man to whom they were prepared to listen was Prince Ivan Khovansky, an Old Believer, a braggart and a rogue, who was in league with the Miloslavsky. Instructed by Sofia he played on their fears. He told them that under the regency of Natalya and with Matveev as chief minister, the foreigners would quickly gain power and destroy Orthodoxy. The *streltsi* would lose their privileges and become serfs. The rumors spread rapidly and the *streltsi* neared explosion point. Sofia waited before unleashing them. She was evidently in complete control of the situation. With her uncle, Ivan Miloslavsky, Khovansky, and a trusted band of *streltsi* with whom she had direct contact, she was turning the anger of the *streltsi* against the Naryshkini. She planted rumors among them and soon every *streltsi* was convinced that the Naryshkini had poisoned Tsar Fedor and were preparing to murder Tsarevich Ivan. She was waiting now only for the return of Matveev.

On May 11, Matveev reached Moscow. Natalya greeted him as a father and savior. All the boyars, except the Miloslavsky, and numerous representatives of the church and the people of Moscow called to express pleasure at his return. *Streltsi* of all regiments of their own accord conveyed their respects to him. The tensions in the city suddenly relaxed. Misled by the warmth of his welcome, Matveev evidently thought that the reports he had received had exaggerated the situation. He also underestimated the abilities of Sofia. Arousing the *streltsi* afresh with rumors, she was preparing to strike.

On the morning of May 15, while Matveev was attending a meeting of the Council of Boyars in the Kremlin, two horsemen, Alexander Miloslavsky and Peter Tolstoy, both in close league with Sofia, galloped into the *streltsi* quarter. "The Naryshkini have strangled Tsarevich Ivan!" they shouted. Alarms were sounded and, grasping their weapons, the *streltsi* began making for the Kremlin, calling for the heads of the traitors.[4]

Matveev was leaving the council chamber when he was told that the *streltsi* were in the outer suburbs of the city. He ordered the Kremlin gates to be closed, but it was too late. The *streltsi* were already surging into the square in front of the Granovitaya Palace. They halted at the foot of the Red Staircase, the grand entrance to the palace, and began clamoring for the Naryshkini to be handed over to them.

Matveev learned from their shouts that they believed that Tsarevich Ivan had been murdered. He turned to Natalya and advised her to show herself to the mob with Peter and Ivan. She hesitated, intimidated by the howling mob of troops, but she knew she had no alternative.

Holding the hands of the two boys, Natalya stepped onto the staircase where all could see her. The *streltsi* fell silent. Raising her voice she called to them: "Here is the Lord Tsar Peter Alexeevich! Here is the Lord Tsarevich Ivan Alexeevich! Thanks be to God they are well and have not suffered at the hands of traitors!"[5]

The *streltsi* were bewildered. A few of them mounted the staircase and, face to face with Ivan, asked him if he was truly alive and unharmed. He stammered a reassurance, and they slowly walked down the staircase to rejoin their silent comrades.

At this point a group of *streltsi* began demanding the surrender of certain boyars whom Sofia had listed. Others took up the shouting and the mob again became threatening. Matveev now stepped forward, accompanied by the Patriarch. He spoke to them quietly, reminding them of their great deeds in the past and asking how they could threaten violence against those nearest to their Tsar. They heard him in silence. They had seen Ivan alive and well and realized that they had been tricked by lies. The Patriarch admonished them. The revolt was dying away and they were turning to disperse to their quarters.

Suddenly they were aroused to a fury. Prince Mikhail Dolgoruky, jointly with his father the commander of all *streltsi* regiments, had been infuriated by this mutiny. He now spoke to them from the head of the Red Staircase. In the heat of anger he abused them, threatened them with the knout, and ordered them to dismiss immediately. His curses and threats stung them to action. They rushed the staircase, seized him and threw him over the balustrade onto the pikes of their comrades below. They hacked his body to pieces, bespattering the mob with blood.

Another band of *streltsi*, led by Sofia's men, now appeared from the shadow of the palace wall and began shouting for Matveev's head. Others took up their cry. Natalya dropped Peter's hand and threw her arms around Matveev in an attempt to protect him. But the *streltsi* brushed her aside and threw him over the balustrade onto the pikes below.

The *streltsi* had now become savage and uncontrollable. They stormed the Red Staircase and began searching the palace for Ivan Naryshkin and others against whom their hatred had been aroused. They found several of their victims whom they cast down onto the pikes below the staircase. One of Natalya's brothers, Afanasy Naryshkin, was found and hacked to death. But their anger mounted when they failed to find Ivan Naryshkin and Natalya's three younger brothers. All four were hidden in the apartments of Tsarevna Natalya, Peter's eight-year-old sister, which they had not searched. As night fell the *streltsi* withdrew to return to their own quarters. They posted guards to prevent anyone escaping and swore to return next day, threatening a general massacre if their victims were not surrendered.

At dawn next day the *streltsi* returned. Again they raged through the Kremlin, killing all who stirred their suspicions. Still they could not find the Naryshkini. Returning on the third day they gave their ultimatum. They would kill all boyars in the Kremlin if Ivan Naryshkin was not surrendered. Sofia then approached Natalya and declared loudly for all to hear: "Your brother will not escape the *streltsi*. Nor is it right that all should perish on his account."[6]

Natalya had endured three days of terror. The life of her son and her own life had been in constant danger. Now she feared a massacre of boyars that would lead to the death of her son. She had no choice but to give up her brother. She ordered personal servants to summon him. He came and behaved bravely as he received the last rites. Natalya then took from Sofia's hands the holy ikon of the Mother of God and, weeping bitterly, blessed him with it. He then walked out to the *streltsi* who surged forward with yells of triumph. For hours they tortured him, trying to extract confessions that he had poisoned Tsar Fedor and was plotting to seize the throne for himself. He refused to answer. He was nearly dead when, his arms and legs broken and hanging grotesquely, they dragged him to the Red Square and hacked the body to pieces.

The *streltsi* gathered again at the Red Staircase. They declared their loyalty to the Tsar, the Tsarevich, and the Tsarevni, and dispersed to their quarters. But having plundered and terrorized the city with impunity, they were still unruly. Sofia and Khovansky, whom she had appointed commander of the regiments, were the only people whom they heeded. On the prompting of her agents they petitioned, on May 23, that Peter and Ivan should occupy the throne jointly. The Boyar Council and the hurriedly convened Assembly of the Land promptly agreed their request. Two days later on another petition Tsar Ivan was declared senior to Tsar Peter. On May 29 the *streltsi* announced that they wished Sofia to be regent during the minority of the Tsars. The Patriarch and boyars at once begged her to accept the office and she consented.

Sofia had now attained the position of power for which she had struggled with such determination. She had dominated the Kremlin during the *streltsi* terror. She alone could have restrained them, but she had ensured that the massacre continued since she wanted not only Matveev but also Ivan Naryshkin and certain others killed. She had displayed courage and inhuman ruthlessness, but her triumph was not enduring.

All others in the Kremlin and in the city, except those close to Sofia, had been terrified of the *streltsi*. Contemporary reports make no mention of Peter.[7] He was at this time just ten years old, but advanced beyond his years mentally and physically, and the experience marked him indelibly. He did not forget and he was to punish the *streltsi* savagely.

Sofia found almost at once that her position was challenged. She had used the *streltsi* and took it for granted that she could rely on Khovansky as their commander. But he too was ambitious and unscrupulous. He boasted that he held the real power in the land. Sofia acted promptly to dispose of this threat. On August 19, 1682, she took the two young Tsars with her to Kolomenskoe. From there she sent couriers into the provinces with the report that Khovansky was planning to kill the Tsars. She called on the boyars and gentry to come to their defense with men and arms. She then moved on to the Troitsa, the renowned fortress-monastery. From there she sent a detachment of

troops who arrested Khovansky and his son and summarily beheaded them.

Learning that the militia was being mobilized, the *streltsi* took fright. They humbly petitioned to be forgiven for their excesses and prayed for the return of the Tsars to the Kremlin. On November 16, 1682, Sofia, attended by a strong escort, made a triumphant entry into Moscow with the two Tsars. She had secured her position for the time being and could now begin to rule.

Sofia had appointed Vasily Golitsyn as chief minister and he was her guide and support throughout the seven years of the regency. It was a partnership of two remarkable people. Sofia, an able, strong-willed, and fearless young woman, was devoted to the brilliant prince and had complete confidence in his abilities and policies. But the record of these seven years is disappointing. Some attempts at reform were made but they were on a small scale and the dominant impression of the regency was of harsh measures especially against runaway serfs and Old Believers. In foreign affairs Sofia and Golitsyn were more active.

On ascending the throne the Tsar usually confirmed treaties made by his predecessor. Once Ivan had been proclaimed Tsar jointly with Peter, Sofia sent embassies to Stockholm and Warsaw for this purpose. The Swedes welcomed the Russian envoys since they came to confirm the Treaty of Kardis (1661) whereby Sweden held the Baltic territories and barred Russia from access to the Baltic Sea.

The envoys to Warsaw met with no welcome. They came to confirm the Treaty of Andrussovo (1667) which provided for an exchange of embassies to negotiate a permanent peace between Russia and Poland. All past attempts to agree such a peace had failed, because the Russians had refused to honor the undertaking to return Kiev to the Poles. But Poland and Austria were now at war with Turkey and a major defeat by the Turks and the threat of Turkish invasion had made King Sobieski of Poland desperately anxious to secure Russian help against their common enemy. Negotiations were drawn out, but in 1686 he agreed to yield Kiev to Russia permanently in return for firm undertakings by Moscow to declare war on the Turkish Sultan and the Crimean Khan, to defend Polish territories against Turkish invasion, and to mount a campaign against the Crimean Tatars in the following year.

Sofia and Vasily Golitsyn were jubilant over the cession of Kiev. The conditions of the new treaty were onerous, but they and the Russian people as a whole accepted them readily. The Turks and Tatars were hated enemies not only because they were infidels, but also because of their incessant raids in which they laid waste the land and carried off the young people to sell into slavery. In the seventeenth century Russian slaves were to be found chained to the oars of galleys in every Mediterranean harbor.

Sofia at once ordered mobilization of the army and preparation for the campaign against the Crimean Khan. In May 1687 the Russian force of nearly one hundred thousand men began moving southward. Vasily Golitsyn was supreme commander, but he lacked experience and went in fear that the Tatars, moving swiftly on their small sturdy horses, might take him by surprise. His excessive caution and the hardships of the march undermined the morale of his troops. Then at Bolshoi Lug, not far from the Dnieper River, the Russians found that the tall feathergrass of the steppes was on fire. Golitsyn at once ordered a retreat. He sent reports to Moscow that the Tatars, seeing the might of the Russian army, had fled to the Crimea after setting fire to the steppe, and that Russian troops had chased them as far as Perekop. He had in fact lost some forty-five thousand men on the march without once sighting the enemy. But when he returned to Moscow, on September 14, 1687, Sofia hailed him as a victor.

Rumors had reached the Russians that the Cossacks, not the Tatars, had fired the steppe. Suspicion fell on Hetman Samoilovich who was even said to be secretly in league with the Tatars. He had expressed himself strongly against the alliance with Poland and the war on the Crimean Tatars. He regarded Poland as the main enemy and he feared that the Ukraine would suffer Tatar reprisals. His opposition to Sofia's policies led to his fall from favor and, unknown to him, his chief lieutenant, Ivan Mazepa, whom he had befriended and advanced, was plotting to displace him. Mazepa's approaches to Golitsyn had their effect. Only the Cossack elders could elect the Hetman, but they did not disregard Golitsyn's advice. Mazepa became Hetman of the Cossacks of the Ukraine, and he was to play a treacherous role in the years to come.[8]

A Polish campaign against the Turks had proved as abortive as Golitsyn's Crimean expedition. The Austrians and Venetians had, however, gained considerable victories which had awakened the hopes of Orthodox Christians in Southern and Eastern Europe that liberation was at hand. But more than the Turkish yoke they dreaded liberation by the Roman Catholic Austrians, and they sent pressing pleas to Moscow that the Russian armies should come to their aid and liberate them. For their part Sofia and Vasily Golitsyn were concerned that the Austrians, Venetians, and Poles should not make a separate peace, leaving Russia alone to face the Turks and Tatars. They were thus anxious to mount a second expedition against the Crimean Khan as a means of keeping their allies in the war.

At this time desperate appeals for armed support were reaching Moscow from the Russian settlements on the banks of the Amur River and its tributaries. In their movement across Siberia to the shores of the Pacific Ocean the Russians had settled the Amur region in the 1630s and 1640s and by the mid-century their fortified towns were numerous. The Chinese were, however, determined to evict them, and for some forty years they had been struggling to hold their settlements. But Sofia was concentrating all resources on the second Crimean campaign and could not spare troops or arms to send to the distant Amur River. She sent an embassy to make peace. The Russian and Chinese envoys met near Nerchinsk in Transbaikalia in 1689 and after long argument a treaty was signed in Nerchinsk, the first to be signed by China with any foreign power. By its terms the Russian settlers had to withdraw from the Amur basin, and the Russian advance in this region was halted for nearly two centuries.

In February 1689 the Russian army, again commanded by Vasily Golitsyn, began its southward march. At the Samara River, Mazepa and the Ukrainian Cossacks joined him, bringing his strength to 112,000 men. Nearing Perekop the Russians engaged the Crimean Tatars and defeated them. But Golitsyn now found that heat, shortage of water, and loss of horses were weakening his forces. He decided to retreat and suffered further losses of men on the homeward march.

The second campaign, like the first, had cost some twenty thousand lives and achieved nothing. But again his reports to Moscow told of great victories. Sofia accorded him and his troops a triumphal entry into the city and prepared a proclamation of the special rewards and decorations for all who had taken part. She was astonished and furious when Tsar Peter refused to sign it. Moreover, angry about the two abortive campaigns and the spurious reports of victory, he refused to receive Golitsyn when he rode to Preobrazhenskoe to receive the formal congratulations and thanks of the Tsar.

For seven years Sofia had ruled as regent, but the Tsars had now come of age, which was taken to happen on their marriage. She had long feared this inevitable development and in 1687 had assumed the title of *Gosudarynya* or Sovereign in a bid for supreme power. She had even through her agent, Shaklovity, whom she had made commander of the *streltsi* after the execution of Khovansky, tried to arouse their support for her coronation on September 1, 1687, the Russian New Year's Day. But the *streltsi* had shown no enthusiasm and given no support.

Tension mounted between the two parties of Sofia, Vasily Golitsyn, and the Miloslavsky on the one hand and Peter and the Naryshkini on the other. On July 31, 1689, General Patrick Gordon noted in his diary that "the heat and bitterness are ever greater and greater, and it appears that it must soon break out." A few days later he wrote of "rumors unsafe to be uttered."[9]

Early in August the conflict burst into the open. Sofia and Shaklovity, fearing an attack by the Naryshkini, had assembled some seven hundred *streltsi* in the Kremlin and the Lyubyanka. Peter and his mother were at Preobrazhenskoe. On the night of August 7–8 two *streltsi* rode there to warn Peter that Sofia was planning to kill him. Peter galloped at once to the Troitsa Monastery. On the following day his mother and wife, the boyars and his two "play regiments" as well as one regiment of *streltsi* joined him there.

From this stronghold Peter sent orders for all colonels and ten *streltsi* from each regiment to report to him in person. Gradually the people rallied to him. Sofia begged the Patriarch to intercede in what she called a family quarrel. He agreed, but on reaching the Troitsa he remained there, supporting Peter's cause. On August 29 Sofia herself took the road to the monastery, hoping to talk with Peter, but on his orders she was turned back and had to return to Moscow. The foreign officers were in an invidious position. Sofia had ordered them to remain in Moscow, but some had already gone to Troitsa. On September 4, Gordon and the remaining officers took the same road and this was, as Gordon noted in his diary, "the decisive break."[10]

Sofia was now alone. Vasily Golitsyn remained at his country estate and, when it was clear that she was beaten, he made his way to the Troitsa. But Peter refused to receive him and, having confiscated his estates and stripped him of the rank of boyar, exiled him to the Arctic. Learned and advanced in his ideas, he might have served Peter well, but he was fortunate to escape torture and execution through the intervention of his cousin, Prince Boris Golitsyn, who was close to Peter. Shaklovity and others who had served Sofia were executed.

Peter now wrote to his half-brother, Ivan, proposing that Sofia should no longer be allowed to interfere in affairs of state. To this and other proposals Ivan readily agreed. Some three weeks later Sofia was escorted, protesting loudly, to the cells prepared for her in the Novodevichy nunnery where, after her bold struggle for freedom and power, she was doomed to end her days.

VI

Peter Alexeevich

1689–1725

The Romanov dynasty had made a faltering start. Of its first five Tsars, all were minors when they came to the throne, and three were physically backward and ailing. The succession had been a continuing source of anxiety. But the dynasty had fulfilled the basic need of the young nation that there should be a Tsar on the throne. Moreover, Tsar Alexei had grown to be an impressive Autocrat, who established the Romanovs more securely. But then the dynasty produced Peter, one of the most dynamic and creative rulers in history.

Born in the Kremlin Palace on May 30, 1672, Peter displayed strength and vitality as a small child and he developed rapidly. He was three and a half years old when his father, Tsar Alexei, died. He may have noticed that his mother became tearful and anxious, but his daily life did not change noticeably. Tsar Fedor showed no desire to victimize his stepmother and half-brother. At the age of seven Peter was removed from the care of the women of the *terem* and entrusted to tutors. His first tutors are not known, but from 1683 to 1690 a clerk from one of the *prikazi*, named Nikita Zotov, who was later to win renown as a drunkard, gave him lessons. His formal education was, however, neglected; he could read and write, but his spelling, grammar, and handwriting were always to be appalling.

The happy and stable routine of his childhood was shattered by the revolt of the *streltsi* which made a deep and lasting impact on him. He was then ten years old, but mentally and physically developed well beyond his age. Suddenly he found himself in the midst of bloodshed and savagery in which Matveev, Naryshkin uncles, and others close to him were hacked to pieces. The *streltsi*, raging through the Kremlin, had threatened a general massacre in which he, too, might have been killed. For the first time in his life he experienced danger and fear. The terror of these days was probably the cause of the mad rages that were to seize him in later years, making it unsafe to be near him, and of the twitching which contorted his handsome face.

This experience also marked the beginning of his aversion from Moscow. He was never to feel at ease in the city which was the ancient seat of the Orthodox Tsars, the spiritual and temporal center of Russia. Later he was to avoid Moscow; months and even years were to pass when he did not set eyes on the Kremlin. Finally he was to move the capital to the new city which he himself built and which looked out to the Gulf of Finland, the Baltic Sea, and the West.

During the regency of his half-sister, Sofia, Peter was free most of the time to pursue his own interests. She was taken up with Vasily Golitsyn, her chief minister, and the government of the country, and she paid no special attention to him. He had to be present on formal occasions when, seated beside Ivan, his half-brother and co-Tsar, he took part in church festivals or received foreign envoys in audience. He escaped as soon as he could from these functions and then he was more or less his own master.

Peter was now at the age when the noise and excitement of playing at war make a strong appeal, and he devoted himself earnestly to war games. Perhaps he had in mind Sofia, the Miloslavsky, and the *streltsi* as real personal enemies against whom he had to prepare. His first troops were his companions, the *komnatnie stolniki*, or stewards, appointed to attend him, and increasingly he drew recruits from among his father's grooms and falconers. He drilled them on a small parade ground which he had had laid out in the Kremlin. As Tsar he was able to draw on the state arsenal for weapons. At first he had wooden cannon, but soon he had enlisted into his army a foreign gunner, Simon Zommer, and under his direction he arranged a full artillery display to celebrate his eleventh birthday.

His mother, Tsaritsa Natalya, had continued to live in the Kremlin after the death of Tsar Alexei. But she was uneasy there. While Sofia was regent, she escaped from Moscow as often as possible, spending her time at Preobrazhenskoe and other country residences. Peter was delighted with this arrangement. He was always eager to get away from the oppressive Kremlin and to engage in military exercises in the open country, especially now when his games were growing in scale. In 1687 he established his military headquarters at Preobrazhenskoe and began recruiting in earnest. Tsarevna Sofia and Vasily Golitsyn were taken up with preparations for the first Crimean campaign and did not interfere. Soon he had two regiments at full strength, named the Preobrazhensky and Semyonovsky after the neighboring villages which served as their respective headquarters, and he trained and exercised both regiments unceasingly in maneuvers and mock battles.

At the same time Peter's interests were broadening. His formal education had come to an end, but he was constantly learning. He liked using his hands and could never see a craftsman at work without himself mastering the craft. He quickly qualified as a stonemason, smith, carpenter, and printer.

Two incidents at this time were important in his future development. Prince Yakov Dolgoruky returned from Paris, where he had been Russian envoy, bringing an astrolabe. Peter was fascinated, but could find no one among his people to instruct him in its use. Finally in the Foreign Quarter he met a Dutchman, Franz Timmerman, who explained how it worked. Timmerman became his tutor in the study of mathematics, geometry, and military science.

The second incident was more momentous. Shortly before his seventeenth birthday Peter was visiting a village near Moscow and in a storehouse on the estate of a Romanov forebear he noticed a boat unlike the flat-bottomed boats plying the Russian rivers.

"What kind of boat is that?" he asked Timmerman, who was constantly at his side.

"An English boat," the Dutchman replied.

"What is it used for? Is it better than our Russian boats?"

"Yes, if it had a new mast and sails, it would move not only with the wind, but against the wind as well."[1]

Peter was fascinated and could not rest until the boat had been refitted and he was shown how to sail it on the Yauza River. Karsten Brandt and Kort, two Dutch boatbuilders from the Foreign Quarter, were taken into his personal service. With them and other companions Peter set out for Lake Pleshchev, some fifty miles north of Moscow, which provided a suitable expanse of water. Here during the winter he set to work with them to build three yachts and two small frigates.

On his mother's insistence he returned to Moscow in January 1689. He could not bear to be away from his boatbuilding. His mother had, however, found him a bride, Evdokiya Lopukhina, and was anxious that he should marry her without delay, thus indicating that he was no

longer a minor and that the regency of Sofia had no further legality.
Tsaritsa Natalya also hoped that marriage would settle him and distract
him from boatbuilding and other pursuits which she considered dangerous and unbecoming for the Tsar. As a dutiful son he married
Evdokiya on January 27, 1689.

Peter remained with his mother and his young wife for a short time.
As soon as he could, he hurried away to help in the boatbuilding. Again
his mother called him back. He protested in a letter: "Your unworthy
son, Petrushka, sends his respects. As to your instructions to return to
Moscow, I am ready to obey; only work—I have work to do and he
whom you sent has seen it and will report to you about it."[2] But he returned and then escaped again to the lake. In the late summer, he
remained with his mother in Preobrazhenskoe. He realized now that he
must be at hand because tension between his supporters and Sofia and
the Miloslavsky was mounting.

By this time, moreover, Peter was more prepared to be away from
Lake Pleshchev. He was thinking of future plans. He had talked with
foreigners about the sea and sailing ships and suddenly the small English boat and the yachts, tacking against the wind, had made them real
to him. The vision of Russian ships sailing the seas fired his imagination.
A seventeen-year-old boy, born hundreds of miles from the sea, Tsar of
a nation of landsmen and peasants, he dreamed of being a sailor and
creating a navy. It became a mighty obsession.

The little English boat had served a momentous purpose and now
was forgotten. Many years later it was found rotting in a storehouse.
But it was destined to be preserved, so that generations of Russians to
come could look on it respectfully and call it, in Peter's own words,
"the grandfather of the Russian navy."

In August 1689 the conflict with Tsarevna Sofia erupted. She had
wielded the powers of regent for seven years and had sought desperately to usurp the supreme power, but could find no support even among
the *streltsi*. The title of Peter and Ivan to the throne was beyond challenge. Sofia was imprisoned under guard in a nunnery and the Naryshkini,
the family of Peter's mother, returned to power.

Peter himself entered Moscow on October 6, 1689. The bells of the
city rang out in welcome and the people joyfully celebrated the return
of their young Tsar. He was, however, in no mood to celebrate. He returned to the Kremlin with reluctance. He was not ready to rule as
Autocrat and for the next five years he left affairs of state to his mother
and the small group of ministers he had appointed while at the Troitsa
Monastery.

At this time Peter embarked on a new stage in his education as he
began frequenting the Foreign Quarter. There he found men who

could answer his questions and instruct him in the crafts and sciences of the West. But he had to exercise some restraint. His mother insisted that he attend to his formal duties as Tsar. He was also under the stern watchful eye of Patriarch Ioakim, a conservative Muscovite, venerable and forbidding in aspect like an Old Testament prophet. Ioakim was unrelenting in his hostility toward heretic foreigners and was horrified when he saw the young Tsar in the company of Timmerman and others. Moreover, he reflected the mood of the Muscovites at this time. Sofia and Vasily Golitsyn had extended patronage to foreigners in a way that incensed most Russians. In an outburst of xenophobia, soon after the fall of Sofia, a Muscovite mob had seized a foreigner in the city and burnt him alive. All Russians looked on Peter as the Tsar who would cleanse the country of the foreign blight, and soon they were to find that they were gravely mistaken.

Patriarch Ioakim died in March 1690. His successor, Adrian, Metropolitan of Kazan, was equally conservative, but a mild man, lacking authority. In any case Peter had already embarked on his Western tutelage in earnest. His visits to the Foreign Quarter were more frequent and the friendships he formed there, especially with General Patrick Gordon and Franz Lefort, strongly influenced him.

Patrick Gordon, a Scot from Aberdeenshire, had entered the Russian service as a major in September 1661, when Alexei was Tsar. By distinguished service, especially against the Crimean Tatars, he had risen to the rank of general. An honorable, conscientious, and brave man he had won the respect of the Russians, and his petitions to be allowed to retire to Scotland were all firmly rejected because he could not be spared. He was also cultured, combining the abilities of a man of action with the learning of a scholar. Already in his mid-fifties when he became Peter's companion, he took pleasure in instructing and guiding his dynamic eighteen-year-old master.

Franz Lefort, son of a prosperous Genevan merchant, differed completely from Gordon. In revolt against the dour Calvinistic life of Geneva, he had come to Russia in search of adventure. He had served under Gordon who had commended him for bravery under fire. By nature Lefort was high-spirited, pleasure-loving, idle and irresponsible. He had captivated Peter by his charm and gaiety. He was able to talk fluently, if superficially, about Western science, institutions, and life, and he was without equal as a drinking companion.

Peter now gathered around him a motley company of eighty to two hundred members of different trades, faiths, and tongues. The inner circle, comprising his favorites and those whom he regarded as colleagues, included Gordon, Lefort, Andrei Vinius, Jacob Bruce, and other foreigners. This company, taking the place of the traditional court of the Tsars, went everywhere with him in pursuit of military and naval experience, and diversion. Peter spent his days working hard on training exercises or as a gunner, smith, or boatbuilder, and his evenings banqueting with members of his company. All needed the capacity to drink deeply, for the young Tsar had a strong head and an iron constitution. Often these evenings ended in debauchery and drunkenness on a vast scale. But at dawn the following morning, while his companions were still deep in drunken slumber, Peter would rise to work furiously through the day. It was a pace too hectic for some of the company. General Gordon usually took to his bed for two or three days after these orgies, and Peter visited him or sent medicines to speed his recovery.

Fireworks provided another source of entertainment. Displays often went on for five hours without a break. As Peter mastered pyrotechnics, the displays became more elaborate as when on a white pavilion of flame a representation of Hercules, tearing open the lion's jaws, was outlined by fireworks. Peter also reveled in buffoonery which was often cruel and extremely gross. It included the "All-joking, All-drunken Assembly" of which his old tutor, Nikita Zotov, was president or "Prince-Pope." The drunken assembly observed ceremonial which mocked the church and the patriarchate in a way that distressed his people. Peter himself was deeply religious, although he did not follow the devout routine of his father and did not share the bigotry of his people. His mockery of the church was in part youthful irreverence and in part an expression of his anger against the conservatism and incompetence of the hierarchy and the clergy and their influence on the nation. He was later to recognize that the church, as distinct from the Orthodox faith, was a retrograde force in Russian life and then he began to reform it.

Diversions and drinking consumed only a small part of his time and energy. Throughout the winter of 1689–90 he was preparing for maneuvers. The summer of 1691 was devoted to planning "the great and terrible battle," waged in the autumn between the army of Generalissimo Prince Romodanovsky, comprising the Preobrazhensky and Semyonovsky regiments, and the army of Generalissimo Ivan Buturlin, comprising *streltsi* regiments. Peter took an active part in Romodanovsky's army which was victorious. He hastened from the field of battle to Pereyaslavl to assist Karsten Brandt and his team of carpenters to complete the two frigates and three yachts. Master Shipwright Peter Alexeevich, as he was known in the yard, also laid down the keel of a ship of war and throughout the winter he labored from dawn until late every night, eating his food in the shipyard and sleeping only when exhausted. On May 1 the ship was launched with full ceremony. Nothing ever gave him so much satisfaction as the launch of a ship, especially one which he had helped to build with his own hands.

In July, Tsaritsa Natalya and the court journeyed to Pereyaslavl to witness maneuvers on the land and water which he directed. But already he had passed beyond this stage of his naval training. He was planning to visit Archangel to examine seagoing ships and to sail the White Sea.

Archangel was then the center of Russia's trade with the rest of Europe. Every spring as soon as the ice broke, foreign merchantmen began crowding the wharves. Throughout the brief summer the port was the scene of frantic activity as the Uspensky market was cleared of goods and the ships were unloaded and loaded to sail before ice closed the river and sea.

To Peter, who paid his first visit to Archangel in summer 1693, the port was a revelation. The great merchant ships fascinated him and when a number of English and Dutch ships sailed in convoy, escorted by a Dutch warship, he sailed with them in a small yacht, the *St. Peter*, which had been made ready for him. He sailed nearly two hundred miles before he reluctantly turned back.

The experience of Archangel deepened his obsession with the sea and ships. He examined every ship in port and spent hours questioning captains and seamen. He was learning and, always constructive, he was planning ahead. He gave orders for a new wharf to be built at Solombala and laid down the keel of a ship to be constructed there during the coming winter. Finally he wrote to Nicholas Witsen, Burgomaster of Amsterdam, who acted on occasion as agent for the Tsar, to purchase for him a forty-four gun frigate to be delivered in the following summer.

Returning to Moscow, Peter busied himself with turning blocks and preparing rigging as well as casting cannon to be mounted on the ship under construction at Solombala. But on January 25, 1694, his mother died. The grief of early widowhood, the horror of the *streltsi* revolt, and constant anxiety for her son, especially during the regency of Sofia, had aged her prematurely. She had been ill since her visit to Pereyaslavl. According to Patrick Gordon, Peter was "exceeding melancholy and troubled" by her death.[8] He did not attend the funeral and for three days he did not leave Preobrazhenskoe or see anyone. But he could not stand still to grieve for long. He had to be active and soon he was immersed in plans for his next visit to Archangel. But her death marked the end of a stage in his life. She had kept him in touch with Muscovite ritual, ensuring that he was present as Tsar on ceremonial occasions. After her death he ignored this function. On April 8 he accompanied Tsar Ivan in the Easter procession; this is the last reference in the court records to his participation in Kremlin ceremonies. The Foreign Quarter now became the center of his interests and his court moved between the Quarter and Preobrazhenskoe.

The visit to Archangel in the summer of 1694 was highly successful. The *St. Paul*, the keel of which he had laid down at Solombala, was launched. The forty-four gun frigate, ordered from Holland and called *The Holy Prophesy* arrived on July 11, and he was delighted with her. He sailed her to Svyatoi Nos at the entrance of the White Sea and back to Archangel. Yet again his mind was racing ahead to new projects. By the time he returned to Moscow he was actively planning a major venture to the south.

The second expedition against the Crimean Tatars, led by Vasily Golitsyn, during Sofia's regency, had not ended with an armistice or a peace agreement. Russia was thus still formally at war with the Crimean Tatars and the Turks. The Russian government, distracted by the Tsar's activities, had taken no further action, and Russia's allies, Poland and Austria, were complaining strongly that Russia was failing in her obligation to prosecute the war vigorously. Also Moscow was receiving reports from Hetman Mazepa in the Ukraine, that the Zaporozhsky Cossacks were restless and urging that the Tsar should send an army to remind them of their allegiance.

Peter had an added, and to him more important, incentive for launching a campaign to the south. This was his driving ambition to create a navy. The White Sea was frozen over for some eight months of the year. Of the two other seas on which he could realize his ambition, the Baltic was closed to him by the Swedes and the Black Sea by the Turks. He found himself committed to some action against the Crimean Tatars and the Turks. He decided therefore to challenge the Turks at Azov, which commanded access to the Sea of Azov. Here he would have warm water harbors in which to build his fleet, and then, having seized Kerch, he could challenge the Turks for command of the Black Sea.

The Ottoman Porte was then still a formidable power. Peter was, however, confident after large-scale maneuvers in the autumn that his army, trained and led by foreign officers, could take Azov. His plan of campaign was that Boyar Sheremetev with 120,000 men and a detachment of Cossacks, led by Mazepa, would march against the Crimean Tatars and incidentally prevent their going to the aid of the Turks at Azov. Peter with his chosen regiments and some thirty thousand troops would proceed against Azov.

This first attempt to take Azov was a failure and might have ended in disaster had General Patrick Gordon not taken precautions. But the defeat was salutary for Peter; it suddenly matured him and at the age of twenty-three he became a responsible Tsar and began his rule as Autocrat. He blamed no one for the miscarriage of the campaign and he acknowledged the reasons for it. One reason was that the command of the Russian army had been divided between three generals—Gordon, Lefort, and Artemon Golovin. In practice "Bombardier of the Pre-obrazhensky Regiment Peter Alexeev" filled the role of supreme commander, but he refused to assume it openly and to command in person. Another reason was lack of experienced engineers, and he wrote at once to the Austrian Emperor and also to Denmark and Brandenburg, asking each to send him six to ten competent engineers. The most important reason for failure had been lack of warships to prevent the Turks taking supplies and reinforcements to the Azov garrison by sea. Peter at once set about remedying these faults and planning a new campaign to take place in the following summer.

The building of a fleet was a tremendous undertaking. Russia had no tradition of shipbuilding and lacked both facilities and trained workmen. Moreover, Peter was planning not a squadron but a fleet of twenty-five galleys, thirteen hundred river barges, and numerous small craft. He had to decide on the site and build the shipyards, assemble materials, enlist shipwrights and carpenters, and train crews. All had to be done and the vessels built and made ready during the five winter months. It was a striking demonstration of the scale on which he thought and worked. It was also an early proof of the dynamism of the young Tsar, for by the end of April all vessels had been launched and many were already proceeding down the Don from Voronezh, where he had established the shipyards.

Early in June the Russian galleys anchored at the mouth of the Don River, effectively blockading Azov. By land the artillery began bombarding the garrison. A few weeks later the Austrian engineers and gunnery experts, sent in response to Peter's letter to the Emperor, arrived. They inspected and approved the extensive siege works carried out by the Russians. The bombardment continued. A council of war decided that a general assault should be made on July 22, but on July 19, waving their turbans and lowering their banners, the Turkish garrison surrendered.

In Moscow, news of the capture of Azov brought everyone rejoicing into the streets and the churches. Victory over the mighty, Ottoman Porte was unbelievable. The Patriarch wept with joy as he read the official report of this defeat of the heretic Turks. Meanwhile Peter was busy drawing up plans with the advice of the Austrian engineers for the rebuilding and fortification of Azov. He also inspected the northern shore of the sea and finally chose Cape Taganrog as the site of the new harbor.

On his return to Moscow he marched in procession through the city and under the triumphal arch, especially erected on his instructions. The whole ceremony bewildered the Russians. They were accustomed to holy ikons, borne by church dignitaries, resplendent in their robes, and long services of thanksgiving in the cathedrals. This traditional religious character was absent from Peter's triumph. The arch was classical in style, embellished with allegorical statues, dominated by immense figures of Hercules and Mars. But most horrifying of all to the people of Moscow was to see their Tsar, not in the place of honor, but following behind the gilded sledge of Admiral Lefort and wearing a German cloak of black and with a white feather in his hat. He was on foot and marched the full distance of the triumphal route.

Peter, now aged twenty-four, had grown to be a magnificent figure of a man. He was nearly seven feet in height and powerfully built. His face round, his eyes open and intelligent, he would have been strikingly handsome but for the distressing twitch and the habit of rolling his eyes in a frightening way. Another characteristic which set him apart was his dynamic energy. He was constantly on the move. He did not walk but rushed and his companions had to break into a run to keep up with his long swift strides. His energy was not merely physical; it was also mental. He was constantly learning, planning, and building. At the same time he was singleminded and determined. He had been concentrating on the creation of a navy and the training of the army to the exclusion of all else. But his vision was now broadening.

On his return from Azov, Peter was actively planning two great projects, both revolutionary and involving great problems for Russia, but both were at the same time simple and logical developments of his grand enterprise. The first was to begin building his navy and, stemming from it, the second was to send young Russians abroad to study seamanship, navigation, and shipbuilding, and to visit the West himself for the same purpose. Within five months work on the navy was under way, many young Russians were already abroad, and he himself was on the point of departure.

The new shipbuilding program imposed heavy burdens on all classes of the Russian people. Three thousand families from the Kazan region and three thousand *streltsi* with their families were sent to colonize Azov. A labor force of twenty thousand men was assembled from the Ukrainian towns to build the new harbor at Taganrog. The already large labor force at Voronezh was greatly augmented for the new shipbuilding program. Responsibility for building the ships was imposed equitably on the boyars, gentry, senior churchmen, and the monasteries, each producing one or more ships or parts of ships according to the number of serfs owned. The norm was ownership of eight thousand serf families in respect of which one ship had to be built, rigged, and armed. Thus the Patriarch owned private estates, containing 8761 serf families; he had to build one ship in respect of eight thousand households and pool his remaining 761 households with those of two metropolitans, an archbishop, and twelve monasteries to produce another ship. Merchants in the capital and provinces were responsible for building twelve ships;

they petitioned the Tsar to have the number reduced, and Peter at once increased it to fourteen ships. He would allow no exceptions. Failure to have the ships ready for service by April 1698 meant confiscation of all property. Nearly all landowners contracted with foreign shipwrights, engaged in the work at Voronezh, for the construction of their ships.

The Russian people grumbled and accepted these new burdens. But they were distressed by Peter's order that their young men must train in England, Holland, and Venice. To all but a handful of Russians the countries of the West were unknown and sinister, and the Tsar was condemning those sent away for training to be corrupted and seduced from the Orthodox way of life. The rumors that the Tsar himself was going abroad distressed them even more. The Tsar had never traveled beyond his own frontiers, except on rare occasions of war. They did not understand why he wanted to go. Already for many of them Peter was the "Tsar-Stranger" who had broken away from their cherished traditions. But they felt too that he was deserting them, that he would disappear or suffer some deep change, and their distress had in it an element of pathos, as though they were children about to be orphaned.

Peter was not concerned or even interested in the reactions of his people. He was absorbed by his immediate plans. Each young Russian training abroad had to obtain a certificate of proficiency from the host country; he had to take one soldier with him and ensure that he too received training; he had also to engage and bring back with him to Russia two skilled mariners. For himself Peter saw nothing strange or dangerous in his plans to travel to the West. He was a forerunner, obliged to learn so that he could teach. As Tsar this was his special duty, for, as he said, "a monarch should feel ashamed to lag behind his subjects in any craft."[4]

The problem was how he could travel without being committed to the diplomatic formalities which he found tedious and which would hinder his work. The problem was resolved by the decision to appoint a grand embassy to the courts of Western Europe with which he could travel incognito. The capture of Azov had committed him to war with Turkey and he knew that Russia alone could not stand against such a mighty power. The purpose of the embassy was to negotiate a grand alliance of Russia, England, Denmark, Prussia, Holland, Austria, and Venice against Turkey.

Peter personally directed the preparations for his embassy. He wrote out in his own hand lists of what he required for his navy, including such details as types and quantities of blocks and tackles, navigation instruments, and cannon. His ambassadors were to enlist personnel, especially ships' captains and officers "who have themselves been sailors

and have reached their rank by service and not other means."[5]
The embassy grew rapidly until it numbered more than two hundred
fifty persons, including a group of thirty-eight "volunteers" among whom
Peter was listed under the name of "Peter Mikhailov."

The incognito was hardly effective. All Europe knew that the Tsar was
traveling with the embassy. One speculation was that he was making a
pilgrimage to Rome and hopes were high there that he would be converted, thus uniting the Eastern and Western churches. The Austrian
resident in Moscow reported to Vienna that the embassy was "merely a
cloak to allow the Tsar to get out of his country and travel in freedom,
and has no other serious purpose."[6] Other theories circulated. But the
reason for his tour was simple, as were the reasons for most of his
actions: he was visiting Western Europe to study in the shipyards and
to learn all that was relevant to the creation of a navy. This remained
his chief purpose, but his eager questing mind was to range widely.
The tour was to prove a turning point in his reign, and Macaulay did
not overstate when he wrote that "his journey is an epoch in the history
not only of his own country but of ours and of the world."[7]

The embassy departed from Moscow on March 9, 1697. It was delayed at Riga by flooding of the Dvina River. An incident occurred
there, when Peter was inspecting the defenses of the city, which gave
rise to recriminations and which he was later to use as an excuse for
declaring war on Sweden. From there the embassy with Peter and a
few chosen companions impatiently traveling ahead proceeded by way
of Mitau, the capital of the Duchy of Courland, Koenigsberg, and
Berlin. He inspected fortifications and in Pilau and Koenigsberg studied
gunnery with the artillery expert of the Elector of Brandenburg,
Frederick III, soon to become the first King of Prussia.

In Courland the Duke feasted the embassy, discreetly showing respect
to the Tsar. Baron de Blomberg wrote that "open tables were kept everywhere with trumpets and music attended with feasting and excessive
drinking all along, as if his Tsarish Majesty had been another Bac-
chus."[8] The Russians with their brutish manners did not make a
good impression, and he noted that the foreign officers in the embassy
usually referred to them as "the baptized bears."[9]

Conspicuous by his height and his obvious authority, Peter found
himself surrounded by staring crowds. He suffered acutely from this
curiosity. In the small fortress town of Kustrin a band of Frankfurt
students broke into the house where he was resting in order to set eyes
on the Tsar. He dreaded a repetition of this incident and drove through
Berlin, sitting tightly in the corner of his carriage to avoid being seen.

At Koppenbrugge he was prevailed on to dine with the Electress
Sophia Charlotte, a remarkable woman of beauty and intelligence. It
was his first contact with the gracious and cultivated aspect of Western

life. Shyness overwhelmed him when confronted by her and he covered his face with his hands. Later he relaxed and the dinner, lasting four hours, proved a merry occasion. Sophia considered him a remarkable man with a good heart and noble instincts. Her final judgment, written two months later, was more circumspect: "He is a ruler both very good and very evil at the same time," she wrote. "His character is exactly the character of his country. If he had had a better education, he would be an exceptional man, for he has great qualities and unlimited natural intelligence."[10]

Peter was now nearing Holland and he was impatient to set to work in the shipyards. At this time Holland was at the height of her power and prestige, renowned especially as a naval and mercantile nation. Here he believed he would be able to study shipbuilding at its best while also recruiting experts and purchasing equipment.

With eighteen companions Peter rushed ahead to Zaandam, then the center of a flourishing shipbuilding district. Zaandamers, serving in Moscow, had spoken as though this was the foremost shipbuilding town in Holland. But he found Zaandam disappointing, and he hated the great crowds which shadowed him wherever he went. He traveled to Amsterdam to join the embassy on its arrival on August 16. There he had his first meeting with Nicholas Witsen, a wealthy patron of the arts and sciences who shared his passion for ships and who acted unofficially as Dutch minister for Russian affairs.

Witsen, as a director of the East India Company, proposed to Peter that he would find it more convenient and profitable to work in the Company's yards. He added that the directors had agreed to build a new frigate, so that he could study the whole process of ship construction. This proposal excited Peter. He hastened back to Zaandam the same evening to collect his tools and next morning he started work under the direction of a master shipwright.

During the next four months Peter worked and studied in the shipyards. He laid down his tools only for special visits, once to go to Utrecht to meet William III, on another occasion to examine the work of the celebrated anatomist, Professor Ruysch, whose techniques for preserving corpses fascinated him. He traveled to The Hague where his embassy sought to negotiate the grand alliance against Turkey. Embassies from the leading European powers had gathered there for the Congress of Ryswyk. But the Russian project made no headway. All Europe now wanted peace with Turkey, for conflict over the Spanish succession was threatening. France and the balance of power, not the infidel Turks, preoccupied the West. News of Turkish defeats by Prince Eugene and by Russian troops near Azov made Turkey seem a far less formidable enemy, however, and the failure of the diplomatic mission did not seem so calamitous to the Russians.

Meanwhile Peter's disappointment in Dutch shipbuilding methods was growing. His master shipwright and other Dutch experts worked by rule of thumb and were unable to teach him the principles of ship construction. Already he was looking toward England as the country where he would learn the basic principles. His interest was intensified by the gift from William III of a magnificent new yacht, the *Royal Transport*. Admiral Lord Carmarthen, who had designed it, wrote to him about its graceful, speedy lines. Peter was now intent on going to England without delay. On January 8, 1698 with a suite of sixteen companions he went on board the *Yorke*, flagship of Vice-Admiral Sir David Mitchell who commanded the small squadron, sent to take him across the Channel. The crossing was an exciting experience for Peter. He was at sea in a large ship of war for the first time and, although the weather was stormy, he stayed on deck, avidly studying the seamanship and handling of the great ship.

London was at this time one of the largest and wealthiest cities in Europe. The Great Fire of 1666 had destroyed the city between the Tower and the Temple, but new mansions, now of brick and stone, had risen from the ashes within a few years. The genius of Sir Christopher Wren had had full play in the rebuilding of fifty-one churches and his masterpiece, St. Paul's Cathedral, towered majestically over the city. But the forest of masts of the ships moored in the Pool of London interested Peter most of all. For a month he remained in London, living in a house in Norfolk Street off the Strand. He visited watchmakers and learned to repair watches. He even found time to observe the English method of making coffins, which was more economic in its use of timber, and he sent a coffin to Moscow to serve as a model.[11]

Accompanied by two companions and by Admiral Mitchell Peter paid an informal call on the King at Kensington Palace. He had long admired William III, but no report has survived of their meetings in Utrecht or in Kensington. If they were attracted to each other, it was the attraction of opposites. William was cold and restrained, ailing and dour; Peter was tempestuous and impulsive, explosively energetic and healthy. They were alike only in their purposefulness and determination. At their meeting William persuaded Peter to sit for Sir Godfrey Kneller, the foremost portrait painter in Europe at the time. Kneller's portrait, which hangs in Kensington Palace, shows the lively, open, handsome face of the young Tsar in his prime, but his expression is both chivalrous and benevolent, and the picture contains no suggestion of the fierce will, the savage anger, and the volcanic energy which were to make his reign so outstanding.

Early in February Peter moved to Deptford, then the center of important docks and shipyards. He was lodged with his suite in Sayes Court, the country house of the diarist, John Evelyn. It was a fine house with a magnificent garden, but the Russians were, according to Evelyn's bailiff, "right nasty" and caused extensive damage.[12] For Peter this was the crucial stage of his training when he was mastering the principles underlying all that he had learnt by practice in Russia and in Holland. A journeyman-shipwright, employed at Deptford at the time, testified that "The Tsar of Muscovy worked with his own hands as hard as any man in the yard."[13]

At Deptford and in London Peter visited churches freely and also went to Quaker meetings. But the Anglican church interested him most because it was part of the English way of life which manifested a spirit of enterprise and independence so different from the humility and submission encouraged by the Orthodox Church in Russia. He had numerous discussions with Gilbert Burnet, Bishop of Salisbury, who was strongly and favorably impressed by him. Later, when he came to write his *History of His Own Times,* after receiving horrifying reports of the suppression of the *streltsi,* his opinion was somewhat revised. He then wrote: "After I had seen him often and had conversed much with him, I could not but adore the depth of the providence of God that has raised up such a furious man to so absolute an authority over so great a part of the world . . . Man seems a very contemptible thing in the sight of God while such a person as the Tsar has such multitudes put, as it were, under his feet, exposed to his restless jealousy and savage temper."[14]

During these weeks Peter was often in the company of Peregrine Osborne, Marquis of Carmarthen, who was high-spirited, a sturdy drinker, and an able shipdesigner and seaman. Through him Peter granted a monopoly of the import of tobacco into Russia, a deal which provided him with ready money to pay for the equipment that the Russians were buying to take back with them. He spent hours at Woolwich Arsenal, Greenwich, and at the Tower of London which then housed the Royal Society and the Mint. The English coinage had recently been reformed, as a result of proposals made by Isaac Newton and John Locke. Russia had a severe coinage problem and two years later Peter reformed his coinage on the English model. Meanwhile he and his companions had been engaging English seamen and ships officers and experts in every field. Sometimes he found that Englishmen while willing to serve in Russia demanded terms too high. But he did engage a mathematician from Aberdeen University, named Henry Farquharson, who with two young students from Christ's Hospital, Stephen Gwyn and Richard Grice, later established the School of Mathematics and Navigation in Moscow.

The visit to England was now drawing to a close. The King had been a considerate host. He had given Peter the free run of naval and military establishments. He had invited him to inspect the fleet and to observe maneuvers in the Solent. On board the flagship *Humber* Peter excitedly watched the great ships of war maneuver, fire their broadsides and veer to attack again.

England had delighted him. He had met such men as Mitchell and Carmarthen, and he carried away with him a great respect for English engineers, gunners, and, above all, shipwrights. He always acknowledged that, in naval matters, "If he had not come to England he had certainly been a bungler," and frequently observed that "The English island is the best, most beautiful, and happiest there is in the whole world."[15]

Returning to Amsterdam, Peter found the embassy surrounded by men and equipment. More than seven hundred officers, seamen, engineers, and artisans had been engaged and vast quantities of arms and equipment purchased. Ten ships had to be chartered to transport them to Russia. He, himself, planned a leisurely journey with visits to Vienna and Venice. Reports reached him, however, that the *streltsi* had again rebelled and he was disturbed that Romodanovsky had not put down the revolt with sufficient severity. He was more disturbed to learn that he and others in Moscow, having had no news for him, were ready to believe that he was dead and had been near to panic. He sent letters, castigating them for behaving like "old women," and then set out on his travels. He hastened to Vienna on receiving news that the Emperor and the Venetian Senate were discussing proposals for peace with Turkey. He realized soon after arriving in Vienna that he could not hold the Emperor from coming to terms with the Sultan. He had indeed failed not only to forge a grand alliance against the Turks but also to prevent the collapse of the existing alliance. The political purpose of his embassy had, however, been a secondary purpose. Now he was eager to go on to Venice, renowned at this time for its galleys.

On July 15, Peter was on the point of departing from Vienna when post arrived from Moscow. It brought alarming news of another outbreak of the *streltsi*. Romodanovsky reported that four regiments were marching on Moscow and that he had sent troops, commanded by Generals Gordon and Shein, to halt them. The letter had taken a month to reach Vienna and for all Peter knew the *streltsi* might have occupied the Kremlin. Putting aside his plans to visit Venice, he set out on July 19 with all haste for Moscow. He was almost at Cracow when he learned that the *streltsi* had been defeated and that one hundred thirty had been executed, while 1860 were held under arrest.

Peter traveled at a more leisurely pace after receiving this report. On July 31 he reached Rawa and there he had his momentous meeting with Frederick-Augustus, Elector of Saxony and now King Augustus II of Poland. Augustus was a handsome, powerfully built man, but self-indulgent and deceitful. He had numerous mistresses and was said to have fathered over three hundred illegitimate children. He had had ambitions of winning military renown, but in two campaigns in Hungary had displayed neither courage nor ability. He had been elected to the Polish throne, thanks to large-scale bribery, to the presence of Saxon troops, and to the support of the Tsar and the Emperor. Peter, who was simple and straightforward in personal relationships, was impressed by Augustus and was soon to find that his new ally was weak and treacherous.

The Great Northern War had its beginnings in this meeting at Rawa in August 1698. The idea of a Northern League against Sweden was not new. Thirty years earlier Ordin-Nashchokin had proposed it as a national policy and, as with so many of the plans of his father's great minister, Peter was now carrying it into action. But the meeting with Augustus was timely, for Peter, having seen his proposals for a crusade against the Turks miscarry, was ready to turn northward. By concentrating Russia's strength against Sweden he would be able to break through to the Baltic Sea and there establish ports and his navy. This policy was to dominate most of his reign.

The Western tour was coming to an end. He had set out primarily to obtain the knowledge and equipment needed to build his navy. But with his roving curiosity and capacity for learning, he had ranged far more widely. He had expected to see the technical superiority of the West, but had also been impressed by the trade and industry, the wealth and the intellectual vitality, and the cultured world of Holland, England, and Austria. Everything in the West had contrasted with the lethargy and conservatism of Russia. His people did not want to depart from their medieval way of life, dominated by the church. But he was determined now that they should change and that Russia should be transformed into a modern nation.

As he hastened toward Moscow, his practical mind was translating his impressions into policies of reform. At the same time a cold savage anger consumed him. The *streltsi*, who had terrorized him as a boy, had rebelled twice while he had been abroad. They were a dangerous force, who might be incited again by the Miloslavsky, and they were never to be trusted. He had made up his mind to deal with them once for all, so that he could devote himself to his new policies, free from fears of their rebellion. As a contemporary diarist in Moscow wrote: "It had come to pass that Muscovy was to be saved by cruelty, not by pity."[16]

On the evening of August 25, 1698, Peter entered Moscow quietly and unexpectedly. He was avoiding the lengthy ceremonial which had always greeted the Tsar on his return to the city. He did not remain in the Kremlin or call to see his wife and young son. He visited Anna Mons, the daughter of a German wine merchant in the Foreign Quarter, and then rode to Preobrazhenskoe where he spent the night. But news of his return spread rapidly and at first light next morning crowds of people made their way to Preobrazhenskoe to greet him. All wanted to set eyes on their Tsar and to pay him homage. He received them all and, when they prostrated themselves on the ground in Muscovite fashion, he lifted them up and kissed them, for he disliked this servile practice.

Then, as his subjects crowded about him, Peter took a pair of scissors and began cutting their beards. All present, except the Patriarch and two elderly boyars, suffered the treatment. The Patriarch and nobles were shocked and the simple people were horrified. The beard was fundamental to their Orthodoxy and to salvation. At the beginning of the century a few young nobles had begun shaving, but the Patriarch had sternly condemned the practice and Tsar Mikhail had legislated against it. The present Patriarch, Adrian, had proclaimed from the pulpit that "God did not create men beardless, only cats and dogs . . . the shaving of beards is not only foolishness and dishonor, it is a mortal sin."[17] Peter now outlawed the beard, but a few months later relaxed the ban when he saw that a beard tax would help the treasury. Next he ordered the wearing of Western dress. The flowing Muscovite robe reaching to the ground and with wide sleeves was cumbersome and interfered with work. He had adopted Western clothes for efficiency and convenience, and his people must follow his practice in readiness for the great labors ahead.

With this assault on two of the main symbols of old Muscovy, Peter launched a new era in Russia's history. It was an era when old traditions were displaced and new ideas forcibly introduced, when the conservatism and lethargy of Muscovite life were attacked, and the barriers against Western ideas and techniques were struck down. It was an era of war and hard labor for everyone from the Tsar to the humble peasant. Peter did not spare himself and labored harder than any of his subjects. It was, moreover, his era, for he created it. Many of his reforms had been outlined and planned long before his reign; in time they might have been implemented. But he could not wait and he plunged his people into a revolution.

Peter's purpose was to reform and revitalize Russia so that she would stand as a great power on equal terms with the Western powers not only in military strength but also in trade and industry, in government and civilization. His reforms, his assaults on old Muscovite traditions, and his military and naval campaigns were all directed to this end. It involved him in constant war and war became the source and pressure behind many of his reforms. But to Peter war was an instrument of policy, unavoidable in achieving his basic aims. He had no love of war and no hunger for military renown or personal glory. He was indeed a selfless man without personal vanity. He was a reformer and builder and of necessity he became a conqueror.

The two immediate tasks to which Peter now gave his attention were to get rid of his wife and to deal with the *streltsi*. He had married Evdokiya in obedience to his mother's wishes, but had never felt the slightest interest in her. A typical product of the Muscovite *terem*, she was narrowly Orthodox and conservative and completely out of sympathy with all that he thought and did. From abroad he had sent instructions that she should be shorn as a nun, the normal method of disposing of a wife, but she had resisted. She feared in particular, that she would be separated from her son, Alexei. Her resistance was to no purpose. The boy was given into the care of Peter's sister, Tsarevna Natalya. On September 23 a humble carriage took Evdokiya from the Kremlin to the Suzdal Pokrovsky Nunnery, where she became a nun under the name of Elena.

The purging of the *streltsi* was a bloody and barbarous affair. Within a few days of his return from abroad, Peter had ordered Boyar Shein to assemble all *streltsi* who had been involved in the rebellions and had not been executed. He was not satisfied with the investigations that had been carried out and was convinced that his half-sister, Sofia, and the Miloslavsky had been behind the new outbreaks. With memories of their uprising in 1682 when they had murdered so many and had terrorized the city and now, seeing them as a threat to himself and to the nation at a time when he was impatient to launch new policies, he approached the new investigation in a mood of cold fury.

In Preobrazhenskoe fourteen torture chambers were prepared. The main interrogation began on September 17 and continued until mid-October. The procedure was that the accused was questioned and if, as usually happened, his evidence was considered incomplete, he was raised on the gallows, his arms pulled out of joint and he was knouted. Between strokes of the knout he was questioned further. Many *streltsi* proved stubborn in spite of this torture and were exposed to fire in attempts to make them confess. Several women were implicated by the evidence thus extracted and they too were knouted and tortured in the same way.

The investigations were continued remorselessly day by day, enveloping Preobrazhenskoe in a haze of fire and blood and the village echoed with the screams of the victims. Peter was convinced that Sofia and the Miloslavsky had instigated the rebellions, but no conclusive evidence was obtained. He even questioned Sofia personally, but she denied all charges. Toward the end of September, 196 of the rebels were hanged from gallows erected at various points in Moscow. Some two weeks later another mass execution took place, 144 and two days later 278 *streltsi* being hanged, the majority from beams extruding from the crenellations of the Kremlin walls.

In all 799 *streltsi* met their deaths by hanging, beheading, or breaking on the wheel. The winter had set in early and the icy cold fixed in rigid permanence the horror of the Tsar's justice. Frozen corpses hung from the Kremlin walls and over all the gates through which the people passed on their daily business. At the execution place (*Lobnoe Mesto*) on the Red Square, headless bodies lay grotesquely beside pools of frozen blood and on the wheel were the bodies unnaturally bent of those whom death had overtaken more slowly. For nearly five months the bodies remained on display as a grim warning of the fate of rebels and traitors.

Further interrogations and executions took place in the following months, but on a smaller scale. In June 1699 Peter disbanded the remaining sixteen regiments of the Moscow *streltsi*. He dispersed these men to distant parts of the country and they were forbidden to serve again as soldiers. He had thus eradicated the undisciplined and rebellious force which could challenge the throne, and now he relied on his own loyal guards regiments.

Since his return from abroad Peter had been eager to inspect progress on the construction of the navy. Now, having dealt with the *streltsi*, he felt free to leave Moscow and on October 23, 1698, he set out for Voronezh. He found that the small river town had been transformed into a great sprawling shipbuilding center. Twenty ships had been launched and many more were at advanced stages of construction. Shipwrights of many nations were directing the work. But all were working under great difficulties. Shortage of labor was the chief problem. Peasants fled in hundreds and sickness also decimated the labor force, until it was but half the size needed. Other problems troubled Peter who in a moment of despair wrote: "A cloud of doubt covers my mind, whether I shall ever taste these fruits or whether they will be like dates which those who plant them never gather."[18] But he put his doubts aside and, personally laying down the keel of a sixty-gun ship, the *Predestination,* he worked furiously with his own hands to help speed the creation of the navy.

In February 1699 Peter hastened to Moscow on receiving news that his favorite and close friend, Lefort, was ill. One evening during Lent, Lefort who did not believe in abstinence at any time caught a chill after a drinking bout. Debauchery had underminded his constitution and on March 2 he died, aged forty-three. Arriving in Moscow, Peter was overwhelmed by grief on finding that his favorite was already dead. Lefort received a state funeral of greater magnificence than that granted to any Russian, except only the Tsars and the Patriarchs. Peter himself wore deep mourning. Two days later he returned to his shipbuilding. He had much to do and, as after the death of his mother, he could not stand still to grieve.

Peter was now increasingly impatient to negotiate a peace with

Turkey. The time was ripe to launch his attack on Sweden jointly with Augustus of Saxony and Poland, but he refused to commit himself to the campaign in the north until he had secured his position in the south. At Karlowitz Lord Paget, the English ambassador in Constantinople, had as mediator brought about agreement between Austria and Turkey. Having made concessions to the Austrians, the one enemy whom they feared, the Turks were in no hurry to make peace with the Russians. Peter seethed with impatience. Finally, however, the Turks proposed that a Russian envoy should be sent to Constantinople to negotiate. Peter appointed Councilor E. I. Ukraintsev as his envoy extraordinary and decided to send him by warship.

The forty-six gun frigate, *Krepost*, newly launched and fitted out, was chosen for the mission. On August 6 Peter himself sailed with the small fleet which escorted the frigate as far as the entrance to the Straits of Kerch. There the Turks, alarmed by the unexpected arrival of so many Russian ships of war, were prevailed on with difficulty to provide an escort for the frigate. In Constantinople the little ship made an even greater impression and some Turks recognized that they were dealing with a new Russia.

The months following his return from Kerch were for Peter a time of agonized waiting. Augustus sent agents to Moscow to impress on him the importance of launching hostilities against Sweden without delay and by December 1699 at the latest. King Christian V of Denmark sent a special envoy to Moscow to propose an alliance and immediate action against Sweden. To each envoy Peter avowed his eagerness to march, but confirmed his determination not to embark on war in the north until he had reached an agreement for peace, or at least a lengthy armistice, with the Ottoman Porte in the south.

The negotiations in Constantinople were, however, unduly protracted and Peter could never be sure that they would not break down. Because of this danger he had received the embassy from the King of Sweden, sent to Moscow to confirm existing treaties between the two countries. He had solemnly gone through the formalities of confirming these treaties while secretly discussing with Danish and Saxon agents the plans for their combined assault on Sweden. Repeatedly he sent instructions to Ukraintsev in Constantinople to hasten the negotiations, but the Turks would not be hurried. Only on August 8, 1700, did he receive word from Ukraintsev that agreement had been reached. On the following day the proclamation of war on Sweden was made from the Bedchamber Porch in the manner of the Muscovite Tsars.

Only toward the end of 1699 had Peter set about creating an army. The navy and other matters had claimed his attention and, after his success at Azov, he was confident that he could recruit, train, and equip his army to defeat the Swedes. He had decided, moreover, to break from the Muscovite practice of conscripting untrained peasants to serve for a campaign and then disperse to their villages. He called for volunteers who were to serve as regular troops, receiving the same pay, rations, and drink allowance as the guards. The response was good. Within three months twenty-nine new regiments, with a combined strength of 32,000 men, had been formed. Foreign colonels, many of whom had commanded Russian troops at Azov and in earlier Crimean campaigns, commanded the new regiments and were responsible for training their men in Western military methods. According to two foreigners, the new Russian army was an impressive force and, when brought to its planned strength of nearly 64,000 men, it would be formidable.[19]

In this hasty and strenuous work of creating a new army, one man was absent who would have been at Peter's right hand. General Patrick Gordon had noted in his diary on December 31, 1698: "In this year I have felt a sensible failing of my health and strength—but Thy will be done, O my gracious God."[20] In September 1699 he commanded the Butyrsky Regiment in the procession in honor of the Swedish embassy. A few days later he took to his bed and his strength slowly ebbed. Peter visited him several times. Toward the end of November he began to fail rapidly. Calling on November 29 Peter found him on the point of death. The Jesuit priest who had given the Last Sacraments moved away from the bedside as the Tsar entered. "Stay where you are, Father," he said. "Do what you think fit. I will not hinder you." A few minutes later convulsions racked the dying man. Peter held a mirror to his face, but there were no signs of breathing. He closed his eyes, kissed him, and his own eyes filled with tears, he left the house.[21] Gordon received a state funeral, attended by all Russians of importance. Peter himself walked in the funeral procession of this Scot whom the Russians had respected and who had faithfully served three Tsars.

As the time approached for the opening of his Swedish campaign, Peter's mood was one of lighthearted confidence. He did not doubt that he would readily conquer Ingria and Karelia and that with access to the Baltic he would then develop his naval plans. But he overestimated the strength of the Northern Alliance. Even as he declared war on Sweden the King of Denmark was, unknown to him, signing a peace with the Swedish King. Augustus of Poland, Peter's one remaining ally, was to prove a liability in the campaign. Peter also overestimated the strength of his hastily trained army. But his greatest miscalculation, and one in which all Europe shared, was in underestimating the new King of Sweden, Charles XII, who was then only eighteen years old.

The accession of a minor to the Swedish throne in 1697 had encouraged Sweden's enemies to take action to settle their scores with her. They expected easy victories, but they were to find that Charles XII, although so young, was an outstanding general who made his mark in the age which produced Marlborough, Prince Eugene, Vauban, and Turenne. He believed himself to be invincible and he dazzled Europe with his bold exploits, his courage, and his hardiness.

The Great Northern War which began with attacks on Sweden by Russia, Denmark, and Saxony was soon to resolve itself into a duel between Peter and Charles. Both monarchs were young and vital and both had shown early promise of remarkable abilities. But in every other respect they differed. Charles was brilliant, arrogant, and in the long run destructive. Peter was exceedingly able and dynamic, but always ready to acknowledge mistakes and to learn. Charles reveled in the excitements and dangers of war; Peter hated war and resorted to it only when it was unavoidable in pursuit of his objectives. Charles was contemptuous of his enemy, but Peter was to prove a greater monarch, a greater general, and a greater man. Painstakingly but inexorably he won through to victory. Russia was to become dominant in the Baltic and to supplant Sweden.

Peter had decided to launch his campaign not by invading Ingria and Karelia, but by taking Narva on the Narova River, some ten miles from the Gulf of Finland. During October the Russian forces took up siege positions and began bombarding the fortress. But Peter was uneasy. He had received news that the Saxon army had failed to capture Riga and that Augustus had raised the siege. Further he was disturbed by reports that Charles XII had landed at Pernau with a force of thirty to thirty-two thousand seasoned troops. Peter made hasty preparations to meet the oncoming Swedes in pitched battle and then before dawn he left Narva for a secret meeting with Augustus. Eight hours later Charles led his army in a direct attack on the Russian positions. At this moment a violent snowstorm enveloped the scene, reducing visibility to a few feet. The main Russian forces gave way to panic and fled from their positions. Thousands were drowned in the Narova River. Only the guards regiments stood their ground. With the whole army in disarray the Russian commanders could only surrender to the Swedes. Charles allowed them to retreat with colors and weapons, but without their artillery, and he held a number of senior officers as prisoners of war.

Peter had suffered a crushing and humiliating defeat. The news spread quickly and all Europe laughed at him. Many charged him with cowardice in leaving his army on the eve of battle. Charles himself considered it contemptible behavior. But considerations of pride, glory, and chivalry played no part in Peter's actions. He was not prepared to risk himself in battle at this stage against the veteran Swedish army. He regarded his defeat not as a disgrace, but a hard lesson in the development of his army and of Russia herself. He made no recriminations, but accepted the mistakes made as his own.

In a fury of activity he set about training and equipping his army anew. His immediate fear was that Charles would follow up his victory by marching on Moscow. Nothing barred his way into Russia and Peter hurriedly strengthened the defenses of Novgorod and Pskov, the two fortified cities that might hinder a Swedish advance. It was soon clear, however, that the Swedes could not invade at this juncture. They were exhausted after the forced marches and the fighting at Narva. Moreover, Russia lay in the grip of a severe winter. But Peter did not relax his efforts. In January 1701, Pleyer, the Austrian resident in Moscow, was reporting to Vienna that the Tsar's army was already twice as strong as before Narva. At the same time Peter was making urgent, but unavailing, attempts to gain the support of England, Holland, Austria, and Brandenburg, and to induce the Poles to join him against the Swedes. But his immediate concern was to prevent Augustus, Elector of Saxony as well as King of Poland, his one ally, from dropping out of the war. In February 1701 Peter and Augustus met at Birze and confirmed their alliance, each giving firm undertakings to fight until the Swedes were defeated. To obtain this assurance, Peter found that he had to guarantee Augustus considerable assistance in troops and money which he could ill-afford.

From Narva, Charles moved his army into winter quarters near Dorpat in Livonia, and there he awaited reinforcements from Sweden. Toward the end of the spring the fresh troops nearly ten thousand strong joined him and he marched to Riga. The Saxon army of 27,000 men with four Russian regiments in reserve was drawn up on the left bank of the Dvina River, ready to take this important stronghold, as Augustus and Peter had agreed. Charles at once crossed the river and routed the Saxons. The Russian regiments fled at the first shot in the engagement. The incident deepened Charles's contempt for the Russians who, he considered, would never learn to fight.

Carried away by his belief in his own invincible generalship and by his scorn for the Russians as soldiers, Charles disregarded Peter as an enemy; he would crush the Tsar when he was ready. Thus instead of following up his great victory at Narva by marching on Moscow, Charles turned south and spent the next six years in Poland. He left his able colonel, Schlippenbach, with a detachment of only eight thousand men to defend Livonia and Ingria. He was confident that this token force could hold off the Russians. But he gravely misjudged his adversary, Peter, and he was to pay dearly for his arrogance.

During these six years when Charles was engaged in Poland, Peter was able to train his men and weld them into an army. They gained experience in action. Boyar Sheremetev who had emerged as Peter's most competent general, defeated Schlippenbach at Erestfer in December 1701 and even more decisively at Hummelshof in July 1702. Sheremetev's victories gave him control of Livonia, and raised Russian morale by demonstrating that the Swedes were not invincible. On receiving Sheremetev's report, Peter exclaimed: "Praise God; at last we are able to beat the Swedes!" and this new confidence spread quickly through his army.[22]

In October 1702 Peter captured the fortress town of Schlusselburg, situated on an island in the Neva River near Lake Ladoga. He took another fortress town, named Nyenskantz at the entry of the Okhta River into the Neva in May 1703. The action involved an attack on a small Swedish squadron in which to his great delight Peter took two Swedish ships. With the capture of Yamburg and Koporie in the summer he had completed his conquest of Ingria, the objective for which he had declared war on Sweden. Russia now had access to the Baltic. But, as Peter well knew, the Northern War was not yet at an end. Charles XII had won brilliant victories in eastern Europe and had created a legend of invincibility. Peter knew that his hold on Ingria and Livonia could not be secure until he had defeated Charles. He did not underestimate his enemy and even expected to lose battles, but not to lose the war. His complete confidence in ultimate victory was demonstrated at this time when he laid the foundations of a new city at the mouth of the Neva River.

The estuary of the Neva was marshy, unhealthy, and desolate. But here on Yanni-Saari or Hare Island, one of the nineteen islands in the estuary, Peter laid the foundations, on May 16, 1703, of the new fortress and port, to be called St. Petersburg after his patron saint. His decision on the site was hasty, but it embodied the instinctive wisdom of a monarch deeply rooted in his country's history and needs. In effect, he was transplanting Novgorod, which with Kiev had been the earliest Russian center of trade and contact with the West, to the Baltic coast. Moscow represented the traditional Russian Orthodox outlook. Early in his reign he had rejected Moscow and now in his new city he was creating the symbol and center of his reformed and reorientated Russia.

St. Petersburg fired his imagination and he lavished attention on plans and buildings. He sailed in the Gulf of Finland and, lead in hand, took soundings. He decided to make Kotlin Island, eight miles to the west of the city, a fortress, later to be called Kronstadt, defending its approaches. The labor force, numbering hundreds of thousands, suffered inhuman hardships and the death-rate was high, but the work continued at his headlong pace. St. Petersburg grew rapidly and within his reign it became a beautiful and important city, which he made the capital in place of Moscow; by the end of the century it had become a world metropolis.

The years 1705 to 1709 were for Peter the most critical of the Northern War. He had captured Dorpat and Narva and had secured his hold on Livonia and Ingria. But he had yet to fight the fateful battle to decide the final outcome of the war. Adding to the general anxiety was the unpredictability of Charles himself. Many rumors that he was about to march on Russia proved false. The Russian and Swedish armies nearly met in a major battle near Grodno in the summer of 1706 but the Russians retreated in good order. Charles then turned to defeat the Saxons and in October 1706 he compelled Augustus to sign the Treaty of Altranstadt. This put an end to the alliance with Russia and Augustus recognized as King of Poland Stanislas Leszcynski whom the Poles elected to the throne under the strong pressure of the Swedes. This treaty alarmed Peter because it meant that he now stood alone against Charles.

The general expectation was that Charles would invade Russia in the spring of 1707. He remained in Saxony, however, until the late summer and then marched slowly through Poland. It was well for Peter that he did not launch his invasion at this time. Following on a rebellion in Astrakhan at the mouth of the Volga River in 1706, which had been suppressed, Peter was faced with more serious uprisings by the Bashkirs and among the Cossacks of the Don and Dnieper. Led by Ataman Bulavin, a major Cossack uprising developed during 1707, threatening to become a challenge on the scale of Stenka Razin's movement of the previous century. But toward the end of 1708 the last of the rebel armies was destroyed and the Russian armies were freed to meet the challenge in the west.

Charles had already begun his invasion of Russia. In July 1708 he had defeated a Russian army at Golovchina, but the fighting had been severe and his casualties were heavy. He then crossed the Dnieper River, but his troops found themselves incessantly harried by Russian detachments. They stubbornly continued their advance, and the Russians fell back slowly before them, leaving the earth scorched. At this point instead of waiting for General Adam Lewenhaupt to join him with his army, Charles turned southward. Learning that Lewenhaupt was crossing the Dnieper, Peter drew up his forces at Lesnaya, where on September 28 they completely routed the Swedish army of sixteen thousand men. Peter was jubilant, but soon afterward he received the disastrous news that Hetman Mazepa had gone over to the enemy.

The treason of the old Hetman shocked Peter. He had always shown him consideration and had ignored secret reports of his double dealing. He always had difficulty in believing that someone he trusted could betray him. His immediate fear was that Mazepa might manage to persuade the people of the Ukraine and the Cossacks to follow him in transferring their support to Charles. But Mazepa's position as Hetman was difficult. The Ukraine was in a constant state of ferment. Resentment of Russian rule, and especially of the heavy burdens imposed by Peter, had been mounting. Mazepa was concerned to preserve the freedom of the Ukraine from further Russian encroachment. But he was far more concerned for his own welfare. He had entered into secret negotiations with Stanislas, King of Poland and then with Charles. Now, seeing that the duel between Peter and Charles was approaching its climax, he switched his support to Charles who, he thought, would be the victor. But for all their discontent the Ukrainians did not follow him.

Charles crossed the Desna River and advanced to Romny. He had suffered two major disappointments. General Lewenhaupt had joined him from Lesnaya with the battered remnants of his army and without the supply train on which the Swedes were depending. Then Mazepa arrived with some two thousand Cossacks instead of the army of over twenty thousand men which the Hetman normally commanded. At the same time the Russians were shadowing them from the north and attacking them in swift well-executed movements. The Swedes found now to their cost that the Russians were no longer the raw recruits whom they had ignominiously defeated at Narva nine years earlier.

In April, Charles moved farther south, intent on taking Poltava, an important town on the Vorskla River. Learning of this move Peter rejoined his army and assumed the supreme command. On June 26 Russians and Swedes joined battle. Peter fought with conspicuous courage. A musket ball knocked off his hat and another glanced off the iron crucifix around his neck. He was constantly in the thick of the fighting, encouraging his men. Charles fought with his usual disregard for danger. He had been wounded in the foot and had to be carried on a litter, but he insisted on being taken to the centers of bitterest fighting where he could exhort his men to greater efforts.

The Russian troops were, however, seasoned and disciplined. They drove back the Swedes, and breaking their lines forced them to flee from the battlefield. The Swedish army had numbered sixty thousand; half had lost their lives in the advance eastward and into the Ukraine. The remnants of this army, numbering only 16,947, were taken prisoner at Poltava or to the south as they tried to escape. Charles, Mazepa, and a few companions managed to get away and to find refuge on Turkish territory.

This was Peter's great moment of victory. He attended a service of thanksgiving on the field of battle and then he celebrated. He was exultant, but not arrogant. The Swedish generals were brought to his tent and he sat them down at his side. He showed them great courtesy and especially to Rehnskjold, praising him for his bravery and presenting him with his own sword. After the salute of cannon to the Russian victory, Peter rose and proposed a toast to his teachers in the art of war. "Who are your teachers, sire?" asked Rehnskjold. "You are, gentlemen," Peter replied. "Then well have the pupils returned thanks to their teachers," commented Rehnskjold.[23]

Peter wrote promptly to his colleagues in Moscow, giving them news of the victory. In one of these letters he expressed succinctly the chief reason for his great joy and summed up the significance of Poltava for him. "Now," he wrote, "with the help of God, the final stone in the foundation of St. Petersburg has been laid."[24]

Among the first letters Peter wrote from the field of battle was one to his mistress, Catherine Skavronskaya. The letter was brief: "Little Mother, good-day. I declare to you that the all-merciful God has this day granted us an unprecedented victory over the enemy. In a word, the whole of the enemy's army is knocked on the head, and you will hear about it from us. Come here and congratulate us. Piter."[25] She had already become his close companion. In 1712 he married her and in 1724 she was formally crowned as his Empress.

Catherine was born in 1685 near Dorpat in Livonia. She belonged to the family of a peasant, Samuel Skavronsky, but was probably illegitimate. When she was three her mother died, apparently leaving her alone and destitute. The local pastor took her into his home and two years later Ernst Gluck, the Lutheran pastor of Marienburg, engaged her to look after his children and help with domestic work. When she was seventeen a Swedish dragoon married her, but he was probably recalled immediately to his regiment. She was never to see him again.

At this time Sheremetev's army was approaching Marienburg. He laid siege to the fortress, threatening to destroy it completely if the garrison did not surrender. In desperation the Swedish commander decided to blow up the fortress. He kept his plan secret, but warned Gluck who with his family, including Catherine, escaped to the Russian camp. He was taken at once to Sheremetev who received him kindly and, accepting his proposals that he might serve the Tsar as a translator, sent him with his family to Moscow.

During the interview with Gluck, Sheremetev did not take his eyes off Catherine. She was full-figured, dark, and comely. Finally he asked who she was and, on being told that she was a foundling who had just been married, he replied, "That's of no importance. She will stay with me."[26] Catherine kept house for him for some six months. But Menshikov, a brave, quick-witted rogue of humble origin who had served in the Tsar's play regiments and had accompanied him on his Western journey and was now high in his favor, took her for himself. Some months later Peter met her in Menshikov's house and she became his mistress.

Peter was not greatly interested in women. Gossip circulating the courts of Europe attributed to him a sexual life as wild as it was insatiable. The fact was that Peter devoted his energies to his work. He was a conscientious and dedicated monarch and highly critical of Augustus and others who allowed mistresses to distract them from the important things of life. He undoubtedly indulged himself with various women when he felt the need, but such passing incidents claimed little of his time, thought, or energy. By nature he was monogamous. Only four women played any real part in his life. They were his mother, his sister, Natalya, with whom he felt an affectionate bond, Anna Mons, and Catherine who was to be his intimate companion for over twenty years. He had met Anna Mons in the Foreign Quarter when he was only seventeen. She had reigned unchallenged as his mistress and might have become Tsaritsa. She was, however, foolish enough to become betrothed to another man while still his mistress. He was angry, but allowed her to keep the palace and most of the jewelry he had given her, and then he forgot her completely.

Catherine was a more attractive woman and a worthier mate for Peter. She had grown to be a handsome, but not beautiful, woman, remarkable for her goodnature and generosity. Alexander Gordon, another of the Scots in the Russian service, considered that "The reason why the Tsar was so fond of her was her exceeding good temper; she was never seen peevish or out of humour; obliging and civil to all, and never forgetful of her former condition."[27] She provided a haven of affection and maternal care to which Peter could always return from his labors and from which he could set out again refreshed.

Often Catherine accompanied him, enduring hardships without complaint. She had great physical and mental stamina and in the midst of her strenuous life at his side she bore him twelve children.[28] She was with the army on the Pruth and later in the exhausting Persian campaign. She was the idol of the troops who saw in her not only the Tsaritsa, but also the perfect commander's wife. She could review regiments, speaking kindly to the men, showing sympathy and understanding of the soldier's life, and awarding tots of vodka on special occasions.

Peter became dependent on Catherine in many ways. Often she appeared more as a mother than as a mistress and a wife. When agonizing headaches presaged one of his insensate rages and everyone went in terror of him, Catherine alone was without fear. She would call him to her and take his head in her hands and stroke his forehead until he relaxed in sleep. For hours she would sit motionless, holding his head and when he awoke, the convulsions of face and body had passed and he was in the best of humors. Only Catherine could exorcise his furies and on these occasions she alone stood between the Tsar and his people.

Their companionship deepened with the passing years, but was to be overcast toward the end of his life. Whenever separated they wrote to each other, indulging in private jokes and exchanging small presents, such as fresh lemons and figs, oysters, flowers, clothes, and even mint. He addressed her as "Muder" or "Moeder" or in English "Little Mother," and affectionately as "Katerinoushka," referring to himself as "the old fellow." Often their letters expressed an earthy coarseness which was in part a reflection of the manners of the day, but also suggested that they were physically close. Peter himself recognized that fate had bestowed upon him a true mate and he was to express his gratitude to her publicly.

News of the Russian victory at Poltava spread quickly through Europe. Countries which had declined Peter's proposals, supported by liberal offers of money and men, to join with him against Sweden, now sought alliance with the victorious Tsar. In October 1709, Peter met Augustus in Thorn and they readily agreed on the revival of their alliance. Augustus with the Pope's dispensation had disavowed the Treaty of Altranstadt and had been restored to the Polish throne. Evidently Peter had no hesitation in continuing to support Augustus in spite of his treachery and constant failure in the face of the enemy.

Meanwhile Peter was disturbed by the possibility of the Turks declaring war. The Sultan had not forgotten the humiliation of the defeat at Azov and now Charles XII, supported by France, was pressing for Turkish action against Russia. Through his resident in Constantinople Peter demanded the surrender of Charles and when this was refused he issued an ultimatum. The Turks refused to be browbeaten and on November 20, 1710, they declared war.

Peter had been hasty and overconfident in provoking this war, but he was counting on the support of the Orthodox Slavs under Turkish rule and also on the cooperation of the Hospodars of Wallachia and Moldavia with whom he had made secret alliances. But the Orthodox Slavs did not rise in force to support the Russian advance and the Hospodars gave no effective aid. In July the Russian army was at the Pruth River where it repelled a Turkish attack, but Peter now found himself with 38,246 troops, far from supplies and surrounded by a Turkish army of 119,665 men, supported by seventy thousand Tatars from the Crimea. His position was in fact desperate. Fortunately the Turkish Vizir in command was disturbed by the prospect of further casualties and was ready to negotiate. A treaty of peace was signed on July 12, 1711, under which Peter was obliged to surrender Azov and make other concessions. The Vizir, not appreciating the desperate position of the Tsar, had in fact demanded far less than Peter was prepared to concede. Peter was relieved to save his army and to escape capture himself. But the campaign on the Pruth was a severe humiliation, especially after his great triumph over the Swedes.

Poltava had not, however, meant the end of the Northern War. Peter returned from the Pruth determined to force the Swedes to an early peace, but peace was to elude him for a further ten years. If he had concentrated all his forces on crushing Sweden he would probably have gained peace earlier. But, acting now with special caution and eager that Russia should play her part in Western affairs, he became embroiled in intrigues and tortuous diplomacy.

Peter, nevertheless, made effective use of the navy which he had carefully built up since the capture of Ingria and the foundation of St. Petersburg. In April 1713 a Russian galley fleet of ninety-three galleys, sixty brigantines, and fifty large boats, carrying altogether 16,050 troops, sailed from St. Petersburg and, with the support of an army sent by land, the conquest of Finland was completed in the following year. A naval victory off Cape Hango in the same year was a source of tremendous pride for Peter who considered this victory equal in importance to Poltava. In the battle the Russian fleet comprised twenty ships of the line and some two hundred galleys and, having outmaneuvered the veteran Swedish fleet, the Russians pursued and destroyed it. The battle highlighted Peter's achievement which was that in less than ten years he had created a navy which had outsailed and defeated the Swedish navy which had for many decades dominated the Baltic Sea.

The sudden emergence of Russia as the new northern power disturbed the rest of Europe. Holland and England in particular were alarmed that Peter might monopolize their trade with Russia. But other factors now complicated the rivalries in the Baltic. The War of the Spanish Succession had ended and France had become the ally of England and Holland. In 1714, moreover, Queen Anne died and the Elector of Hanover ascended the English throne as George I. He was eager to expel the Swedes from northern Germany and for this reason Peter thought that he would be a ready ally. But George was equally anxious about the growing Russian ascendancy in the north and was not prepared to assist in the final destruction of Swedish power.

Further complications arose from Peter's attempts to establish dynastic alliances with ruling families in the West. In 1710 Anna, the daughter of his half-brother, Ivan, who until his death in 1696 had been co-Tsar, was married to Frederick Wilhelm, Duke of Courland. In the following year Tsarevich Alexei married Princess Charlotte of Wolfenbuttel, but she died shortly afterward. In 1716 Catherine, the other surviving daughter of Tsar Ivan, was married to Charles Leopold, Duke of Mecklenburg. Finally in 1724, Charles Frederick, Duke of Holstein-Gottorp, who was a nephew of Charles XII and was in line for the succession to the throne, was betrothed to Anna, one of Peter's elder daughters, and they were married in May 1725.

The general effect of these dynastic marriages was not, however, to earn goodwill and strengthen Russian influence in the north, as Peter hoped, but to arouse suspicions and antagonism among the other countries of Europe. In fact, Peter's diplomatic offensive probably delayed the ending of the Northern War for several years, and the dynastic marriages were to add sordid chapters to the history of the dynasty and of Russia.

Peter's great objective at this time, however, was alliance with France, sealed by a dynastic marriage of his son, Tsarevich Alexei, with the daughter of the Duke of Orléans or between his daughter, Elizabeth, and the boy-King, Louis XV. In 1717 he visited France to promote this proposal personally. The negotiations were lengthy and involved, and came to nothing. But Peter himself made a strong impression in Paris. The gentleman of the court, attending upon him, wrote that "He is dark and there is a fierceness in his expression. He appears to have a lively mind and a certain grandeur in his movements, but little restraint."²⁹ Marshal Villeroi wrote to Madame de Maintenon that "This Prince, said to be barbarous, is not so at all; he has displayed to us sentiments of grandeur, of generosity, and of politeness that we by no means expected." But several considered that with the noble qualities were mingled savagery and barbarism.³⁰

During his six weeks in Paris, Peter was tireless in inspecting royal buildings, bridges, glass factories, and the Mint. He went several times to the Gobelin tapestry workshops and he engaged workmen to establish similar workshops in Russia. Since his visit to London nineteen years earlier, his interests had expanded. He had achieved his ambition of creating a navy and now he was lavishing his attention on the development of his new city. He made repeated visits to Versailles, Fontainebleau, and St. Cloud, studying the architecture and decoration of the palaces, and the planning of the gardens. His visit to Paris and these palaces were soon to bear fruits in St. Petersburg.

Recognizing that his efforts to create an effective anti-Swedish alliance were making small progress and exasperated by the tortuous diplomacy in which he was enmeshed, Peter was ready to adopt other methods. A new, highly imaginative plan, introduced by Baron Goertz, the Holstein minister, and envisaging direct negotiation with Sweden, appealed to him. Goertz was eager to restore Sweden to her position as a great power, allied with Russia. Sweden was to cede to Russia all the territories which Peter had conquered and with his cooperation would compensate herself at the expense of Denmark and the German states. Goertz presented the scheme to Charles XII who returned to Sweden from Turkey at this time. Charles was impressed and at once made Goertz his minister. But he did not fully understand the policy and certainly did not accept the permanent cession of the territories conquered by the Russians. Goertz hoped that with time he would gain his acceptance. He was also assuming that the Duke of Holstein would ascend the Swedish throne on the death of Charles XII and counted on the Duke's marriage with the Tsar's daughter to cement the Russo-Swedish alliance.

Negotiation between Russian and Swedish ministers at a congress at Lafo, one of the Aland Islands, raised Peter's hopes in 1718, but the negotiations reached deadlock and broke down. In December 1718, however, Charles XII was killed while conducting the siege of the Norwegian fortress of Frederickshald. He had made no provision for the succession and the Swedes, who hated Goertz and the Holstein party, elected Charles's sister, Ulrica Eleanora, to the throne. England, Denmark, Prussia, and Saxony hastened to sign treaties with the new Swedish government, as a check to Russia's expanding power. George I sent an English squadron into the Baltic to cooperate with the Swedish fleet in an attempt to compel Russia to accept England's mediation.

Peter responded by breaking off diplomatic relations with England and mounting new attacks on Sweden. In July 1719 a Russian fleet landed Russian and Cossack troops on the Swedish coast and they caused widespread devastation. Another Russian army had landed near Stockholm and had ravaged the surrounding districts. Further destructive raids took place in 1720 and 1721. Finally, in April 1721, through the intercession of Campredon, the French ambassador in St. Petersburg, who had previously been ambassador in Stockholm, Russians and Swedes resumed negotiations at Nystadt.

Peter was on his way to inspect the disputed frontier near Vyborg when couriers from Nystadt overtook him. They reported that on August 30 his envoys had signed the treaty of peace with Sweden on his terms. The Swedes had formally ceded in perpetuity the Baltic states of Livonia, Esthonia, Ingria, part of Karelia, and the Vyborg district, all of which he had conquered by his own arms. For his part the Tsar had agreed to return Finland to Sweden, to pay compensation for Livonia, and to grant the Swedes certain duty free rights in Riga, Reval, and Arensburg.

The Treaty of Nystadt had set the seal on his great victory. The Northern War had been a long cruel struggle but now he had gained his objectives; Russia had a secure foothold on the Baltic and ports from which her ships could sail. He now returned with all haste to St. Petersburg. He sailed into the Neva with trumpets sounding, drums beating, and cannons firing. The news flashed through the city and the people hurried to the Troitskaya wharf to welcome their Tsar. He attended a thanksgiving service in the Church of the Holy Trinity and then on the square he spoke to the vast crowd.

Peter at once busied himself with arrangements for celebrating the peace. Proclamations were to be made throughout the tsardom and the peace was to be thrice-celebrated; once on receiving the news, a second time on October 22, and a third time on January 28, 1722.

At a joint meeting of the Senate and the Holy Synod as the date of the second celebration approached, it was unanimously decided to petition the Tsar on behalf of the nation to take the title of Emperor and the Great. Menshikov took the petition to Peter who showed reluctance. On October 22 Peter with his family, his court, and all officers and ministers attended a victory service in the Church of the Holy Trinity in St. Petersburg. The treaty and its ratification were read and the Archbishop of Pskov, Prokopovich, delivered an oration in praise of the Tsar. Then the whole Senate came before him and the Great Chancellor, Count Golovkin, spoke of his heroic endeavours "Through which alone and by your tireless labors and leadership, we, your loyal subjects, have stepped from the darkness of ignorance onto the theater of fame of the whole world and, so to speak, have moved from nonexistence to existence, and have joined in the society of political peoples—for that and for winning a peace so renowned and so rewarding, how can we render our proper gratitude? And so that we may not be with shame before the whole world, we take it upon ourselves in the name of the All-Russian nation and of all ranks of the subjects of Your Majesty, humbly to pray you to be gracious to us and to agree, as a small mark of our acknowledgment of the blessings that you have brought to us and to the whole nation, to take the title—Father of the Fatherland, Peter the Great, Emperor of All Russia!"[31]

The Senators and the whole congregation shouted "*Vivat!*" thrice. The crowds outside the church took up the cry which echoed through St. Petersburg and through Russia. The people who had obeyed their Tsar unwillingly, but had endured their hardships and had learned and served, now united in celebrating the fruits of their labors and in paying tribute to the Father of their Fatherland, Emperor of All Russia, Peter the Great.

On his return in August 1698 from his first visit to the West, Peter had embarked on a policy of change and reform. No aspect of Russian life went untouched and the spate of ukazi bewildered his people. Their Tsar was like an elemental force, upturning their lives. He had started with his assault on their beards and on Muscovite costume, both powerful symbols of the traditional way of life. But a minor reform which heralded the new era was his reform of the calendar. The Russian calendar was calculated from the creation of the world and the year began on September 1. Peter now adopted the Julian calendar and he ordered everyone to celebrate the new year and the start of the new epoch on January 1, 1700.

Working under pressure during the rest of his reign, Peter launched reforms and new projects one after the other, returning to them repeatedly, modifying, canceling, and then propelling them further toward fulfilment. It was a wasteful method, but he had few ministers on whom he could rely and had to supervise and direct everything himself. In the years after Poltava he was able to legislate more carefully. He worked still under pressure, but it was the pressure of the massive task that he had shouldered and not of the urgent threat of war. He had no overall scheme; he was a practical man, working by trial and error. By the end of his reign, however, the new institutions of military, civil, and ecclesiastical administration had acquired an impressive coherence.

In the first stages the Northern War had concentrated his attention on the immediate needs of his armies and, above all, on finance. The war made unprecedented demands on the nation's resources. He had launched his war on Sweden with an army of some forty thousand troops. During the next ten years some three hundred thousand men were called up and the military strength was maintained at one hundred thousand. By the end of his reign the regular army exceeded two hundred thousand in addition to one hundred thousand Cossacks and a large force of Kalmyks, Bashkirs, and other native troops. Military expenditure increased from an estimated 2.3 million in 1701 to 5.2 million rubles in 1724, and in the same period the national revenue increased from 3 million to 8.5 million rubles.

Peter resorted to numerous expedients to raise the finance so urgently needed for the war. The coinage was debased by reducing its silver content, but this led inevitably to depreciation of the currency. He seized on ideas for new taxes. Alexei Kurbatov, a serf, wrote a paper, proposing a new stamp duty, which came to Peter's notice. The duty was imposed and proved profitable. Kurbatov became a leading *pribylshchik*, the name given to the new officials whose task was to devise sources of revenue, and was later promoted further. Meanwhile taxes multiplied. Hats, boots, hides, harnesses, beehives, watermelons, cucumbers were some of the items which now attracted taxes. At the same time the number of state trading monopolies expanded greatly.

In 1710 Peter ordered a review of the system of direct taxation. The household was the unit on which the main direct tax was levied, based on the census of 1678. After long consideration he decided that a poll tax should take the place of the tax on households, and, levied on the basis of a new census, the poll tax produced more satisfactory results.

While raising new taxes, Peter was also tireless in his efforts to build up Russia's economic strength. He encouraged prospecting for minerals and was prompt to utilize mineral resources. He established heavy industry in Russia. He had begun developing iron foundries early in his reign, primarily to equip his army. Twenty or so small foundries were working at the time of his accession. He expanded several of them, but also established fifty-two new foundries, including thirteen large and well-equipped works which opened up the important industrial region of the Urals.

In light industry his efforts were at first directed exclusively to supplying his army and navy. He established textile mills to produce cloth for uniforms, and then factories to produce sailcloth and ropes, and he organized the lumber industry. As the pressures of war relaxed he began encouraging other manufactures. Glass and china works were set up in St. Petersburg in 1715, followed by new factories to produce silk and velvet textiles, stockings, and other luxury goods.

The founding of most of these new industries was accompanied by delays and setbacks, arising from lack of workmen, from bad management, and generally from the inexperience of the Russians. His achievements were nevertheless remarkable. At his death 233 new industrial undertakings were in production and Russia was manufacturing a wide range of goods which she had formerly imported. Peter had also paid close attention to developing trade since his first visit to Archangel in 1693. Gradually he had made St. Petersburg the center of Russia's trade with the West. Russian and foreign merchants resisted, but Peter had his way and St. Petersburg superceded Archangel. Moreover, as a result of his numerous measures encouraging and protecting Russian merchants and developing natural resources, Russia's foreign trade quadrupled in value during his reign.

The old Muscovite administration suffered from overcentralization, slowness, corruption, and incompetence. Peter tried to eliminate these faults but had only partial success. Corruption and extortion were engrained in Muscovite life and, although he waged constant struggle against both failings and imposed punishments of extreme severity, he could not eliminate them. But in the process of numerous reforms he transformed the administration, and the basic system which he instituted endured until 1917.

The administrative reform began in 1707 with the division of the country into eight provinces. The old *prikazi* or central ministries gradually fell into disuse. The new provinces were intended to provide greater efficiency in financing the army. But the country was left virtually without a central government. In February 1711 Peter took the first step toward filling this gap. As he prepared to leave for the Pruth campaign, he established the Senate to exercise power in his absence. But the inadequacy of the Senators, who were inexperienced, venal, and constantly quarreling either among themselves or with the powerful provincial governors, prevented the new institution functioning as he had envisaged. He appointed an "Inspector-General or Supervisor of Ukazi" and later even detailed guards officers to ensure that Senators carried out their duties and behaved themselves. He himself lectured them on the need to despatch business promptly and on dignity of conduct. He punished those who misbehaved and in 1719 alone five Senators were heavily fined. Gradually, however, the Senate came to play an important role in coordinating the administration of the country and in acting as the central office, ensuring control over the collection and allocation of finance. The Senate was further strengthened by the appointment of Menshikov, Golovkin, Apraksin, and other leading men of the time. In 1722 Peter created the office of Procurator-General, responsible to the sovereign alone. Gradually the Senate began to function more effectively.

Peter next gave his attention to the replacement of the old *prikazi* which were neither suitable nor competent to deal with the mass of new public business and could not relieve the Senate of its financial burden. Most countries of Northern Europe at this time made use of the collegial system which in England was represented by the Board of Admiralty. The system appealed to Peter, especially because the collegial board would reduce the dangers of corruption and of the domination of one man, and because group decisions would probably be sounder than the arbitrary judgments of a single minister. For five years he studied reports on the system. He enlisted experienced administrators from abroad to guide and train his people, and in 1717 he established nine colleges. Disputes between foreigners and Russians and among the Russians themselves nearly brought state business to a standstill in certain colleges. But, as with the Senate, to which they were subordinated in July 1721, the colleges gradually began contributing significantly to the administration of the country.

Service and ability were the criteria by which Peter had rewarded and promoted men, and he gave careful consideration to the application of these criteria throughout the army, the navy, and the civil departments. In January 1722 he introduced the Table of Ranks which transformed the social and service conditions of the landowning class as a whole. The table separated the military from the civil branch of service and classified all officers and officials in fourteen parallel grades. Everyone had to start at the lowest grade and earn promotion. All persons, whether Russian or foreign, could acquire the titles and privileges of nobility by reaching a certain grade in the hierarchy of rank. Titles of nobility were not abolished, but they became distinctions, conferring no rights or privileges, and even at court rank gained by service took precedence over other titles. Inevitably the old landowning nobility complained about the low-born newcomers who had precedence and took command over them. But it was Peter's purpose to attract the newcomers and to broaden the composition of the landowning class in the interests of the nation. In this he was fairly successful and his Table of Ranks remained in force until 1917, although in later years it was to develop the faults of an entrenched bureaucracy.

From the time when he had made his first tour of the West and had sent the first groups of young Russians to study abroad, Peter had been concerned about the education of his people. Education was essential not only to enable them to serve efficiently but also to raise Russian society to Western standards. Many of the young Russians whom he sent abroad failed through laziness or debauchery to study properly but most returned with the certificate which he required as evidence that they had completed their apprenticeship. The foreign officers and experts, engaged in increasing numbers to serve in Russia, had as their main duty "to teach the Russian people without reserve and diligently"[32] and in general they honored their terms of service. Moreover the Russians were quick to learn in every field and Peter was soon able to rely on Russian ships, armaments, and manufactures in great variety. But laziness and reluctance to learn were widespread, and his attempts to introduce elementary education met with passive resistance and evasion.

In 1701 the first Russian secular school, the School of Mathematics and Navigation, had been founded in Moscow by Henry Farquharson. It had moved later to St. Petersburg and been renamed the Naval Academy. Farquharson's school had flourished, but other schools, established by Peter in Moscow and St. Petersburg, had attracted few pupils. As in every other field he found that compulsion was necessary. In 1716 he decreed that children of landowners must attend one of three special schools in St. Petersburg—the Naval Academy, the Engineering Academy, or the Artillery Academy—and this system proved successful in imposing a degree of education on the landowning class as a whole.

Peter's innovations in education and in other fields had all tended to diminish the authority and influence of the church. Since early in his reign he had felt that the church and Orthodoxy were a retrograde force in Russian life. He had major reforms in mind, but he approached them carefully. On the death of Patriarch Adrian in 1700, he did not appoint a successor, mainly because of the danger that a strong Patriarch would rally the general opposition to his reforms. He had made Stefan Yavorsky, a learned monk from the Ukraine, the Metropolitan of Ryazan and then had appointed him to the new office of "Exarch of the most holy patriarchal throne, guardian and administrator," with the special task of cleansing the church of various abuses. Yavorsky, however, became increasingly critical of Peter and his policies, and after Poltava Peter turned to another learned churchman, Feofan Prokopovich, who supported his work with zest. Early in 1721 he issued the Spiritual Regulation, composed by Prokopovich but revised in every detail by Peter himself. This regulation, applying to the church the collegial system, established the Holy Governing Synod, responsible in place of the patriarchate for the spiritual and temporal affairs of the church. The

Holy Synod was given special tasks of reform, combating superstition, spreading knowledge of the Gospel and establishing schools. His program of reforms brought a revolution in the Orthodox Church, but it was a revolution of customs and institutions, not of doctrine. Quickly absorbed into the life of the church and the nation, most of his reforms endured.

The range of Peter's interests and activities was amazing, and it appeared to grow in the later years of his reign. He reformed the Cyrillic alphabet, commissioned books and translations of foreign works, and encouraged the printing of books of all kinds in Russia. He had himself collected books during most of his reign and especially during his visits to the West. His personal library covered a wide variety of subjects, including history, science, medicine, law, religion, and military and naval affairs. This library was to provide the foundation of the library of the Russian Academy of Sciences. The Academy had been proposed to Peter by the German philosopher, Leibnitz, who was one of his keenest admirers. Peter's interest had been further stimulated by his visits to the French Academy in 1717. He gave close attention to the charter and arrangements for the Academy, which were completed in January 1724, but the Russian Academy was finally established after his death when his widow, Catherine I, inaugurated it.

The training of doctors, erection of hospitals, the care of illegitimate and unwanted children, the organization of fire-fighting services, the planting and maintenance of gardens were some of the projects to which he gave active attention. In the last years of his reign he was working on plans for the instruction of his people on the principles of good citizenship and the creation of an ordered society, based on law and honest service. But while he did not live to launch this program of instruction, he made considerable change in Russian social life. To accustom his people to mixing as in Western countries, he decreed in November 1718 that receptions should be held at regular intervals. Lists of hosts were drawn up and provision had to be made for dancing, card-playing, and polite conversation. Stiff and awkward at first these receptions quickly became part of the life of the city. But their main importance was that, since Peter insisted that women must play a full part in such occasions, women were for the first time emancipated from the gloom and idleness of the Muscovite *terem*.

Like his predecessors Peter was beset by anxieties over the succession to the throne, but his problem was more obstinate and tragic in its outcome. Tsarevich Alexei, his son by his marriage with Evdokiya Lopukhina, had grown to manhood as a craven weak individual with the outlook of an old Muscovite. To him rallied all the embittered conservatives who hated the new Russia and it became clear that on succeeding to the throne he would endeavor to erase the work to which his father had dedicated his whole reign.

During the first eighteen years of his life Alexei saw little of his father who was taken up with the Northern War and the needs of his armies. He was not completely forgotten. On his father's instructions he was taken to witness the storming of Nyenskantz and Narva and was later sent to Smolensk to direct the preparation of army supplies and the mobilization of recruits. Such experience was intended to supplement his formal education and to equip him for the responsibilities of the throne. At this stage, although surrounded by people antagonistic to Peter, Alexei evidently held his father in awe and took pride in the new army and its victories over ancient enemies. He tried anxiously to please him, but was soon plagued by a sense of his own inadequacy. He began to dread meeting his father and he drank heavily to escape his fear and weakness.

Peter treated his son harshly during these formative years. Driven by his own sense of service, he sought to harden the boy to the tasks ahead. Noting his submissiveness and timidity he handled him with Spartan firmness, withholding the warmth and kindness that he might have shown; when later he tried to show him sympathy and understanding it was too late. Peter, titanic in strength and physique and relentless in purpose, overwhelmed his son without realizing it. He expected too much of a boy who was to prove weak in health, will, and courage, who broke under the weight of his demands and example, and who in the end was no more than a pitiful drunkard.

Toward the end of the summer of 1709 Alexei was sent abroad to study. He went to Dresden and then to Karlsbad to take the waters. At this time he had his first meeting with Princess Charlotte of Wolfen-buttel who was soon to become his wife. She was then sixteen years old, a charming, natural, and dutiful girl. She found Alexei clever and attrac-tive; he was impressed by her, but was deeply antagonistic to the idea of marriage with a foreigner and a Protestant. He did not dare, however, to express opposition to his father's will, and they were duly married on October 14, 1711. She accompanied him to Thorn where he was in-structed to arrange army supplies and river transport. He then had to join the army for the campaign in Pomerania. She waited alone in Elbing and, since no one had thought of providing her with money, she was al-most destitute. Menshikov found her there and was shocked by her predicament. He gave her money and reported to Peter who ordered her to go to St. Petersburg.

Charlotte was homesick and miserable after these months of loneliness and privation and the prospect of traveling alone to Russia terrified her. Instead of obeying the Tsar's orders she fled to her old home in Braun-schweig. Peter was angry when he learned of her flight and wrote expressing his disapproval, "for we would never have thwarted your wish to see your family, if only you had informed us beforehand."[33] In February 1713 he went to see her and readily forgave her. She then made the journey to St. Petersburg and settled with Alexei in the small palace built for them on the bank of the Neva. But here her life was miserable. Alexei ignored her except when he was drunk and then he was coarse and abusive and ill-treated her. She was eight months pregnant when in June 1714 he suddenly departed for Karlsbad to take the waters again. She bore him a daughter, named Natalya, but was deeply hurt by his indifference toward her and the child on his return to St. Petersburg. She was even more distressed soon afterwards when she learned that he was living with a peasant girl, named Efrosinia. Charlotte was already pregnant again and on October 12, 1715, she gave birth to a son, christened Peter. She had joked with the Tsar about fulfilling his wish for a son and now she took a sad pride in having pleased him. Four days later she began to fail, and she knew she was dying. She was anxious that her death should not be attributed to grief and unhappiness, and she repeatedly expressed her gratitude to the Tsar for his many kindnesses to her. Although ill himself at this time, Peter visited her and tenderly they took leave of each other. During her last hours Alexei was at her side and so distraught from grief and remorse that he fainted three times. At midnight on October 22, 1715, Charlotte died; she was just twenty-one years old.

Returning from her funeral in the Cathedral of St. Peter and St. Paul, Alexei was handed a letter which his father had written some two weeks earlier while in Schlusselburg. "A Declaration to my Son" was its heading and it faced Alexei with an ultimatum. Opening with a reference to the Swedes whom the Russians had learned to beat, the letter continued:

> But, when considering this joy granted by God to our country, I think on the line of succession, a bitterness almost equal to my joy consumes me, seeing you unfit for the handling of state affairs (and God is not to blame, for he did not deprive you of intelligence, nor did he take away from you bodily strength; for, although not very strong by nature, still you are not weak); worst of all, you wish to hear nothing of military matters, through which we have come from darkness into light, and while before we were not known in the world, now we are respected. I do not teach that you should be eager to fight without cause, but to love this subject and in every way possible to further and learn it, because this is one of the two factors essential in governing, namely, order and defense . . . And having no desire, you do not learn anything of military matters and you know nothing of them . . . You give weakness of health as your excuse for being unable to endure military hardships. But that is not the reason! For I do not desire labors, but willingness, which no illness can prevent . . .

Considering with grief and seeing that in no way can I incline you to good work, I have written this last testament to you, deciding to wait yet a little to see whether *without hypocrisy* you will change. If not, then know that I will cut you off wholly from the succession like a gangrenous growth, and do not imagine that because you are my only son I write this merely to frighten; in truth by the will of God I will do it, for as I have not spared and do not spare myself for my country and my people, how should I spare you who are useless? Better a worthy stranger than an unworthy son![34]

Alexei was terrified. He consulted with the small band of those who were close to him, seeking a way out of his predicament. On October 31 he replied in a letter of cloying humility and hypocrisy, asking to be allowed to renounce the succession to the throne. Peter was not satisfied. He recognized that such a renunciation could readily be disclaimed after his death.

On January 19, 1716, Peter sent him "a further last warning," castigating him for ingratitude and opposition.

"Everyone knows that you hate the works which I have carried out for the people of my nation, without sparing myself, and that finally after my death you will destroy them. And so, to remain as you desire, neither fish nor flesh, is impossible; thus, either change your nature and without hypocrisy be worthy to be my successor, or become a monk, for without this my soul cannot be easy, and especially since now my health is poor. And so, on receiving this, reply promptly by letter or in person, giving your decision. And if you do not do this I will treat you as a criminal."[35]

Alexei replied promptly that "I desire the monastic state and ask your kind permission thereto," and signed himself "Your slave and unworthy son, Alexei."[36] Again Peter was uneasy, suspecting that, when the time came, the monastic vows would be set aside. Moreover, he was still nursing the hope that his only son might mend his ways. Before departing for Copenhagen and Paris, he called on Alexei and found him in bed, feigning illness. He spoke kindly to him, commenting on his decision to become a monk he said, "That's not easy for a young man. Think again without haste, then write to me what you want to do . . . I'll wait another six months."[37]

Alexei did not reply. Spared the awful presence of his father, he spent his time drinking. A letter from Peter demanding a decision reduced him to a state of panic. Often he had thought of fleeing abroad, but had never found the courage for such a drastic action. Now in desperation he made the decision.

On September 26, 1716, Alexei set out from St. Petersburg accompanied by his mistress, Efrosinia, her brother and three servants. A friend had promised to find him somewhere to hide. Near Libau he met his aunt, Tsarevna Maria Alexeevna, returning from taking the waters. He told her that he was traveling to join his father, and she gave him her blessing. Alexei then began weeping and muttered that he wished that he had somewhere to hide. But his aunt offered no comfort. "Where could you go from your father; he would find you no matter where," she answered. He did not tell her of his flight.[38]

From Libau, carefully covering his tracks, Alexei traveled to Vienna, where he threw himself upon the mercy of the Emperor, his brother-in-law. He was by this time hysterical. When questioned by the Imperial Vice-Chancellor about his relations with his father, he grasped at the opportunity to exonerate himself, but he was excited and confused, maintaining at one moment that his father was ruthless and bloodthirsty, and the next that he was good at heart and just. Finally he was told that the Emperor would extend his protection and intercede with his father, but that he must remain hidden in the mountain fortress of Ehrenberg in the Tyrol.

Two months passed before Peter, then in Copenhagen, realized that his son had fled and was in some secret hiding place. He at once sent trusted guards officers to search through Europe. He was sure, however, that Alexei would be found in Austria under the Emperor's protection. He was distressed by this final breakdown in his relations with his only son and also felt the disgrace to Russia and to himself as Tsar, especially at this time when relations with the Emperor were strained.

Within three months one of Peter's officers had located Alexei's hiding place in the Tyrol. Peter sent an envoy to Vienna where he was received in private audience and told the Emperor that the Tsar knew where his son was hidden and requested him to surrender him to his father. The Emperor found himself in an acutely difficult position. He was loath to withdraw his protection since Alexei had convinced him that this would mean sentencing him to death. At the same time he was unwilling to interfere between father and son, and was himself afraid of the Tsar and his armies. He decided to remove the Tsarevich to a new hiding place in Naples. Alexei set out with an imperial secretary and one servant who was Efrosinia, dressed as a page. In spite of the secrecy surrounding their movements, however, Peter's officers shadowed them all the way.

Peter was at this time in Paris. The problem of his son plagued him constantly. Finally he sent Count Tolstoy to Vienna to confront the Emperor again with his request for the surrender of the Tsarevich. Tolstoy carried out his instructions and warned the Emperor that the Tsar was ready to take drastic steps if his son was not surrendered. The imperial government knew what this meant, for Russian troops were present in strength in Poland and along the Silesian frontier. Tolstoy also threatened that, if the Tsarevich did not return, the Tsar would lay a curse upon his son, Peter, and the Duchess of Wolfenbuttel, the mother of the Emperor and mother-in-law of Alexei, was horrified by this threat to her grandson. The pressures mounted and the Emperor finally acknowledged that Alexei was under his protection and promised to persuade him to return voluntarily to Russia. Tolstoy accompanied the Emperor's messenger to Naples, where face to face with the Tsarevich, he gave him a letter from his father. The letter read:

> My son, it is known to all what disobedience and contempt you have shown to my wishes and that neither words nor punishment have made you obey my instructions, finally deceiving me and invoking God at your parting from me. Then what did you do? You ran off and like a traitor placed yourself under foreign protection. This has been unheard of not only among our children but even among our true subjects! By this act what shame and grief you have inflicted on your father and what disgrace on your country! And so I am sending to you now for the last time a message which Tolstoy and Rumyantsev will report to you. If you will obey me, then I assure you and promise before God and his judgment that you will suffer no punishment; but I will show you my best love, if you obey and return. But if you refuse, then as your father by the power given me by God I will curse you through eternity, and as your Sovereign I will declare you a traitor, and I will neglect no means to bring you to justice as a traitor and vilifier of your father, in which God will aid me in my right. Remember that I have done nothing to you by force, and if you had so desired all would have been now as you wanted. What you wish, do![89]

Alexei was overwrought and refused to return. But Tolstoy by threats and promises left him no alternative. The most telling threats were that he would be parted from Efrosinia and that Peter would himself come to Naples to get him. Finally he agreed and at the end of January 1718 he arrived in Moscow.

On February 3 Alexei was summoned as a prisoner to the audience chamber of the Kremlin Palace. In the presence of his father, all ministers, nobles and the church hierarchy he made a solemn renunciation of the succession and swore to recognize as heir to the throne the new Tsarevich, Peter Petrovich, born to Catherine on October 29, 1715. The whole assembly then proceeded to the Uspensky Cathedral where he swore the oath on the holy relics.

Peter was still not satisfied. He suspected some conspiracy. Alexei had given the names of his closest associates and after interrogation several of them had been executed. Meanwhile Alexei had returned with his father to St. Petersburg where he was allowed to live in freedom in a house adjoining Catherine's palace. Here he waited impatiently for the return of Efrosinia. She had been allowed to travel at leisure because she was pregnant. She arrived in St. Petersburg in mid-April and was taken to the Petropavlovsky Fortress where presumably she gave birth to her baby.

Four weeks later, when Peter was at Peterhof, she was brought before him from the fortress and he questioned her. She spoke readily and openly on all that Alexei had said to her and to others and, whether moved by hatred, contempt, or mere indifference, she could not have done more to damn him.

Alexei had, she said, written many times to the Emperor, vilifying the Tsar and his policies. He had rejoiced over reports of a revolt in the army and over the illness of the Tsarevich, Peter Petrovich. He had repeatedly told her how he longed for his father's death. On ascending the throne he would live in Moscow, leaving St. Petersburg deserted. He would abandon the navy, leaving the ships to rot. Efrosinia's evidence contained countless instances of his perfidy and treason. Confronted by his mistress, Alexei could only confess. He was placed under arrest and taken to the Petropavlovsky Fortress to await trial.

Peter was determined that he himself should not try his son. He ordered senators, ministers, and senior officers to form a court and to judge the Tsarevich honestly without fearing him, especially if they considered that the crimes of the Tsarevich merited only lenient punishment. This civil court consisted of 127 of the leading men of the day. The first examination took place on June 19, 1718, when Alexei was raised on the scaffold and received twenty-five strokes of the knout. Three days later Peter sent Tolstoy to question him further on certain points in his evidence. The questions Tolstoy was to ask suggested that Peter was anxious to probe and understand the reasons for the failure in his relations with his son. But Alexei's answers did not help to clarify the basic reasons for his failures or his fear of his father.

On June 24 Alexei suffered his second examination and received fifteen strokes of the knout. His evidence in both examinations confirmed the charges of treason laid against him. The full court assembled and unanimously passed sentence of death. But Alexei, who had suffered forty lashes of the knout in five days and had been savagely flayed, was already failing. On June 26, in spite of the sentence of death, he was examined again under torture and Peter himself was said to have been present. Later on the same day he died. He received the state funeral of a Tsarevich and was laid to rest in the Cathedral of Saints Peter and Paul.

Although committed in the West during most of his reign, Peter always had in mind the policy of expanding Russian interests in the countries to the east and south. He was eager to develop trade with

China, Central Asia, Persia, and India. But his attempt to initiate commercial relations with China by sending an embassy, led by Guards Captain Lev Izmailov, to the Emperor in 1719 achieved nothing. The Chinese were not interested in trade with Russia. Peter nevertheless pressed ahead with exploration of the Pacific coast to the north of China. He had already annexed Kamchatka and the Kurile Islands. In January 1719 he sent an expedition by land to chart the shores of the Sea of Okhotsk and to establish whether Asia and North America were joined by land. When the expedition returned without having solved this problem, he sent Captain Bering on the voyage which many years later resulted in the discovery of the Bering Strait. But Peter died without learning the solution to this mystery which had for so long intrigued him.

Trade with Persia and India was also constantly in his thoughts. His first attempts to penetrate into Central Asia and Persia met with setbacks. In 1717 a Russian expeditionary force of 3500 troops, commanded by Bekovich Cherkassky, was annihilated by the Khan of Khiva. Meanwhile, seeking closer relations with Persia, Peter had appointed Artemy Volynsky, a cavalry officer, as his ambassador in Isfahan. Volynsky's instructions were to gather intelligence about the strength of the Persian army and the route to India; he was also to persuade the Shah that the Tsar, rather than the Turkish Sultan, was his natural ally and that Persian trade, taking advantage of Russian waterways, should be routed through St. Petersburg. The Persians were already alarmed, however, by reports of Russian power and by the Tsar's expeditions into Central Asia. They believed that Russian forces were massing to attack them and the Shah was anxious to be rid of Volynsky before he could report fully on the weakness of his regime.

On leaving Isfahan, Volynsky was made Governor of Astrakhan. From there he was tireless in urging Peter to launch a campaign against Persia which was on the point of collapse. Peter, however, showed caution; he had not forgotten how close to disaster his impetuous campaign on the Pruth had brought him in 1711. In September 1721, however, an incident took place which decided him on action. The Lesghian mountaineers, led by Daud Bek, invaded the Persian provinces and a small band of warriors captured the important town of Shemaha, the center of Russian trade with Persia. The Lesghian raid caused heavy damage to Russian merchants, but it also demonstrated how weak the Persian defenses were.

Volynsky at once urged Peter to send troops without delay to protect Russian interests. Further reports that Persia was on the point of collapse made Peter fear that the Turks might forestall him by occupying the Persian provinces adjoining the Caspian Sea.

Peter sent troops ahead to Astrakhan and on May 13, 1722, he himself, accompanied by Catherine, set out to command his army. He had trouble with some of the wild mountain tribesmen and, although all finally swore loyalty, he had to take special precautions against surprise attacks. He took Derbent without opposition, but he was worried by the heat and lack of provisions. Many of his troops fell ill from the heat and from eating melons and fruits to which they were not accustomed. He had intended to march as far south as the Kura River, which flowed into the Caspian south of Baku, and to establish there a stronghold which would dominate the caravan trade routes to India and Persia from the Caucasus. Heat, illness, and the hostility of the Daghestan mountaineers made him give up these plans. He ordered his army to retreat to Astrakhan where he arrived early in October. But he continued his campaign, sending strong detachments southward which in 1723 captured Resht and Baku.

The Persians, threatened now by the Afghans, were desperate for Russian help and the Shah sent an envoy to St. Petersburg to negotiate. The treaty, signed there on September 23, gave Russia the provinces on the southern and southwestern shores of the Caspian in return for undertakings to expel the Afghans from Persia and to maintain the Shah on his throne. Peter was pleased with this result. But he was soon to find himself faced with the threat of war with Turkey. The Lesghian mountaineers turned to the Sultan for protection, while the Armenian and Georgians appealed to the Tsar for support against the Turks. Meanwhile the English ambassador in Constantinople was making strenuous efforts to persuade the Turks to declare war on Russia. This pressure had some result in that the Turks demanded the withdrawal of the Russians from the Caspian provinces and the Caucasus. Peter refused to be intimidated and in April 1723 he ordered preparations for war against Turkey. But neither side wanted war and they welcomed the mediation of the French ambassador. By the Treaty of Constantinople, signed on June 12, Russia and Turkey agreed on the limitations of their respective possessions in the region.

During the Persian campaign Peter had suffered several bouts of illness and he had to spend a month quietly in Astrakhan before returning to St. Petersburg at the end of the campaign. He had always enjoyed robust health, but now suffered from strangury and stone, which had probably been troubling him in some degree over the years. The complaint now became chronic and was soon to contribute to his death.

Peter was over fifty years old, but despite his tempestuous life, his dynamic energies and his capacity for work were unimpaired. John Bell, a Scot who accompanied him on the Persian campaign, noted that "he could despatch more affairs in a morning than a house full of Senators could do in a month."[40] His daily routine was rigorous. He rose at 4 A.M., or earlier, in St. Petersburg, going at once to his cabinet where Makarov, a humble clerk in Volodga whose ability Peter had recognized and who had become his chief secretary, was awaiting him. He worked through the morning in his cabinet and then went to the Senate or to one of the colleges to supervise and give instructions. After dinner he usually inspected the Admiralty shipyards or new buildings in the city on which he lavished so much care and thought. He worked even longer hours when he had on hand a task of special importance. In November 1721, for instance, when revising the draft of the naval code, he worked on it for fourteen hours a day until it was completed. He always carried a notebook in which he jotted down any idea or suggestion that seemed useful. "Dispatch to Siberia for information in Kamchatka" and "A short history of present day and ancient affairs for the instruction of young people after the alphabet" were two notes, but many were so cryptic as to be intelligible only to the writer.[41] It was by harnessing his great energies and his capacity for detailed work in such a rigorous routine that he managed to accomplish so much.

During these years the relationship between Peter and Catherine matured and deepened. He had married her privately in November 1707, and they were together as much as his campaigns and frequent journeys permitted. They disliked the separations that disrupted their lives. "Praise God, all is merry here," he wrote to her from Reval in 1719, "but when I come to a country house and you are not there I feel so sad." In another letter he wrote: "But when you state that it is miserable walking alone, although the garden is pleasant, I believe you, for it's the same for me: only pray God that this is the last summer we'll spend apart and that we may be always together in future."[42]

Catherine had been with him in the campaign on the Pruth and again during the Persian expedition, and had earned his special gratitude on both occasions by her steadfast companionship despite discomforts and dangers. He had acknowledged his indebtedness to her after the Pruth campaign by publicly celebrating their marriage (February 19, 1712) and two years later he instituted a new decoration, the Order of St. Catherine, commemorating her conduct when she had behaved "not as a woman, but as a man."[43] After the Persian campaign he resolved to proclaim her services to the nation.

On November 15, 1723, Peter declared in a ukaz that "Our best beloved spouse, consort, and Empress, Catherine has been a great support to us and not only in this, but also in many military operations, putting aside womanly weakness, of her own free will she has been present with us and has helped in every way possible . . . and for these labors of our Spouse we have decided that by virtue of the supreme power given us by God she shall be crowned which, God willing, is to take place formally in Moscow in the present winter . . ."[44] A severe attack of strangury compelled him to postpone the ceremony, but on May 7, 1724, the coronation took place. Peter, always so careful in his expenditure on himself, spared no expense for this occasion. Catherine's robes were magnificent, her cloak embroidered in gold with the imperial double-headed eagle, and her crown ablaze with priceless jewels.

From the Red Staircase, where as a boy forty-two years earlier Peter had stood with his mother in mortal fear of the *streltsi*, the coronation procession moved with slow dignity to the Uspensky Cathedral. There during the elaborate magnificence of the Orthodox ceremony, Peter placed the imperial crown on the head of the peasant-girl who was his wife. He then retired to the palace while she proceeded to the Arkhan-gelsky Cathedral to pray at the tombs of the Muscovite Tsars. In the evening Peter and Catherine presided over a vast banquet at which guests were presented with a medal, struck for the occasion, bearing on one side profiles of Peter and Catherine and on the other the portrayal of Peter, placing the crown on her head and the words *"Crowned in Moscow 1724."*

The succession to the throne was never far from Russian minds and the coronation of Catherine was taken by many as an indication that Peter intended her to succeed, for their infant son, Peter, had died in 1719. On February 5, 1722, Peter had by ukaz abolished the Muscovite custom whereby the Tsar had presented his chosen son as his heir. He had invoked the example of Ivan the Great and had provided that the Emperor should appoint to the throne whomsoever he thought fit. This ukaz caused widespread anxiety. In the opinion of many Russians the heir should be his grandson, Tsarevich Peter Alexeevich, but Peter clearly had no intention of allowing him to succeed. Now it was feared that he might appoint some foreigner to occupy the throne of the Tsars. Other possible contenders were Catherine, Duchess of Mecklenburg, and Anna, widow of the Duke of Courland, the two daughters of Tsar Ivan, Peter's half-brother, and Catherine's three surviving children—Anna, Elizabeth, and Natalya. But the Russian throne had never been occupied by a woman and the prospect was far from popular. Peter did not share this prejudice, however, and may well have intended in promulgating this ukaz that Catherine and then his own daughters should succeed.

Peter spent most of the year 1724 in St. Petersburg. He was busy with numerous projects and took special interest in the new buildings under construction in what was already a beautiful city. The reform of the church in all branches of its administration and the creation of the Academy of Sciences were his other chief preoccupations. But attacks of strangury became more frequent and severe. Toward the end of the summer the pain was unbearable. His physician, Blumentrost, anxiously consulted with other doctors and on their advice Peter agreed to an operation. An English surgeon, named Horn, performed it, cutting open the lower abdomen and through to the bladder from which blood and urine flowed freely. Peter endured the surgeon's probing with fortitude, although without anesthetics the pain must have been excruciating. The two doctors at his side during the operation had their hands crushed as he grabbed them in spasms of agony. The operation gave him only temporary relief and he was confined to his bed by further attacks during the following weeks. But then medicines gave him full relief. He began to think that he was cured. He at once set out on strenuous journeys, visiting the Olonetsky ironworks and the Ladoga Canal then under construction. Blumentrost frequently advised him to live more quietly, but he was incapable of taking life easy or resting when he saw so much to be done and when time was so short.

Returning from Olonets on November 5 he sailed at once for Lakhta on the Gulf of Finland to inspect an armaments factory. He was nearing Lakhta in a storm when he saw a boat run aground and in danger of capsizing. He sent a sloop from his own yacht, but his men were unable to refloat the vessel, the crew of which was in danger of drowning. Unable to watch any longer Peter himself went in a skiff to help. He jumped into the freezing water and waded to the boat with a rope and helped to refloat her. The twenty men of the crew who had been saved from drowning were on his orders put ashore and accommodated in peasants huts while they recovered from exposure. Peter went on to inspect the factory at Lakhta, but he had been severely chilled and suddenly he was seized by stomach convulsions and fever.

Returning to St. Petersburg he found himself involved in a domestic crisis which distressed him and aggravated his illness. Catherine's chamberlain, William Mons, and one of her ladies at court, Matrena Balk, who were brother and sister of the Anna Mons who had been his mistress long ago, were found to be guilty of serious corruption. They had taken bribes and extorted large sums from petitioners. Catherine had probably been aware of their peculations, but was too easygoing to take any action. Further, Makarov, Peter's trusted cabinet secretary, was implicated.

Throughout his reign Peter had raged and fought against corruption among his people. He had punished severely all who were found guilty, no matter how eminent, but now he had found that those close to him and his wife were corrupt. Catherine begged him to pardon her chamberlain and lady in waiting.[45] Peter would not relent. Mons was executed; Matrena Balk was knouted and exiled to Siberia. At once Peter issued a new ukaz, condemning to death without mercy all who, holding positions at court, used them for personal gain, especially by extorting bribes for passing petitions to the Emperor or Empress.

During the next few weeks Peter tried to follow his usual crowded routine, but he was clearly ill and his strength was ebbing. On January 16, 1725, he suffered an attack of strangury so severe that he cried out in agony. Doctors gathered around him but could do nothing. A chapel was set up near his bedchamber and priests prayed constantly for his recovery. But the hopes of the vast majority of his people that he would recover were already fading.

On January 26, 1725, Senators, members of the colleges, the army high command, the guards, and naval officers assembled at the palace to keep vigil, and many were in tears. Twice Peter rallied and gave orders for an amnesty for criminals. But then he sank into a coma. By the evening of January 26 all hope had gone and the archbishops of the Holy Synod administered the last rites. But still Peter clung to life. About 2 P.M. on January 27 he called for pen and paper, but his writing was indecipherable except for the words "Give all to . . ." He asked for Tsarevna Anna, his eldest daughter, but then he lost the power of speech. He lingered unconscious until the morning of January 28 when at 6 o'clock Peter, the greatest of the Romanovs, and one of the outstanding rulers in history died.

VII
Catherine I
1725–1727

Peter had so dominated the nation by his personality and dynamic purpose that his death was an awesome event for all Russians. An elemental force which had shaped and dictated their lives was suddenly removed. He had been unique and irreplaceable, and now they lacked even the security of knowing who would succeed to the throne.

By an ukaz of February 5, 1722, Peter had asserted the right of the Autocrat to nominate whomsoever he chose as his successor. He himself had failed to exercise this power and the succession was to give rise to a series of crises.

In the years from his death in 1725 until 1762, when Catherine II seized the throne, Russia had no fewer than seven Autocrats, and the succession was decided by palace revolutions. The old nobility and the new aristocracy of men of ability, created by Peter, struggled for power through their candidates for the throne. But the decision was not made by the Assembly of the Land or by the Senate. The Preobrazhensky and Semenovsky Guards Regiments were the decisive authority. Recruited mainly from the gentry, the guards had become a privileged elite. They had been united by their fervent devotion to Peter and by regimental pride. Their power extended far beyond their military duties as the personal troops of the sovereign. Peter had called on them to exercise authority in policing and administrative matters, and had made them an important arm of government. Now contenders for the throne depended on their support.

As Peter lay dying, the urgent question in every mind was who should succeed. The great majority of Russians expected that Tsarevich Peter Alexeevich, the son of Tsarevich Alexei and grandson of the dying Emperor, would ascend the throne. He was the sole remaining male representative of the Romanov dynasty. He had the full support of the old nobility. Through his father who was remembered as the opponent of Peter's policies, he was seen as standing for the old Muscovite way of life. In fact, the old nobility did not advocate reversal of the policies of Peter and return to the Muscovy of Tsar Alexei; they were concerned simply to recover their power and prestige, and as a first step they were determined to remove the arrogant newcomers whom Peter had raised to high office. As Tsar the son of Tsarevich Alexei would, they believed, aid them in this purpose. But the new aristocracy realized that they would be the first to suffer if Tsarevich Peter became Tsar. Menshikov and Tolstoy in particular feared this event, for they had been implicated in the prosecution and death of Tsarevich Alexei. They were, moreover, men of energy and ability who were more than a match for the old Muscovite families.

Catherine, Peter's widow, was their choice for the throne. Opponents held against her that she was of humble origin and not even a Russian, that she had been no more than a camp-follower when Peter had made her his mistress, and that her subsequent marriage to him was of doubtful legality. There was also strong prejudice against a woman occupying the throne of the Tsars. But Catherine had the support of the guards and the army generally. She had campaigned at Peter's side and her bravery and concern for the troops had won their respect and affection. Menshikov and Tolstoy reminded members of the nobility, the Senate, the Holy Synod, and the *Generalitet* (those holding positions in the four highest grades, established by the Table of Ranks) that on the direction of the Emperor she had been crowned and that all had sworn allegiance to her. Tolstoy also claimed that "she had learned the art of ruling from her husband, who entrusted to her the most important state secrets."[1] But it was the support of the guards that ensured her accession.

Guards officers came voluntarily to her when Peter first fell ill, and declared their personal devotion. The troops also demonstrated their loyalty. Taking no chances, however, Catherine paid from her own purse the sixteen months backpay owing to them. Guards officers who had been granted leave to work on their estates were recalled to their regiments to pray for the recovery of the Emperor. In St. Petersburg all sentry posts were reinforced and infantry detachments maintained patrols.

On the night of January 27, Senators, members of the Synod, and all senior officials gathered in the palace to discuss the succession. The two factions faced each other. Prince Dmitri Golitsyn, seeing the strength of the support for Catherine, proposed as a compromise that Tsarevich Peter should ascend the throne and that during his minority Empress Catherine and the Senate should be entirely responsible for the government of the country. But Tolstoy firmly rejected this proposal. A group of guards officers who were present loudly cheered his demand that Catherine alone must succeed.

At this time the rolling of drums resounded around the palace. It was then found that both regiments of guards were drawn up in the courtyards. Repnin expostulated: "Who has dared to order them here without my knowledge? Am I not the Field Marshal?" His rival, General Buturlin, who was, jointly with Menshikov, Lieutenant Colonel of the guards, the sovereign being always their Colonel, answered, "I ordered them home in accordance with the wishes of the Empress, to whom every subject, not excluding even you, owes obedience!"[2]

Violent arguments broke out between the factions, continuing for some hours. But all came to recognize that the presence of the guards, loyal to a man to Catherine, had decided the matter. By 4 A.M. the meeting had reached agreement. Apraksin announced that, by virtue of her coronation and the oath of loyalty sworn to her by all ranks of the people, the Senate declared Catherine Empress and Autocrat with all the powers that had belonged to her husband.

The proclamation of the death of the Emperor Peter on the morning of January 28 was followed immediately by the announcement that Catherine was now Empress. In St. Petersburg the news was received quietly. Trouble was expected in Moscow, the old capital, where Peter's Westernizing reforms, symbolized by the ascendancy of the new capital of St. Petersburg, were resented. Moscow's loyalty was likely to be with Tsarevich Peter. Troops were stationed in Moscow as a precaution, but in the event the news was accepted quietly, except by a few individuals who were promptly seized.

Menshikov was jubilant. The succession of Catherine had delivered him from the threat of disgrace and exile. A prince whose wealth and power none could rival, he was now at the pinnacle of his extraordinary career. He came of humble origins and had, it was said, sold pies in the streets of Moscow as a boy.[3] His father had served as a corporal in the Preobrazhensky Regiment and Menshikov himself had been one of Peter's original play soldiers. He was a lively and entertaining companion, known to everyone as Alexashka. He accompanied Peter on his grand embassy to Europe in 1697–98 as a sergeant and *denshchik* (orderly and personal attendant) and then as the Tsar's private treasurer. Peter had developed an affection for him, but it was not until a few years later, early in the Northern War, that he had discovered Menshikov's remarkable abilities, his courage, and capacity for bold initiatives. He alone of Peter's companions mastered the craft of shipbuilding; he displayed great talent as a field commander, and he gave enthusiastic and unquestioning devotion to Peter and his policies. He had then begun his meteoric rise to high office.

At the same time, however, Menshikov was a rogue, hated and feared by many at court and throughout the country. He was greedy for power and wealth and unprincipled in their pursuit. He needed to serve a strong master who could control him. Peter waged a relentless campaign against corruption among those in authority and on many occasions he threatened Menshikov with severe punishments. Discovery of his misdeeds infuriated the Tsar who "often kicked him publicly and beat him like a dog, so that bystanders concluded him undone, but always next morning the peace was made up." Indeed, Menshikov was so adept in winning forgiveness that many believed that he used witchcraft for the purpose.[4] But he owed his escape from the full weight of the Tsar's anger mainly to Catherine who had been his mistress before Peter had taken her for himself and who interceded many times on his behalf.

Menshikov had been ennobled as Prince of Izhora and had received vast estates and other rewards for his work, especially during the Northern War. But wealth, honors, and power had inflamed his greed and ambition. Peter had become more and more disappointed in his old companion and had withdrawn his trust and friendship. In the last year of his reign he dismissed Menshikov from office as President of the War College and was considering far more drastic punishment. Menshikov was saved by Peter's death and now with Catherine alone on the throne his greed was unleashed. He was restored to the presidency of the War College, but he wanted also the office and title of Generalissimo and the vast region of Baturin, which Peter had refused him. He was to gain both objectives, but his power and arrogance intensified the hatred and fear which so many felt toward him.

Catherine sought to restrain him for time to time, but without success. She was herself under his influence and dependent upon him. She was like him in needing a master to serve. She had proved an admirable companion to Peter and the perfect commander's wife but, uneducated and self-indulgent, she could never be a commander. She could not make decisions and important matters were held up for months awaiting her signature. Rumors circulated about her excessive drinking and her numerous lovers, especially Peter Sapieha and Reinhold Lowenwolde, and her licentious way of life.

Catherine gave some early indication that it was her intention to rule, but she was without doubt prompted by Menshikov. In April 1725 she ordered that the Senate should in a body report to her every Friday on business in hand. It was soon clear, however, that the Senate was not to wield real authority. A dispute arose over the demand of Major General Munnich, in charge of the construction of the Ladoga Canal, for fifteen thousand troops to complete the project. The Senate agreed after long debate to meet this demand, but then found itself overruled by Menshikov who obtained instructions from the Empress in support of his decision. The Senators were infuriated. Several among them began actively discussing plans to curtail Menshikov's authority, but they were powerless.

Unrest spread at court, through the city, and into the country. Rumors were current of plots to place Tsarevich Peter on the throne, supported by the Ukrainian army which was commanded by Prince Mikhail Golitsyn, the brother of Prince Dmitri Golitsyn, then the most active representative of the old nobility in St. Petersburg. Recognizing that the general unrest might readily erupt in civil war, Menshikov, Apraksin, Tolstoy, and others agreed to set up a small council, superior to the Senate, which would govern the country.

By an ukaz of February 8, 1726, the Supreme Privy Council was appointed. The six members were Prince Menshikov, Count Apraksin, Count Golovkin, Count Tolstoy, Prince Dmitri Golitsyn, and Baron Ostermann, all of whom had held high office in Peter's reign. But within the Privy Council three men—Menshikov, Golitsyn, and Ostermann—held the power. Menshikov was the dominating member, but he needed his two colleagues.

Prince Dmitri Golitsyn was one of the most learned and cultured Russians of the time. He had in 1697, when already over thirty, traveled in Italy and other parts of Western Europe. He had since amassed a valuable library and had made a study of Western political philosophy. Under Peter the Great he had served as governor in Kiev and later as a Senator, but he had attained no higher office although distinguished for his intelligence and practical ability. His rough outspoken honesty may have offended Peter, but a more important factor was his fundamental opposition to the reforms. At heart Dmitri Golitsyn remained a Muscovite boyar, who wanted Russia to be modernized within the framework of the old Muscovite order, preserving the rights of the nobility and limiting the powers of the Autocrat. His alliance with Menshikov was a temporary and uneasy expedient, for he was sworn to get rid of the newcomers of whom Menshikov was the most outstanding.

Vice-Chancellor Ostermann, the son of a Westphalian pastor, had risen to prominence by his industry and brilliant intelligence. He was devious and so skilled in negotiations and intrigue as to be indispensable.

It was said of him that he always had gout in his right hand when called on to sign a document that might commit him in the future.

The Privy Council had power to legislate by decree on matters of internal and external policy, to supervise all Colleges, and in general it was to serve "to relieve Her Majesty of the heavy burden of ruling."[5] Catherine took little part in the meetings of the council which became in fact the supreme governing body. The Senate was demoted by decree in March 1726 from the "Governing" to the "High" Senate. Menshikov's rival, Yaguzhinsky, who had held the powerful office of procurator-general of the Senate, was not only omitted from the Privy Council but was also transferred, and the office of procurator-general was left vacant. Others who had held high office under Peter seethed with resentment over their exclusion, but could do nothing. The membership had been carefully planned, mainly by Menshikov himself, who had at a stroke triumphed over rivals and over the Senate. But even he was unable to prevent Catherine appointing the Duke of Holstein to the council by special decree. The Duke, Charles Frederick, had, in May 1725, married Tsarevna Anna and, taking advantage of the high regard in which the Empress held him, he and his minister, Bassevitz, were interfering more and more in Russian affairs.

In its policies the Supreme Privy Council endeavored to carry on the work of Peter the Great. Inevitably, however, there was a decline in activity. The dynamism of Peter's leadership was no longer felt and the nation was exhausted after the tempestuous years of his reign. The urgent need was to relieve the people of some of the pressures which he had imposed. The poll tax still weighed heavily on the peasantry, many of whom were unable to pay and, indirectly, on the gentry whose estates suffered. In 1724, twenty percent of the poll tax had remained uncollected and this figure was increasing. Unrest and threats of popular uprisings were widespread. The council found itself compelled to reduce the poll tax and to enact other measures intended to lighten the burdens of the people and the conditions of military service. The council also canceled many treasury trading monopolies and eased conditions of trade. But there was a marked reduction of tempo in national life.

Throughout these months concern about the succession was growing at court and throughout the country. Catherine's robust peasant strength, worn down by childbearing, by her strenuous life with Peter, and latterly by drink and debauchery, was clearly declining. Early in April 1727 she fell seriously ill. Her condition deteriorated rapidly and on May 6 she died.

On the following day the imperial family, members of the Supreme Privy Council, of the Holy Synod, the Senate, and the *Generalitet* assembled in the palace to hear the reading of the final testament of the Empress. It was rumored then and later that this testament was a forgery, but according to the journal of the Privy Council it bore Catherine's signature.[6] It was an attempt to establish an order of succession and to eliminate the uncertainty which Peter's ukaz, asserting the right of the Autocrat to nominate his successor, had caused.

According to this testament Prince Peter Alexeevich was to succeed to the throne. He was to take no part in state affairs during his minority, when the government would be carried on by the Supreme Privy Council, enlarged to include the Tsarevni, Anna, Duchess of Holstein, and Elizabeth. If Peter died without heirs then Anna and her descendants, and failing her Elizabeth and her descendants, were to succeed. No mention was made of the daughters of Ivan V, the half-brother of Peter the Great. At this stage, however, the urgent concern was that the nation should have a Tsar. Without delay the accession of Emperor Peter II was proclaimed and all Russians joined in celebrating the event.

VIII

Peter II

1727–1730

The new Emperor, Peter II, was eleven years and four months old, but advanced physically and mentally for his age. The Supreme Privy Council was to carry on the government while he was a minor and, since Menshikov dominated the council, he might have been expected to be content with the arrangement. But he had dynastic ambitions, and may indeed have had designs on the throne itself. When Catherine I was still Empress, he had recognized that Peter's claims to the succession could not again be denied. He had therefore transferred his support to him and had also obtained Catherine's approval for the marriage of his daughter, Princess Maria A. Menshikova, to him. It appeared to be an astute move, and on May 25, less than three weeks after the death of the Empress, they were formally betrothed.

Menshikov had already taken action to ensure his control over the young Emperor. He did not allow him to reside, exposed to all kinds of influences, in the imperial palace on the other side of the Neva River from Vassilevsky Island where Menshikov himself lived in magnificence. He had the boy moved into his own palace where he could keep him under his eye. As his tutor he appointed Andrei Ostermann, who had always been his dependable ally and who, as a foreigner, promoted by Peter the Great, was unlikely to become allied with the old nobility.

At the same time Menshikov himself sought to draw closer to the old nobility. As a newcomer, suddenly possessed of great wealth and power, he knew that he was resented by the old boyar families which had always treated him as an outsider. But through marriage with the imperial family and alliance with the Golitsyns, with whom he believed he had a sound understanding, he hoped to gain acceptance. He now cultivated the Dolgoruky, giving them influential appointments. Prince Alexei Dolgoruky became chamberlain at the court of Princess Natalya, the sister of the Emperor; Prince Ivan Dolgoruky, the son of Prince Alexei, was also brought to court, although he had been in disgrace for expressing opposition to the betrothal of Menshikov's daughter to the Emperor. Other members of the Dolgoruky family were also advanced. While forging new alliances, Menshikov disposed of rivals. Among them were the Duke and Duchess of Holstein who felt compelled to leave Russia in July 1727. In Kiel the Duchess, Anna Petrovna, the daughter of Peter the Great, gave birth to a son and soon afterward, in May 1728, she died.

As Generalissimo, the commander-in-chief of the army, and with his authority over the Privy Council and the Senate established, with the Emperor under his direct personal control and his daughter betrothed to him, Menshikov appeared to be in an unassailable position. The Saxon ambassador reported that "Never did anyone so shake with fear even before the deceased autocratic Emperor Peter I, as they are forced to tremble now before Menshikov."[1] But there is no security for those in power under an Autocrat, and especially when the Autocrat is an uncontrolled and stubborn boy.

While adept in manipulating the leading men in the government and at court, Menshikov at once met with difficulties in handling the Emperor. The boy was wilful and knew that he stood beyond coercion and punishment. He was not interested in the lessons which Ostermann had carefully planned for him. He quickly developed a strong respect and affection for his tutor, but he pursued his own pleasures in spite of Ostermann's strictures. He had three favorite companions. He was fond of his sister, Natalya, a gentle, serious girl, one year older than himself, who had a restraining influence on him. He delighted in the company of his young aunt, Elizabeth Petrovna, the daughter of Peter the Great, who was then seventeen years old. She was very pretty with fair hair and bright blue eyes, and her irrepressible gaiety made her an entertaining companion. It had even been suggested that he might marry her in due course and Peter himself welcomed this prospect.

But his closest companion was Prince Ivan Dolgoruky, who was nineteen years old and could always find pleasant ways of spending the time. He shared Peter's passion for hunting and they spent days together on horseback. Often Peter was up all night, taking part in some escapade, engineered by Ivan Dolgoruky. He would fall into bed in the early hours of the morning and sleep through most of the day.

Menshikov and Ostermann considered, not unreasonably, that this was not a way of life that would train and equip him for manhood and the responsibilities of the throne. Ostermann admonished him and as his tutor tried to impose some discipline; his efforts were ignored, although evidently not resented. But Menshikov's assumption of the role of father and his admonitions were resented, and it was soon evident that Peter and his sister hated him. They probably regarded him as one of those directly responsible for the death of their father. Peter had also been antagonized by his betrothal to Menshikov's daughter whom he disliked. Most of all they resented the power which he wielded over them personally and over the court and the country. His companions fostered this hatred. Elizabeth Petrovna was hostile toward Menshikov, especially for· compelling her sister, Anna, to leave St. Petersburg and to return to Kiel. Prince Ivan Dolgoruky and other members of the Dolgoruky family were his staunch enemies and used every opportunity to incense Peter against him.

Open conflict broke out between the stubborn boy and the all-powerful Generalissimo as a result of an incident when Peter was twelve. A guild of masons sent him a gift of money, which he ordered to be taken to his sister. Menshikov intercepted the messenger and directed him to take the money to his cabinet saying that "The Emperor is still very young and does not know how to handle money properly." Learning of this, Peter faced Menshikov and in a fury asked him how he dared to interfere with his instructions. Menshikov was taken by surprise and explained that because the treasury was empty he had taken custody of the money, intending a better use for it. Peter's fury was not abated by this excuse. "I will teach you that I am Emperor and that I am to be obeyed!" he shouted and he walked out of the chamber.[2] Soon afterwards at court on the name day of Princess Natalya, Peter turned his back on Menshikov and took obvious pleasure in humiliating him publicly. Similarly he ignored his betrothed, Princess Maria Menshikova.

Menshikov was infuriated by this treatment. He knew now that the Dolgoruky were not to be won over, but were his inveterate enemies and that they were inflaming the Emperor against him. But his anger was also directed against Ostermann, who had informed him that both Peter and his sister were well disposed toward him. Since Ostermann had misinformed him in this way, he assumed that he was secretly working against him. Menshikov had a meeting with Ostermann when he charged him with deceit and even threatened that he would be broken on the wheel for seducing the Emperor from Orthodoxy.

Ostermann was in a difficult predicament. He enjoyed the respect and goodwill of the Emperor and his sister, and he had many enemies at court, including the Dolgoruky. He had supported Menshikov in the past, but he had to think of his own survival when Menshikov fell from power, and he was too astute not to see that this would soon happen.

Menshikov evidently believed that he could recover the Emperor's goodwill. On September 3 he planned a magnificent ceremony on his estate in Oranienbaum on the occasion of the consecration of a church he had built. He was especially anxious that the Emperor himself should attend so as to demonstrate to the court and the foreign ambassadors in St. Petersburg that relations between them were friendly. In spite of his humble petitions and special arrangements, however, the Emperor stayed away. On September 5 Menshikov counted on seeing the Emperor at Peterhof at the celebration of the name day of Elizabeth Petrovna. But Peter went off hunting in order to avoid him, and Natalya, his sister, escaped through a palace window on learning of his arrival. On the same day the Privy Council met in the absence of Menshikov and directed that the Emperor's personal property should be removed from Menshikov's palace. This was done on the following day and the Emperor took up residence in the Summer Palace on September 7. He also on this day sent instructions that the guards were to obey orders only from him, conveyed through Guards Majors Yusupov and Saltykov.

On the morning of September 8, Guards Major Semen Saltykov arrived at Menshikov's palace and informed him that he was under arrest on the order of the Emperor. Menshikov fell to the ground in a faint on hearing this news and recovered consciousness only after a surgeon had let blood. His wife, son, and sister hastened to the palace to petition for pardon, but the Emperor and Elizabeth Petrovna paid no heed to their tearful pleas. In fact, news of the fall of Menshikov was received with rejoicing and, apart from his own family, not one voice was heard in his defense. At a special meeting the Privy Council sentenced him to be stripped of all offices and decorations and to be confined to his estate in Oranienbaum. In the following April further charges against him were considered. He was found guilty on all counts. His remaining property was confiscated and he was deported to Berezov in Siberia, where he died in 1729.

The expectation in St. Petersburg after the fall of Menshikov was that the Supreme Privy Council would govern until the Emperor came of age. Within the Council Prince Dmitri Golitsyn would be the leading member, enjoying the confidence of Peter and the court. Golitsyn certainly merited this confidence, for he had consistently supported Peter's cause. His brother, Field-Marshal Prince Mikhail Golitsyn also deserved recognition for his competent management of the army in maintaining order in the Ukraine. But Peter actively disliked the Golitsyns. He was especially hostile to Dmitri Golitsyn who, although a man of ability, culture, and integrity, was too blunt and outspoken to be a courtier and had probably offended him. His expedient understanding with Menshikov may also have prejudiced Peter against him. Whatever the reason, he did not find favor, and the way to high office and power was dependent on the favor of the boy who was Emperor.

For a time Ostermann was the most powerful man at court. He had access to the Emperor and continued to enjoy his affection and respect. But his position remained exceedingly difficult. He was unable to carry out his duties as tutor, because Peter refused to attend lessons or to study. The Dolgoruky were chief among his many enemies at court and their influence over the Emperor was growing so rapidly that he feared for the future. The young Prince Ivan Dolgoruky was an undesirable companion for a boy, but Peter would not be parted from him. In desperation Ostermann asked to be relieved of his duties, but Peter begged him with tears to remain as his tutor and adviser.

In January 1728 Peter departed with his court from St. Petersburg. Extensive preparations had been made for this move and the Emperor was welcomed with magnificent ceremonial in Moscow. He had come for his coronation, but many believed that he would remain in the old capital. A profound significance was attached to this move. Peter himself had said: "I do not want to go to sea, like my grandfather,"[3] and it was now believed that he was deliberately turning his back on his grandfather's reforms. Many old boyar families were still hostile to Peter the Great's city. It was far from their estates and maintaining homes there involved them in heavy expense. They and indeed most Russians were also emotionally attached to Moscow; they took a certain pride in St. Petersburg, but Moscow was for them the heart of the nation and its real capital. There was, however, no general demand for a reversal of Peter the Great's policies.

Another factor, which was expected to influence Peter to turn his back on St. Petersburg and all that it stood for, was his meeting with his grandmother. The nun, Elena, whom Peter the Great had compelled in 1698 to take holy orders, but who had always referred to herself as Tsaritsa, was surprisingly still alive and now emerged from her seclusion. She had written pressing her grandson to come to her in Moscow. She had always been a conservative, narrowly Orthodox, Muscovite, completely out of sympathy with the new policies, and was now expected to impose her outlook on her grandson. When the meeting took place, however, soon after the Emperor's arrival in Moscow, it proved a cold, uncomfortable occasion. Peter and his sister, Natalya, accompanied by Elizabeth Petrovna, had no point of contact with this elderly nun, who came from a different age, almost a different world. Also she admonished the young people severely for leading feckless lives and for endangering both their health and their souls. In the coming months Peter avoided her as much as possible and the fears which Ostermann and others had had about her influence proved unnecessary.

On arrival of the court in Moscow, Peter had appointed Prince Vasily Lukich and Prince Alexei Grigorievich Dolgoruky to the Supreme Privy Council. He also made his inseparable companion, Prince Ivan Alexeevich Dolgoruky, the Ober-Kamerger or Lord Chamberlain of his court. These promotions sharpened their challenge to the Golitsyn and to Ostermann. Natalya, his sister, alone was able to exercise restraint over him and through her Ostermann tried to curb the excesses of the boy's way of life. But Natalya was not strong and, falling ill in the summer of 1728, she died on November 22.

By indulging him and pandering to his passion for hunting, the Dolgoruky gradually brought Peter completely under their influence. At the beginning of September 1729 he set out from Moscow with them and six hundred and twenty hunting dogs and did not return to the capital again until November. Soon afterward the announcement was made that the Emperor would marry Catherine, the seventeen-year-old daughter of Prince Alexei Grigorievich Dolgoruky, and they were betrothed with full ceremony on November 30.

Among the Dolgoruky, however, there was misgiving about this marriage. Certain members of the family spoke of the unpopularity of Menshikov, who had planned a similar marriage with the Emperor, and they expressed fears that the same fate might befall them. Also strong antipathies had developed within the family. Prince Alexei detested his son, Prince Ivan, and his sister now betrothed to the Emperor also hated him. In the savage struggle for power even family loyalties were swept aside.

Preparations went ahead nevertheless for the marriage. On January 6, 1730, the ceremony of the blessing of the waters took place on the Moscow River. On the following day the Emperor fell ill and it was soon apparent that he had smallpox. His condition declined rapidly and on January 19, the date appointed for his marriage, he died, aged fourteen years and three months.

IX

Anna

1730–1740

The sudden death of the boy-Emperor shocked and agitated the nobility and gentry. They had come crowding into Moscow for his wedding and now they awaited his funeral. For the third time in the past five years the succession to the throne was a matter of urgent and anxious concern. Their anxiety was all the more acute because Peter II was the last of the male line of the Romanovs. His death seemed to threaten the extinction of the dynasty. Awesome tales of the Time of Troubles, which had followed on the passing of the previous dynasty, were recalled. There were, in fact, several Romanovs of the female line alive and eligible. But in the midst of the winter, when the old city lay under heavy snow above which the cupolas and crosses of the cathedrals and towers of the Kremlin glistened in the cold air, the Muscovites, huddled around their stoves, were apprehensive of the future.

The Supreme Privy Council met at once and in secret. It now had five members, but for these special meetings Field-Marshal Prince Mikhail Golitsyn, Field-Marshal Prince Mikhail Dolgoruky, and Prince Vasily Dolgoruky attended. The most forceful member was Prince Dmitri Golitsyn. Confident in his own superior intelligence and ability and his noble birth he saw himself as the champion of the old Muscovite nobility. He grasped now at the opportunity to revive their authority, while limiting the autocratic power and the elevation of favorites to positions of high authority.

At the start of the Privy Council's meetings Prince Alexei Dolgoruky advanced the claim of his daughter to the throne on the ground that she had been betrothed to the Emperor. He produced "a certain letter as the testament of Peter II."[1] It was in fact a forgery which Ivan Dolgoruky had signed and which he had planned to use with the support of Field-Marshal Vasily Dolgoruky to rally the guards. The Field-Marshal disapproved of the plot, however, and the Privy Council brushed aside the alleged testament as not deserving serious consideration.

The two surviving branches of the Romanov family were the daughters of Peter the Great by his second wife, Catherine, and the daughters of his half-brother, Ivan V. The pretensions of Peter's first wife, Tsaritsa Evdokiya, to the throne were rejected by the Privy Council. The claims of Tsarevna Elizabeth and' of her nephew, the young Duke of Holstein, to the succession were undeniably strong. Prince Dmitri Golitsyn had, however, never approved of the marriage of the Emperor with the humble peasant girl who became Catherine I. He maintained also that, since the children had been born before Peter's marriage with their mother, they had been born out of wedlock. He rejected the line of succession, provided in the testament of Catherine I, as having no validity since she herself had had no true title to the throne. The male line from Peter the Great had died out, and it was, he argued, necessary to turn to the senior branch of the dynasty, represented by the descendants of Ivan V. Of the three surviving daughters, the eldest, Catherine, Duchess of Mecklenburg, was not acceptable because the Duke, her husband, a contemptible and troublesome creature, was alive. But the second daughter, Anna, widow of the Duke of Courland, seemed suitable.

Anna was the victim of Peter the Great's policy of dynastic marriages. At the age of seventeen she had been married to Frederick William, Duke of Courland, but in January 1711, only a few weeks after their wedding, the Duke had died. Anna had spent the next nineteen years in Courland as the widowed Duchess without power or money. The dukedom had passed to Ferdinand, uncle of Frederick William, but he lived in Danzig and took no interest in it. The Russian resident in Courland, Peter Bestuzhev-Ryumin, who was Anna's lover, managed the affairs of the duchy. He was displaced in her affections by Ernst Johann Buhren or Biron, the grandson of a groom, who had risen in the service of Duke Jakob III of Courland. Biron had studied for a short time at the University of Koenigsburg, but had been expelled for some misdemeanor. He had attracted Anna at first by his expert horsemanship and he was soon wielding a strong influence over her.

Anna would have remarried, but was prevented by the rivalries over the duchy. Several petty princelings considered marriage with the young widowed Duchess, with Courland in mind as a dowry. Anna herself had ardently pressed Empress Catherine for permission to marry Count Maurice of Saxony. But Catherine would not consent, fearing that the marriage might weaken Russian influence in Courland, which Poland claimed as a fief of the Polish crown. Anna had thus remained a widow and throughout her years in Mittau she lived in penury. She depended almost entirely on small grants that she was able to beg from St. Petersburg. She wrote to Catherine, Menshikov, Ostermann, to the Golitsyn and the Dolgoruky, asking for money. Her letters, ill-composed and ungrammatical were, as befitted a poor relation, couched in the humble terms of a supplicant. She had created the impression in St. Petersburg of being sensible, restrained and, above all, submissive.

At 10 A.M. on January 19, only a few hours after the death of Peter II, members of the Senate, the Holy Synod, and the *Generalitet* gathered in the palace. The Chancellor, Count Golovkin, announced to them that the Privy Council considered that Anna should succeed to the throne. All present voiced their approval and there was general satisfaction that she had been chosen. But neither Golovkin nor any other member of the Privy Council mentioned the plans, which they had been discussing secretly, to limit her powers. Rumors nevertheless circulated and the silence of the councilors excited speculation.

Prince Dmitri Golitsyn was the author of the eight "Conditions," on the basis of which Anna was to ascend the throne. The "Conditions" required her to promise solemnly that she would not marry or nominate a successor to the throne and that she would maintain the Supreme Privy Council of eight members. Further, she had to undertake that without the consent of the Privy Council she would not declare war or conclude a peace, impose taxes, or confer army, naval or civil ranks above the equivalent of colonel in the Table of Ranks, that she would not deprive members of the nobility of property or honor without trial, that she would not grant estates, or confer titles on Russians or foreigners, and that she would not expend state revenues. She had to acknowledge, too, that the guards and other forces were under the command of the Privy Council. The letter, which she had to sign, ended with the words, "And if I do not fulfill this promise then I will be deprived of the Russian crown."[2]

In proposing such drastic restraints, Dmitri Golitsyn was seeking to secure the nobility and also the gentry from arbitrary onslaughts on their property and position such as they had suffered at the hands of Ivan the Terrible and Peter the Great and to ensure that they participated in the government with the Autocrat. His "Conditions" contained the seed of what might have developed into a movement toward constitutional monarchy, as had happened in England. The Supreme Privy Council might have become a cabinet, answering to the Assembly of the Land (*Zemsky Sobor*) which might have served as a parliament, or the combined Senate, Holy Synod, and the *Generalitet*, now often convened to consider matters of special importance, might have developed into the parliament. But this seed did not take root. The nobility and the gentry were without a sense of community of interest. Even the ancient nobility lacked coherence as a class. Rivalries and petty greed robbed them of the capacity to act together. Other classes opposed them, fearing that with power they would be a greater scourge than the most savage Autocrat.

January 19th was a day of frantic activity in Moscow. Peter II had died in the early hours of the morning and by the evening Prince Vasily Dolgoruky was on his way to Mittau. His task was to inform Anna of her election to the throne and to secure her signature to the "Conditions." He traveled in haste. Like other members of the Privy Council he was worried that Anna might learn, before he had secured her signature, that the "Conditions" represented the will only of the council and not of the nation as a whole. Indeed, guards had been posted on all the gates of Moscow to prevent anyone taking the road to Mittau. But Yaguzhinsky, the former procurator-general and now a bitter opponent of the council, managed to send a messenger who evaded the guards, and warned Anna against accepting the "Conditions." Dolgoruky arrested this messenger in Mittau and had him sent back to Moscow in chains. Yaguzhinsky, too, was arrested on the orders of the Privy Council. Meanwhile, despite this warning, Anna had signed the "Conditions" as well as a letter of acceptance of the throne drafted by Vasily Dolgoruky, which stated also that she would set out from Mittau on January 29.

In Moscow hostility toward the Privy Council was growing. No one wanted to be ruled by an oligarchy and especially by this council of eight members of whom four were of the Dolgoruky and two were of the Golitsyn families. At least the council's composition would have to be broadened and made more representative. But there was also general objection to this form of government, which had reduced Poland and Sweden to weakness and insignificance. Russians feared that their nation would suffer in the same way if the Privy Council had extensive powers. All were convinced that Russia must have an absolute monarch to ensure the order, unity, and strength of the nation.

On February 2 the Senate, Synod, *Generalitet*, and leading members of the provincial nobility and gentry, some five hundred men in all, were summoned to the Kremlin Palace by the Privy Council. The letter and the "Conditions," signed by Anna, were read aloud to them. They reacted with hostile silence. The assembly was invited to propose reforms. It was a gesture by Golitsyn to win general support. Petitions for reforms began to pour into the palace. The proposals were wide-ranging but they dwelt especially on the need to broaden the membership of the council, revealing the general concern that one or more families of the old aristocracy should not dominate it.[3]

On February 10 Anna arrived in the village of Vsesvatskoe on the outskirts of Moscow, where she remained for several days. A battalion of Preobrazhensky Guards and a detachment of horseguards came of their own accord to swear loyalty to her. Anna received them and, despite the "Conditions" she had sworn to observe, declared herself to be Colonel of the Preobrazhensky and Captain of the horseguards, presenting to each of the guards a tumbler of vodka with her own hands.

On February 15 Anna made her ceremonial entry into Moscow. All ranks of the people were summoned to the Uspensky Cathedral to swear the oath of allegiance. Feofan Prokopovich, Archbishop of Novgorod and the senior member of the Holy Synod, insisted on a new oath of allegiance, which referred to the absolute power of the Autocrat and made no mention of the council or "Conditions." Prince Dmitri Golitsyn tried to forbid the new form of oath, but his fellow councilors, fearing demonstrations of popular support, agreed to its use. In his address to the Empress in the cathedral, Feofan, who had a powerful voice and great eloquence, dwelt on the Russian tradition of devotion to the person of the Autocrat.

Anna had been so long absent from Russia that she was not aware of the factions striving for power. She was now closely guarded by Vasily Dolgoruky who allowed no one to approach her directly. She probably did not realize that at this time a bitter struggle was raging over the "Conditions" which she had promised to observe. Suddenly she was made aware of the position.

Within the Privy Council the Golitsyn and the Dolgoruky had decided to arrest Golovkin and Ostermann and certain of their leading opponents. But on February 25, before they had time to act, Prince Vasily Dolgoruky hurriedly summoned them into the presence of the Empress. In the great audience chamber they found Anna and assembled before her some eight hundred of the leading men in the land. In their names a petition was read aloud, expressing the fears of her subjects that observance of the "Conditions" would encourage the enemies of the nation and bring disaster. They asked for approval to convene a special assembly to make recommendations on the institution of an effective system of government.

Prince Vasily Dolgoruky suggested to Anna that she might discuss this proposal first with her Privy Council. She was, however, prepared to approve the proposal for such a commission. At this stage an uproar broke out. Guards officers and other members of the company loudly demanded full restoration of the autocracy. Anna was evidently confused by these conflicting demands. But she acceded to a new request that the guards officers and others in agreement with them should have an interval in which to prepare a new petition, and she promised to grant them audience after she had dined. She then invited members of the Privy Council to join her and they were thus prevented from consulting together or taking action during this critical interval.

The petition which she heard on her return to the audience chamber was a straightforward request that she should rule as her predecessors had ruled, that she should destroy the "Conditions," and further that she should abolish the Supreme Privy Council and revive the Senate as instituted by Peter the Great. The petition had a hundred and fifty signatures appended.

Anna appeared astonished. "What!" she exclaimed. "Were the points which were brought to me in Mittau not in accordance with the will of the whole people?"

"No!" came the answer from the crowd.

"This means," she said, "that you, Prince Vasily Lukich, have deceived me!"

The "Conditions" and the letter which she had signed in Mittau were then brought to her and in front of the assembled company she tore them up.[4]

The confirmation that Russia would continue to be ruled by an absolute monarch was received with general relief. On the night of February 25 the Aurora Borealis spread across the horizon, bathing the city in lurid red light, like blood.[5] To the highly superstitious Russians this was a dire augury and many were to claim later that it had presaged the *Bironovshchina*, the terror caused by Biron, Anna's favorite. For Prince Dmitri Golitsyn the phenomenon had a special meaning, for he said to a small circle of friends: "The banquet was ready, but the guests were not worthy. I know that I will be the sacrifice for the failure of this business. So be it: I suffer for the fatherland; even now I have only a little time and those who now force me to weep will have to weep longer than me."[6]

Anna was thirty-seven years old when she arrived in Moscow. She was an imposing but an unattractive woman, coarse and masculine in her features and her tastes. A Holstein courtier who had seen her six years earlier described her as "handsome and she carries herself in a way that makes one feel respect for her." But in an account of her ceremonial entry into Moscow, Princess Natalya Sheremetev who, as the betrothed of Prince Ivan Dolgoruky, was probably not an impartial witness, wrote, "It was terrible to see: she has a repulsive face; she is so tall that when she walks among her officers she is a head taller and she is exceedingly fat."[7]

Her life in Mittau had been restricted and unenviable. She had been merely a pawn in the political game, played by Russia, Prussia, and Poland over Courland. Constant humiliation had made her hard, proud, and vengeful. She had longed for money and power. Now she was Empress with absolute power, free at last from restraints and penury, and free to indulge her tastes.

Anna had a passion for shooting and riding. Loaded guns were kept by the windows of the palace and she would fire at passing birds. She collected animals and birds, but on occasions she had the cages and aviaries opened so that she could practice her skill with gun and with bow and arrow. Her stables contained some forty horses which she often rode to the hunt. In three months of one year she killed by her own hand nine stag, sixteen deer, four boars, a wolf, 374 hares, 68 wild duck, and sixteen sea-fowl.

Hating solitude, she demanded constant diversion. She kept in attendance on her a number of women who could be counted on to chatter incessantly. Often when she heard of a woman renowned for her lively tongue, she would send for her and maintain her at court. Thus she wrote to the governor in Pereyaslavl: "Seek out in Pereyaslavl among the impoverished gentry and townspeople maidens who would be similar to Tatiana Novokshchenova for she, so we believe, will soon die, so that this would be a successor. Thou knowest our pleasure that we maintain those who are about forty and talkative . . ."[8]

Anna also delighted in maintaining a large troupe of freaks, dwarfs, and buffoons. Any human creature who was malformed and sufficiently grotesque could be sure of a place at court. The Tsars had always maintained dwarfs and jesters, and the custom was not peculiar to Russia, but was the fashion in all the courts of Europe in this age. Anna's delight in the deformed and grotesque was, however, extreme and, as in the pleasure she took in humiliating and mocking others, it was sadistic. Members of the corps of buffoons were sometimes lined up and ordered to kick each other in turn, and to carry out other degrading capers. Blood flowed and injuries were frequent during these bizarre performances for the entertainment of the Empress.

The pleasure she took in humiliating others also showed in her demeaning of members of old noble families. Prince Nikita Volkonsky was made a court buffoon with the special duty of looking after the imperial white rabbit. But Prince Mikhail Golitsyn was subjected to a far more degrading ordeal. He had married a Roman Catholic and had changed his own faith, hoping to keep his marriage and conversion secret. But

Anna, a bigoted Orthodox believer, discovered his secret and was out-raged. He was made to become a jester and was cruelly humiliated before the whole court, as when he was seated upon a large basket of eggs and required to hatch them, cackling like a hen all the time. Golitsyn's wife died, no doubt from remorse over the persecution of her hus-band. Anna decided then that, although he was now fifty, he should marry again and that she would provide him with a new wife and a magnificent wedding. She chose for his bride a Kalmuck named Anna Buzheninova, who was so ugly that she was a court freak.

The winter of 1739–40 was exceptionally cold and on the frozen Neva, midway between the old Winter Palace and the Admiralty, an ice palace was built for the couple. Constructed entirely of ice, the palace was thirty-three feet in height by eighty feet long, and twenty-three feet deep. It was surrounded by trees, carved from ice, and ice birds perched on the branches. In the elaborate decorations and furniture, no detail was overlooked. The bedchamber had a fourposter bed with pillows and bedclothes, and even two pairs of slippers, all made of ice. The reception and dining rooms were fully furnished, every item in-cluding plates and mock foods being carved from ice. Four small cannon and two mortars were fashioned from ice and fired several times, using half an ounce of powder for each charge, without bursting.

The wedding procession and celebrations were fantastic. Golitsyn and his bride were carried in a large iron cage, strapped on the back of an elephant. The guests, numbering more than three hundred, followed, some in sledges drawn by reindeer, dogs, oxen, swine, and goats, and some riding camels. A feast was laid out in Biron's palatial riding school. Natives from all parts of the Russian Empire had been brought to St. Petersburg for this wedding. All were now served with their special native dishes and they danced to their own music. When the banquet was over, the married couple were escorted by the noisy throng to their palace. They were conducted to their bedchamber, dis-robed, and put into their ice bed. Guards were posted at the door to see that they did not escape before morning.[9]

Court life in Moscow and St. Petersburg was coarse, cruel, and often grotesque. In the reign of Anna, however, it began to acquire a certain crude magnificence. The court of the Tsars had always displayed a barbaric splendor. Richard Chancellor, the English sea captain, who visited the court of Ivan the Terrible, had been deeply impressed by the profusion of gold and riches. But the display, demonstrating the wealth and power of the sovereign, barely hid the squalor of Muscovite life. Peter the Great had noted the great contrast between Muscovite manners and standards of living and those of the courts and capitals of England and France. He had founded St. Petersburg, determined to create a rich port and a beautiful city where cultured civilized living would be possible. His city had grown impressively and after 1712, when he had declared it to be the capital of Russia, it had begun to acquire the spaciousness and grandeur worthy of the capital of a vast and growing nation. After his death, however, St. Petersburg had languished. It had revived when early in 1732 Anna moved the court there again from Moscow and she introduced new fashions.

After her years of penury in Mittau, Anna, with the national revenue at her disposal, gave full reign to her extravagance and she delighted in opulent entertainments. In Courland she had witnessed the efforts of German princelings to imitate the fashions of Versailles. Now as Empress she sought to emulate Versailles on a grand scale and, according to Manstein, "to have her court the most brilliant of all Europe."[10] Firework displays, which were a feature of all European courts, were mounted in St. Petersburg with a skill and magnificence unequaled elsewhere. Balls, banquets, fêtes, and masquerades were frequent events. Court dress became richly Westernized. Peter the Great had campaigned against the old Muscovite robes with long coats and wide sleeves which hampered the wearer, especially on board ship. But his own taste had been for the Dutch coat and breeches which, while practical, were far from elegant. Anna required all at court to wear the finest clothes, imported from abroad, and no one was permitted to appear twice in the same dress at court functions. The results were, however, often ludicrous. "The richest coat would be sometimes worn together with the vilest uncombed wig; or you might see a beautiful piece of stuff spoiled by some botcher of a tailor; or, if there was nothing amiss in the dress, the equipages would be deficient."[11] Among some of the old Muscovite families and among the people murmuring was soon heard over the new ostentation and extravagance.

In the midst of her diversions Anna did not feel wholly secure on the throne. She had not forgotten that members of the old nobility had tried to impose restrictions on her power as Autocrat or that the gentry and others had at the momentous meeting on February 25, 1730, sought opportunity to promote reforms which would undoubtedly have had the same result. The guards alone had come forward as the ardent supporters of absolutism, and she had promptly raised two new regiments, the Izmailovsky and the cavalry guards. But this was not enough to make her feel secure and her mistrust of the Russian nobility and gentry remained. She had lived much of her life among Germans and was herself more German than Russian in outlook and sympathies. Now she relied increasingly on Germans in her service. Soon all the most senior positions in the government and the army were held by Germans.

Anna nevertheless heeded certain of the demands made by the nobility and the gentry. On March 4, 1730, she abolished the Supreme Privy Council and revived the Senate. In practice, however, these changes were little more than gestures. The Senate was not allowed to exercise real authority, and the Privy Council was promptly succeeded by a new central executive. Known as the Cabinet of Her Imperial Majesty, it functioned unofficially at first, but on November 10, 1731, it was formally instituted. Ostermann was its main author and was soon known as "the first Cabinet Minister." With his clear but devious mind and his remarkable instinct for survival, he had on plea of illness absented himself from the Privy Council during the secret discussions on the "Conditions." Soon after the accession of Anna he had, in the words of a contemporary, "thought it was high time to be entirely cured of his convenient disorder. His eyes which had been out of order, now saw clearer than before, and he felt himself to be in a condition to do any service that should be required."[12] He gained the confidence of the Empress and was soon one of the most influential men in the country.

Among the new Senators were the members of the Dolgoruky and Golitsyn families who had served on the Privy Council, but they did not retain their positions for long. Anna's vengeance fell most heavily on the Dolgoruky. All princes of the family were seized and charged with various crimes. They were found guilty of having distracted Emperor Peter II from his studies, of having ruined his health with hunting parties and wild living and of having in this way caused his premature death. All were banished or imprisoned. Subsequently certain members of the family were recalled to the imperial service, but then they were faced suddenly with new accusations. Found guilty, Prince Vasily Dolgoruky and his son, Prince Ivan, were broken on the wheel and executed; two other members of the family were quartered; others were put to death by different means.[13]

On the return of the court to St. Petersburg in January 1732, Anna gave attention to army reforms, primarily to meet the complaints of the gentry about conditions of entry into the army and length of service. Peter the Great had required that they should serve until old age, injury or ill health made them unfit for service. In future they could retire after twenty-five years of service, begun at the age of twenty. Further the landowning nobility and gentry had complained that their estates languished because all male members of their families were away on military duties. Anna now provided that the head of the family should be able to nominate one son to remain on the estate, free from compulsory service.

Anna appointed Count Munnich to be President of the War College, Field-Marshal, and commander-in-chief of the army. He had served Peter the Great, winning his praise for resolving the engineering problems in building the Ladoga Canal, completed after Peter's death. A man of considerable ability, Anna chose him to implement a series of reforms in the army. He established the Corps of Cadets which was housed in the vast palace, built for Menshikov, in St. Petersburg. Cadets were drawn from the Russian and Livonian nobility and the sons of serving foreign officers. They were educated and trained to enter the army as officers. He reviewed the pay of Russian officers so that they received the same as foreign officers. He revised army regulations and in many ways raised standards of discipline and conditions in the army, but efficiency and morale were not improved, for his discipline was harsh and impersonal and he inspired none of the comradeship which had made the army so effective under Peter the Great.

While Ostermann directed foreign affairs and much else and Munnich commanded the armed forces, Anna felt free to indulge her favorites. Biron, her lover, who had followed her to Russia, was foremost among them. On the occasion of her coronation in Moscow (April 28, 1731) she had made him a count. His position and power had grown rapidly from this time. In 1737 the Diet of Mittau under pressure from St. Petersburg had elected him Duke of Courland. But he remained in Russia at the side of the Empress and became detested and despised by all Russians.

Arrogant, ambitious, umbrageous, greedy, obsessed with pomp and ceremony, and cruel, Biron was a man of whom nothing good was ever said by his contemporaries, except that he was a fine horseman. He had engineered the cruel execution of six or seven of the Dolgoruky at a time when Anna seemed about to make use of their services. He was behind the *Kantselyariya Tainikh Rozysknykh Del* (The Chancery for Secret Investigations) which was responsible for the interrogation, torture, and punishment of Russians suspected, on the slightest evidence, of being critical or hostile to the Empress or her favorites. More than twenty thousand were exiled to Siberia and thousands died under torture or at the hands of executioners. Indeed, the latter part of Anna's reign has come to be known in Russian history as *Bironovshchina*, the rule or terror of Biron.

Anna clearly had a strong affection for this companion of many years. She indulged him and allowed him great authority, but she did not allow him to dominate her completely or to interfere freely in affairs of state. Biron resented Ostermann and Munnich, but was never able to have them dismissed or to override their authority in their respective fields. Moreover, in Count Karl Augustus Lowenwolde, another intimate friend since her years in Mittau, Anna had a second lover. She had appointed him to be Colonel of the new Izmailovsky Guards Regiment, while Keith, a Scot of long service in Russia, was its Lieutenant Colonel, and Biron's brother, Gustavus, was only Major. But Biron exercised power enough to arouse the hatred of the Russian people against the court and increasingly toward the Empress herself.

During her reign, when foreign policy was under the direction of Ostermann, Russia entered into two wars, and her relations with neighboring powers continued to be complicated by the dynastic unions with the houses of Holstein and Mecklenburg. Both wars were waged in pursuit of the two traditional purposes of foreign policy, namely, the reunion of all Russians, many of whom were still under Polish rule, and the extension of Russia's frontiers to their natural geographical limits which, since Peter had established Russian power on the Baltic Sea, meant the Black Sea in the south. But, although the Russian army won resounding victories, losses in lives and equipment were heavy, and the outcome advanced Russia no closer to her two objectives.

Since the last years of Peter the Great's reign, Russia had been at war with Persia. Ostermann, who had always had misgivings about this costly venture, negotiated a peace, surrendering to Persia the provinces, annexed by Peter in 1723. But he considered this justified because a conflict with France over the succession to the Polish throne was threatening and war with Turkey, France's ally, was an ever-present danger.

Russian policy was based on alliance with Austria and Denmark against France. Friendly relations between Russia, Austria, and England had been resumed after the death of King George I in 1727, and on the accession of Anna, France tried to secure an understanding with Russia, hoping to weaken the alliance with Austria. Ostermann was, however, opposed to this policy, pointing to the conflict that was inevitable with France over the Polish succession, and he won the day.

On February 1, 1733, King Augustus II of Poland, the ally of Peter the Great in the Northern War, died. The European powers at once became involved in intrigues over the election of his successor. For France, Roman Catholic Poland was the main bastion of her eastern defenses and it was French policy to maintain a strong influence in Poland. The French candidate for the throne was Stanislas Leszczynski, whom Charles XII had made King of Poland but who had been forced to abandon the throne after the Russian victory at Poltava. Leszczynski's daughter was now married to Louis XV, which was a further reason for the intensive French diplomacy to secure his election. Moreover, he had visited St. Petersburg and had promised Anna the Duchy of Courland in return for her support. In Vienna he had undertaken to recognize the pragmatic sanction if Emperor Charles VI would help him to gain the Polish crown.

After some hesitation, however, Russia and Austria decided that Frederick Augustus, son of the late King and Elector of Saxony, should be their candidate. In August 1733 Russia, Austria, and Saxony made an agreement to use military force, if necessary, to ensure his election.

They were taken by surprise when on September 12 Leszczynski was suddenly elected to the throne.

Ostermann was disturbed by this demonstration of French influence and took prompt action. An army of twenty thousand Russian troops, commanded by Anna's Irish general, Count Peter Lacy, advanced into Poland to the Vistula River. Leszczynski fled with his closest supporters to Danzig. The Poles, under Russian and Austrian pressure, then elected Frederick Augustus to the throne as King Augustus III. The Russian army next laid siege to Danzig and, after terrible losses, took the city. Meanwhile the Austrians, engaged by the French and their allies, Spain and Sardinia, had suffered defeats and appealed to St. Petersburg for support. Lacy marched his army into Saxony and advanced toward the Rhine. His approach brought an end to hostilities. By the Treaty of Vienna (1735) Augustus III was confirmed as King of Poland and soon afterward Leszczynski abdicated. Ostermann had ensured that Poland should not be dominated by interests hostile to Russia.

France was, however, a powerful enemy and at once exerted diplomatic pressure in Constantinople to arouse the Turks to action against Russia. French influence was an important factor in the outbreak of the Russo-Turkish War of 1735-39. The Turks now complained of Russian intervention in Polish affairs, which had, they alleged, damaged Turkish interests. The defeat which they had inflicted on Peter's army in the Pruth campaign in 1711 encouraged them to believe that they could readily gain further victories. For their part the Russians had not forgotten the humiliation of the Pruth campaign, and they were emboldened by the reports of their ambassadors in Constantinople, which portrayed the Ottoman Porte as being in decline and unprepared for war.

Anna finally yielded to the persuasion of Munnich and others who were anxious to embark on war. At first, however, Ostermann maintained that the army, commanded by Munnich, which had crossed the Don in August 1735, was marching against the Crimean Tatars and not against Turkey. Only in the spring of 1736 did Russia declare war on Turkey.

The Russian army advanced on two fronts, the main force under Munnich against Perekop and a smaller force commanded by Lacy against Azov. Munnich succeeded in overcoming the strong defenses of Perekop on the isthmus linking the Crimea with the mainland, and then took Bakhchisarai, the capital of the Crimean Khans. Lacy captured Azov and a strong detachment, commanded by the Russian general, Leontev, took Kinburn. The Russians had won a series of resounding victories, but at heavy cost in lives, resulting in part from the fierce resistance of the Tatars, but in part too from poor organization and grossly inadequate provisioning of the Russian forces. By the end of the summer all Russian troops had withdrawn into the Ukraine.

The campaign of summer 1737 was crowned with further success when the important fortress of Ochakov was captured. But the campaign of the following year was disastrous. In May 1738 Ostermann called on the French ambassador to mediate for peace with the Turks, but they refused to negotiate. The campaign of 1739 resulted in the Russian conquest of Moldavia. At this time, however, Austria began suing for a separate peace and Ostermann hastened to open negotiations with the Turks. But the Treaty of Belgrade, which ended the war in 1739, yielded small gains in return for the heavy losses of life and the crippling expense that Russia had suffered. Ostermann led the Russian negotiations but was no match for the French ambassador in Constantinople, who served Turkish interests. The Russians demanded the cession by Turkey of the Black Sea littoral from the Danube to the Kuban, including the Crimea. The Turks vigorously rejected this demand, and Ostermann managed to secure only Azov and a short strip of adjoining territory. The fortress of Azov was, moreover, to be razed to the ground and assurances given that Taganrog would not be fortified. Further, he had to accept confirmation of the ban on Russian ships sailing the Black Sea.

The outcome of the war had caused bitter disappointment. It intensified the anger and discontent which had been mounting among Russians of all classes throughout Anna's reign. They were constantly affronted and humiliated by the power and the unbridled arrogance of the clique of German favorites. Biron in particular treated everything and everyone Russian with a contemptuous superiority which caused deep offense. At the same time heavier taxes were extorted mercilessly and both landowners and local officials were held personally accountable for arrears. The war against Turkey, far from being over in one summer campaign, had dragged on for four years and had been a serious drain on resources. The personal extravagance of the Empress and the expenditure of her court added significantly to the strain on the economy. Burdens of taxation and service had been heavy under Peter the Great, but he had demanded that revenues should be expended in the national interest.

Now the Russians, observing the waste and ostentation of the court, grew more resentful as taxes increased and as the methods of governors and officials, under pressure from the government, became more brutal in enforcing tax collection. The anger did not, however, erupt in rebellion. Secret agents were everywhere and the smallest complaint could lead to interrogation, torture, and banishment or execution. Opposition groups were not allowed to develop, but as the reign neared its end the mood of the Russian people was growing explosive.

Childless and aging prematurely, Anna was frequently ill during 1739–40. She suffered severely from gout and stone. As her health declined, the succession became a matter of concern. Her sister, Catherine, had married Charles Leopold, Duke of Mecklenburg; their daughter, Anna Leopoldovna, was born in 1718. Biron had planned to marry his son to her, but this plan had been frustrated by Ostermann and by Anna Leopoldovna herself, who in 1740 had married Anthony Ulrich, Prince of Brunswick-Bevern-Luneburg. Their son, Ivan, was born in August 1740.

Anna was near death when, on October 16, 1740, she designated the infant, Ivan, to be her successor. At the same time she appointed Biron to be regent until the boy came of age. All was arranged at her bedside by Biron and others close to her, but without reference to the Senate, the Holy Synod, or representatives of the Russian people. On October 17 Anna died, and there were few in Russia who mourned her.

X
Ivan VI

1740–1741

The proclamation of the death of the Empress and the accession of Ivan VI was heard by the Russian people in angry silence.[1] All felt that the nation had been humiliated and degraded during her reign by the German adventurers. Arrogant, contemptuous of everything Russian, and insatiably greedy for wealth and power, they had plundered and abused the people and the country. Hostility toward all foreigners, but especially against the Germans in the imperial service, had mounted dangerously. But the Russian people had not rebelled. Anna had been the daughter of a Tsar and so had legitimate title to the throne. The guards regiments had supported her, ensuring that she wielded absolute power as Autocrat; they had soon found ample reason to regret their action but they, too, had hesitated to rise against the legitimate Empress.

The two-month-old infant, proclaimed as Emperor Ivan VI, had, however, only a tenuous claim to be descended from the Tsar. He was the great-nephew of the deceased Empress. His father, Prince Anthony Ulrich of Brunswick, was a German; his mother, Anna Leopoldovna, was the daughter of another German, the Duke of Mecklenburg, but her mother had been Russian and daughter of a Tsar. To most Russians, however, Anna Leopoldovna was German and the Brunswicks were a German family. Moreover, since she and her husband quarreled and were often estranged, Anna had appointed Biron to act as regent until the Emperor came of age.

The prospect of Biron exercising the autocratic power was insupportable. The general hatred of Anna's favorite grew daily. He behaved so offensively and stupidly that even his compatriots detested him, and they recognized the danger that he might provoke a popular uprising which would sweep them aside. But Biron's greatest mistake was to antagonize the guards. Fearing that the Preobrazhensky and Semenovsky, the proud regiments raised by Peter the Great, would rebel, he ordered other army units to the capital as a counterbalance and made preparations to send guards detachments to distant parts of the country, probably far to the south where they could defend the frontiers against Tatar incursions. He also had in mind a longer-term plan to recruit guardsmen not from the nobility, from which they had always been drawn, but from lower classes, a change so fundamental as to amount to disbanding the regiments.

Their existence threatened, the guards were ready to rise. A detachment of the Preobrazhensky, led by Munnich who commanded some respect among them, entered the palace in the early hours of November 9, 1740, and arrested Biron, who was in bed and had to be carried away wrapped in a blanket. A proclamation, made in the name of the Senate, the Holy Synod, and the *Generalitet*, appointed Anna Leopoldovna as regent in his place. Biron's regency had lasted just twenty-two days.[2]

The new regime was, however, hardly more acceptable. Anna Leopoldovna was a debauched and stupid woman without the least understanding or capacity for ruling a vast empire. She would stay for days in her bedchamber, disrobed and indulging her unnatural passion for her lady-in-waiting, Julie Mengden. She also had a lover, Count Lynar, the Saxon Minister in St. Petersburg, and for some perverse reason she was planning to marry him to Julie Mengden. Taken up with sensual pleasures, she left all affairs of state to Field-Marshal Munnich, who had become chief minister. But he was no match for his rival, Ostermann, who gained the regent's confidence. On January 28, 1741, an ukaz restored Ostermann to the position of first minister and limited Munnich's authority to the army and the Ladoga Canal. Incensed by this treatment, Munnich at once tendered his resignation and to his chagrin it was accepted.

Ostermann now had no direct rival, but he ruled in the midst of intrigues, instigated by Austria, France, and Prussia. The War of the Austrian Succession had broken out in 1740 and Russia, despite popular discontent and economic decline due to misgovernment and

gross extravagance since the death of Peter the Great, was still a formidable power. Austria and France were competing anxiously for
Russian support and their ministers were active in St. Petersburg. An
important factor in the displacement of Munnich had been his hostility
toward Austria and his support for France and Frederick II of Prussia.
Ostermann, the author of the Austro-Russian treaty of 1726, pursued
the policy of alliance with Austria. In St. Petersburg the French ambassador, Marquis de la Chetardie, and the Swedish minister, Count
Nolcken, intrigued to reverse this policy. Since he was so firmly entrenched, the only method was to take advantage of popular discontent
to promote a coup which would place Tsarevna Elizabeth on the throne.
They believed, mistakenly as they were to learn, that she was pro-
French. But they were not mistaken about her bitter hostility toward
Ostermann himself, whom she regarded as having treacherously betrayed the family of her father to whom he owed everything.

In return for Swedish support Nolcken demanded the return of the
Baltic territories gained by Russia in the Northern War, but Elizabeth
firmly rejected such terms. Sweden, encouraged by France, then went
so far as to declare war. The pretext was to relieve Russia of the rule of
foreign ministers, but the Swedes were in fact taking advantage of the
apparent disarray of the government. At Vilmanstrand in August 1741,
however, they were soundly defeated by the Russian army under the
command of Field-Marshal Lacy. De la Chetardie pursued his purpose
by intrigue. Elizabeth's French physician, Armand Lestocq, served as
the intermediary between them. But beyond lending her two thousand
ducats instead of the fifteen thousand requested by her, he took no part
in her coup and, indeed, was surprised to learn later that it had taken
place.[3]

The impetus behind the conspiracy, overcoming the reluctance of
Elizabeth to embark on the drastic action of seizing the throne, came
not from foreign ambassadors, but from the Preobrazhensky and from
her close companions. The revolution itself was an expression of Russian
exasperation and hostility toward the German adventurers who ruled
the country. The banishment of Biron had removed the most offensive
member of this group, but the fact that Germans still held the most
important offices and commands remained a national humiliation. Russian
pride was wounded further by their open assumption that, if the
foreigners were banished, the Russians would prove incapable of governing the country.

The conspiracy would nevertheless have taken further time to develop
had Ostermann not provoked a crisis. On November 23, 1741, Elizabeth
was summoned before the regent, Anna Leopoldovna, who revealed
that she and Ostermann knew of the plot and had decided to arrest
Lestocq. On the following day the guards received orders to prepare

immediately to move to the Swedish front. Elizabeth herself was not held under arrest or sent under guard to a nunnery, nor was Lestocq taken at once into custody. It was clear, however, that this was her last opportunity to act, if she was to escape relegation to a nunnery and if Russia was to be relieved of the intolerable regime of Anna Leopoldovna.

After months of hesitation, Elizabeth now took the initiative and she acted decisively. After midnight on November 24-25, she traveled swiftly by sledge to the Preobrazhensky barracks. With her were Lestocq, Mikhail Vorontsov, her chamberlain, Herr Schwarz, her old music master, Alexei Razumovsky, her lover, and Alexander and Peter Shuvalov, two gentlemen of her household. On her dramatic appearance in the barracks, holding a silver cross in front of her, the guards welcomed her with enthusiastic oaths of support and loyalty. At their head Elizabeth then traveled to the Winter Palace where the regent, her consort, and the infant, Ivan VI, were arrested in their beds. Detachments of guards took Ostermann, Munnich and others into custody. There was no resistance or bloodshed.

Elizabeth intended at first to send Ivan VI and the Brunswick family back to their duchy, but a revolt in their support by certain guardsmen and others made her realize that they would always be a threat to her security on the throne if allowed their freedom. She then banished Anna Leopoldovna and her consort to Kholmogory on the Northern Dvina River, not far south of Archangel.

Ivan VI was imprisoned in the fortress of Schlusselburg, where for some eighteen years he grew up in solitary confinement in an isolated casemate of the fortress where only his guards had access to him. Separated as a small child from his family, Ivan did not know love or companionship. He was dressed in rags and often hungry, and his warders, escaping their boredom in drinking bouts, often ill-treated him.

Elizabeth did not know of this ill-treatment and would not have allowed it. She had been saddened by Ivan's plight and on the one occasion when she had him brought to St. Petersburg so that she could see and talk to him, she was reduced to tears. But she considered him to be too great a threat to her throne to be freed.

Peter III, who lacked all capacity for sympathy or kindness and was sadistic, ordered that if Ivan misbehaved by calling himself a prince or angered his warders, he was to be put in chains and beaten. He added the sinister instruction that, should anyone seek to release him, he was to be killed.

After seizing the throne, Catherine II intended holding Peter III imprisoned in Schlusselburg and for this reason she ordered that Ivan should be moved to Kexholm. The death of Peter III made this unnecessary and Ivan was brought back to his old prison.

In August 1762 Catherine went to see Ivan for herself. She found that "apart from his painful and almost unintelligible stammering, he was bereft of understanding and human intelligence."

In July 1764 the unfortunate innocent who had been Ivan VI was murdered by his guards, apparently as a result of an attempt to release him, but surrounding circumstances suggest that his death might have been engineered from St. Petersburg.[4]

The tragic story of Ivan VI began with the arrival of Elizabeth at the Winter Palace. On the morning following his arrest, Elizabeth made a ceremonial entry into the palace. St. Petersburg rang with cheers, for this was a popular and bloodless revolution. The Senate, the Holy Synod, the *Generalitet*, and other senior representatives of the nobility, the gentry, and the army then fervently took the oath of allegiance to Elizabeth, as Empress and Autocrat.

XI

Elizabeth

1741–1761

Elizabeth's accession awakened a new spirit among the Russian people. She was the daughter of Peter the Great whose memory they now venerated, because he had brought the nation "from the darkness of ignorance onto the theater of fame of the whole world." She put an end to the German domination and restored to Russians their sense of national pride. For these reasons and through her own personality she revived their sense of personal identity with their sovereign, which was a vital source of the strength and unity of the nation.

In her foreign policy she was tenacious and singleminded in maintaining Russian interests. Internally the twenty years of her rule were a period of stability and relative prosperity. Her reign, although later overshadowed by that of Catherine II, was a time of growing strength and of preparation. For many Russians, too, it was a time of gaiety and happiness, rare in Russia's history.

Historians have usually portrayed Elizabeth as a vain, fickle, and amorous woman. They have relied mainly on the despatches of foreign ministers in St. Petersburg, many of whom were prejudiced because thwarted in their plans and anxious to explain away their failures.

Most of them reported to their capitals that, with Elizabeth on the throne and native Russians appointed to all high offices, the Russian Empire would speedily disintegrate and Russia would no longer be a factor of importance in European affairs. But under Elizabeth's rule Russia not only did not disintegrate, but became stronger and her role in Europe became dominant.

Elizabeth, the youngest daughter of Peter the Great and Catherine, was born in December 1709, on the day that Peter made his triumphal entry into Moscow after his victory at Poltava. She took after her father in her physique and energy and in her honesty and sense of duty. From her mother she inherited her beauty, sensuality, and her easygoing nature. During childhood she was neglected by her parents; her father was constantly rushing away to inspect some new project or to embark on a campaign and often her mother went with him. Elizabeth grew up in the midst of the new Westernizing reforms but her education, such as it was, was left to churchmen who taught her in the spirit of old Muscovy. She was extremely religious and throughout her life she was strict in observing the Orthodox rites. Her lack of formal education showed in such matters as her ignorance of the fact that England was separated from the continent by the Channel. She disliked reading, except devotional works, and then she insisted on large type, for she firmly believed that excessive reading of small type had hastened the death of her sister, Anna Petrovna. On the other hand she had learned enough English, German, and French to be able to address the ambassadors in their own languages, and when she was brought to consider state matters she displayed a shrewd commonsense. Her upbringing had in fact given her a deep love for Moscow and old Russia. Like her predecessors she was crowned in Moscow, but she remained there for a year, and Muscovites had never seen the court more gay and splendid than during this period. She returned to Moscow for long visits throughout her reign and she was loved not only for her brilliant court but also for her piety in worshiping at the holy shrines of the old city. But she was also devoted to St. Petersburg and all that it stood for. Indeed, she resembled her grandfather, Tsar Alexei, in embracing the old and the new currents which were flowing through Russia.

Elizabeth resembled Tsar Alexei also in her goodness of heart. She could be quick-tempered, like him, and she was forthright and severe when she saw Russian interests threatened or her dignity or vanity were affronted. But generosity and what a contemporary called "her tender, indeed bewitching, kindness" were among her most attractive qualities.[1] She liked to create happiness around her and "like a good godmother" she took a personal interest in the problems of young people.[2] She would, for instance, arrange the weddings of her servants, herself dressing the bride and providing the wedding banquet, and then watching the pleasure of the guests.

In character she contrasted sharply with Empress Anna, for she was neither malicious nor sadistic. In removing Anna's German favorites from office she did not allow them to be tortured or executed, although Ostermann and Munnich were condemned to death and had to go through the ordeal of being prepared for execution, receiving the imperial pardon at the last moment. She did not share or give way to the xenophobia which had mounted dangerously by the time of Anna's death. She adhered firmly to her father's rule that foreigners should be engaged, but should not be allowed to displace Russians from senior positions.

Elizabeth detested cruelty and tried to moderate the savageries, which were taken for granted in Russia at this time. She had vowed before seizing the throne that she would abolish the death penalty, so freely imposed in Anna's reign. In her ukaz of May 17 she honored this pledge. Again in 1754 she refused to approve the new criminal code, prepared by a special commission and endorsed by the Senate. She considered the new code to be savage and she maintained her refusal to make it law even in the face of strong pressure from the church hierarchy.

As a young woman Elizabeth had been renowned for her beauty and at the time of seizing the throne, when approaching her mid-thirties, she was radiant. She was tall and massive but shapely in build, and she moved with a wonderful lightness and grace. None could compare with her in dancing and horseback riding. She had lively blue eyes, a full, well-shaped mouth, and her skin was so clear that she had no need of the cosmetics which Russian women usually applied with heavy hands. Her hair was fair, but for some perverse reason she often dyed it and her eyebrows black. She was exceedingly vain about her beauty. She dressed magnificently and extravagantly, refusing to wear a gown more than once. At her death more than fifteen thousand gowns were found in her wardrobes, as well as two trunks filled with silk stockings, and masses of unpaid bills.

By nature she was lazy and slovenly and wildly undisciplined. Her way of life had been irregular since childhood. Often she did not go to bed until dawn and then slept late into the following day. She ate, dressed, and arose as and when the spirit moved her. She was indolent and had a strong aversion from affairs of state and from work of any kind. Days and even weeks went by without her ministers being able to come near her to discuss urgent matters. She was nevertheless an Autocrat who commanded the respect and loyalty of her people. She was not corrupted by her indolence, extravagance, and indiscipline. She retained a basic simplicity and integrity, and she had a strong sense of her duty to the nation and to the memory of her father. Often, too, she showed a commonsense and an instinctive wisdom which were more profound than the devious reasoning of her ministers. She imposed her personality on her epoch and accomplished far more than her successors conceded in laying the foundations of a cultural renaissance in Russia.

At this time St. Petersburg and its court were still evolving, unlike Moscow where tradition and the church had imposed a rigid ceremonial. The court life of St. Petersburg was directly dictated by the tastes and character of the Autocrat. The court of Empress Anna had displayed a crude magnificence and the grotesquerie to which she was so much addicted. Fear of secret agents and denunciations, especially during the *Bironovshchina*, had made it oppressive. The court of Elizabeth was gay and more tasteful in its magnificence. The heavy fear-laden atmosphere was replaced by a new spirit, reflecting the warmth, kindness, and pleasure-loving nature of the Empress herself.

Elizabeth had lived a secluded life within her own small court while Anna was Empress. She was popular and, as discontent mounted under the rule of the German favorites, she was watched closely by Anna's agents on suspicion of plotting to seize the throne. She had many supporters who urged her to act, but she knew that the time was not ripe, and she behaved circumspectly. Anna would probably have forced her to take the veil and retreat into a distant nunnery, but Biron's intercession saved her from this fate. For Elizabeth the ten years of Anna's rule were a time when she had to curb her natural gaiety and gregarious tastes. Once she herself was on the throne she indulged to the full her passion for banquets, balls, masquerades, and theatrical displays.

The theater, first introduced into Russia toward the end of Tsar Alexei's reign, had not at once attracted a following. Peter had looked on the theater solely as a means of educating his people,[8] but they had not shown interest. The theater remained a court entertainment. German and Italian troupes had played in St. Petersburg during Anna's reign and she had in 1732 directed Rastrelli to include a theater in his plans for the new Winter Palace.

Elizabeth's enthusiasm for the theater was unbounded, and during her reign theaters began to flourish not only at court but also in other parts of the country. In 1749 the first Russian tragedy written by a Russian playwright, the actor-manager-dramatist Alexander Sumarokov, was performed, and his many dramas were soon being presented regularly. Lomonosov, the great Russian polymath, and other Russians wrote plays which were eagerly presented. In Yaroslavl, Fedor Volkov, a brilliant actor-manager, established a theater with its own company of actors. It was so successful that Elizabeth heard of it and Volkov and his company were to perform often at court. By an ukaz of August 30, 1756, she established a state theater with a generous budget and a permanent site on Vassilevsky Island, adjoining the quarters of the Corps of Cadets who were regularly called on to assist in theatrical productions, and Sumarokov was appointed to be its first director. But while Elizabeth and the court encouraged Russian dramatists and players, the classical dramas of Racine, Molière, Voltaire, and others were the main attraction and were performed at least twice a week.

Elizabeth took even greater pleasure in Italian comic opera and ballet. Lavishly produced, with singers and dancers from Italy, France, and Germany, the comic operas became the center of court life for a time. The palace was constantly filled with the sounds of music and not only Italian and German music but also the plaintive songs of the Ukraine.

Elizabeth's greatest pleasure was, however, the masquerade ball. Every Tuesday during winter these masquerades were held and usually she insisted on the men dressing as women and the women as men. She herself sometimes wore the uniform of an officer of the guards, but more often she put on the simple costume of a Dutch seaman in which she appeared to special advantage. But it was also an act of piety, for her father had dressed in this fashion in the shipyards of Amsterdam; he had then taken the name of Peter Mikhailov, and Elizabeth, when dressed as a seaman, insisted on being called Mikhailovna.

The young Grand Duchess, Catherine, enjoyed these evenings. She noted in her *Memoirs*, however, that "the men disliked these reversals of their sex and were in the worst possible humor, because they felt hideous in their disguises. The women looked like scrubby little boys, while the more aged had thick short legs which were anything but attractive. The only woman who looked really well and completely a man was the Empress herself. As she was tall and powerful, male attire suited her. She had the handsomest leg I have ever seen on any man and her feet were admirably proportioned. She dressed to perfection, and everything she did had the same special grace whether she dressed as a woman or a man. One felt inclined to look at her and turn away with regret because nothing could replace her."[4]

Night after night the court was ablaze with dramatic and operatic spectacles, balls, banquets, or masquerades. Elizabeth was always magnificently robed, and members of her large court were often impoverished by their efforts to follow the fashions which she set. Behind the gallant façade, however, the Empress and the nobility lived in what a leading Russian historian called "golden poverty."[5] All but the most powerful and wealthy nobles returned from the palace to houses which were small and bare, with ill-fitting doors and windows through which the winds whistled, while water flowed down the walls from condensation or leaks in the roofs. Elizabeth lived little better in her palace. The stove in her bedchamber had enormous cracks in it. Her personal furniture was sparse and simple, and such was the shortage of beds, chairs, and tables that, when the court moved on one of the frequent visits to Moscow and to other parts of the country, all such furniture had to be transported with her. Such discomforts did not, however, trouble her.

Elizabeth was in fact an enthusiastic patron of architecture and the marriage of her taste and vitality with the genius of her architect, Rastrelli, produced the great memorials of her reign. Bartolomeo Francesco Rastrelli had designed all the larger government buildings and had supervised all the major architectural activity in Russia during the previous twenty years.[6] His real opportunity to express himself came with the accession of Elizabeth, who put him to work on a grand scale. The new Summer Palace which he built for her, carefully merging Russian and Western styles, was the most magnificent and attractive palace in St. Petersburg.[7] He then built the Anichkov, the Vorontsov, and the Stroganov palaces. Under Elizabeth's personal direction he rebuilt Peterhof, expanding it vastly while preserving the original palace, which her mother, Catherine I, had built. He was also responsible for the Cathedral of St. Andrew in Kiev and of the Smolny Convent in St. Petersburg, which she commissioned. His last major work for Elizabeth was the rebuilding of the Great Palace at Tsarskoe Selo and the Winter Palace in St. Petersburg which, with his new version of Peterhof, established the basic Russian baroque style of the residential architecture of the Russian Autocrats for the years to come.

A woman of great beauty and vitality, Elizabeth was reputed to have had countless lovers. Allowing for the exaggerations of court gossip, and the courts of eighteenth-century Europe were hotbeds of gossip and intrigue, this was probably true. She was a woman of generous affectionate nature and highly sexed, and not one to exercise self-restraint. But the man whom she evidently loved sincerely was quite unlike the courtiers and favorites of the age both in origin and in character. He was a simple peasant from the Ukraine, named Alexei Razumovsky. As a boy he had tended sheep but the local priest, attracted by his handsome face, his gentle nature, and his fine voice, had taken him under his care and taught him reading, writing, and singing. An imperial courier, traveling from Budapest to Moscow, stopped at the village and, attending the service in the local church, was transported by the magnificent voice of the young Razumovsky. The courier persuaded him to go to St. Petersburg and he was soon one of the leading singers in the court chapel. Elizabeth, then Tsarevna, was at once attracted by this young singer and had him appointed to her small court. On becoming Empress she made him a count and a field marshal and in 1742, on the advice of her spiritual adviser, Father Dubyansky, a devout and wise priest who had great influence over her, she married her favorite in great secrecy.[8] The marriage was evidently childless, although after her death imposters came forward, claiming them as their parents.

Sudden riches and elevation to the highest offices did not change Razumovsky. When made a field marshal he roared with laughter and assured his friends that he would not expose Russian soldiers to such dangers as to command them in battle. Simple honesty and a certain shrewdness kept him from interfering unwisely in state affairs. At times he drank too much and then he became boisterous and inclined to horseplay, but normally he was a man of quiet dignity and courtesy. Elizabeth was devoted to him and showed him every consideration. He suffered from gout and when he was confined to his apartments she would cancel all court functions and nurse him anxiously.

As was the custom, Razumovsky's family came to court to share in his good fortune. His mother, an old peasant woman, was decked in a fashionable gown and respectfully received, but she stayed only briefly, preferring to return to the humble village where she had spent her life. Razumovsky looked after his younger brother, Kyril, sending him to be educated in the universities of Berlin and Paris. Kyril learned rapidly and acquired many Western tastes and interests. He married, under pressure from the Empress, Princess Ekaterina Naryshkina, who was her cousin. As a very young man he was appointed to be the first president of the Academy of Sciences and was later made a count and Hetman of the Cossacks of the Ukraine. Like his elder brother, he was a patron of Russian writers and dramatists, and kept open house for actors, dancers, and musicians. Indeed, while both Alexei and Kyril Razumovsky owed their fortune entirely to the favor of the Empress, they earned the goodwill of nearly all who came into contact with them, because they were unfailingly amiable, generous, and shrewd.

Alexei Razumovsky held the affection of the Empress until his death. It was as well, however, that he was good-natured and unpossessive, for he was soon obliged to share her with other, temporary, favorites. Her voluptuous nature was not to be satisfied by any one man. At Easter 1750, for instance, Grand Duchess Catherine noted that the Empress was out of temper, because at church she had found herself between four favorites, Alexei Razumovsky, Ivan Shuvalov, the newly appointed Gentleman of the Bedchamber, a chorister, named Kachenevsky, and Cadet Beketov. Catherine commented that "It must be admitted that anyone but Her Majesty would have been embarrassed with less than that. To deal with four men and conciliate them all is not a task that everyone could accomplish."[9] As she grew older, Elizabeth was increasingly attracted by young men, often half her age. But Alexei

Razumovsky evidently bore this with composure, content to stay in the background as her trusted confidant and companion.

Ivan Shuvalov, the chief favorite of the latter part of Elizabeth's reign, was like the Razumovsky, amiable, unpretentious, and generally liked. He was, however, highly educated and an able and cultured patron of the arts and of education in Russia. He corresponded with Voltaire and the Encyclopaedists and had such an enthusiasm for French culture that he was probably more responsible than any other man for introducing it and the French language into Russian court life. He promoted secondary schools and took the initiative in establishing the University of Moscow and the Russian Academy of Arts in St. Petersburg, both modeled closely on the French institutions.

The Shuvalovs had been among those who formed part of Elizabeth's small court when she was Tsarevna. They belonged to the gentry and, while the family had not won special renown, they apparently gave special attention to education. Like Ivan, his two cousins, Peter and Alexander Shuvalov, who now became influential at court, were well educated. In character, however, both were unattractive. They were insatiably ambitious and ruthless in cultivating favor and eliminating rivals. They were feared and hated at court. Alexander Shuvalov as head of the Secret Chancellery was particularly dreaded. One of his eyes was half closed and whenever he was excited or angry one side of his face twitched convulsively, adding to his sinister appearance.

Peter Shuvalov was the outstanding member of the family. He was vindictive and unscrupulous but he also had a brilliant inventive mind. He married Elizabeth's favorite lady-in-waiting and through her and the influence of his young cousin he quickly gained Elizabeth's confidence. He was rapacious and amassed a vast fortune, but in the process he introduced many measures which benefited the national economy and the army. The national finances were disorganized and the nation suffered from chronic budget deficits. Arrears of poll-tax mounted annually. Peter Shuvalov promoted a sweeping reform of taxation policy by reducing the poll-tax and increasing indirect taxes, especially on salt and alcohol which were state monopolies. By these and other measures affecting trade he revived the economy in some degree so that the heavy expenditure involved by the Russian campaigns in the Seven Years' War could be borne. He was responsible for the abolition in 1753 of most of the internal tariffs and duties which had severely hampered trade. As Grand Master of Artillery he improved the general level of efficiency and personally invented a new type of howitzer. He contributed also by army reforms and by ensuring that the army, thirty thousand strong, was ready for service.

Alexei Bestuzhev-Ryumin was Elizabeth's chief adviser and responsible for foreign policy for most of her reign. He was appointed Vice-

Chancellor in 1741 and Chancellor three years later. He was probably of English origin. His forebear seems to have been a Kentish yeoman, named Gabriel Best, who went to Russia in 1403 and whose son was made a boyar by one of the Muscovite Grand Dukes. Alexei's father had won the favor of Peter the Great and had later become the adviser and lover of Anna in Courland. An able diplomat and a distinguished chemist whose tonic or elixir was much in demand, Alexei Bestuzhev was by nature secretive, irascible, and ruthless. Already in his fifties when he attained high office, he was feared at court as a man of sinister influence. But, although an unattractive man, he was honest and devoted to the interests of his country. For this reason Elizabeth, who was said to have disliked him as a person, retained him in office for so long, ignoring the attempts of the agents of Prussia and France to have him dismissed.

Bestuzhev had been the personal enemy of Ostermann, but in power he pursued the same policy of supporting Austria against Prussia and France. He based his policy on alliances with the maritime powers, England and Holland against Prussia, and with Austria and Poland-Saxony against the Ottoman Porte. But he had to apply to the full his talent for intrigue to maintain this policy in the face of the opposition at court.

Frederick of Prussia, having seized Silesia in the Austrian Succession War, was eager to strike again, this time to take Bohemia. But he could not be sure how Elizabeth, guided by Bestuzhev, would react. His own minister in St. Petersburg, Mardefeld, and the Frenchman, de la Chetardie, plotted unscrupulously to bring about the dismissal of Bestuzhev and to draw Russia into alliance with Prussia and France. Their success seemed probable at one stage. Many had regarded Elizabeth's accession as a triumph of French diplomacy and now her French physician, Armand Lestocq, and de la Chetardie were expected to wield strong influence over her. Baron Mardefeld in close concert with the Frenchman disbursed bribes wherever they seemed likely to further the Prussian cause.

Frederick II had a further agent in St. Petersburg who, he believed, would bring strong influence to bear on the Empress. This was Princess Johanna of Anhalt-Zerbst, who had accompanied her daughter, the future Catherine II, to Russia to marry the Grand Duke Peter, the heir to the Russian throne. The young Grand Duke was already a fervent admirer of Frederick and marriage with the Princess of Anhalt-Zerbst was widely expected to consolidate Prussian influence in the Russian capital. Bestuzhev had opposed the marriage for this reason and had hoped that a Saxon princess would be summoned to marry him. Elizabeth had, however, made her decision without consulting him. But Bestuzhev was soon able to demonstrate to her the perfidy of the pro-Prussian party at court.

All who were opposed to Bestuzhev's policies were in the habit of gathering in the apartments of Princess Johanna where they gossiped and plotted, but their lack of success in displacing Bestuzhev brought increasing disgruntlement among them. De la Chetardie in his despatches vented his spleen on the Empress whom he described as frivolous, indolent, incapable of dealing with affairs of state, and much else besides. He also reported on his discussions with Princess Johanna, of whom he wrote highly as the special agent of the King of Prussia. Although suspecting that Bestuzhev intercepted his despatches, he was so confident that no one could break the cipher in which they were sent that he took no further precautions. Bestuzhev, however, not only managed to break the cipher, but also assembled in a dossier copious extracts from these despatches which he presented to the Empress.

Elizabeth was shocked. Like her father she was honest in her personal relationships and both surprised and infuriated by deceit and betrayal. Her anger was now tempestuous. De la Chetardie, with whom she had been on very friendly terms, was given twenty-four hours in which to leave Russia. The Prussian ambassador was declared *persona non grata* and had to leave. Princess Johanna was severely reprimanded and some months later was sent home. Grand Duke Peter and his young German wife were placed under close supervision, and two of their Holstein attendants were expelled from Russia in the following year.

Bestuzhev had triumphed over the pro-Prussian party at court for the time being. He now worked to consolidate the alliance with England which formed the basis of his foreign policy. The Anglo-Russian treaties of 1747 had provided that Russia would station an army in Courland and send another to the Rhine in return for British subsidies. An army under General Repnin had begun its march to the Rhine in January 1748 and, although not involved in action, its presence had served England well in inducing France to sign the peace of Aix-la-Chapelle in 1748. But these treaties had now expired; England and France were about to come to grips over their colonial territories. George II of England was increasingly anxious for the safety of Hanover which lay exposed to Prussian attack.

Bestuzhev's most difficult task was to prevail on Elizabeth to enter into a new treaty with England. She was actively hostile toward Frederick, but she also felt an instinctive mistrust of England. Early in 1750 new proposals came from London. For three years Elizabeth delayed her reply to the English note. Bestuzhev was exhausted by the negotiations with the English, who were driving a hard bargain and raising pettifogging demands, and by his efforts to win the approval of the Empress.

In June 1755 a new ambassador, Sir Charles Hanbury-Williams, arrived in St. Petersburg. His instructions were to obtain immediate agreement. A suave, elegant diplomat with a talent for intrigue he managed to secure Elizabeth's approval of the new alliance, which she signed on September 16, 1755. Its terms required Russia to provide an army of fifty-five thousand men to defend Hanover against Prussia in return for a substantial annual subsidy. When two months later the treaty had to be ratified, Elizabeth again hesitated, suspicious of England's good faith and reluctant to sacrifice Russian troops in England's cause. Finally on February 1, 1756, ratifications were exchanged.

A few days later incredible news reached St. Petersburg. It confirmed Elizabeth's worst suspicions and it crushed Bestuzhev. This news which confounded most of Europe was that George II of England and Frederick II of Prussia had secretly joined in alliance under the Treaty of Westminster. It had happened only two weeks before the final ratification of the Anglo-Russian treaty. Both monarchs had displayed a cynical disregard for their existing alliances, equaled only by the effrontery with which they now tried to justify their new treaty. A spectacular reversal of the pattern of European alliances now took place. Austria managed to bring France, her traditional enemy, into a defensive alliance against Prussia, and Russia later joined this alliance, confronting Frederick with three powerful enemies.

Bestuzhev, his influence waning and his position as Chancellor in jeopardy, at once set about salvaging what he could of his policy. In his hatred of France and his opposition to Russia joining the Franco-Austrian alliance he still had some common ground with Hanbury-Williams. They now joined forces in opposing the Shuvalovs and Mikhail Vorontsov, the vice-chancellor, who were pro-French.

Elizabeth had been seriously ill in 1755–56 and, although she recovered, many believed that she would not live much longer. Factions at court turned their attention increasingly to the young court of the Grand Duke and Duchess. The Shuvalovs anxiously cultivated the Grand Duke who hero-worshiped Frederick of Prussia; Bestuzhev and Hanbury-Williams paid assiduous attention to Catherine. Bestuzhev had displayed intense hostility toward her from the day of her arrival in Russia, believing that, like her mother, she must be an agent and supporter of the Prussian King. He had come to recognize, however, that she was, unlike her mother, highly intelligent and uncommitted, and that she might one day be influential.

The real power still rested in the hands of the Empress who was inflexible in her hostility toward Frederick of Prussia. She was guided and influenced, however, by the Conference of Ministers. This Con-

ference had been set up on the instigation of Bestuzhev himself after
the setback of the Anglo-Prussian alliance. Elizabeth had welcomed
the proposal, for she felt the heavy burden of responsibility for foreign
affairs and she hoped that the Conference would shield her from the
pressure of the intrigues surrounding her. The Conference met twice
in February 1756 and agreed on the basic principles of Russia's opposition to Prussia in alliance with Austria and France. Bestuzhev argued
furiously against the inclusion of France, but to no purpose. Unknown
to him, Mikhail Vorontsov, with Elizabeth's approval, was already negotiating a treaty with France. Bestuzhev was now Chancellor only in
name, but still he fought to retain his position and, despite the efforts
of the Shuvalovs and Vorontsov, Elizabeth refused to dismiss him.

In August 1756 Frederick invaded Saxony, thus unleashing the Seven
Years' War on Europe. The Russian army began to mobilize and toward
the end of the winter it was massed ready to march on Prussia. Field
Marshal Apraksin was appointed commander-in-chief. A lazy, self-indulgent, but amiable man, he seemed unlikely to lead the army to victory.
He was, however, a friend of both Bestuzhev and of the Shuvalovs and he
was one of the most senior officers available. As though anxious to avoid
action, he advanced slowly and reluctantly. But he was in an unenviable
position. The Empress was ailing and not expected to live long; Grand
Duke Peter, the heir to the throne, was violently opposed to the war
against his hero, Frederick. Apraksin knew that success against the Prussians would earn him the antagonism of the Grand Duke and certain
disgrace after he had ascended the throne. Apraksin felt that he was
being called on to commit political suicide.

In St. Petersburg the Empress and her ministers openly suspected him
of deliberate delaying tactics, and messages demanding action harried the
unfortunate commander. In June a Russian force, led by General Fermor,
the second in command, captured Memel and on August 19 Apraksin
won a great victory over the Prussians at Grossjaegersdorf. There was
general rejoicing in St. Petersburg. The Prussians were in retreat and
the road to Koenigsburg lay open. But then came the report that Apraksin had not only failed to press home his advantage, but had retreated
across the Nieman River to take up winter quarters in Poland. The confusion and anxiety in the capital were at this time further overcast by the
news that the Empress had had a severe stroke.

On the morning of September 8 Elizabeth was attending divine service
in the small church with its single gilded cupola, close by the palace in
Tsarskoe Selo. The service had just begun when she moved out of the
church alone and, as she stepped from the porch, she fell to the ground
unconscious. A group of peasants, walking to the church, stood bewildered at a respectful distance from her, not knowing what to do.
Members of her suite hurried from the church. Doctors were sum-

moned and let blood, but failed to revive her. For two hours she lay in the shadow of the cupola before screens and a couch were brought and she was carried into the palace. When later in the day she regained consciousness she could only speak indistinctly and her mind seemed clouded. But, while all at court were expecting daily to hear that the end had come, she began to recover rapidly and by the end of the month she appeared to have recovered fully.

Elizabeth devoted her remaining energies to the prosecution of the war against Prussia. Apraksin's retreat from his victory at Grossjaegersdorf was incomprehensible. She sent an ukaz, ordering him to advance into East Prussia and to engage the enemy. Apraksin complained of lack of supplies and equipment and the exhaustion of his men. His complaints were largely justified, but Elizabeth believed that he was avoiding battle. Bestuzhev was suspected of sending him secret instructions to this effect. Elizabeth now listened to the old Chancellor's enemies, who alleged that he was pursuing an independent policy in liaison with the young court. On February 14, 1758, when he failed to attend the meeting of the Conference of Ministers because he was ill, Elizabeth sent for him. Bestuzhev slowly dressed and made his way to the palace. As he entered the conference room, he was arrested. Field-Marshal Apraksin, too, was relieved of his command at this time and placed under arrest.

In these last years of Elizabeth's reign, when her health was failing, gloom and anxiety began to spread through St. Petersburg. The future was unsure and the prospect of Grand Duke Peter succeeding to the throne filled every Russian with apprehension. He was outspokenly pro-German and at the same time mentally unstable. His accession held the threat of the return of the German domination of Anna's reign, and also of weak government and insecurity.

Meanwhile Elizabeth continued to demand vigorous action against Prussia. She felt that Russian arms had been disgraced after Grossjaegersdorf and she was angered by the criticisms which her allies were making about the inaction of the Russian army. She had appointed Fermor as the new commander-in-chief and by January 1758 he had completed the occupation of East Prussia. He then marched into Brandenburg, intending to join with the Austrian army at Frankfurt on the Oder. Turning aside to lay siege to the fortress of Kustrin, he was astonished to receive reports that Frederick, at the head of the Prussian army, had made forced marches from the south to defend his hereditary territory and was about to attack him. Fermor moved his troops into strong positions at Zorndorf. There on August 25 the two armies joined in one of the bloodiest battles in modern times. In nine hours of fighting the Russians lost 10,886 men killed and 12,788 wounded, and the Prussians suffered similar casualties. But the battle was indecisive.

In St. Petersburg Elizabeth was deeply disappointed by the reports of this battle. For a time she even considered going to the front to lead her army in person. She accused Fermor of irresolution and of failure to pursue the Prussians after the battle. The criticisms were not just, but she was incensed by the terrible casualties among her soldiers and the mounting cost of this war which remained unresolved. Also she felt herself to be surrounded by deceit which she could scotch only by decisively beating Frederick. In fact, an extraordinary situation had developed in the capital. While Elizabeth was giving all her thought and strength to prosecuting the war, Frederick had at her court a team of spies and agents who kept him informed not only about Russian policy but also about the detail of Russian tactics. On occasions he knew the military orders sent by the Empress and the Conference of Ministers before they reached the commander-in-chief. His agents were Grand Duke Peter, Mikhail Vorontsov, the Shuvalovs and Keith, the new English ambassador, who by hand of diplomatic couriers passed information promptly to Frederick in Berlin. Grand Duchess Catherine had never shared her husband's enthusiasm for Frederick and Prussia and she was openly contemptuous of him, the Shuvalovs, and Vorontsov for their disloyalty to the Empress and to their country.

Elizabeth's health deteriorated steadily during 1759–60, but her determination to wage the war against Prussia remained as strong as ever. Fermor was advancing with his army across the Vistula River and into Saxony to join there with the Austrian army. In April 1759 he suddenly received an ukaz from the Empress, relieving him of the command and appointing in his place Count Peter Saltykov. Russian officers and troops were alarmed and Frederick rejoiced on receiving this news. Saltykov was an odd little old man without great military experience, who wore a plain white kaftan instead of the usual highly decorated uniform of a general. But the Russians quickly learned to respect their new commander-in-chief who acted with energy and decision which raised morale, and Frederick's rejoicing was shortlived. At Kunersdorf near Frankfurt, Saltykov, supported by Austrian auxiliaries, routed the Prussian army. Of his army of forty-eight thousand men, Frederick could muster only three thousand after this battle. Saltykov lost some sixteen thousand men, but this was the price to be paid for such a victory.

News of the Russian victory resounded throughout Europe. In St. Petersburg Elizabeth attended a thanksgiving service and the people rejoiced; in Vienna and at Versailles the victory was celebrated with equal enthusiasm. Frederick was in despair and contemplated suicide. He appealed to England to mediate on his behalf and, counting on the uneasy relations between Russia and her allies, Austria and France, and even more on Elizabeth's known hatred of shedding the blood of her troops, he believed a peace to be possible. But he failed utterly to understand Elizabeth. To the English ambassador who conveyed peace proposals in

December 1759 she replied firmly that she would never make peace without her allies and then she would consider only such items as would guarantee an honorable and lasting peace. She made it clear, moreover, that she would never trust Frederick and that she would not rest until Prussian power had been finally broken. But again her determination was thwarted. Saltykov had become dilatory and the campaign of 1760 proved abortive. The allies themselves began pressing her to make peace, but she refused. She knew that her army had only to invade Prussia now to deliver the final blow. For the campaign of 1761 she appointed Alexander Buturlin as commander-in-chief. He was the most senior officer in the Russian army, having served under her father in the Northern War and the Persian campaign. But now he was old and drunken, and he proved inadequate. The capture of Schweidnitz and Kolberg by Rumyantsev and the occupation of Berlin nevertheless brought Frederick to the point of unconditional surrender. He was saved not on the field of battle, nor by his cynical and devious diplomacy, but by the death of the Empress.

Elizabeth was ailing and, although only fifty-two years of age, she was an old woman. Her legs were so swollen that she was unable to walk. She had always been very religious by nature and now she spent most of her time in prayer. Her other concern was the prosecution of the war. But she worried, too, about the succession. She knew that her nephew, Grand Duke Peter, was pro-Prussian, that on her death he would reverse her policies, and that he was incapable of ruling. Her one solace was the infant Paul, the son of the Grand Duke and of Catherine, his wife, and on him rested her hopes that all would be well in the end.

Elizabeth lingered for months. She suffered fevers and further strokes, and her strong constitution pulled her through after each attack. But on December 23, 1761, she suffered a particularly severe stroke. She recovered consciousness on the following day and twice repeated with her confessor the deeply moving *Otkhodnaya*, the prayer for the dying. Then, shortly after 4 P.M. on Christmas Day, the doors of the bedchamber were opened. Prince Nikita Trubetskoy, one of the oldest Senators, came out into the anteroom which was crowded with notabilities, churchmen, and courtiers. Many were already on their knees praying and others were unashamedly weeping. Trubetskoy, himself, was in tears as he formally proclaimed the death of the Empress and the accession of Emperor Peter III.

XII
Peter III
1761–1762

Grief and despondency lay over St. Petersburg and the whole country. All Russians felt the death of Elizabeth as a personal loss, but deepening their grief was the sense of hopelessness, evoked by the prospect of the new reign. It showed in their faces and they even gave voice to it. The guards, marching to the palace to take the oath of allegiance, murmured aloud among themselves and, according to one who was present, it "sounded so menacing and alarming, so desperate."[1]

The new Emperor was, however, jubilant. While St. Petersburg was in mourning, he celebrated his accession and freedom. His conduct was crude and offensive to all Russians. He was tall and thin with a long sheepish face, and he was constantly talking and laughing loudly. During the weeks when the body of the Empress lay in state and the people crowded past the open coffin in the solemn ceremony of leave-taking, Peter held rowdy drunken parties and insisted that all guests should wear their brightest clothes. On the occasions when he appeared at the lying-in-state he behaved oafishly, joking with the ladies in attendance, ridiculing the priests, and making an unseemly noise. At the state funeral he played childish games which disrupted the solemn procession to the cathedral.

One of his first acts as Emperor was to order an armistice with Prussia. He then invited Frederick to draft his own peace terms. The resulting treaty restored to Prussia all the territories occupied by the Russian army. The war had never been popular, but the Russian people had accepted the immense effort and the casualties, and took pride in their victories over the Prussians. The army in particular was incensed to find its sacrifices and victories brusquely cast aside. But the new Emperor went on to offend the army further. He introduced Prussian uniforms to be worn in place of Peter the Great's uniforms in which all Russians took special pride. He also made a fetish of discipline and constantly drilled the troops in the rigid Prussian style. He went on to form a regiment of household guards, composed entirely of German and foreign soldiers, which posed a direct threat to the Preobrazhensky and Semenovsky regiments. Further, he prepared for war against Denmark which had the sole purpose of recovering Schleswig for his Duchy of Holstein which, as he made abundantly clear to his new subjects, meant far more to him than Russia ever would. Thus the army found itself under orders to prepare for a campaign which had nothing to do with Russian interests and which they did not understand. Moreover, since Frederick had agreed to join in this venture, Russian officers and men would be marching side by side with Prussians whom they had so recently fought with great bitterness and had defeated.

Peter demonstrated his contemptuous disregard for Russian interests, traditions, and loyalties not only in his treatment of the army but also of the church. He had been brought up in the Lutheran faith until the age of fourteen when he was received into the Russian Orthodox Church. But he remained a Lutheran at heart. He was without respect for the faith of others and incapable of understanding how deeply the daily life of every Russian was rooted in Orthodoxy. In church he would disturb the congregation and mock the officiating priests, often poking out his tongue at them. He criticized the rich vestments of the Orthodox clergy and the opulence of the Russian churches. He directed that many of the ikons should be removed, that priests should shave their beards, and that in future they should dress somberly like German pastors. He had a Lutheran chapel built in the palace and decreed freedom of worship for all Protestants. Finally he issued an ukaz confiscating church property and providing for a scale of payments to be made from the treasury for the maintenance of the clergy. His ukazi brought a storm of protest from the clergy and the people, which he disregarded. Protestants and Roman Catholics in the foreign embassies expressed amazement at his treatment of the established church.

While Peter antagonized the Russian people and in particular the

Orthodox Church, the two main pillars of support for his throne, Catherine, his consort, carefully cultivated them. From the first day of her arrival in St. Petersburg she had embraced Russia ardently, taking care that the Empress and others should observe her ardor. She studied the language and was notably devout in her observance of Orthodoxy. During the lying-in-state she maintained a vigil, kneeling in prayer by the open coffin for hours every day. The French ambassador observed sagely that she "more and more captures the hearts of the Russians."[2]

Catherine's Russian career had started in January 1744 when as the Princess Sophia of Anhalt-Zerbst she had departed with her mother from Zerbst, bound for St. Petersburg. The urgent summons from the Empress had not stated the purpose of their visit, but they knew that the Empress was anxious to have the Grand Duke married. She had chosen Catherine because of her link with the Holstein family and also because it was important that the bride should come of a family that was noble but insignificant and unlikely to involve Russia in further European commitments.[3]

Halting in Berlin on their journey, Catherine and her mother were received by the King. He carefully briefed Princess Johanna in whom he saw a valuable agent, well placed to influence the Empress in his favor. But he also observed with curiosity this young princess who might one day occupy the throne of Russia as the Emperor's consort, and he was evidently impressed. Catherine was then a spirited, highly intelligent girl of fifteen, slender in build and neither pretty nor plain. She was dark in coloring with brown hair. She had a broad forehead, a rather long face with a strong almost pointed chin, and a smiling but controlled mouth. Her face was not remarkable and only her chin and her firm mouth gave indication of the strength of will and the purposefulness which played an important part in her extraordinary career.

Grand Duke Peter, whom she was to marry, was a tall, frail, unhealthy youth. Born in Kiel in 1728 he was only three months old when he lost his mother, Anna Petrovna, the beloved sister of Empress Elizabeth. His father had neglected him and had himself died in 1739. Through childhood he had suffered neglect, and ill-treatment, and he had grown to be capricious, cruel, cowardly, and boastful.

Elizabeth had sent for him immediately after her coronation. She was fervently devoted to the memory of her father and sister, and was determined to cherish this nephew as a mother and, since he was the grandson of Peter the Great and in her view the only surviving male of the Romanov dynasty, he was to be brought up as her successor. From the time when he arrived in Russia she had lavished care and affection on him, but he had always been an exceedingly difficult, unlovable boy. He was backward and infantile and slow to learn from his tutors. She soon recognized that he would never be fit to rule, but she could not bring herself to disinherit him or to send him back to Holstein. She sought comfort in the hope that he would have a son worthy of the succession. For this reason she was urgently planning his marriage, although he was only sixteen.

From their first meeting, Catherine was amazed by Peter's childishness and inadequacy, but she humored him. She was tremendously ambitious and she never lost sight of the fact that he was the heir to the throne and her career. In July 1744 Catherine and Peter accompanied the Empress on a pilgrimage to Kiev and soon after their return to Moscow Peter fell ill with smallpox. Elizabeth herself nursed him devotedly through this loathsome and highly infectious illness, for although vain about her beauty she was a woman of courage and generous affection. Catherine was not able to see him until February 1745. She found then that he had grown taller and thinner and his skin, puffed and hideously pock-marked, made him repulsive to her. Again she mastered her feelings, but as the wedding day approached she spent hours weeping unhappily.

Elizabeth's impatience to have them married increased. The health of the Grand Duke was weak. If he were to die, the deposed boy-Emperor, Ivan VI, alive in the grim fortress of Schlusselburg, would be restored to the throne; the succession would be lost to the family of Peter the Great, and the German favorites would again rule Russia. Nothing could be allowed to delay his marriage with Catherine and the birth of a son and heir to the throne.

The wedding took place with great magnificence on August 21, 1745. A court ball followed in the evening, but soon after the ball had begun the Empress impatiently led the bride and groom off to their apartment. Ladies-in-waiting undressed Catherine and put her to bed. She sat alone, unsure what to do. According to her *Memoirs* she was so innocent at this time that she knew nothing of sexual relationships.[4] After a time Madame Krause, the new maid appointed by the Empress to ensure, if not to supervise, the consummation came to tell her that the Grand Duke would join her as soon as he had supped. Two hours later he appeared. He remarked with a laugh that the servants would be surprised in the morning to find them in bed together. Clearly he had no idea that he had a duty to perform. When next morning Madame Krause questioned them about their first night of marriage, she learned nothing to encourage the hopes of the Empress.[5]

The winter of 1745–46 passed in the usual round of entertainments. Catherine enjoyed dancing and she had made friends with certain members of her husband's suite. Her relations with Peter were, however, far from intimate; indeed, two weeks after their wedding Peter told her that he had fallen in love with a Fräulein Korf, and he made it clear that she was far more beautiful than his wife. Catherine had bouts of weeping, especially after Princess Johanna had been sent home. She had never been close to her mother, who had been jealous and waspish and had shown her no affection, but as her mother she had nevertheless been someone close to her in this strange country where she felt exposed and insecure.

As the months passed without signs of pregnancy, the Empress began to observe Catherine with cold suspicion. She felt that she had been badly let down by Princess Johanna and she suspected that Catherine was also working for, or at least sympathetic towards, the Prussian King. But the real reason for her mounting hostility was Catherine's failure to become pregnant. Elizabeth blamed her entirely. The possibility that Peter might be impotent and unable to consummate the marriage did not occur to her. He had had several boyish infatuations for young women at court, which made him seem normal and mature. In any case it was in her view the wife's duty to guide and inflame the passions of her husband.

One morning in May 1746 the Empress suddenly stormed into Catherine's apartments in a fury. She accused her of deceit and betrayal of Russia's interest, of having affairs with gentlemen of the Grand Duke's suite, and of failing to ensure that her marriage was consummated. This angry meeting was the beginning of a long persecution for Catherine. A trusted lady-in-waiting, Maria Choglokova, was appointed to watch over her and to ensure consummation. Choglokova who was young, married, and constantly pregnant, seemed particularly suited to this function. Bestuzhev, at this time convinced that Catherine was a Prussian agent, drafted instructions which reflected the extent of Elizabeth's suspicions. The first instruction was to ensure that Catherine practiced Orthodoxy with true devotion and "not just for the sake of appearances."[6] The second and most important instruction was that Choglokova should guard "the marital fidelity between both Imperial Highnesses" and impress on Catherine that she had been elevated to imperial rank solely in order that she should produce an heir to the throne.[7] Fourthly, she had to prevent Catherine interfering in political matters and take care that she conducted all correspondence, even with her father and mother, through the Ministry of Foreign Affairs. Similar instructions applied to Peter and the members of their respective courts with whom they were friendly were all removed.

Catherine was lonely and bored. Peter was an inadequate companion. He spent his time playing the violin badly, training and ill-treating packs of dogs in his apartments or playing with toy soldiers, and he drank heavily. Catherine found outlets for her mental and physical energies in riding, dancing, and reading. But for some six years her way of life was unnatural for a young woman of her passionate temperament. In 1752, however, she conceived a fondness for a young chamberlain of the grand ducal court, named Sergei Saltykov, whom she considered to be "handsome as the dawn." Saltykov paid ardent court to her, although he had only two years earlier married one of the Empress's ladies-in-waiting. Choglokova evidently turned a blind eye on the affair, for she had by this time come to understand that Catherine was not at fault for her failure to become pregnant.[8]

The Grand Duke laughed about Saltykov's pursuit of his wife, but showed no concern. When on December 14, 1752, Catherine set out with the court on a visit to Moscow, she was pregnant, but the journey brought on a miscarriage. In the following May she was again pregnant, but again she miscarried, this time due to horseback riding and a hunting excursion. In February 1754 she found herself pregnant for the third time and now she was required to rest and live quietly. The Empress appointed the sinister Alexander Shuvalov to be chamberlain of the grand ducal court and he watched over her. On September 20, 1754, after an exhausting labor she gave birth to a boy, who was at once christened Paul. The Empress bore him away in triumph to a specially prepared nursery, and forty days passed before Catherine was allowed a brief glimpse of her child.[9]

The grand ducal couple were by this time completely estranged. Peter preferred the company of Elizabeth Vorontsova, the niece of the Vice-Chancellor, and Catherine was carrying on her affair with Sergei Saltykov. But Peter's attitude had changed from one of indifference to one of active hostility, and this was intensified by political disagreement. Catherine had tried to stand aside from the factions and intrigues at court. She had, however, developed a new maturity and independence after the birth of her son. She had read widely and Montesquieu's *Esprit des Lois,* the *Annals* of Tacitus, and Voltaire's *Essai sur les Moeurs et l'Esprit de Nations* had made a deep impression on her, preparing her for the role of enlightened Autocrat. But she had also shed some of the loyalties which she had brought with her from Anhalt-Zerbst. She had been antagonized by Peter's unreasoning enthusiasm for Frederick of Prussia and she regarded Holstein as unimportant. The Shuvalovs, who now curried favor with Peter, were her enemies, but she no longer saw Bestuzhev as her archenemy and now welcomed him as an ally.

In the months following the birth of Paul she felt a desperate need for friends and allies. Sergei Saltykov had been posted as Russian minister to Hamburg, and on the few occasions when she had seen him before his departure it was brutally clear that, having seduced her, he had lost interest. But in June 1755 the new English ambassador, Sir Charles Hanbury-Williams, had arrived in St. Petersburg and on his staff a young Polish count, Stanislas Poniatowski, soon made her forget Saltykov completely.

A member of the powerful Czartoryski family, which led the pro-Russian party in Poland, Poniatowski was tall, good-looking, gentle, highly educated, and intelligent. Hanbury-Williams had become friendly with his family during visits to Poland, and had invited him to join his embassy as secretary to gain experience. Catherine and Poniatowski were strongly attracted to each other on sight. Within a few weeks of their meeting she was creeping from her apartments, dressed as a man, to ride to secret assignations with him. It involved passing through the Grand Duke's apartment, but as he usually retired to bed drunk, the risk was not great; in any case he was busy paying court to Elizabeth Vorontsova and disinterested in his wife's movements.

After the formation of the Anglo-Prussian alliance when Bestuzhev and Hanbury-Williams were still working together, united now only in their opposition to France, and to the Shuvalovs and Vorontsovs, who were pro-French, Catherine's position was misunderstood by many at court. She was the personal friend of Hanbury-Williams and indebted to him for facilitating her affair with Poniatowski. Many took this to mean that she supported his pro-Prussian policy. Hanbury-Williams himself reported to the Prussian King that she was a dependable ally. But Bestuzhev knew otherwise. He had persuaded her to write person-ally to Apraksin, urging him to march on the Prussians without further delay. He knew that she had little influence on policy, but he counted on her support after Elizabeth's death and he knew that Apraksin would read her appeal in this light. Bestuzhev had even prepared a plan whereby on her husband's accession she would wield power directly with him and not merely through her influence, if any, on him. Another of his plans was to prevent Peter's accession and to ensure the election of the infant Paul as Emperor with Catherine serving as regent. She politely rejected his proposals as being impracticable at this stage. But the more important reason was that her ambition had hardened and she intended to possess the absolute power alone, sharing it with no one, not even her son.

On December 9, 1757, Catherine gave birth to a daughter named Anna Petrovna by the Empress after her eldest sister, the Grand Duke's mother. It was generally accepted at court that Poniatowski was the father of the child. Peter, himself, had expressed great surprise on learn-ing that she was pregnant again. A few weeks after the birth of this daughter, Catherine was distressed to learn of the arrest of Bestuzhev and Apraksin. A matter of even greater concern to her was the im-minent recall of Poniatowski to Poland, which she was powerless to stop. Moreover, the Grand Duke had now begun talking openly of sending her back to Zerbst and of making Elizabeth Vorontsova his wife.

Catherine suffered from intolerable loneliness and isolation at this time and she grew desperate. On the advice of Ivan Shuvalov, the favorite who alone of the Shuvalovs was not ill-disposed toward her, she wrote to the Empress, throwing herself on her mercy. Protesting that "her soul was in danger" she had already enlisted the sympathy of the Empress's confessor. He appreciated her predicament and was sympathetic, as were most of the clergy, for she had always worshiped respectfully and humbly in the Orthodox rite. He spoke to the Empress in such terms that she sent Alexander Shuvalov to ask if she would be well enough for an audience the following night.

Catherine was summoned to this dramatic meeting after midnight on April 13, 1758. As she entered the Empress's chamber she noticed that the Grand Duke was present as well as Alexander Shuvalov. She at once threw herself at Elizabeth's feet, begging tearfully to be sent home to Zerbst since she could not bear the hostility of her husband and the disfavor of the Empress herself. To be returned to the petty court of Zerbst was the last thing that she wanted, for it would mean the denial of all her ambitions, but she calculated, too, that such an appeal would arouse the sympathy of Elizabeth herself. To the charge that she had sent orders to Apraksin, contrary to the instructions she had been given, she replied spiritedly and convincingly. She noted that the Empress was softening toward her. The Grand Duke, who had been watching her angrily, now began to abuse her aloud. She replied with dignity, noting at the same time that his abuse had the effect of making Elizabeth more tender toward her. Finally Elizabeth ended the audience, quietly promising her that they would meet alone together and talk intimately. The second meeting took place toward the end of May. No record of it has survived, but it marked the beginning of a warm and friendly relationship between the two women. The threat of being ignominiously returned to Zerbst was lifted. She was no longer in disfavor, and her dignified conduct, which quickly became known to all at court, had won her general approval.

Catherine continued, nevertheless, to lead a lonely life. No one had taken the place of Bestuzhev as her ally, nor of her friend, Hanbury-Williams, for she did not admit his successor, Sir Robert Keith, to her confidence. The departure of Poniatowski in August 1758 grieved her, and a few weeks later the death of her infant daughter, whom all regarded as his child, deepened her grief. But, although isolated at court and without direct influence, she was attracting wide and sympathetic support from Russians of all classes by her loyalty to the Empress, by her open opposition to Prussia, by devotion to the Orthodox Church and her respect for Russia and her people.

Now aged twenty-nine, Catherine had developed into a distinguished rather than a beautiful woman. She possessed, however, what a contemporary described as "sheer magic of personality" which captivated the crowds and appealed irresistibly to most of those who came into contact with her.[10] Poniatowski had succumbed at their first meeting. A few months after his return to Poland, a guards officer, Grigori Orlov, came under her spell, and he was able to play a vital part in her bid for power.

There were five Orlov brothers and all were heroes to their brother officers and men of the guards regiments. They could boast neither noble ancestry nor wealth, but all were striking in physique and beauty, and renowned for their dashing courage.[11] Grigori and Alexei were the most outstanding of the brothers. Alexei had far more intelligence and initiative, but Grigori was of the stuff that makes legends. In the savagery of the fighting at Zorndorf he was wounded three times, but continued to command his men and his fiery courage made them idolize him. He was known, too, for his conquests of women, and Catherine was quick to yield to his dashing appeal. But she was now older and wiser, and she saw in him not only a lover but an important ally who would rally the guards behind her when the time was ripe.

Catherine was also fortunate at this time in gaining other influential allies. Nikita Ivanovich Panin, the former Russian ambassador in Stockholm, had in 1760 been appointed tutor to Grand Duke Paul. A precise, courtly man, Panin was also very able and devoted to the interests of his country. He was representative of the small liberal group of the nobility who favored a system, limiting the powers of the Autocrat, on the lines of the oligarchic council in Sweden, and the parliamentary system in England. His plan was to arrest Peter when the time came and to make Paul Emperor with Catherine acting as regent until he came of age.

Another ally was the young Princess Dashkova, who late one evening toward the end of 1761 burst upon Catherine with impassioned protestations of loyalty. This Princess had been before her marriage Catherine Vorontsova, the youngest sister of the Grand Duke's mistress and she was also his goddaughter. She was, however, unlike her plump and stupid sister, for she was small, highly intelligent, and learned, and alive with nervous energy, but all too ready to be carried away by her enthusiasms and loyalties.

Catherine and Grigori Orlov were now carrying on their affair in the greatest secrecy. The Empress was failing and the capital was astir with rumors and intrigues. Late in June 1761, however, at the time when she was approaching the most crucial stage of her career, Catherine became pregnant. There could be no pretense that the Grand Duke was the father of the child, but, as was not difficult with the fashions of the day, she kept her pregnancy secret.

The death of Empress Elizabeth placed her future in jeopardy. Peter had repeatedly stated that after his accession he would send her away to Zerbst, dissolving their marriage so that he could marry his mistress. Meanwhile, in the first weeks of his reign his behavior had given violent offense to Russians of all classes. The English minister, Keith, was heard to say on one occasion to a Russian lady, "Really, your Emperor must be mad to misbehave as he does!"[12]

In certain of his enactments, however, Peter revealed some sanity. On February 21, 1762, he abolished the Secret Chancellery and directed that no one should be interrogated or arrested on political charges until the Senate had investigated the case and given approval. He also ended the persecution of Old Believers and granted them freedom of worship. He approved measures to promote domestic and foreign trade. He reduced the price of salt which weighed heavily on the peasantry and also extended some protection to them from industrial serfdom. But his most important reform was to release the gentry from the duty of service, making their service voluntary in future and also granting them the right to resign from the army except in time of war.

Such measures, holding promise of magnanimous and liberal policies, and designed to win him the support of his people were, however, overcast by the sense of humiliation felt by most Russians over the peace with Prussia which was announced with ceremony and had to be celebrated for three days. Moreover, the army was seething with discontent as preparation for the Danish campaign neared completion. But Peter seemed wholly unaware of the hostility with which his subjects regarded him.

Catherine remained quietly in the background during these first months of her husband's reign. She rarely went out and avoided his dinners and drinking parties. She was unwilling to expose herself to the contempt and rudeness which he now showed her in public. But also she was nearing the end of her pregnancy and on April 11, 1762, she gave birth to Grigori Orlov's son, an event which passed off without the Grand Duke knowing about it.

Grigori Orlov's son bore the name of Alexei Grigorevich Bobrinsky. The name Bobrinsky derives from the Russian word *bobr*, meaning a beaver. The family explanation of this name was that Catherine, anxious to keep all knowledge of the impending birth from her husband, the Emperor, worked out a scheme to get him out of the palace when her labor started.

Peter enjoyed fighting fires and there was a standing order that he was to be informed immediately of any outbreak of fire in the city so that he could direct operations. Catherine had a trusted servant, named Shkurine, who had a timbered house on an island in the Neva, facing the Winter Palace. He came to her aid by agreeing to sacrifice his house. On April 11, as Catherine felt the first pains of labor, a signal was given from a window of the palace. Soon afterward dense smoke began to rise from Shkurine's house. The Emperor was alerted about the fire and at once rode over the bridge to direct the fire-fighting. While he was away, Catherine was safely delivered of this son, who was smuggled out of the palace, wrapped in a rug of beaver skins.[13]

Already around Catherine a number of conspiracies were developing. All involved her in some degree, but she made no attempt to coordinate them and, indeed, seemed to play a passive role. Dashkova was plotting feverishly without revealing her plans and Catherine, while encouraging her, handled her with great caution. Panin, too, was active with his plan to arrest Peter and elevate Paul to the throne, a plan which she did not welcome, but she said nothing to discourage him. She was depending chiefly on the Orlov brothers. By mid-June they had won over all the guards officers with a few exceptions and were actively sowing disaffection more widely in the army. Another conspirator of great influence was Count Kyril Razumovsky. He plotted quietly, confiding his plans to Catherine who kept them secret even from the Orlovs.

During June, as troops prepared to leave for the Danish campaign, popular anger and discontent mounted dangerously in St. Petersburg. Peter was in Oranienbaum, intending to leave from there with his troops. On June 19, Catherine attended a theatrical performance in Oranienbaum, returning to Peterhof on the same evening. It was the last time that she saw her husband.

The tension erupted a few days later. A corporal of the Preobrazhensky Guards was interrogated after asking an officer when the Emperor was to be dethroned. This led to the arrest of a certain Captain Passek who was a friend of the Orlovs and a supporter of Catherine. Grigori Orlov told Dashkova who was alarmed, but Panin dismissed the arrest of Passek as being of no importance. At some stage, however, the Orlovs decided to take action.

On hearing of what was happening, Kyril Razumovsky sent for Taubert, the keeper of the printing press of the Academy of Sciences, of which Razumovsky was president. He told Taubert to go down to the cellars to supervise the printers who were waiting to produce overnight a manifesto, proclaiming the overthrow of the Emperor and the accession of Empress Catherine. Taubert asked to be excused from such a dangerous task. Razumovsky dealt with him brusquely. "You already know too much," he said. "Now your head as well as mine is at stake. Do as I tell you!"[14]

During the night of June 28, 1762, Alexei Orlov and a brother officer rode to Peterhof, arriving at 6 A.M. Alexei Orlov went to Catherine's bedside and awakened her. "It's time to get up. All is ready for you to be proclaimed," he said. Learning of what had happened, she did not hesitate. She quickly put on a black dress and with her trusted maid,

Shargorodskaya, she set out in the waiting carriage on her momentous journey.

Grigori Orlov met them a few miles from St. Petersburg. Catherine transferred to his carriage and continued the journey at a brisker pace. Near the village of Kalinkina Grigori galloped ahead to alert his colleagues of the Izmailovsky Regiment who were quartered there. Catherine approached more slowly, but as soon as she arrived officers and men gave her a tumultuous welcome. The whole regiment at once swore the oath of allegiance to her as Empress Catherine the Second. Shortly afterwards, Razumovsky, Colonel of the Regiment, arrived and he knelt respectfully to kiss her hand in token of his allegiance.

Accompanied now by Razumovsky, Alexei and Grigori Orlov and the Izmailovsky, Catherine rode to the barracks of the Semenovsky Regiment. Again the whole Regiment eagerly swore allegiance to her. Among the Preobrazhensky, however, were certain officers who knew nothing of the conspiracy and tried to hold their men to the oath of loyalty to Peter, but the troops swept them aside.

As Catherine proceeded down the Nevsky Prospekt, escorted by the noisily exultant guards, the townspeople joined in welcoming her. The procession came to a halt at the Kazan Cathedral. Catherine dismounted from her carriage and with the Orlov brothers, Razumovsky and a crowd of guards officers she attended a short service in which priests pronounced the blessing on her as the "Autocrat Catherine the Second" and on "the heir to the throne, Tsarevich Paul Petrovich." As with the guards regiments, there was no attempt to proclaim Paul other than as heir and successor to his mother.

Catherine rode on to the Winter Palace where Panin hurried to her with the eight-year-old Grand Duke whom he had snatched from his bed on learning of the coup. Sentries had been posted, but they admitted to the palace all members of the Senate, the Holy Synod, heads of colleges, army officers, and others who wished to kiss the hand and swear loyalty to the new Empress. About midday Razumovsky's manifesto was proclaimed to the people.

In the midst of this excitement and success Catherine and her supporters were careful to take all precautions, especially in mounting sentries and maintaining patrols. But in the city there was no disorder or rioting. Members of foreign embassies walked freely in the streets and all reported on the good conduct of the crowds. Officers were sent to the troops in Livonia and to the naval fortress in Kronstadt to proclaim the manifesto and administer the new oath of allegiance. There, outside the capital, trouble was most likely.

Catherine had, meanwhile, settled in the Winter Palace in the apartments which Elizabeth had occupied. When she appeared on the balcony she found herself wildly proclaimed by the troops, crowded in the forecourt. At first she had not recognized them. Quartermasters, acting on their own initiative, had brought from their stores the old uniforms introduced by Peter the Great. The troops had at once torn off their hated Prussian uniforms, forced on them by Peter III, and they had stood with great pride cheering their Empress. It had been a small incident, but indicative of the upsurge of national feeling, released by this revolution.

On the morning of June 28 Peter had inspected the troops in Oranienbaum and then had set out with his large suite to celebrate his name day with the Empress in Peterhof. Only when he and his suite arrived there and found that Catherine had gone to St. Petersburg, had they realized that something was amiss. On the advice of the Chancellor, Vorontsov, of Munnich and others he had agreed to set out for the city, but from a young lieutenant of the Preobrazhensky Regiment, who was in charge of a boat carrying fireworks to Peterhof, they learned that all in the city were excitedly hailing their new Empress. This was the first direct news Peter had of the revolution. He agreed now to send a colonel of his suite to Kronstadt to bring a force of three thousand men by sea to Peterhof. He then slumped into a state of lethargy. By this time, however, the Kronstadt garrison had sworn the oath of loyalty to Catherine. When later Peter was rowed in a galley to Kronstadt, he was halted at the entrance to the harbor by a midshipman who threatened to fire on him. Peter was terrified and hurried back to Oranienbaum.

Meanwhile from St. Petersburg, Catherine, now wearing the uniform of a guards officer, mounted on a white horse, and holding a saber, set out at the head of her army for Peterhof. Alexei Orlov rode ahead with an advance guard of hussars. He surrounded Peterhof, meeting with no opposition from the Holstein guards whom he disarmed. On arriving, Catherine was handed an abject letter from Peter, asking her forgiveness, resigning all rights to the throne, and begging to be allowed to retire with Elizabeth Vorontsova to Holstein. Catherine would not consider allowing him to reside in freedom in Holstein, plotting against her. She sent General Izmailov and Grigori Orlov to him, demanding first that he write out and sign a declaration of abdication. He readily signed away the throne and was then brought under strong guard to Peterhof where he was stripped of his Russian uniform, insignia, and sword. Catherine appointed Alexei Orlov in charge of a guard to take Peter to Ropsha and to hold him there until the fortress of Schlusselburg had been made ready for him.

Catherine's revolution had been an easy triumph. She was now eager to return to St. Petersburg to consolidate her position and to begin her reign. On the morning of June 30 she entered the capital to be greeted by an unprecedented welcome. The whole population lined the streets as, still wearing a guards uniform and mounted on her white charger, she led the Preobrazhensky, the Semenovsky, and the Izmailovsky through the city and finally halted at the Winter Palace. It had been an extraordinary revolution.

XIII

Catherine II

1762–1796

Catherine had attained her ambition. She was Empress and Autocrat of the vast Russian Empire. But she had to hold her throne and to rule, and with the acclaim of the whole nation ringing in her ears she did not appreciate at first the magnitude of the task.

The most dangerous threat arose out of the extraordinary paradox of her triumph. A German without a drop of Russian blood in her veins, a Protestant convert to Orthodoxy, and a usurper, she had been swept to the throne of the Romanovs on a wave of patriotic feeling by a people strongly xenophobic, especially in their hatred of Germans, bigoted in their devotion to Orthodoxy and in their suspicion of converts, and staunchly conservative in their traditions. By feats of personality and calculation she had convinced the Russians that she was one of them, and with such force that they eagerly entrusted her with the maintenance of all that they treasured in their national life. But popular enthusiasm could wane and strong policies would incur hostility, such as had mounted against Peter III.

A more serious danger arose from the fact that the guards and the people of St. Petersburg looked upon her as the Empress they had created. The Muscovite Tsars had succeeded by hereditary right and all Russians had accepted them as appointed by God. But Catherine was always to be in the position of supplicant, seeking and buying goodwill and the support of those who maintained her on the throne.

During the first weeks of her reign Catherine was mainly concerned with preparations for her coronation. Peter had not given special thought to this ceremony, although Frederick of Prussia had written to him, stressing its importance. Catherine did not make this mistake. She recognized the religious significance of coronation to her people. She saw also the opportunities that it would provide for magnificent celebrations and for her to appeal to her subjects, and she had an extraordinary talent for projecting herself on such public occasions.

The Russian Autocrats were always crowned in the Uspensky Cathedral in Moscow. Catherine gave instructions for the streets of the old capital to be covered with green fir branches, for special viewing stands to be erected at every vantage point, and the buildings to be gaily draped. For the occasion, moreover, she made Moscow the center of government, moving the Senate and several colleges there. It seemed that she intended restoring Moscow to its former pre-eminence, and this appealed strongly to popular sentiment. Moscow was still the holy city and there was general rejoicing that the new Empress was showing proper respect to Mother Moscow.

Catherine had appointed Prince Trubetskoi in charge of arrangements, allocating fifty thousand rubles for the purpose. But coins to the value of six hundred thousand rubles were sent to Moscow in oak barrels for the personal disposal of the Empress. She took special care over the amnesties to be granted to prisoners and exiles. In these and other preparations she was already demonstrating her great capacity for work and her concern for detail, which were to be important factors in her reign.

Throughout Moscow, popular excitement mounted in anticipation of this great public event. On September 13 Catherine made her ceremonial entry into the city. The people crowded at the windows and on the roofs of buildings and lined the streets, acclaiming her. Nine days later the coronation took place. Twenty bishops, thirty-five archimandrites, and other churchmen chanting psalms, and the guards regiments, brilliantly accoutered, escorted her to the Uspensky Cathedral. After the magnificent ceremony, conducted by the Metropolitan of Novgorod, she proceeded to the Arkhangelsky and Blagoveshchensky Cathedrals in the Kremlin to pray before the holy relics. She then returned to the palace and there received the congratulations of the nobility and the foreign ambassadors. With prodigal hand she bestowed the Orders of St. Andrew and of Alexander Nevsky, bejeweled swords, new titles, and other rewards on all who had supported her. The Orlovs were treated with special generosity and all were created counts.

Catherine was delighted with her coronation and the acclaim of her people. To her ambassador in Warsaw she wrote: "It is impossible to describe to you the joy which the masses of the people show here on seeing me. I have only to make an appearance or to show myself at a window and the cheers are renewed."[1] She was always at her best on such great public occasions. She carried her imperial robes as though born to them. She responded to acclamations with easy smiling grace. She gave gifts and honors with a personal kindness which made the recipients her slaves. Her charm cast a spell over individuals and crowds alike.

From the moment of her accession and throughout these celebrations Catherine did not even momentarily relax her determination to strengthen her grip on the throne. The immediate threat was that two dethroned Emperors were alive and might be seized on as figureheads to rally malcontents, especially among the oppressed peasantry. Catherine knew that only death could remove this threat and within two years both Emperors had died by violent means.

Peter had been taken to Ropsha on the evening of June 29, 1762. He was an abject figure and, suffering from shock, he fainted away several times. But, although under close guard, he received every consideration. Catherine gave instructions that he was to have his violin, his favorite dog and attendants and, when he complained that he could not sleep, his own bed was at once sent from Oranienbaum. But he was cantankerous and abusive, making the lives of the duty officers a torment.

Catherine was still undecided whether to incarcerate him in the fortress of Schlusselburg or to hold him in some place farther from St. Petersburg. Suddenly, on the evening of July 6, the question was resolved for her. She received by hand of a frightened courier a grubby piece of paper on which Alexei Orlov had scribbled a message, apparently in a state of drunken remorse. The message was that Peter was "no longer in this world"; he had perished in a brawl among the officers of his guard.[2] There may have been a plot to murder him, but no evidence of such a plot has survived, nor apparently was Catherine directly implicated in his death. She appears to have played the passive role, as in the revolution, of waiting on others to take the action she desired. But once Peter was dead she acted decisively, and on the following day she signed a manifesto, proclaiming the death from natural causes of the former Emperor. Two years later the unfortunate Ivan VI, imprisoned for most of his life in Schlusselburg, was cruelly murdered by his guards. Again she was not implicated directly, but she did not disguise from her confidants her relief and delight over his death.[3]

In these first months of her reign Catherine found her great skill in handling people put to severe test. She needed all the support she could find and drew around her everybody of ability and experience, retaining, where possible, the services of those who had sided with her husband. She recalled Bestuzhev, the former Chancellor, from exile, but kept Vorontsov in office. Count Nikita Panin was her chief adviser. She had few men of his caliber on whom to rely but, knowing his ideas on limiting the power of the Autocrat and on the rights of Paul to the throne, she handled him with special care.

The most troublesome problems were, however, posed by her intimate supporters, Dashkova and Grigori Orlov. They were possessive toward her and each was fiercely jealous of the other. Dashkova was, moreover, a bitter opponent of all the Orlovs. The nineteen-year-old Princess made enemies fearlessly and in her arrogance, her high moral principles, and her conceit, she was a constant source of discord. She resented in particular the special attention which Catherine showed to Grigori Orlov, and also the role that he had played in the revolution. She was sincere in her high morality, as in her idolizing of Catherine, and her realization of her friend's moral lapse, especially with someone she hated, depressed her.

On the march to Peterhof to crush the Emperor finally, Dashkova had ridden at Catherine's side. She, too, wore the uniform of a guards officer and she reveled in the drama of the occasion. She had busied herself in Peterhof in issuing orders, inspecting sentries, and tirelessly taking it upon herself to represent the Empress. Entering Catherine's apartment she was shocked to find Grigori Orlov lounging on a sofa and casually opening state papers. She demanded to know on what authority he was reading such important papers.

"The Empress asked me to open them," he replied.

"I doubt it," she said heatedly. "No action has to be taken on them for a few days yet and the Empress will appoint people to deal with them officially. Neither you nor I are qualified for that work."[4] Dashkova then swept out of the room. When she returned later, Grigori was still reclining on the sofa with the papers. But Catherine was with him and clearly she acquiesced in what he was doing.

Dashkova was, in fact, too unbridled in her enthusiasms and prejudices to be an easy friend and ally. She lacked the amalgam of hypocrisy essential for success at court. Her own family, and especially Chancellor Vorontsov, considered her to be dangerous. He wrote that "her capricious and intemperate behavior and opinions will so anger the Empress that she will be sent from court and through her downfall our family will incur unjust public disgrace."[5] Catherine was soon obliged to admonish her for taking too much on herself. Dashkova flared up in anger, and Catherine handled her with the gentle patience which was part of her power over people. But also Catherine recognized her exceptional abilities and later as Director of the Academy of Sciences she was a brilliant success.

Grigori Orlov caused Catherine greater anxiety. He still saw her as his mistress and the woman whom he had made Empress. Proud, ambitious and not highly intelligent, he did not appreciate her strength of character and her abilities, and he resented his new position as her male courtesan. His role was the more galling because he could now claim so little part in her life. Already she had established her own disciplined routine of rising at 5 A.M., working fifteen hours a day and falling exhausted into bed at night. A few minutes snatched from this crowded day was usually all that she could spare her lover. But Grigori saw power within his grasp through marriage with her. He began pressing her to marry him, but received only evasive answers.

Persistent rumors were heard in Moscow and St. Petersburg that the Empress would marry again and that her choice would be Grigori Orlov. Bestuzhev gathered signatures to a humble petition that she should take a husband, indicating that Grigori Orlov would be the popular choice. But many Russians had misgivings. The Orlovs had lost much of their popularity through arrogance and abuse of their new-found eminence. Catherine was alarmed to learn of a conspiracy to murder them. A gentleman at court, named Khitrovo, was the leader, and interrogation established that he was a loyal and devoted subject and that, provided that she married someone worthy of her and the throne, he was in no way opposed to her taking a second husband. But he considered that marriage with one of the Orlovs would bring disaster. Catherine did not punish him for conspiring, but merely sent him from the court, to live quietly on his country estate. She also issued a general instruction, forbidding idle gossip on this subject of her remarriage and, as people at court and in the cities realized that she did not intend to marry again, the rumors ceased.

Grigori Orlov became more moody and boorish. He threatened to resign from the imperial service and, although she had power to command, she gently dissuaded him. He courted other women to provoke her. She humored him because she knew that he might be dangerous, but also because she had a deep affection for him. He had completely displaced the gallant Pole, Stanislas Poniatowski, who was in Warsaw and wanted to marry her, not for the throne, but because he sincerely loved her. She temporized, giving no answer to either suitor. She had, in fact, resolved that, although they might serve as her lovers, neither Grigori Orlov nor Poniatowski would ever share her throne, for love of power transcended all else in her life.

Catherine was, indeed, insatiable in her ambition. She was not content with attaining the throne and wielding absolute power over the Russian Empire. Power and position had extended her horizons. She was determined now to achieve fame that would resound throughout the civilized world and would make so great an impact on her age that her contemporaries and generations to come would acclaim her. Ambition on such a scale has a certain grandeur which commands admiration. To a remarkable degree, moreover, she achieved her ambition, although her achievement was in many fields no more than an imposing façade.

A genius for publicity and promotion was one important reason for her success. She considered presentation to be an essential instrument in the art of government. She took pains in herself drafting ukazi and manifestoes and also in her public appearances to appeal to her people and to create the image of herself as their wise and humane Autocrat. As time passed and she felt more secure, she became more concerned about her impact upon the rest of Europe and in projecting herself as the most enlightened of monarchs. Many of her manifestoes were specially translated for European distribution. Within Russia the imperial voice was heard without challenge or competition, but this did not apply in the rest of Europe and she had to take care not to appear to be stridently protesting her own virtues. Astutely she secured the services of an influential chorus which included the leading publicists, artists, and intellectuals of the day. She won their support by flattery and generosity. A typical instance was her kindness to Diderot, which was soon the talk of Europe. He was plagued by money troubles and proposed selling his library. She at once bought it, but left it in his possession, and then appointed him librarian of his own library at a handsome stipend. Many of the leading writers and artists of the day enjoyed her patronage; in fact anyone who showed her affection, rendered her service, or sang her praises found her to be extravagantly generous.

The most influential of her correspondents and allies, however, was Voltaire, and he led the chorus in her praise in Europe. Now close on seventy, Voltaire kept up a vast correspondence and received distinguished visitors from all countries at Ferney, his wealthy estate on French soil but conveniently near to Geneva. He was already a legend as the sage whose wit, energy, and fearless denunciations of injustice and tyrany inspired the young men of the day. To them, as Goethe later testified, he "governed the whole civilized world."[6]

Voltaire had long been interested in Russia. He had written the *Histoire de Charles XII*, dwelling in detail on the Northern War, and as early as 1745 had tried to prompt Empress Elizabeth to commission him to write a history of her illustrious father. For twelve years she had delayed her answer, mainly because of her suspicion of this irreligious Frenchman who never went to church. Ivan Shuvalov had finally negotiated the commission and the second volume of the *Histoire de l'Empire de Russie sous Pierre le Grand* had appeared in 1763.[7]

Within a few weeks of her accession Catherine began making approaches to Voltaire. He was reserved toward her at first, because she was an usurper who seemed unlikely to hold her throne and because she was rumored in the West to have been implicated in the murder of her husband. By flattery and acts of generosity to his friends, however, she won him to her cause. The correspondence which they began in 1763 continued until his death fourteen years later. She took great care over her letters to him because they were "always in some degree documents of state," representing what she wanted him to pass on to his many influential friends.[8] She fired in him the vision of herself as the Empress of the Enlightenment, who would bring about the salvation of Russia by applying the principles of justice and tolerance which he had tirelessly proclaimed. He clung to this image of her although as the years passed he must have known that behind the façade of enlightenment she was an extreme reactionary.

The project which first aroused his enthusiasm was her *Nakaz* or Instruction for the recasting of the laws of Russia. This was her fanfare to the rest of Europe, announcing that a new era was beginning in the East. She planned to summon a grand legislative commission, comprising representatives of governmental institutions and deputies from all social classes and races of the Empire to carry out a radical reform and reordering of the Russian legal code.

In January 1765 Catherine began working on the *Nakaz* for the guidance of the legislative commission. She methodically devoted three hours to it each day and finished it two years later. To the Russians it was a document of startling novelty. She had drawn on the advanced philosophical ideas then current in the West. Of the 526 articles of the *Nakaz*, as finally published, 250 were taken directly from Montesquieu's *L'Esprit des Lois* and one hundred articles came from Beccaria's *Of Punishments and Crimes*. She had copied the articles literally. She made no claims to original or creative intelligence. As she wrote frankly when sending a copy of the *Nakaz* to Frederick of Prussia, "You will see that, like the crow in the fable, I have decked myself in peacock's feathers; in this work merely the arrangement of the material and here and there a line or word belong to me."[9]

The *Nakaz* was nevertheless a remarkable document. Chapter 1 asserted that "Russia is a European nation." Chapter 2 stated that "the Sovereign is absolute . . ." and contained the characteristic statement that "the intention and end of monarchy is the glory of the citizens, of the state, and of the Sovereign." Many articles showed that she recognized the evils at the root of Russia's problems. She pointed to the insupportable burdens of the peasantry and especially to the taxes imposed by nobles "who seldom or never reside in their villages" and were "without the least regard to the means by which the peasants may be able to raise this money." She stressed that misery and oppression of the people were the reasons for the depopulation of vast areas of the country. Other articles defined political freedom and equality, condemned corruption, and the use of torture in obtaining evidence.[10]

By June 1767 deputies of various races, ranks, and creeds from every part of the Russian Empire had assembled in Moscow. Moslem Tatars and Bashkirs, Buddhist Kalmyks and pagan Samoeds mingled with Orthodox Russians of every class, except the serfs, the largest and most sorely oppressed class, which was not represented at all. Catherine made a state entry into the city and on June 30 with magnificent ceremony formally opened the legislative commission in the ancient Granovitaya Palace. The *Nakaz* was read aloud to the deputies who interrupted with outbursts of applause. They were, however, confused by these instructions which were alien to Russian thought and experience. Moreover, when they settled to work, they were divided into various committees which complicated the proceedings. Reports by deputies on the wishes of their people took up so much time that they had to be abandoned. The commission moved to St. Petersburg at the end of the year but, burdened by its procedure and the impossibility of its task of reforming and codifying the law, it had already ceased to function. At the end of 1768 the commission was prorogued. Deputies dispersed to their homes to await a further summons, but no summons ever came.

The grand legislative commission had thus failed completely in its declared purpose. It had, however, served Catherine in projecting her image and especially in winning her the acclaim of the rest of Europe. Voltaire declared in a letter to her that the *Nakaz* was "the most beautiful monument of the century. It will bring you more glory than ten battles on the shores of the Danube, for it is in the end your work; your genius conceived it, your fair hand has written it . . ."[11] In Russia, after the dissolution of the legislative commission, the *Nakaz* was kept under lock and key; in Europe by contrast it circulated in twenty-three versions. When in 1771 the French prohibited the import of two thousand copies of a French translation, the seal was set on her renown as the truly enlightened monarch of the age.

Meanwhile the *Nakaz* no longer reflected her own ideas and became merely a gambit in her great promotion campaign. As Grand Duchess she had been enamored of the advanced ideas then current in France. She had probably cherished dreams of developing Peter the Great's reforms further, of creating in Russia a society of freemen, ruled by law and watched over by herself as benevolent Autocrat. But on mounting the throne the experience of power and responsibility and, even more, concern for her security, made her abandon such idealistic plans. She owed her throne to the nobility and gentry and she took care to ensure their continued support. She knew that the peasantry were oppressed and felt sympathy for their sufferings, but they could not be of direct use to her. Far from relieving them of their burdens, therefore, she met the demand of the landowning class for wider powers over them. In 1765, for instance, when embarking on the *Nakaz* she granted landowners the power to sentence their serfs to hard labor in Siberia. They had had the power to exile serfs to Siberia in Elizabeth's reign, and many serfs had pioneered new lives for themselves in this virgin expanse. But in future they were to be condemned as convicts to hard labor without hope of freedom. In August 1767, when the deputies were pondering the lofty injunctions of the *Nakaz*, Catherine approved an ukaz, submitted by the Senate, which condemned to the knout and exile with hard labor for life any peasant who petitioned or complained against his landowner. In Peter the Great's reign, serfs had frequently exercised their right to petition against ill-treatment, and he had made strenuous efforts to ensure that such petitions were investigated and that action followed. By this monstrous ukaz Catherine had quietly expunged the sole remaining right of the serfs, condemning them to suffer in silence. Indeed, in her reign serfdom developed into its extreme form as an institution of slave labor.

Unrest among the oppressed peasant masses waxed dangerously. At a crucial stage in her reign when at war with Turkey and menaced by Sweden, it erupted suddenly in the terrible rebellion known as the *Pugachevshchina*, after its leader the Don Cossack, Emelyan Pugachev. Uniting serfs, Cossacks, and Asiatic nomads in Eastern Russia in what rapidly developed into a social revolution, it swept like a steppe fire toward Moscow, threatening to reduce her throne to ashes.

Pugachev had served with bravery in the Russian army and then had deserted. He took refuge with Old Believers in the Ukraine and finally escaped down the Volga to the Irgiz River, several hundred miles farther to the east. In May 1773 he suddenly turned up at the head of a motley band of troops in the Orenburg region. He now proclaimed that he was the Emperor Peter III who had made a miraculous escape from Ropsha before Catherine's henchman could murder him. Peasants and Cossacks believed his story. The simple people were always credulously ready to accept false Tsars. There had already been three or four imposters claiming to be Peter III, but all had been caught and executed before they could cause trouble. Pugachev was to prove more dangerous because he was an inspiring leader and also because his appearance coincided with the spreading of a curious rumor that Peter III had intended liberating the serfs and giving them the land that they worked, and that the Empress had prevented him.

Pugachev's first supporters were drawn from the Yaik Cossacks who were mainly Old Believers in revolt against the Orthodox Church and against the imperial government. They were joined by the Bashkirs, Kalmuks, Kirghiz, and other Tatar tribes as well as by industrial serfs from the mines and foundries of the Ural region. By autumn 1773 he had extended his authority along the Volga and in the Urals, repelling detachments of government troops sent against him, and laying siege to Orenburg.

Pugachev's strength grew day by day. He now set up his own court, apeing the imperial court. He gave his leading courtiers such names as Orlov, Panin, and Vorontsov, and produced an heir whom he called Grand Duke Paul. He even appointed, in a startling inversion of Catherine's reputed custom, six concubines to serve him as maids of honor. He issued his own ukazi, proclaiming his intention of killing off the nobility, distributing the land among the peasants, and locking Catherine away in a nunnery. No program could have appealed more strongly to the people and it released a destructive fury to which Pugachev gave the lead. He brutally murdered all landowners and officers who fell into his hands, enlisting into his army the peasants and troops.

Savage rebellions, led by Cossacks, the wild, treacherous, marauding horsemen of the southern and southeastern borderlands, had broken out in every century. Stenka Razin had defied Tsar Alexei for two years, and Peter the Great had crushed a similar revolt, led by Bulavin. On each occasion the rebellion had drawn its strength from the support of the peasants, fighting for freedom from the burdens of serfdom and for the land which they worked. Pugachev's movement was, however, far greater in scale and it was waged from the outset as a war for peasant liberation against the landowning nobility. The fact that the nobles had been freed from all duties of service and the false hopes aroused by Catherine's early manifestoes, followed by her ukazi which finally crushed their hopes of liberation, had added to the bitterness of the serfs.

Excited by a desperate urge for vengeance and freedom, peasants throughout Eastern Russia set fire to the houses of their landowners, savagely killing them and their families, and their hated overseers.[12] Smoke from burning mansions and forests, fired by peasant bands, hung like curtains on the horizon. Local uprisings had been numerous since Catherine had come to the throne. They had, however, been put down promptly by detachments of troops. The chief rebels had been cruelly knouted and executed or, their nostrils torn out with iron pincers and their cheeks branded with hot irons, they had been sent to hard labor in Siberia. But Pugachev's rebellion was far more formidable. His army was fifteen thousand strong and growing rapidly. In Moscow where many landowners had taken refuge, a feeling of panic spread as all awaited the dreaded news that his army was marching on the city.

Catherine was well aware of the gravity of this revolt and of the dangerous mood of the peasantry in all parts of the country. But with her army fully engaged against the Turks, she could spare only small detachments instead of the great punitive expedition needed to put down the rebellion. She was deeply disturbed, but she remained gay, poised, and active, displaying nothing of the stress that she felt. In December 1773 when the menace of Pugachev was mounting dangerously, she welcomed Diderot in St. Petersburg. She dined with him every night of his visit, lasting several weeks, and sat late talking with him on freedom and the rights of man. In his enthusiasm as he expounded his ideas, he even slapped her on the knee, a familiarity which astonished the court, but she took no offense. At this time she also had frequent meetings with Melchior Grimm, the gallicized German whose bulletin of literature and gossip, *Correspondence Litteraire*, was read in all the courts of Europe. He was to become her most regular correspondent, the influential vendor of her news and views, and her main agent in carrying out commissions in Paris and elsewhere.

News of Pugachev's rebellion spread quickly through Western Europe. Catherine was anxious to play down its importance. Writing to Voltaire in January 1774 she dismissed Pugachev as a mere "highwayman," and she complained that the newspapers were making too much fuss of him. But in a later letter she confessed to him that "for more than six weeks I have been obliged to devote my uninterrupted attention to this affair."[13]

In the early months of 1774 Catherine was at a serious disadvantage. The rebellion was spreading and Pugachev was preparing to march on Moscow. The Turkish Grand Vizir had massed a mightly army and, with civil war raging over a large part of Russia, he was confident of victory. But Catherine had in Suvorov a general of genius. At Kirsova, with a force of three thousand men, he routed twelve thousand Turks and again at Kozludji he defeated a Turkish army of forty thousand men. The decisive victory was won by Rumyantsev, who surrounded the main Turkish army at Shumla, compelling it to surrender. On July 21 the famous treaty of Kuchuk-Kainardji was signed.

Catherine acted promptly. She ordered Count Peter Panin to march eastwards without delay to suppress the rebels. Panin drove Pugachev toward Chernoyarsk, and he escaped only by swimming across the broad Volga. But he now appeared to lose his zeal and his capacity for leadership. His followers, dreading the conflict with the imperial army, began deserting. Finally a group of his closest lieutenants betrayed him in return for pardon for themselves. They delivered him, bound hand and foot, to an advance detachment, commanded by Suvorov, who took him to Simbirsk. From there he was taken in an iron cage to Moscow where he was tried and in January 1775 publicly beheaded.

Catherine had insisted that the rebels must be treated with humanity. She refused to allow torture and she displayed the greatest clemency to all the rebels, except the leaders. She recognized that peasant unrest continued to be acute and that it might readily lead to further rebellions on a similar scale. Indeed, she knew that the enslavement of the peasants under serfdom must inevitably lead to a great cataclysm which would sweep across Russia in a destructive wave. Soon after the execution of Pugachev she wrote to her minister of justice concerning the peasants that "If we do not consent to diminish cruelty and moderate a situation which is intolerable to the human race, then sooner or later they will take this step themselves."[14] She clearly counted on it happening later rather than sooner. While acknowledging the cruelty and inhumanity, she made no attempt to combat or moderate it. In the early part of her reign she was dependent on the support of the landowning classes who perpetuated serfdom. But this dependence had diminished. Indeed, the Pugachev revolt had brought them rallying around her throne for protection. This factor, together with the prestige of her victories over the Turks and the strong support of the army gave her the strength and opportunity to meet this great challenge of her reign. But she evaded it and even went to reactionary extremes in extending the powers of the nobility and the gentry and in enormously increasing the number of peasants condemned to serfdom. At the same time her public protestations of humane principles and the rights of man became more frequent and vehement. She took special pains that they should be publicized in Western Europe so that she could bask in the false glory of being the enlightened Empress.

By contrast with the hypocrisy and oppression of her internal rule, Catherine's foreign policies were crowned with great successes, although at times her concern for immediate glory limited her vision and her capacity for statesmanship. On becoming Empress her first thought had been to secure peace. Her avowed opposition to Peter III's pro-Prussian policy had been no more than an expedient, allowing her to appeal to the strong anti-Prussian feelings of the Russian people. In fact, she had embarked on a policy, known sometimes as the Northern System, involving the reorientation of Russia's alliances. This system, devised by Panin, provided for a coalition of all the northern non-Catholic countries, but including Poland, under the leadership of Russia and opposed to the southern Catholic alliance of Austria, France, and Spain. But the countries in the northern alliance had interests too divergent to allow them to work in harmony, nor would they accept the leadership of Russia.

The Polish succession posed the first major problem of foreign policy after her accession. Catherine wrote to Stanislas Poniatowski, her former lover, of her wish that he should be King of Poland. His devotion to her personally and his gentle indecisive nature would make him an admirable Russian puppet, and he would do nothing to stem what she called "the fortunate anarchy" which kept Poland weak and subservient.[15] Again Austria and France were intriguing to secure the election of their candidate, this time the Elector of Saxony. Catherine and Frederick of Prussia concluded a general defensive alliance on March 31, 1764, and agreed a secret convention, designed to ensure that Poland remained weak. The election took place in August. Russian troops had entered Poland in the previous May to make sure that the Poles elected the Russian candidate, and Poniatowski duly became King Stanislas Augustus of Poland. But the new Russo-Prussian alliance and Russia's complete domination of Poland alarmed and antagonized Austria and France, who now applied all their influence in Constantinople to bring the Ottoman Porte to war against Russia.

Alarmed by the growing power of Russia, the Sultan was ready to heed the appeals from dissident Poles and the advice of the French and Austrians, and toward the end of 1768 he declared war. During the winter of 1768–69 Turks and Russians hurriedly mobilized their forces. The main Russian army, commanded by Prince Golitsyn, advanced toward Moldavia to prevent the Poles supporting the Turkish army and to threaten Turkey in the Balkans. In September, Golitsyn won a victory in capturing the fortress town of Khotin on the Dniester River. But Golitsyn inspired no confidence as commander. Catherine appointed Prince P. A. Rumyantsev in his place and General Peter Panin, brother of her chief minister, took command of the army, posted near Bender. Both were very competent generals. Indeed Catherine was fortunate to have in her service a number of able commanders, of whom Rumyantsev and Suvorov were quite outstanding, and for this she was indebted to Elizabeth who had first given them opportunity and experience in the Seven Years' War, and who had revitalized Peter the Great's army.

Catherine also gave urgent orders for the refitting of ships and the construction of new squadrons in the Baltic shipyards. She enlisted the services of three English admirals and a large number of English officers and seamen. In September 1769 two Russian squadrons sailed from the Baltic and, after revictualling in English ports, passed into the Mediterranean. Never before had Russian ships of war sailed along the European coast. Many in the West were alarmed and saw in it something portentous, and Catherine took care to aggravate their fears by her propaganda.

The purpose of this naval expedition was to challenge the Turks in the Aegean Sea, to force the Dardanelles, taking Constantinople, and then joining up with the Russian armies on the northern shores of the Black Sea. This ambitious plan succeeded to a remarkable degree, and might have succeeded completely but for the limitations of the Russian commander-in-chief. This was Alexei Orlov, who had no naval experience and was too impetuous to command on such a scale, but he had under him three able admirals in the Russian, Spiridov, and the two Englishmen, Greig and Elphinston. Off Chios the Russian squadrons engaged and defeated the far stronger Turkish fleet. The Turks then took refuge in Chesme Bay. Admirals Elphinston and Greig at once barred their exit from the bay and sent in fire ships which destroyed the whole Turkish fleet. The Russians were now masters of the Aegean, but Alexei Orlov failed to press his advantage by sailing with all speed to force the Dardanelles. The Battle of Chesme was nevertheless a signal naval victory, comparable with Peter the Great's defeat of the Swedish navy at Hango fifty-six years earlier. Catherine celebrated with magnificent festivities in which all Russians joined wholeheartedly. She was also prompt to spread the news through Western Europe, and to Voltaire she wrote a special account of the battle in her own hand.[16]

Couriers were soon bringing to St. Petersburg reports of further great victories on land. Rumyantsev had advanced into Moldavia and had captured Jassy, the capital. Next he had defeated a far stronger Turkish army at Fokshani, and had inflicted total defeat on the Turks at Kagul on the Pruth, thus confirming Russia's conquest of the Turkish provinces north of the Danube.

In the midst of her jubilation, however, Catherine was compelled to exercise restraint. Such tremendous victories threatened her with war on a scale which was beyond the strength of the nation. Austria and France were both alarmed by these demonstrations of Russian power and in particular by the danger that Russia would seek to conquer the Balkans. Frederick of Prussia was disturbed by the very real danger of another European war, for if Austria marched against Russia, Prussia would be involved, and France was bound to intervene. This was not part of Frederick's plan. He took the initiative of meeting with Joseph II of Austria and then of proposing that Catherine should limit her Turkish conquests and recompense herself at the expense of Poland.

Meanwhile in the campaign of 1771 Prince Dolgoruky had conquered the Crimea. This had been for centuries the base from which the Tatars had invaded Russia, at times threatening to take Moscow and, apart from causing terrible devastation, they carried off thousands of young Russians to sell as slaves. At any other time the conquest of the Crimea would have led to the wildest celebrations among all Russians, but now the country lay in the grip of a terrible plague. Brought from the Turkish front, it raged most seriously in Moscow. Each day some eight hundred people were dying in the city. Corpses lay piled in the streets. The living were in a state of terror and opposed all attempts to enforce quarantine regulations. They took refuge in superstition, believing that only the intercession of the saints could help them. The holy ikon of the Mother of God, near the Varvarskaya Gate of the Kremlin, was reputed to work miracles. Crowds gathered in prayer before the ikon, and the contagion spread. Catherine's efforts to enforce order in the old city were ineffectual. Finally, she sent Grigori Orlov, who took prompt measures to which she publicly attributed the decline of the plague. It was, however, the onset of winter which checked the contagion. By mid-November deaths had fallen to 150 a day and by January 1772 the plague had halted. But during 1771 more than 133,000 people in Moscow, Kiev, and other parts of Russia had perished in its horrible agonies.

Adding to the strains of war and plague at this time was the difficulty of establishing mastery over Poland. The Polish confederates, fighting against Russian control, were acting with new boldness and even managed to kidnap the King, Stanislas Augustus, at one stage. They were, moreover, receiving aid from France and Austria and their resistance was growing in scale. Catherine realized that the subjection of Poland might become a serious drain on Russian resources. She readily accepted, therefore, the proposals of Frederick of Prussia for a partition of Poland in which Austria would share. The treaties of partition were signed in July 1772 and in the following year the Polish Diet, meeting under the shadows of Russian guns and with many of its members in Russia's pay, formally approved the partition. Russia gained a large part of White Russia which was populated by Russians and was, in fact, Russian 'territory. But neither Prussia nor Austria could claim similar justification for their gains.

During the Turkish war and the Pugachev rebellion Catherine had felt acutely the loneliness of her position. She needed a man who would not only satisfy her sensual demands but would also be a companion and partner, but a partner who would not diminish her power and prestige. Grigori Orlov had been a satisfactory lover, but had fallen far short of the man she needed. He was a gallant officer but uneducated and without capacity for government or diplomacy. Desperately he had tried to remedy these defects. He threw himself into the study of physics and astronomy, but he made slow progress and lost interest. Since Catherine corresponded with Voltaire and Diderot, he began corresponding with Jean-Jacques Rousseau, whose philosophy she detested. He made himself the patron of Lomonosov and on his death he bought his papers and library from the widow, which he had classified in a special library, built for the purpose. But he remained unsuitable for high office.

For nearly ten years Catherine had kept him at her side, bearing with his moods and tempers. She knew she could never depend on him except in such an emergency as the plague. In fact, his success in restoring order in Moscow in 1771 marked the peak of his career. But his personal relations with Cahterine had long been declining and she decided to make the break. She appointed him as her representative at the conference with the Turks at Fokshani in the spring of 1772. She did not expect great results from this conference and was confident that he could do nothing to damage Russian interests there. Perhaps she was merely concerned to make sure that he was absent from court at this time, for within a few weeks of his departure a new favorite, Alexander Vassilchikov, a handsome young guards officer, had taken up residence in the palace as his successor.

Learning of this change, Grigori Orlov raged like a madman. He set out at once, without thought for the conference, and rode in a fury on the long journey to St. Petersburg. All at court waited in fear of his arrival. Catherine herself had new, especially strengthened locks fitted to the doors of her apartments and those of her new favorite and posted extra sentries throughout the palace. Grigori reached Moscow, but as he was leaving he was handed special orders from the Empress, which halted him in his headlong journey. Her orders were that he was to retire to his estate at Gatshina and to remain there, and officially he was in quarantine, having come from the plague area in the south. Grigori obeyed, his fury suddenly spent. Moreover, he accepted her generous terms of dismissal. She deprived him of all military ranks and appointments which gave him command of troops, and banned him from appearing at court. But she bestowed on him a palace, a gift of two hundred thousand rubles, a life pension of fifteen thousand rubles, and authority to choose from crown lands an estate with ten thousand peasant serfs.

The dismissal of Grigori Orlov caused a major upheaval at court. Many expected that he would soon be restored to favor. But Catherine had no intention of reviving the relationship. She was relieved at the same time that the other Orlov brothers continued to serve loyally and that the danger which she had greatly feared, that they might join with Panin in some plan to place Grand Duke Paul, who had now come of age, on the throne in her place, did not materialize. But Catherine's life, the court, and indeed the whole country, was soon to be excited by a new favorite, who proved to be one of the most brilliant and bizarre characters in Russia's history.

The office of favorite had become established and influential during the reigns of the Empresses who had followed after the death of Peter the Great. In the reign of Catherine, however, the office became notorious because, craving the attentions of handsome, virile young men, she never allowed it to fall vacant. Indeed, she established a certain routine in making these very personal appointments. Any young officer or courtier, who caught her eye and impressed her as equipped for the duties of favorite, was first examined by her personal physician, the Scot Dr. John Rogerson, for she had a horror of venereal disease. The young man was then tested by her lady-in-waiting, Countess Bruce, or later, after the Countess had been found guilty of excess of zeal in fulfilling her duties, by Madame Protassov, who reported to Catherine on his prowess as a lover.[17] Having passed these tests he became personal adjutant-general to Her Imperial Majesty, and was established in an apartment which communicated with hers by way of a special staircase. He received an installation present of ten to twenty thousand rubles, an estate with several hundred peasants, and a monthly stipend. His duties were to escort the Empress and to be available when she required him. In later years, after Catherine had discovered that certain of her favorites had been unfaithful, they were confined to the palace and watched carefully. But none of these tests or restrictions was ever applied to Grigori Alexandrovich Potemkin, who was a law unto himself.

In childhood Potemkin had suffered from the furies of his father who was at best a morose, difficult man, insanely jealous of his intelligent and spirited young wife. His parents could not afford tutors for him, but he was given some education by the village deacon and, after 1746, when his father died and his mother moved to Moscow with his five sisters, by a cousin named Kislovsky, who was a senior civil servant and treated him as his own son. Potemkin showed unusual brilliance in his studies. He was attracted especially by theology and thought seriously of taking holy orders, but equally he was drawn to a military career. While still a boy he entered the newly established University of Moscow; he won the gold medal for the outstanding scholar and was presented to Empress Elizabeth. Suddenly, however, he lost all interest in study and in 1760 was expelled for laziness. He joined the Horse Guards as a private and in due course was commissioned.

The excitements and splendor of life in the capital swept him up and, although poor by the standards of most of his fellow officers, he joined in their wild extravagant life. He was soon closely involved with the Orlovs, and he joined eagerly in their conspiracy to place Catherine on the throne. He was active during the revolution and was among those who received rewards for their support. Moreover, he received a minor appointment, giving him access to the court.

Now aged twenty-three, Potemkin was very tall, but slender in build, brown-haired, and striking rather than handsome in feature. He was widely read, intelligent, and a brilliant conversationalist. He could enliven any company by his sense of humor, his gift of mimicry, and his pleasant singing voice. Soon he was a member of Catherine's small inner circle of intimates. She was charmed by his company. Once, talking of his talent for mimicry, she asked whether he could impersonate anyone. He at once gave a perfect imitation of her way of speaking, even reproducing her strong German accent. It was an entertaining performance, but impertinent. Laughing heartily she forgave him. She was already strongly attracted by this elegant young officer who had a bold imagination and fine intellect, allied with tremendous energy and ambition and who, moreover, was clearly in love with her. But suddenly he lost one eye and withdrew from court.[18]

For a year and a half he lived like a hermit on his small estate. He read and meditated and refused to see any one. Catherine enquired frequently after him and finally her gentle persuasion brought about his return to court.

During the next ten years Catherine made use of his abilities and advanced him in the army, preparing him for high office. He was assistant to the chief Procurator of the Holy Synod, and then served as Protector of the Tatars and other Asiatic races of the Empire. In 1768 he was appointed a chamberlain of the court, an office bringing him into closer contact with her. He was eager, however, to distinguish himself as a soldier and volunteered for active service on the outbreak of war with Turkey. He fought with outstanding bravery, gaining promotion and decorations and the praise of his commander-in-chief, especially for his inspiring leadership of the cavalry.

Potemkin hastened to St. Petersburg to report to the Empress on conditions at the front. It was presumably during this short visit that he declared his love. She was herself already enamored of this dynamic young giant, known as "Cyclops" at court. She granted him permission to write personal letters to her, and it was a significant concession, for an elaborate protocol surrounded the Empress. Potemkin returned to the front and, while engaged in the siege of Silistria, he received a cryptic letter from her which he took to signify the beginning of their affair.[19]

Potemkin hastened to St. Petersburg, arriving in January 1774. He was staggered to find, however, that Vassilchikov was still apparently established as favorite. He asked urgently for a private audience. Catherine was then at Tsarskoe Selo, some twenty miles from the capital. There he had a long meeting with her from which he returned in a radiant mood. Vassilchikov was, in fact, about to be removed. Gentle, good-looking, and intelligent, he was entertaining company, but no companion to support her in bearing the heavy burdens of the throne. He had given her a period of quiet after the storms of Grigori Orlov, but now she was bored with him. She did not act precipitately, however, for the favorite was a person of influence at court. In particular she took care to avoid disturbing Panin, who was known to be alarmed by the prospect of someone as impetuous, ambitious, and energetic as Potemkin in office.

Meanwhile Vassilchikov remained officially the favorite. Potemkin seethed with impatience. He became taciturn and moody, and absented himself from court. Catherine was anxious as to what this furious, unpredictable man might do next. Finally he retired into the Alexander Nevsky Monastery and, knowing his strong religious bent, she began to fear that she had lost him. She sent Countess Bruce to the monastery to tell him that, if he returned to court, he could count on receiving the greatest favors. He put aside his monastic robe, shaved off his beard, and returned with the Countess. Catherine delayed no longer. Vassilchikov retired to Moscow, laden with presents. Potemkin was installed in his place. A few days later he appointed Lieutenant Colonel of the Preobrazhensky Guards, of which the sovereign was always the colonel; this was the first of the innumerable honors to be showered upon him.

Potemkin had by this time lost his slim, elegant figure. He was aged thirty-four, ten years younger than Catherine, and the British ambassador reported that "his figure is gigantic and disproportioned, and his countenance very far from engaging."[20] But he possessed a magnificent compelling vigor which made Catherine's passion for him understandable. "I have put away a certain excellent but very boring citizen [Vassilchikov]," she wrote to Grimm, "who has been immediately replaced, I know not how, by one of the greatest, the most strange, and the most amusing eccentrics of this iron age."[21] Deeply in love and supremely happy in the passionate fullhearted devotion which he gave her, she was like a woman transformed. They spent part of every day alone together and, when apart, they exchanged notes. Catherine's brief note—"My little father, my pigeon I love you to excess"—was typical. Some of her terms of endearment—"Little Parrot," "My Golden Pheasant," "Kitten"—were charmingly absurd as applied to this one-eyed giant of a man. At times, after a quarrel, she would cajole him with mock insults; one note ended with the words, "I am, however, full of tenderness for you, Giaour, Muscovite, Cossack, Pugachev, Golden Cockerel, Cat, Pheasant, Golden Tiger, Lion in the Jungle."[22]

Potemkin was not an easy lover. He had moods of depression, of fury, of mad jealousy, and it was Catherine who wooed him. Often she was the patient supplicant, begging not only his smiles, but even his company. One note, typical of many, read, "My little father, I came to see you to tell you how much I love you, but found your door locked."[23]

Catherine had surrendered herself almost completely to Potemkin and it was said that they were secretly married.[24] She consulted him on everything and usually she followed his advice. He worked furiously on a number of major projects and with his capacity for work and his abilities as soldier and administrator he added to the renown of her reign. But in the midst of this tempestuous affair she still retained a certain commonsense. She was at pains to restrain him in his dealings with the Orlovs and with Panin who resented his power. He was invariably gentle and courteous toward inferiors, but could be insufferably arrogant and rude to equals. But he listened to her advice and took care not to provoke hostilities.

The union of this remarkable couple was, however, devoid of

harmony, although they loved each other deeply. Catherine remained at heart an orderly, disciplined German princess. Potemkin was distinctively Russian in his furious excesses, his moods of exuberant joy followed by deepest depression, his tremendous bouts of work, alternating with spells of lethargy when he would lie for hours on a couch, wearing only a dressing gown and biting his fingernails, often prey to the most morbid thoughts.

Potemkin, who overawed all at court and was a legend in his own lifetime, was perhaps understood only by Catherine. She recognized the deep conflict within him between the deeply religious man who longed to humble himself before God, and the dynamic, ambitious giant who in his pride saw himself surrounded by inferiors. But he clung to power and, after some two years in office as favorite, he took care to preserve his authority by an arrangement which forms one of the most extraordinary chapters in his relations with Catherine.

Incessant quarreling had begun to overcast their companionship. Potemkin saw that it might, moreover, lead to his final departure from court. His plan was that he should gradually withdraw from being her lover, while remaining her partner and in effect co-regent. At the same time, since her lusting nature would always demand to be satisfied, he himself would choose her future lovers, taking care that they were devoted to him. Catherine evidently acquiesced in this arrangement which would ensure his continued strong support, but give her calm in her personal life in place of their exhausting passions.

In the first months of 1776 the court and foreign ambassadors in St. Petersburg were obsessed by rumors that Potemkin was falling from favor. He appeared moody and unapproachable, and he spent less time with the Empress than usual. The Orlovs and Panin in particular awaited further signs of the end of his reign. They were delighted when, in June, Catherine presented him with the Anichkov Palace on the Nevsky Prospekt, for this could only mean that he was moving from his apartments in the imperial palace. Then Potemkin obtained leave to tour the Novgorod region of which he was governor. In his absence a young Ukrainian named Zavadovsky was installed as personal adjutant-general to the Empress.

Potemkin's return to court was awaited with trepidation. All expected him to explode in fury on finding himself displaced. His return was, however, quiet and Catherine received him with her usual warmth. The court was amazed and confused, for far from being dismissed or disgraced, he still reigned supreme, while another met the sensual needs of the Empress. Zavadovsky was in fact no more than a male concubine, chosen by Potemkin. Indeed, he now became director of her love life and he was to appoint and dismiss all her lovers, with one exception, during the next thirteen years, and there were some fifteen of them. Potemkin himself had innumerable mistresses and the five beautiful daughters of his sister, Maria Engelhardt, became the leading women of his entourage. All loved him as he loved them, and his relations with them continued even after they had made the brilliant marriages which he helped to bring about by his influence and generosity. But the bond between Catherine and him remained inviolable. In fact, the elimination of the stormy passion from their relations led them into a harmonious relationship in which they complemented one another.

The time of splendor in Catherine's reign, when she became known as the Semiramis of the North, properly began after Potemkin had taken his place as her partner and co-regent. Under his exuberant influence she embarked on many new projects and she planned on a grander scale.

The court of St. Petersburg was already renowned for its magnificence at the time of her accession. The Asiatic opulence of the Muscovite court had become refined and civilized by Western influences, especially during the reign of Elizabeth. But it was the scale and richness of the entertainments and appointments of the imperial court that overwhelmed foreigners, and Catherine surpassed all her predecessors in elegance and extravagance. In celebrating the birth of a son to Grand Duke Paul, she gave a banquet which so impressed the English ambassador that he reported on it in detail, remarking in particular that "the dessert at supper was set out with jewels to the amount of upward of two million sterling."[25] At balls and masquerades, held frequently during the winter, as many as eight hundred guests took part. All were richly adorned in the latest fashions from the West and laden with jewelry. They crowded into the twenty vast reception rooms of the palace which covered with snow and its windows ablaze with lights, became a sight of unearthly splendor.

Catherine, herself, dressed magnificently and her jewels were celebrated throughout Europe. She usually wore a crown of diamonds, the ribbons of two orders, the bejeweled collars of three other orders, and the Stars of St. Andrew and St. George. But she reserved this ostentatious display for special celebrations, when she required the whole court to be magnificent.

In private life she dressed simply. Her favorite garment was a long loose coat with wide sleeves which she had adapted from the Muscovite kaftan. Comte de Segur remarked with Gallic malice that she wore it to hide her corpulence and it was true that with the passing years she had put on weight, but she liked her loose robe for its comfort and simple dignity. At ease in the Hermitage, the private apartments and galleries which she added to the Winter Palace, she pursued her special interests. She kept up an extensive correspondence with her ambassadors, friends, and agents abroad, and she was abreast of the latest developments in literature and the arts, especially in England and France. Literature was her first interest, but in the architecture of her reign she expressed most fully her taste and achievement. Building gave Catherine pleasure. She saw also that the handsome mansions, palaces, and churches which she erected would stand for future generations to admire and acknowledge as evidence of the grandeur of her reign. She had in St. Petersburg, moreover, a beautiful and impressive city where she could continue the work of Elizabeth in making it the great capital, the equal of any in Europe, that Peter the Great had envisaged.

Catherine's reign was indeed a golden age of art and architecture in Russia. She expended vast sums on erecting numerous buildings and in collecting and commissioning works of art. Her favorites and the wealthy nobility followed her lead. She was fortunate also in having at hand a number of outstanding architects. Vallin de la Mothe, a Frenchman brought to Russia by Elizabeth, built the Hermitage in the neo-classical style which she preferred to the baroque and rococo of previous reigns. In the Hermitage galleries she assembled a vast collection of works of art which her agents purchased for her regardless of cost and which later included the renowned private collections of Sir Robert Walpole, Baron de Thiers, and Count Heinrich Brühl. Foreign architects came eagerly to carry out the generous commissions of the Semiramis of the North. She delighted especially in the work of the Scot, Cameron, who built new apartments for her at Tsarskoe Selo, as well as the Agate Palace and the Cameron Gallery. His classical style had a strong influence and soon members of the nobility were following Catherine's lead in erecting Palladian mansions and in laying out English gardens of extensive lawns and groves.

Catherine's reign was remarkable, too, for the emergence of several talented Russian architects and artists. Ivan Starov worked in the style of classic simplicity and the new Alexander Nevsky Cathedral which he built so impressed Catherine that she commissioned him to build the Taurian Palace which was his masterpiece. In its design and the grandeur of its conception it was one of the wonders of Europe, and Catherine considered it worthy of Potemkin, who had become Prince of Tauris after the conquest of the Crimea, and for whom she had commissioned this palace. Among the artists who contributed to the splendor of her reign were Dmitri Levitski, the son of a Ukrainian priest, who became the leading court painter, Borovikovsky, a Cossack, and Shibanov, a serf belonging to Potemkin.

Literature was, however, Catherine's greatest interest. All her life she had a geniune ambition to be a writer and dramatist. She was happy with pen in hand and said that the sight of a freshly cut quill always made her fingers restless. Her literary output was extraordinary, bearing in mind her burdens as Empress and her vast correspondence, extending over the thirty-four years of her reign. Her literary works alone, as published by the Russian Academy of Sciences, fill twelve large volumes. In 1769 she launched under her own editorship a new literary magazine, called *Vsyakaya Vsyachina* or *All Sorts*, modeled directly on *The Spectator* of Addison and Steele, and containing mild satires on Russian life. Three years later she started writing plays, finishing no less than five plays in that year. The plays were comedies of manners and their most important effect was to inspire Fonvizin, the leading Russian dramatist of the day, to write *Nedorosl* (*The Minor* or *The Simpleton*), which was the outstanding play of the whole era. She had a second burst of playwriting which began in 1786 and lasted for four years. Again she was a forerunner and exercised a profound influence by introducing Shakespeare to the Russian stage.

The Russian theater came to life during Catherine's reign. Her Hermitage Theater was the leader of fashion. Many other theaters were, however, also active, apart from the magnificent theaters in Tsarskoe Selo and in the Taurian Palace. Certain of the great nobles maintained their own private theaters with companies composed of domestic serfs, trained for the stage. The theaters of Count Sheremetev and Princes Yusupov, Prozorovsky, and Naryshkin were even said to rival the imperial theaters in the magnificence and quality of their productions. It was, however, far from being a golden age of the Russian theater. Foreign models dominated and the Russians imitated them slavishly. Moreover, censorship, often exercised personally by Catherine, shackled expression and suppressed all attempts to lay bare or to examine the social problems lying at the root of the general unrest. The writers and dramatists who persisted in pursuing forbidden subjects were cruelly persecuted.

For all her industry and her astonishing output, Catherine's literary works were devoid of talent. She never mastered the Russian language and her writings in French had to be severely edited by others. Her contribution was to introduce new ideas and fashions and to stimulate her people, although she was at pains to impose severe restrictions on them and in later years, after the outbreak of the French revolution, she became increasingly tyrannical. But in some degree her renown as patron of the arts and even more as a patron of learning was deserved.

The Academy of Sciences, planned by Peter the Great and instituted by his widow, Catherine I, had taken root, but much remained to be done. Catherine II gave her attention to the Academy early in her reign. She created the new office of director, responsible to her personally. But Vladimir Orlov, the first director, and Domashnev, the second director, were both young and inadequate. For seventeen years the Academy stagnated. In 1782, however, she made Princess Dashkova the director of the Academy and it proved a brilliant appointment, although motivated mainly by her anxiety to ensure that the turbulent princess had no time to make trouble. Dashkova developed the Department of Geography, promoted exploration and published charts. She embarked on an important program of publications. She was especially concerned to raise the prestige of the Academy abroad. On her instigation also the Russian Academy was established in addition to the Academy of Sciences, for the study and development of the Russian language.

The 1780s brought new military and diplomatic triumphs which raised Russia's prestige. On two occasions Catherine played the role of arbiter of Europe's destinies. The first was when Prussia and Austria appealed to her mediation in their dispute over the successor to the Elector of Bavaria. Next Catherine played the leading role in organizing the armed neutrality of continental maritime powers against English domination of the seas during the American War of Independence. But her main concern was to consolidate Russia's dominion over the vast lands to the south, known at this time as New Russia. Potemkin was already developing these southern provinces. He founded the town of Kherson and produced schemes for attracting settlers from other Slav countries, including the Balkans. The Zaporozhian Cossacks, whom Peter the Great had condemned for their treachery as "a nest of vipers," had been disbanded in 1775 after the Pugachev rebellion. Potemkin now scattered the remnants of this Cossack horde. While the Crimea remained independent, however, New Russia could never be secure.

On July 23, 1783, Catherine took the bold step of proclaiming formally the incorporation of the Crimea into the Russian Empire. At this time, too, her troops were subduing the Tatars of the Kuban and the Budzhak. A declaration of war by the Sultan seemed inevitable, especially as the Turks had been massing troops on their northern frontiers. The great Ottoman Porte was, however, in decline. The Sultan was intimidated by the new might of Russia and he was anxious to negotiate. Catherine's terms were recognition of Russia's sovereignty over the Crimea, the Taman peninsula, and the Kuban, and the formal acknowledgment of the right of Russian ships to pass freely through the Dardanelles and to sail the Black Sea. The Sultan submitted to these demands and in 1784 the Treaty of Constantinople was signed. It marked the triumphant end to a long chapter in Russian history of endeavor to master the northern shores of the Black Sea and to sail its waters. But Catherine, inspired by Potemkin, was absorbed by a more grandiose plan, which was to partition the Turkish Empire, create a new Kingdom of Dacia, and revive the old Byzantine Empire. In his devotion to the Orthodox Church Potemkin could never forget that Constantinople had been the center of Eastern Christianity until captured by the Turks in 1453. It was his dream to restore the city and revive Byzantium, and it was generally accepted that he would be crowned King of Dacia. Catherine planned that her second grandson, Constantine Pavlovich, should occupy the throne of the Byzantine Emperors.

In January 1787 Catherine set out from Tsarskoe Selo to visit the Crimea. Potemkin made all arrangements and her journey became a triumphal progress of indescribable magnificence which impressed not only Turkey but the whole of Europe. In Kiev, Potemkin, who had ridden ahead, greeted Catherine and together they enjoyed the splendid entertainments provided in the ancient city. But suddenly, because the strong religious tradition of Kiev gripped him, he retired into the Pecherskaya Lavra for Lent, but he maintained control of the arrangements through a stream of couriers. At Kherson Catherine was joined by Emperor Joseph II of Austria who had traveled incognito to accompany her on part of her journey. The entry of the Empress into Bakhchisarai, the former capital of the Khans, was the occasion for an astonishing display which, like so much on this Crimean tour, "resembles the dreams of the Thousand and One Nights" as Catherine herself wrote.[26] The climax came when she drove to the heights of Inkerman and saw below the new town and harbor of Sevastopol. Forty warships lay at anchor in the harbor and, as the Empress caught her first sight of the scene, all of the ships fired salvoes in her honor.

Potemkin was the hero of the whole journey. Catherine and everyone in the enormous party expressed amazement that he had accomplished so much, especially in the Crimea. Comte de Segur, who traveled with the Empress, wrote that "It seemed incredible to us that at a distance of 800 leagues from the capital and in a country so recently conquered, Prince Potemkin had found it possible in two years to raise such an establishment, to build a town, construct a fleet, to erect forts, and to assemble such a large number of inhabitants: this was prodigal activity."[27]

The visit of the Empress to the Crimea, the display of Russian strength, and the open declaration of her decision to revive the Byzantine Empire alarmed and provoked the Turks. Catherine had hardly returned to St. Petersburg when the Sultan declared war. Potemkin, who had been waiting impatiently, now ordered his formidable army of one hundred thousand men to march. Rumyantsev commanded operations in the Danubian lands and Potemkin commanded the Black Sea army and fleet. He was too instable and impetuous to make a great general but Suvorov, Samoilov, Repnin, and others serving under him made up for his failings. Turkish attacks were repelled and the key stronghold of Ochakov was captured.

At Kronstadt in the north the Baltic fleet was hurriedly fitted out and was preparing to sail under the command of the British admiral, Greig, when in June 1788 Sweden declared war. Catherine was taken off guard. She had confirmed her alliance with King Gustavus III in 1783. But with the Russians engaged against Turkey, he had yielded to the persuasions of England and Prussia to declare war with the object of recovering Finland. Gustavus was hindered, however, by disaffection among his nobles, many of whom were receiving bribes from Russia. After several indecisive military and naval actions he was compelled to sign the Treaty of Verela in August 1790, confirming the position as it was before his declaration of war.

The Russian army in the south, supported by Austrian troops, won a series of outstanding victories during 1789–91, mainly as a result of the brilliant generalship of Suvorov. The successes of the Russian armies at Fokshani, Rymnik, Bender, Akkerman, Kilia, and Izmail finally compelled the Sultan to sue for peace.

Potemkin had been so occupied with the war and with his extensive projects in the south that his visits to St. Petersburg had become rare and fleeting. Indeed, in his absence, Catherine had taken a new favorite, named Plato Zubov, of whom he disapproved and this had caused discord between them. On April 28, 1791, however, on what was to be his last visit to St. Petersburg, Potemkin arranged a festival in the Palace of Taurida in her honor. This festival was on such a colossal scale that it became legendary as "Potemkin's feast." It began with a banquet provided for the ordinary people in the adjoining squares. To the palace three thousand guests, masked and in fancy dress, were invited. All were assembled when Catherine arrived. Potemkin received her, dressed in a suit of red silk with a cloak of black lace, and his buttons were large solitaire diamonds, while his hat was so heavily encrusted with precious stones that his aide-de-camp had to carry it for him. In the vast hall of the palace the new marble statue of Catherine by Kozlovsky had the place of honor. Dancing, two ballets, and two plays were followed by a banquet at which guests had to be seated six hundred at a time.

Potemkin escorted Catherine as she departed in the early hours of the morning. An orchestra and choir rendered a cantata in her honor while she walked through the palace. Taking leave of her host she thanked him for the magnificent entertainment and Potemkin, falling to his knees, kissed her hand. Both were in tears as though they knew that this was their final parting.

Soon afterward Potemkin traveled again to the south. He was only fifty-two years old, but worn out by excesses of work and pleasure. In Jassy he fell ill of a malarial fever, but insisted on traveling on to Nikolaev. He had ridden only a short distance when he stopped the carriage. He had himself laid on the ground and there, on October 5, 1791, he died.

Catherine collapsed on learning of his death. For weeks she was inconsolable, for she had lost her partner and closest friend, and at the age of sixty-two she felt herself to be completely alone. All who had known or served under him, even rivals and enemies, mourned Potemkin. In his excesses, his flashes of inspiration, his magnificence, and his devotion to Russia and to his Empress he had been a great man. The Prince de Ligne wrote: "He is the emblem of the immense Russian Empire; he also is composed of deserts, of gold mines, and of diamonds— he was the most extraordinary man that has ever lived"; such was the view of his contemporaries.[28]

By the Peace of Jassy, signed on December 19, 1791, the Sultan formally abandoned all claims to the Crimea and confirmed the Russian gains under the Treaty of Kuchuk-Kainardji. He further conceded the coastal region between the Bug and Dniester rivers, where Odessa was soon to rise as the great trading center. But the treaty fell far short of the grandiose plans of Catherine and Potemkin to establish the Kingdom of Dacia and revive the Byzantine Empire. It nevertheless marked the end of the long period during which Turkish power had constantly menaced Russia and this was a momentous achievement.

The last years of Catherine were not, however, a time of serenity. The cost of her magnificence and extravagant generosity, of maintaining her armies and waging the long war against Turkey had laid terrible burdens on her people. In January 1790, the French chargé d'affaires in St. Petersburg reported that:

> The great landed proprietors are beginning to raise their voices in all seriousness, and it has been found necessary to despatch to Moscow Monsieur Sheshkovsky, Chief of the Secret Chancellory, to repress several of them; the people groan in every province to see the best cultivators being continually torn from the land (to serve in the army) and lamenting families being robbed of their sole means of support; money has completely vanished from circulation, and it is evident that the government, under the guise of banknotes, is manufacturing a veritable paper currency; the harvest has been bad, next year's is going to be even worse; no snow has fallen, it is freezing only at intervals, and the grain is fermenting and rotting in the bosom of the earth; the revenues of the crown lands have fallen; trade is languishing; the rate of exchange is sinking steadily; finally, everything proclaims that it is time to finish the war and repair the evils which it has occasioned.[29]

Throughout Catherine's reign the nation had been in the grip of chronic inflation. Revenues had risen impressively. A contemporary Englishman estimated that the national income, which was approximately £1.6 million in 1725, approached £4.4 million under Elizabeth, and £6 million in Catherine's reign. Rapidly expanding trade had made an important contribution in the early years of her rule. But expenditure had risen yet more steeply. Taxes were increased; bank notes were issued; loans were raised abroad. Thus the Russian economy, which had been solvent at the time of her accession, lay under a heavy burden of debt at the close of her reign.

In Poland, unrest and anti-Russian feeling had been mounting since the first partition in 1772. The war against Turkey, which occupied both Russia and Austria, and the French Revolution seemed to the Poles to offer the opportunity to recover the territories which they had lost. Frederick William II, who had succeeded to the Prussian throne in 1786, and was uneasy about the close alliance existing between Russia and Austria, approached King Stanislas Augustus of Poland with proposals for an alliance. Emboldened by this proposal the Poles abrogated the hated Russian constitution and in May 1791 introduced a new constitution of their own. Both Frederick William of Prussia and Leopold II of Austria, who had succeeded on the death of Josef II in 1790, approved the new Polish constitution. Catherine maintained an ominous silence. As soon as the Turkish war had ended, the Russian army marched into Poland and enforced a further partition of Poland in which Frederick William, unable to resist the offer of easy spoils, shared.

Among the Poles a desperate movement developed to expel the Russians. Its leader was the Polish patriot, Thaddeus Kosciusko, who had studied military science in France and had taken part in the American war of independence. The Poles took heart from the fact that Russia, Prussia, and Austria were quarreling among themselves. A general rising in Great Poland and brave fighting in defense of Warsaw forced the Russian and Prussian troops to retreat from the city which they had held under siege for two months. But Kosciusko now found himself threatened by a combined Russian and Prussian force one hundred thousand strong in the west, by an invading Austrian army from the south, and in the east by a Russian army commanded by Suvorov. On October 10, 1794, the Poles were defeated at Maciejowice, and Kosciusko was taken prisoner. In the following month Suvorov captured Warsaw and Polish resistance came to an end.

Catherine now planned the third partition, dividing the spoils with Prussia and Austria, and removing Poland entirely from the map of Europe. Frederick of Prussia had taken the initiative which had led to the first partition, but Catherine had inspired and dominated the second and third partitions of Poland. In supporting Prussian and Austrian demands and in the third partition she had demonstrated her obsession with personal glory and with immediate gains without thought for the future. The policy of successive Tsars had been to recover the lands within Poland's frontiers, inhabited, by Orthodox Russians. She had achieved this traditional objective, but in doing so she had greatly strengthened Prussia and by the final partition she had engendered in the Polish nation an unquenchable hatred of the Russians, when with statesmanship and magnanimity she might have assuaged the old enmity and gained in Poland an ally.

In these last years Catherine's obsession was the threat to her throne, posed by the forces released by the revolution in France. The fall of the Bastille on July 14, 1789, had not greatly alarmed her, but she did not underestimate the significance of the events in France. She recognized, too, that the oppressive conditions which had given rise to revolution in France, were present in more extreme forms in her own empire. She now enforced repressive policies, seeking to suppress the ideas which she had herself introduced with such zest in the early years of her reign. The writings of Voltaire, the old friend and correspondent whom she had revered, were now banned. Everything French was suspect and all newspapers and periodicals believed to be purveying the revolutionary spirit, were closed down.

In May 1790 a storm of imperial anger over the publication of a simple book by a certain Alexander Radishchev demonstrated the extremes to which age and the French Revolution had carried her. A gentle idealist, Radishchev had witnessed the sufferings of the peasantry, especially during the famine of 1786–87, and recognized that basic reforms were needed. Although a respected civil servant, he had written papers and pamphlets, critical of the autocracy, and no harm had come to him. He installed a press in his own house on which he printed *A Journey from St. Petersburg to Moscow*. It was no more than a series of sketches, cast in the form of Sterne's *Sentimental Journey*, then well known in Europe. The chief of police in St. Petersburg, acting as censor, gave permission for its publication after a cursory glance. But the sketches amounted to an indictment of absolutism and serfdom, and one section could have been interpreted as a direct attack on Catherine and Potemkin.

Catherine read the book some weeks after its publication. Furiously she annotated her copy and then ordered the arrest of this "rebel worse than Pugachev." Radishchev was bewildered by the anger of the Empress and by the interest that his book was arousing. His approaching trial was the talk of the day. Foreign envoys in St. Petersburg saw his book as an indication of the widespread disapproval of her regime, felt by the Russians. Interest in the book was so keen that, although it had been strictly banned, copies written by hand circulated clandestinely. As much as a hundred rubles were paid for a copy and some merchants paid twenty-five rubles for an hour's perusal.

At his trial Radishchev was found guilty and sentenced to death. He lay in prison for several weeks, awaiting execution, but then Catherine with a display of clemency commuted the sentence to one of exile in Ilimsk in Siberia. His health broken, in heavy chains, and under close guard he was carried off in a rough open cart on his long journey. But his case had repercussions throughout the country. Alexander Vorontsov, who had been his friend and protector but was not directly implicated, retired from public life because of his disgust with the court. Dashkova, too, asked to be released from the Academy of Sciences. Among the nobility were some whose consciences were troubled by this case of persecution and among the poorer people Radishchev was revered as one who had spoken against oppression.

Meanwhile Catherine averted her attention from the insoluble domestic problems and concentrated on foreign projects which held promise of yet greater glory. She had always been vain, but now her vanity exceeded all bounds. "She is willing," so the British ambassador reported to London, "to give credit to any assertion that she supposes to be in consequence of her own greatness and power."[30] She had not abandoned the grandiose Greek project of reviving Byzantium, and was hoping to gain the support of Britain and Austria for it. She had sent troops against Persia and planned to conquer the whole Caucasus region. She was still dreaming and planning on the scale that Potemkin had inspired. But the Russian people as a whole were disenchanted with their Empress and her magnificence for which they had had to pay so heavily. Toward the end of her reign the splendor was seen to be tarnished and the people were weary.

Catherine herself did not live, however, to pursue her ambitious plans further. She had always enjoyed robust health and even with advancing years she was rarely ill. But death came suddenly. On November 6, 1796, she arose at the usual early hour and attended to business. She broke off to retire to her inner chamber and there, seated on the commode, she suffered a stroke and, after lingering for some thirty hours, she died.

Her life had been an astonishing saga. An insignificant German princess, she had usurped the Russian throne to become Autocrat and the most powerful monarch in Europe. She had reigned with splendor, supported by brilliant men like Potemkin, Rumyantsev, Suvorov, and others, and her foreign policies had been crowned with momentous successes. But her reign had also entrenched and extended the privileges of the landowning nobility and gentry and the evil institution of serfdom. On her death few, apart from those close to her at court, were able to mourn sincerely.

XIV
Paul

1796–1801

Paul succeeded to the throne with relief and rejoicing. He was forty-two years of age, a small ugly man with a strangely flat face and a strident voice which became shrill when he gave way to one of his frequent tempers. He and his family had assembled with ministers and courtiers in the imperial bedchamber as Catherine lay dying. His children on whom she had lavished attention were in tears and most of the courtiers were crying openly. But he had shed no tears for the mother who had treated him with contempt and hostility, and had deprived him of his throne for so many years. It had been strongly rumored that she intended to exclude him from the succession and to make his son, Alexander, her heir. Even as all waited in the bedchamber they were expecting her to recover her senses and by a last testament to displace him. He was, however, spared this final humiliation. She died without regaining consciousness.

Paul had hated and mistrusted his mother since he was a boy. He had not been close to her and indeed had never known her. Empress Elizabeth had carried him away at birth, determined to bring him up herself as a worthy successor to the throne of Peter the Great. In her *Memoirs*

Catherine attributed the estrangement between her son and herself to Elizabeth's action. But she had, in fact, taken no interest whatsoever in him after Elizabeth's death. Her indifference had turned to contempt and then, as he grew older, to open hostility, for he represented a threat to her throne.

Paul hated Catherine not only because she had rejected him and had cheated him of his birthright by usurping the throne, but also because he believed her guilty of the murder of Emperor Peter III, whom he revered as his father. Indeed, he had the body of the martyred Emperor exhumed from its grave in the Alexander Nevsky Monastery and reinterred in the Fortress of Peter and Paul alongside the grave of Catherine. In the somber procession bearing the Emperor's remains to the Fortress, Count Alexei Orlov, who had murdered him and who was now old and failing, was required to walk behind the coffin, bearing the imperial crown. It was a reminder to the people of St. Petersburg that the splendors and triumphs of the thirty-four years of Catherine's reign should not expunge memories of their legitimate Emperor.

At the same time Paul sought throughout his short reign to erase memories of Catherine from the minds of his people. At times he seemed to be trying to exorcise her from his own mind. He refused to wear at his coronation the imperial crown which she had worn. He had inveighed constantly against her extravagance while she was alive, but he did not hesitate to order Duval, the Genevan who served as court jeweler, to make him a new crown, costing several million rubles.[1] His aversion from all the palaces which his mother and her favorites had occupied led him to desecrate or pull them down, or to leave them deserted to fall into ruins. The magnificent Tauride Palace, one of the architectural glories of Catherine's reign, was turned over to the cavalry guards who exercised their horses in its halls.[2] Tsarskoe Selo, one of the most magnificent of the imperial residences, was deserted on his orders. In the savage winters of St. Petersburg it deteriorated rapidly. Its ornamental lakes, lined with marble, became weed-choked marshes. For his own residence Paul had the Mikhailovsky Castle erected on the ruins of the old Summer Palace. The castle was a somber fortress, which reflected his obsessive fear that he would be assassinated. He was, in fact, to reside in the castle for only three weeks before what he feared came to pass.

In character Paul was irascible, instable, impetuous, and eccentric. He had spells of kindness and generosity, but his hatred of his mother and the humiliations and anxieties which he had suffered during her long reign had warped his nature. Many who had contact with him believed that he was mentally unbalanced and even insane. In many ways, however, he was intelligent. Elizabeth had appointed as his tutor Nikita Panin, a man of striking ability who was later to be Catherine's minister of foreign affairs. Nikita Panin and his brother, General Peter Panin, both became close to Paul, and his ideas on government were largely formed under their influence. They also appointed his teachers who gave him a sound general education. He showed ability in mathematics; he learnt to speak French and German fluently and he understood Church Slavonic. He possessed a considerable library and was widely read. But instable and impetuous, he was never able to apply his abilities effectively.

In his domestic life Paul was more fortunate. He had married, at the age of nineteen, the daughter of the Landgrave of Hesse, but she had died in childbirth in 1776. Six months later he married the young Princess of Württemburg, a niece of King Frederick II of Prussia. He traveled to Berlin to meet his bride and there, like Peter III before him, he fell under the spell of Frederick and the Prussian army. His marriage with Maria Fedorovna, as she was called after her baptism into the Orthodox Church, proved stable and fruitful. She was a devoted wife who gave him affection and companionship during the bleak years while Catherine occupied the throne. She also bore him four sons and six daughters.

In 1781–82 Catherine had allowed them to make an extensive tour of Western Europe. They traveled incognito as the Count and Countess du Nord, but were received everywhere with the courtesies due to the heir to the Russian throne. Paul made a good impression at the courts which he visited, and Catherine was annoyed by his success. She had placed her agents among his suite and received regular reports on everything that Paul and his wife did and said. She evidently began to see in him a serious rival, and she was careful to give him no further opportunities to distinguish himself. When she was absent from the capital, she did not appoint him in charge of the city, even less of government affairs, although it was normal practice for the heir to the throne to be in charge. By birth a generalissimo of the Russian armies, she would never permit him to command so much as a regiment in time of war; a grand admiral of the Russian navy, he was not once allowed to visit the naval headquarters at Kronstadt.

Paul was further embittered by the fact that Catherine virtually adopted his first two sons, Alexander, born on December 12, 1777, and Constantine, born on April 27, 1779. She had indeed repeated the behavior of Elizabeth toward Paul. She personally supervised the education and training of Alexander for the throne. For her second grandson, Constantine, she planned a special future: he would succeed to the throne of the great Byzantine Emperor after whom he had been named. Greek nurses, brought especially from the island of Naxos, cared for him as a baby, and Greek children were his playmates, so that as a boy he spoke Greek fluently. In 1786 she planned to take him south to the frontier of the Empire over which she intended him to rule. He caught measles, however, and could not travel with her on the triumphal journey to the Crimea.

The fear that plagued Paul constantly was that Catherine would disinherit him. He knew that this was her intention. She idolized his eldest son, Alexander, who was handsome, charming, and intelligent, and possessed the qualities which she found lacking in her own son. On September 28, 1793, at the early age of sixteen, Alexander was married to a young German princess and everyone expected that at this time Catherine would proclaim him as her heir. The strong opposition of Alexander's Swiss tutor, La Harpe, was evidently the reason why this pronouncement was not made. But, while Catherine was alive, Paul lived under the threat of being disinherited.

Confined to his estate at Gatchina, some thirty miles south of St. Petersburg, Paul lived quietly with his wife, Grand Duchess Maria Fedorovna, and their small court. They kept away from the capital and avoided contact with Catherine's ministers and favorites. Only the Panins and certain others risked incurring Catherine's displeasure by maintaining relations with the "young court," as it was known. Paul valued in particular the friendship of Sergei Pleshcheev, a naval officer who had been trained in England and who was an enthusiastic freemason. Paul had been introduced to freemasonry by Nikita Panin and had been strongly attracted by its mystic rituals and secret signs. He took a close interest in the lodges which were active in Russia at this time.

Paul's fondness for idealistic principles and mystic doctrines indeed led him into an affair which, although platonic, threw the small community at Gatchina into an uproar. The object of his passion was Catherine Nelidov, one of his wife's ladies-in-waiting. She was romantic and devout and was said to have a calming influence over him. But Maria Fedorovna was outraged to see her husband lavishing his attentions on the young lady. Distressed by the disturbance which their friendship was causing, Catherine Nelidov withdrew into the Smolny Convent, but she still visited Gatchina from time to time. On Paul's accession, however, Maria Fedorovna and Catherine Nelidov put their rivalry aside and promised to work together "for the good of the Tsar and the Empire." Later Paul became enamored of a young noblewoman, named Anna Lopukhina, who married Prince Paul Gagarin. She became his mistress, and Maria Fedorovna was obliged to accept their relationship.

At Gatchina, Paul tried to be a good master to his serfs. He was active in improving their conditions, providing schools and hospitals, and even founding small industries. He was devout, but tolerant of other faiths, and built Lutheran and Roman Catholic as well as Orthodox churches. But his great obsession was the army and military dress and parades, and he turned Gatchina into a military camp. He shared to the full Peter III's worship of Frederick and all things Prussian. His private army of some two thousand troops was drilled and paraded daily like a ballet company. All wore Prussian uniforms adapted to his orders. The uniforms were so tight-fitting that officers and troops could not sit and, if they fell down, they could not get to their feet without help. Regimental barbers plaited their hair, setting it in a thick paste made chiefly of lard and flour which gave off an intolerable stench after a time. Details of uniform, the wearing of insignia, the number and positions of buttons, exact obedience to regulations and drill orders were all matters of passionate concern to Paul. He was a savage martinet, obsessed with the paraphernalia of war. Breach of any regulation, no matter how small the detail, made him scream with fury, and punishments were summary and harsh.

On his accession the Winter Palace and other parts of St. Petersburg were suddenly surrounded by sentries and armed patrols. It was as though the army had taken over the city. Wielding absolute power as Emperor, Paul's military parades now became more elaborate and severe. Officers and men dreaded them. Officers found guilty of real or fancied misdemeanors were sent directly from the parade ground to Siberia in one of the sealed carriages held ready for the purpose. Troops were flogged mercilessly for mistakes in drill and breaches of discipline. It was even said that on one occasion Paul, having inspected a regiment, gave the order: "Files, by the right, to Siberia . . . Quick march!"[3]

By contrast with his futile passion for military parades and paraphernalia, Paul's domestic policy was rational in conception, if not in execution. He believed in order and equality among his subjects and was opposed to the privileges of the nobility and gentry. Republicanism was abhorrent to him. He looked upon the absolute sovereign as the keystone of national life. He cherished the ideal of a society reflecting the order of the parade ground, all subjects obeying the same regulations of which the Emperor was the source; only from such unquestioning obedience to the law could the nation flourish. But in his insistence on extreme centralization of government with the Emperor exercising his power through a series of sharply defined central organs, he contributed greatly to the growth of the bureaucratic regime which was to cripple the nation in the years ahead.

One of Paul's earliest and most important ukazi, promulgated on April 5, 1797, the day of his coronation, regulated the succession to the throne. Peter the Great's ukaz of 1722, giving the Autocrat the right to nominate an heir of his own choice, had led to disorder. Paul himself had suffered from the lack of an effective law regulating the succession. His ukaz, establishing the rule of primogeniture, made the eldest son of the Autocrat the legal heir and, if he had no son, then his brothers in order of seniority and their sons would inherit. This law remained in force for the remaining years of the dynasty.

Also on April 5, 1797, Paul issued an ukaz, providing that landowners should not call on their serfs to work their lands for more than three days a week; on the remaining three days the serfs were to be free to cultivate their own lands, and Sunday was to be a day of rest. It is a matter of debate how effectively, if at all, this ukaz was enforced.[4] Like his partial restoration of the right of the serfs to petition the Emperor, however, it gave evidence of his concern to protect the simple people. But with typical inconsistency he also introduced several measures which added to their burdens. Thus he revived the right of merchants to purchase serfs to work in industry; he increased certain taxes paid by the peasantry; most serious of all, he granted extensive state lands with their peasants to favorites and in this way greatly increased the number of privately owned serfs. He ordered that all signs of peasant unrest should be put down with the utmost severity. He even had a manifesto proclaimed, calling on serfs to show complete obedience to their owners and threatening severe penalties to the rebellious.

In spite of his sporadic efforts to reform conditions, Paul was in effect more reactionary than Catherine had been in the last years of her reign. He banned the import of all books and journals. He applied strict censorship to all correspondence and he refused to allow Russians to travel abroad. In his obsession with discipline and conformity he issued detailed instructions on the dress to be worn by men and women, prohibiting fashions which came from revolutionary France. He produced regulations concerning the carriages and number of horses, appropriate to the ranks of their owners. But the worst aspect of his petty repressive rule was his unpredictable temper and his summary removal and punishment of officials, often for no apparent reason. The army, government officials, and the court, were at the mercy of his whims and rages, and all suffered from insecurity and mounting discontent.

In his conduct of foreign policy Paul was no less erratic and, alike to his enemies and allies, bewildering. He had strongly criticized Catherine's expansionist ventures, and on ascending the throne he had sought to free Russia from all military commitments. But he was soon to reverse his policy of non-intervention in France. The revolutionary movement, which he detested, was spreading into Italy and Switzerland, and had to be checked. Also, after the success of Napoleon's campaign in Italy, concluding with the Franco-Austrian Peace of October 1797, Paul had provided refuge for Prince Conde's small army and generous hospitality for Louis XVIII in Mittau. But his decision to join the coalition against France was influenced equally by his quixotic defense of the Order of Knights of St. John of Jerusalem in Malta. Soon after Napoleon's occupation of Malta in June 1798, Paul declared that he had taken the Order under his personal protection and when the Knights elected him to the supreme office of Grand Master of the Order, he accepted. This gave rise to the extraordinary situation whereby the Russian Autocrat, a devout member of the Orthodox Church, became head of a Roman Catholic Order which owed direct allegiance to the Pope of Rome. But Paul's impetuosity frequently led to paradoxical results.

By 1799 Russia was again a member of the coalition of England, Austria, Turkey, and the Kingdom of Naples against France. Paul ordered an army commanded by Suvorov to join with the Austrians in northern Italy. Age, retirement, and increasing eccentricity had not blunted Suvorov's military genius. He gained a number of brilliant victories in Italy and was planning to march on Paris, when he received orders to proceed urgently to Switzerland. He accomplished the heroic feat of leading his army over the Alps by way of the St. Gotthard Pass, but his losses of men were heavy. Moreover, the Austrian army had been defeated at Zürich, and Suvorov managed with difficulty to keep his weakened army intact. Disputes between Russians and Austrians grew bitter and the behavior of Suvorov's troops in Switzerland and Bohemia aggravated relations further between the allies. Infuriated by Austrian complaints, Paul suddenly broke off relations and early in 1800 recalled Suvorov and his army. Soon afterward, as a result of dissatisfaction with English cooperation with Russian forces in Holland and incensed by English occupation of Malta and refusal to give up the island to Russia, he broke off relations with England. He imposed an embargo on English ships which severely damaged Russian trade, and in December 1800 joined with Sweden, Denmark, and Prussia in a new Armed Neutrality, directed against England. Russia and England were now on the brink of war.

Toward the end of 1799 Paul had decided that Napoleon was not, after all, a dangerous adventurer, but the savior of France and Europe. The dramatic change in his opinion was hastened by Napoleon's offer to give him Malta, then about to be seized by the English, and by the unconditional release of all Russian prisoners of war held in France. Now completely under the spell of Napoleon, Paul dismissed the French émigré force of Prince Conde and had Louis XVIII brusquely evicted from Mittau. He was carried away by the prospect of a Russo-French alliance in which Austria and Prussia would join for the partition of Turkey and the destruction of English power. The expansionist policies for which he had criticized his mother now became his obsession. In January 1801 he formally annexed Georgia and he was already planning the conquest of India. Without adequate preparation an expeditionary force of some twenty-three thousand Cossacks was assembled under the command of Vasily Orlov and ordered to advance to Khiva and Bokhara, and thence into India. It was an ill-considered venture and when, after only a few weeks on the march, Orlov and his force were recalled, they had already suffered severe casualties from heat and other hardships.

The reason for the conspiracy which ended in the coup of March 11, 1801, was not, however, Paul's haphazard conduct of foreign policy, nor was it the general worsening of conditions, but his threat to the position of the nobility. They had so recently gained their freedom from the burdens of compulsory service which Peter the Great had imposed. Peter III had released them from this obligation. Catherine's reign had been the golden age of the nobility and gentry in which they had gained all that they had sought. Indeed, in May 1785 she had granted them a charter which confirmed and even extended their rights. This charter guaranteed their exemption from personal taxation, corporal punishment, and state service; they could be deprived of their estates, ranks, and lives only by judgment of their peers; they alone could own estates and serfs.

Paul did not seek to abolish this charter, but he modified certain of its provisions and virtually abolished others. He confirmed that the nobility were free to serve or not, but in practice service, especially in the army, could not be avoided. Exemption from payment of taxes was not questioned, but he would "invite" members of the nobility to contribute toward the cost of state undertakings; to refuse was to court disgrace and worse punishments. One right which was especially valued was immunity from corporal punishment. The savagery of these punishments had not diminished. Flogging by knout or *batogi*, tearing out the nostrils with iron pincers, branding with hot irons were still commonly inflicted on unfortunate peasants and soldiers, and many died from these ordeals.

In January 1797, however, Paul declared that anyone who was deprived of the title of nobility as a result of some misfeasance could no longer claim immunity from such punishments. In Catherine's reign it had been rare for anyone to lose the rank of nobility. But in his tempers Paul frequently deprived offenders of their noble status. His ruling thus made the threat of corporal punishment direct and real.

Unrest among the nobility and gentry grew dangerously. They saw their charter overridden and, as a result of Paul's restrictions on their powers of local self-government in pursuit of his policy of centralizing government, they saw their role in the provinces reduced to nothing. They wondered what further assaults the Emperor would make on their position and privileges. Another source of unrest was his determination to transform the army on the Prussian model. Rigid codes of discipline and administration were introduced with the intention of increasing efficiency and eliminating the waste and corruption which were widespread in the Russian army. Officers and troops found themselves in the straitjackets not only of their Prussian uniforms but also of Prussian discipline. They were, moreover, plagued by the extremely severe punishments meted out for even the most ludicrous misdemeanors. Finally, Paul's contempt for the guards drew upon him the hostility of the strongest and most united section of the nobility. In these and other measures Paul repeated all the mistakes of his father, Peter III, and with the same result that he lost his throne and his life.

From the outset of his reign Paul had antagonized all classes of his people. Rumors of plots to depose him had soon begun circulating. The conspiracy which succeeded, however, was not formed until the autumn of 1799. Count Nikita Petrovich Panin, the son of General Peter Panin, and Count Peter Pahlen, the military governor of St. Petersburg, were its chief instigators. Panin was, in fact, dismissed from the office of vice-chancellor in November 1800 and ordered to live on one of his country estates. He had, nevertheless, played an important part in the conspiracy, especially in approaching Paul's eldest son, Alexander, and obtaining his support for the plan to depose his father.

Count Peter Pahlen evidently directed the operation on the night of March 11, 1801. He brought together the other conspirators. They included a group of guards officers, one of whom was Count Leon Bennigsen, and the three Zubov brothers, of whom Plato had been the last of Catherine's favorites. They met over supper and most of them had drunk deeply before they set out for the Mikhailovsky Castle. They entered without difficulty and made their way to the Emperor's bedchamber.

Hearing noises in the corridor Paul, who lived in fear of plots and assassination, scrambled from his bed and hid in the fireplace behind a screen. At first the conspirators thought that the room was empty. Then one of their number pulled away the screen and saw Paul's bare feet. They dragged him from the chimney in which he had been standing. He was terrified and begged for his life to be spared. In the drunken confusion someone struck him on the head with a heavy gold snuffbox. He fell to the ground and was at once set upon by the conspirators, who finally strangled him with a scarf. Count Bennigsen, who alone was sober, made sure that the Emperor was dead. He had the body dressed and the room set in order. At this point Count Peter Pahlen arrived, having delayed in order to avoid being involved in the actual capture. He and Bennigsen then arranged the proclamation of the death of the Emperor. The official cause was given as apoplexy, a plausible explanation, for Paul had been notorious for his insensate rages.

At court and throughout the city the people were so overjoyed to be free of the harassments of Paul's rule that few worried about the cause of his death. Many in the army and at court were nevertheless disturbed by his sudden end. Certain officers insisted on seeing the body and, although like most people they suspected that he had been murdered, they did not seek to press their enquiries further. All were, in fact, united in welcoming the proclamation of Alexander as their new Emperor.

XV

Alexander I

1801–1825

Alexander was in his early twenties at the time of his accession. He was tall, fair with blue eyes, and strikingly handsome. He had great presence and natural dignity, and seemed born to the role of Emperor. He contrasted sharply with his father and predecessor, Paul, who had been ludicrously ugly and undignified. In personality, too, Alexander was unlike his father. He possessed a charm of manner which recalled his grandmother, Catherine, but a certain shyness and even, on occasion, a stutter, made his charm seem natural and less of an act. He endeared himself to everyone and especially to women. He gave the impression of being simple and straightforward in character. But among all the rulers of Russia and, indeed, of Europe none was more complex and unpredictable.

Alexander, the greatest enigma among the Romanovs, seemed to take on different characters during his reign. The shy young Emperor, burdened by remorse for his complicity in the murder of his father, was remote from the majestic Emperor, acclaimed by the peoples of Europe as he made his triumphal entry into Paris on March 19, 1814. The sensualist, who had many mistresses and was rumored to have had an incestuous relationship with his own sister, was to be universally acknowledged at the Congress of Vienna as the pillar of Christian morality. At Austerlitz, when Napoleon defeated the Russian and Austrian armies, he was overwhelmed by his first experience of battle; he broke down and, sitting on the ground under a tree, he sobbed into his handkerchief until led away by his own officers: the same man, eight years later at Leipzig (October 16–19, 1813), acted so decisively under fire that he saved the allied armies and the French were put to flight. He began his reign as an enlightened and liberal monarch; he closed it as a harsh reactionary, bordering on religious mania. In countless ways he bewildered allies and enemies alike both on the battlefield and at the conference table. Napoleon, whom he vanquished, called him "the Sphinx," "the cunning Byzantine," and "the Talma of the North." Talleyrand, Castlereagh, Metternich, and other statesmen of the age, echoed these epithets. Even his death gave rise to mystery.

Throughout his early life Alexander had been tormented by family divisions. His grandmother, Empress Catherine, had taken him from his parents to supervise his upbringing personally. He was a pretty child, pleasing in manner. Catherine adored him and, although so astute in judging character, she never discerned in the boy his extraordinary talent for dissembling his thoughts and feelings. Certainly he never revealed, and she never appreciated, his longing for contact with his father and mother. When he was seven years old she appointed, on the recommendation of Melchior Grimm, her agent and correspondent in the West, a Swiss, La Harpe, as his tutor. La Harpe was the product of eighteenth-century rationalism and renowned for his learning. His instructions were "to educate the Grand Duke for the throne," using only the French language. It was a strange appointment, but in 1784 Catherine was still regarding and promoting herself as the Empress of the Enlightenment and the choice of an ardent republican as tutor to the heir to the imperial throne was a striking proof of enlightenment.

La Harpe, a man of sincerity, was obsessed by the ideals of liberty and social justice. He lectured the boy for hours on these high principles and the sovereignty of reason. Alexander probably understood only a small part of what he heard, but La Harpe's teaching made a deep impression on him. It aroused the strong idealistic element in his character. He became devoted to the principles of the Enlightenment, and this devotion was to give rise to extraordinary events later in his reign. It was, however, only one element in his complex character and one which was to be perverted into harsh reaction.

After the outbreak of the Revolution in France, Catherine had shed her liberal pretensions and begun to mistrust the Grand Duke's Swiss tutor. She resented also his opposition to her plans for the boy.

La Harpe was no courtier and was genuinely concerned for the welfare of his pupil. In 1793 he had expressed himself against her proposal to have Alexander proclaimed as heir to the throne. He was always anxious that his pupil should have normal relations with his parents. Indeed, in the spring of 1795, after Catherine had finally dismissed him, he went to Gatchina for an audience with Paul at which he implored him to be more kind and friendly toward his sons, Alexander and Constantine. Evidently Paul paid some heed, but he could not rid himself entirely of his resentment and mistrust. Alexander's shyness and reserve seemed to him to betoken dislike, and he also failed to understand that Alexander could be too responsive toward him in case it was reported to Catherine. Paul was sure, too, that he had agreed and had even sought to become Catherine's heir. Rumors and suspicions, carried between the imperial court and Gatchina, constantly poisoned relations between father and son.

In September 1793 Alexander, not yet sixteen, was married to Princess Louise, one of the five daughters of the Crown Prince of Baden. She had been received into the Orthodox Church, rebaptized with the name of Elizabeth, and formally betrothed in the previous May. She was then nearly fifteen years old, but graceful and intelligent. She had, moreover, fallen in love with the tall, slim young man whom she looked on as her prince charming. For the first years of their marriage they were very happy together. Alexander enjoyed the companionship of his affectionate young wife. He needed her sympathetic support, for his relations with his parents had been exacerbated by his marriage, which Catherine had arranged without reference to them. Moreover, Paul could not forgive the fact that Catherine had granted Alexander a larger court than he was allowed at Gatchina; such matters of dignity and protocol were of burning significance to him.

At Easter 1795, Alexander and his brother, Constantine, were allowed to visit Gatchina. Catherine was confident that they would be repelled by the petty tyrant of the parade ground, who was their father. But Alexander, who delighted in the splendor of the court of St. Petersburg and had been fired by the idealism of La Harpe, was equally carried away by his father's military fever. The order and discipline of life at Gatchina appealed to him. Moreover, he felt sympathy for his father's predicament in being deprived of his throne. He shared his disgust over the partitions of Poland. He also came under his mother's influence, and his attitude toward his grandmother hardened. But he dissembled so adroitly that Catherine had no inkling of his true thoughts.

After the death of Catherine, Alexander's enthusiasm for the military life rapidly diminished. His father as Emperor required him to devote himself to drill and parades. He allowed him no special treatment, but seemed to believe that Catherine's spoiled grandson would benefit from the harsh discipline which he inflicted on others. Alexander often found himself to be the victim of his father's insane furies, and his wife, Elizabeth, suffered equally at the hands of her mother-in-law, who did not disguise her dislike. Under this petty tyranny, the young couple stood together and were probably closer to each other than at any other time in their married life. Alexander's feelings for his father were quickly soured, and this was a factor in his decision to support the conspiracy to remove him from the throne. But a further reason was that Paul's erratic rule, and especially the impending war against Britain, the rapprochement with Napoleon, and the campaign to conquer India, were leading the nation to disaster.

On the death of Paul, Alexander ascended the throne without question. His mother, the widowed Empress, in her hysteria on learning the fate of her husband, laid claim to the succession. It was, however, ignored, for Alexander had been declared heir to the throne some time earlier under the new law of the succession. At court and throughout St. Petersburg he was acclaimed. All believed that his reign would be a time of peace, recovery, and reform. Few, if any, paused to consider how disrupted and inadequate had been his training for the supreme office of Emperor. His education had been limited almost wholly to La Harpe's instruction, and even this had come to an end when he had married at the age of fifteen. He spoke fluent English and French, but poor Russian and he hardly knew his own country. He was burdened, too, by a terrible sense of guilt. He had not taken part directly in the murder of his father, but he had given his support to the conspiracy. He may well have believed that Paul would be removed and held comfortably in custody. Indeed it is far from certain that the conspirators themselves had planned to assassinate the Emperor, but his death was nevertheless the responsibility of all of them. He was always to be haunted by this feeling of guilt.

As Emperor, Alexander acted promptly to counteract the worst consequences of Paul's policies. He ordered the immediate recall of Orlov's Cossack force which had been sent to Khiva and Bokhara on the first stage of the invasion of India. He at once restored diplomatic relations with England. His action was timely, for Nelson's fleet had gained a brilliant victory over the Danish navy at Copenhagen on April 2, 1801 (NS), and was preparing for action against other members of the Second League of Armed Neutrality. On June 17, 1801, an Anglo-Russian convention was agreed in St. Petersburg. It was signed subsequently by Denmark and Sweden, and the Armed Neutrality was abandoned. Moreover, in spite of Napoleon's dislike of the new Anglo-Russian accord, a Franco-Russian treaty was negotiated in October 1801.

The new agreements with England and France reflected Alexander's policy of peace. He asserted that peace could be maintained only by understandings between Russia and England, France, and Austria. In a letter to his ambassadors he wrote: "If I ever raise arms, it will be exclusively in defense against aggression, for the protection of my peoples, or of the victims of ambitions that endanger the peace of Europe . . ."[1] His two predecessors, Catherine II and Paul, had on their accessions proclaimed similar policies of Russian neutrality and pursuit of peace. Like them, too, Alexander was to find himself drawn inexorably, and not unwillingly, into the European vortex of war and diplomacy both to further Russia's interests and to maintain the balance of power.

At the same time Alexander made friendly approaches to Prussia and he was to champion Prussian interests throughout his reign. His attitude was in some degree an act of homage to the memory of his father, who had been an extreme Prussophile. It was also influenced, however, by Queen Louise, wife of the Prussian King, Frederick William III, who was a woman of great beauty. He met her and Frederick William on a private visit which he made to Memel in June 1802, and she enchanted him on sight. In the course of a week of banquets, balls, and military parades the two monarchs reached an understanding which was to bewilder not only the chancelleries of Europe but also the Emperor's own ministers.

On his accession Alexander had approached office in a mood of exaltation, mingled with remorse, and with some misgiving, because the problems were so formidable. But he was also eager to embark on liberal reforms and to improve the conditions of the peasantry. His fervor came partly from a need to expiate his sense of guilt and partly from the idealism and sense of mission which La Harpe had awakened in him.

The reign began with a flood of ukazi and manifestoes. He had proclaimed his intention of governing "according to the laws and spirit of Catherine II." He confirmed the rights and privileges, set out in her Charter of the Nobility, which Paul had restricted in practice, and he restored her system of local government. But he had, in fact, disagreed with much that she had done, and this became clear in his subsequent measures. He abolished the security police on which she had depended. He maintained that "all crimes must be provided for, tried and punished by the general laws."[2] He abolished the sovereign's council, which she had established, and appointed in its place a "Permanent Council" of twelve experienced advisers. He set up a commission to pursue afresh the difficult task of codifying the chaotic laws of the land. These measures were, however, merely the beginning of a far broader program.

To assist him in his task, Alexander brought together four young friends in what was known as the "Private Committee." They were

Viktor Kochubey, Prince Adam Czartoryski, and Count Nicholas Novosiltsev, all of whom had spent some time in England, and Count Paul Stroganov, who had studied in France. The "young friends" were, like Alexander himself, enthusiastic about liberal reforms. They dined with the Emperor and Empress on appointed days. After dinner they retired to a room near the private apartments, and began their business meeting. Later in the evening Alexander would join them. He always listened attentively, but made few contributions. This Private Committee, which was never given legal standing, functioned fairly regularly from June 1801 until the end of 1803 or even later. It had considerable influence on Alexander and through him on internal and foreign policy. But its main objectives were never attained. The four friends had worked under pressure to draft a "Charter of the Russian People," to be proclaimed at Alexander's coronation. Their draft was bold and wide-ranging; it contained guarantees of freedom of the individual, of speech and of the press as well as religious tolerance and an independent judiciary. But Alexander did not have it proclaimed. He enjoyed the excitements of enlightened discussion and liberal dreams: he shrank from applying them in practice.

The most onerous task of the four committee members was to make themselves "thoroughly acquainted with all existing constitutions, to digest them, and on the basis of their principles to prepare a constitution for Russia."[3] But their ardent labors resulted in only two administrative reforms, and fell far short of Alexander's grandiose proposals. One reform replaced the colleges of Peter the Great by eight ministries. It was at first taken to impose restrictions on the absolute power of the Autocrat. The change was, however, only nominal, for each of the eight ministers was responsible directly to the Emperor and to him alone. An ukaz proclaimed on the same day, September 8, 1802, sought to make the Senate the highest judicial and administrative organ. This purpose, too, was not achieved.

Alexander was fully aware of the urgent need to improve conditions among the peasantry. The problem was, however, too vast for him and he retreated from difficulties of reforming serfdom. On May 28, 1801, he issued a decree, intended to put an end to the practice of advertising serfs for sale like livestock.[4] But landowners were soon evading this prohibition by advertising serfs as being "for hire," which was understood to mean the same as "for sale." A more important ukaz of February 20, 1803, which raised hopes in liberal circles and among the peasantry that serfdom was now to be abolished gradually, established a new rural class, the free peasants. It applied only to serfs who, by voluntary agreement with their masters and in accordance with the terms laid down, became free men. But serfs found that the price of freedom, ranging from 139 to five thousand rubles for each male, was beyond their reach. The total number of male serfs emancipated during Alexander's reign was only 47,153, a mere one percent of the serf population.

Alexander and Elizabeth had been married for seven years at the time of his accession to the throne. They had been drawn into a close companionship during Paul's reign, when they had been harassed by military discipline and by the Emperor's unpredictable demands. She had proved herself to be a calm and intelligent partner under such stress. As Empress she welcomed the meetings of the Private Committee and encouraged her husband in his reforming zeal. She was happy in the comparative austerity of their way of life for, like Alexander, she had not enjoyed the extravagance and excessive court functions of Catherine II's reign. But clouds gathered over their marriage.

In 1799 Elizabeth had borne a daughter who had died in infancy and there was some doubt as to whether she could have more children. She was not robust in health and suffered often from migraine, fatigue, and colds. By 1801 she was in her twenties and had matured. She was still, and was always to be, devoted to her husband, but increasingly she had to rely on the forbearance and fortitude which were ingrained in her nature.

Alexander was evidently a man of strong sensual needs and as Emperor he did not hesitate to satisfy them with other women. Evidently Elizabeth, so strong in her devotion, could not meet his demands. Rumors of his affairs reached her ears and, apart from the brief visit of her mother, the Margravine of Baden, to St. Petersburg in the summer of 1801, she had only her younger sister, Princess Amelia, at her side to comfort her in her loneliness. But the numerous, more or less discreet, affairs were easier to bear than the official mistress who was soon to come into prominence.

In 1803 Alexander became enamored of Maria Naryshkina, a Pole of great beauty and sensual charm, and a natural courtesan. She had married Lev Naryshkin, a Russian noble holding high office at court. He was complaisant about his wife's affairs and probably found it convenient to condone her entanglement with the Emperor. The court, which was still conditioned by Catherine II's practice of appointing official lovers, readily accepted the Emperor's mistress as a person of influence to be cultivated. Alexander's mother, the Dowager Empress Maria, made a friend of her. No one, least of all Alexander, appeared to sympathize with Elizabeth and the misery of her position. Indeed, her anguish was made the more unbearable by Maria Naryshkina's insolence and effrontery, as when she went out of her way to inform Elizabeth that she was pregnant by Alexander, and she continued to appear at court, flaunting her condition, until shortly before she was brought to labor.

Maria Naryshkina bore several children which Alexander acknowledged as his own, although he knew that she had other lovers.

Elizabeth took refuge in semiretirement from court. She had in 1806 given birth to another daughter, but this child, too, died in infancy. She had to accept that she would never give him a son and a family. Adding to her distress was the court gossip that she received lovers. But she remained staunchly devoted to her husband. She did not blame him or find fault. She waited for him to return to her, and few women would have had such patience.

Elizabeth had to endure not only Alexander's mistress, Maria Naryshkina, but also the antagonism of her mother-in-law, the Dowager Empress Maria, and of the rest of the family. Catherine, Alexander's favorite sister, who was Grand Duchess of Württemberg, was her most active enemy. She was a tiresome woman of great vitality who was ambitious, interfering, vindictive, and indiscreet. Many believed that she had caused the estrangement between Alexander and Elizabeth. This is unlikely, however, for he was not under her influence and often ignored her insistent advice. He was nevertheless extremely, even excessively, devoted to her. His letters, as carefully edited by Grand Duke Nicholas Mikhailovich, reveal a tenderness toward her and at times a passion and an intimacy unusual between brother and sister.[5]

The Franco-Russian treaty of friendship, signed in October 1801, had been part of a general movement toward peace throughout Europe. France had even concluded the Treaty of Amiens with England and similar treaties with other nations. But the peace was no more than an uneasy armistice. Napoleon maintained a blockade against English trade and threatened invasion by massing ships and troops to cross the Channel. Toward Russia he became critical, especially over her close relations with England. It was, however, the cruel murder of the Duc d'Enghien, son of the Duc de Bourbon, on March 21, 1804, that led to the break between the two nations. The murder shocked Alexander and the imperial court at once went into full mourning. He sent a severe note of protest to Paris. Napoleon's reply, prepared by Talleyrand, questioned his good faith in expressing such concern over the death of the Duc d'Enghien, when he himself had failed to investigate the murder of his own father, Emperor Paul, and to punish the assassins. It was a shrewd and cutting rejoinder, which hurt Alexander deeply.

The dominance of Napoleon over Europe, and his restless greed, made enduring peace impossible. By the end of 1804 a new coalition against France was being forged. Alexander had devised an impressive plan to ensure permanent peace, while allowing Russia to acquire vast territories. His idealistic plans, while sincerely intended, usually served also as a façade for Russia's aggrandizement. In November 1804 Novosiltsev traveled to London to present to William Pitt the Emperor's plan for an Anglo-Russian league with the purpose of destroying the Napoleonic regime and creating a new Europe. The scheme provided also that Russia would annex the areas of Poland under Prussian and Austrian sovereignty as well as acquiring Moldavia, Corfu, Constantinople, the Dardanelles, Malta, and other areas. Novosiltsev also requested substantial subsidies as well as certain modifications in the English maritime code.

Pitt was a practical man. He was determined to bring down Napoleon. He expressed warm respect for the high principles and ideals of the Emperor's policy, but he was non-committal about the proposals not directly concerning England and the war against France. On April 11, 1805 (NS), an Anglo-Russian Treaty was signed. The English government allocated five million pounds for subsidies to those monarchs who would put troops in the field against Napoleon. Both England and Russia began pressing Austria, Prussia, and Sweden to join the coalition. Only Prussia clung to a precarious neutrality in the hope that she might secure Hanover, then occupied by French troops.

For some time Napoleon had seemed determined to press on with plans to invade England. Suddenly, toward the end of August 1805, he abandoned these plans and ordered the Grand Army to march into Germany. The allied leaders calculated that Napoleon's army could not reach Bavaria before November. The French advanced at such headlong speed, however, that they took the Austrian army by surprise. At Ulm, on October 19, the Austrian commander, General Karl von Mack, capitulated with twenty-five thousand men.

Napoleon was now in a delicate position. He was four hundred miles from France and winter was approaching. He had just received the devastating news of the annihilation of the Franco-Spanish fleet by Nelson at Trafalgar. The Russian army was still intact and with allied troops it far outnumbered his forces. Kutuzov, the Russian commander-in-chief, was convinced that his tactics should be to avoid direct conflict and to fall back, fighting rearguard actions. In this way he would draw the French farther and farther from their bases and expose them to the hardships of winter. Alexander, under pressure from Emperor Francis of Austria, overruled him. Toward the end of November (1805) the Russian army marched from its headquarters at Olmutz with the purpose of cutting off the French from Vienna. In ordering this advance Alexander made a fearful blunder. At Austerlitz in the course of four or five hours' fighting the Austro-Russian army, some ninety thousand strong, lost twenty-six thousand men and all their artillery, while the French losses were only nine thousand men. For Napoleon it was his most brilliant victory; for Alexander it was a shattering defeat. With Francis of Austria he fled ignominiously from the field.

Two days after the battle, Emperor Francis requested an interview with Napoleon, who agreed to an armistice on the condition that all Russians troops evacuated Austria. He made the further proposal that, if Francis persuaded Alexander to make peace with Napoleon and to enter into alliance with France against England, he would leave Austria intact in the final peace treaty. Alexander withdrew his troops from Austria, but he refused to make peace or to join the alliance against England. On December 26, 1805 (NS), at Pressburg (Bratislava) Francis signed a punitive treaty. Talleyrand had tried to moderate his master's terms, but he had failed to convince Napoleon that a strong Austria was necessary to the balance of European nations.

Meanwhile the Prussian minister, Count von Haugwitz, had come to Pressburg to conclude an offensive alliance with Napoleon. Only two months earlier, in October 1805, Alexander had traveled to Potsdam where Frederick William had exchanged with him eternal vows of friendship. The two monarchs had agreed a convention on November 3 (NS), binding Prussia to present an ultimatum to Napoleon that, unless he made peace, Prussia would enter the war on the side of the allies. After Austerlitz, however, Frederick William made haste to sign a treaty of alliance with Napoleon, and his reward was Hanover. But Napoleon and others regarded him with contempt. Only Alexander accepted his excuses and continued to heed Prussian interests.

Alliance with France, however, cost Prussia dearly. Support of the Continental System crippled her economy and both England and Sweden declared war. Another factor, deeply disturbing to Frederick William and all Prussians, was Napoleon's reorganization of Germany into the Confederation of the Rhine (July 1806), closely allied with France. He had not bothered to consult Prussia or Austria in making this major change. He went on to distress Frederick William further by offering to restore Hanover to England. Among all Prussians the alliance with France was highly unpopular. At court Queen Louise herself led the opposition to it. Frederick William turned again to Alexander and in July 1806 concluded a secret military alliance with him. In the following September he sent an ultimatum to Napoleon, but this was to result in the defeat of the Prussians at Jena and Auerstadt. On October 25 Napoleon entered Berlin.

In mid-October 1806, due largely to French machinations in Constantinople, Alexander found himself at war with Turkey. A large Russian force was nevertheless sent to the west. This force, with some Prussian support, engaged the French in the savage battle of Preussich Eylau, February 8, 1807 (NS). The carnage was terrible and the battle was inconclusive. But now Alexander's fear was that Prussia, already engaged in peace negotiations, would come to terms with Napoleon, leaving Russia to continue the war alone. In April 1807 he held meetings with Frederick William in Memel and the two monarchs signed a new convention, confirming the Russo-Prussian alliance. The French army had been seriously weakened by the grim winter campaigns and especially by the battle of Eylau. The French troops were in rags and hungry; they needed time to recover and re-equip. Intent on taking advantage of their poor condition, the Russian commander, Count Bennigsen, with sixty thousand troops attacked a French corps near Friedland in East Prussia on June 14, 1807 (NS). Victory was within the Russians' grasp, when Napoleon brought up reinforcements. The French recovered and, fighting bravely, put the Russians to flight.

Alexander had to admit defeat and he desperately needed peace. His army in the west had been demoralized by defeats and by lamentable failures in supplies and equipment. His generals had shown incompetence and even in battle had been divided by squabbles and rivalries. He had an army of eighty thousand men tied up in war against Turkey in the south, but he could not weaken this force. Also, he was compelled now to heed the serious strains that had been imposed on his people. England was unwilling to grant further large subsidies and he considered the amounts offered to be grossly inadequate. At his headquarters he was under pressure from his brother, Grand Duke Constantine, from Novosiltsev, Stroganov, and others close to him to sue for peace. They recognized that, lacking barest necessities and led by incompetent generals, the Russian army was bound to fail against Napoleon's army. But Alexander had refused to heed their advice. After the battle of Friedland he changed his mind. He wrote at once to propose an armistice. Napoleon consented. The armistice was signed on June 21, 1807 (NS), and the two Emperors agreed to meet four days later.

The historic meeting of Alexander and Napoleon took place on a sumptuously decorated raft, moored in the middle of the Niemen River, opposite Tilsit. The magnificence and pomp surrounding each Emperor and the brilliance of the uniforms of the Russian and French troops, drawn up on each side of the river, overawed many observers. The two men met alone on the first occasion and talked for three hours.

Alexander had long been curious to meet Napoleon and he evidently fell under his spell. He had obstinately fought against him, but now in one of his bewildering reversals of policy he displayed eagerness to become his ally. For many years alliance with England had been the cornerstone of Russian policy. On the eve of their meeting, Alexander wrote to Napoleon that "An alliance of Russia with France has always been the object of my desires and I am convinced that it alone can guarantee the happiness and peace of the world." When face to face, Alexander's first words are reported to have been: "I hate the English no less than you do and I am ready to assist you in any undertaking against them." Napoleon answered: "If such be the case, then everything can be settled between us."[6]

Napoleon had every reason to be satisfied. He was at the pinnacle of his fortunes. He had crushed and humiliated Austria and Prussia. His great enemy, William Pitt, had died, and against England he now had Russia as his ally. Alexander had publicly recognized his conquests and had bound himself in a secret treaty to offer to mediate between England and France and, in the event of England declining the offer, then to join in the Continental Blockade. The two Emperors discussed grandiose schemes for dividing Europe, the East under Russian and the West under French hegemony. Alexander liked planning on such a scale. When, however, Napoleon proposed erasing Prussia from the map, Russia taking all territory east of the Vistula and Niemen rivers, he refused. He was not prepared to betray his friend, Frederick William, to that extent, although he annexed the district of Belostok.

Napoleon was at his most arrogant when the Prussian King joined their meeting. He acknowledged the charm and beauty of Queen Louise, who evidently offered herself to him if he would deal less harshly with Prussia in his peace terms. But Napoleon was not to be moved. He insisted on the cession to France of all Prussian territory west of the Elbe and on Prussia's Polish provinces being formed into the Grand Duchy of Warsaw. Alexander acquiesced in the creation of the Grand Duchy, although it amounted to a reversal of the policies of Catherine II, and it was to prove a source of anxiety to Russia. The Poles themselves were disappointed, for it fell so far short of what Napoleon had led them to expect. For his part Alexander welcomed Napoleon's offer of support against Turkey.

The three treaties of Tilsit were monuments of arrogance, double-dealing, and deceit. In the atmosphere of goodwill attending their meetings both Emperors may have intended to honor their pledges. Their conduct soon proved otherwise. Alexander nevertheless departed from Tilsit, feeling relieved and exhilarated. "God has saved us," he wrote to his sister, Catherine. "Instead of sacrifices we emerge from the struggle with a kind of luster."[7] To his mother he wrote, "Happily Bonaparte with all his genius has a vulnerable side. It is his vanity, and I have made up my mind to sacrifice my own self-respect to save the Empire."[8]

The Tilsit treaties were far from popular in Russia. As the months passed and their full effects were felt, they were resented increasingly and hostility toward the French mounted. But Alexander had proceeded to carry out his main undertakings. On November 7, 1807 (NS), he had broken off relations with England. Next, on Napoleon's instigation, he invaded Sweden and annexed Finland on March 20, 1808 (NS). But it was soon clear that the policies of the two Emperors were diverging over Turkey, Prussia, and Poland.

On February 2, 1808 (NS), Napoleon wrote to Alexander, outlining a master plan for Russo-French action in Scandinavia, Turkey, and Asia, culminating in the conquest of India. Alexander accepted the plan with enthusiasm and agreed to meet Napoleon in Erfurt to discuss it further. But already Alexander was on his guard and dissembling his real thoughts and intentions. "Bonaparte imagines that I am nothing but a simpleton," he wrote to his sister in September 1808, "but he laughs best who laughs last."⁹ At Tilsit he had been under Napoleon's spell; he no longer labored under it at Erfurt, where he appeared sure of himself and clear about his course of action. An important factor in his new confidence was the advice of Talleyrand, Napoleon's former minister of foreign affairs, who was convinced that by his arrogance and rapacity Napoleon was leading France to disaster. His advice, which Alexander heeded, was that Russia should lead in forming a new coalition against France.

The Congress of Erfurt took place from September 27 until October 14, 1808 (NS), in the midst of magnificence and ceremonial of which both Emperors were masters. Four kings and countless princes and dukes were present. All were minions of Napoleon and anxious to show him every respect. For Alexander, however, the congress was strenuous, involving frequent arguments with Napoleon, and in the convention which they signed on October 12 he showed that he had made few concessions. The Franco-Russian alliance was reaffirmed, but there was no agreement concerning the partition of Turkey. Alexander extracted Napoleon's consent to Russia's annexation of Moldavia, Wallachia, and Finland, but undertook to declare war on Austria if she attacked France.

During these months Francis, Emperor of Austria, had been preparing for war against France. The resistance in Spain to Napoleon's troops had emboldened him, and the friendly attitude of the Russians had encouraged him. But Alexander was playing a double role: he assured the French that he would honor his undertakings; he led the Austrians to understand at the same time that the Russian army would not march against them.

The Austrians opened hostilities in April 1809. The French narrowly escaped defeat in the battle of Aspern and Essling, but on July 6 at Wagram the Austrian army was routed. Again Napoleon imposed harsh conditions on his defeated enemy. The Treaty of Schönbrunn (October 14, 1809) reduced Austria to a second-class power and compelled her to join France against England. During the Austrian campaigns Alexander had rendered no assistance to France. His troops, massed at the Galician frontier, took no part in the fighting. In St. Petersburg opinion was strongly on the side of the Austrians and the terms imposed by Napoleon horrified the Russians. The inclusion of Western Galicia in the Duchy of Warsaw was regarded as part of a deliberate policy of strengthening the Poles against Russia. Hostility toward Napoleon and the French was growing in strength.

Napoleon was concerned to maintain his alliance with Alexander, although disappointed by the Russian failure to lend support against Austria. He had no dependable allies in Europe and was anxious to consolidate his empire and to create his own legitimate dynasty. This made it necessary for him to divorce Josephine and to marry an Austrian or Russian princess who would produce a male heir to his throne. He had decided to seek the hand of Grand Duchess Anna, the fifteen-year-old sister of Alexander. He was ready to accept in its entirety a Russian convention, providing that Poland would never be resurrected, in order to ensure approval of his marriage with the Grand Duchess. But Alexander's reply had still not been received in mid-December when the divorce from Josephine was decreed. Convinced that Alexander was going to reject his proposal, Napoleon suddenly on February 6, 1810 (NS), announced that he would marry Archduchess Marie Louise of Austria. Alexander received this news in two notes, one withdrawing Napoleon's marriage proposal and the other giving notice of his marriage with Marie Louise. The notes crossed with a careful and courteous note from Alexander in which he refused the hand of his sister for two years on the ground of her youth. At the Russian court, however, Napoleon's announcement of his marriage with the Austrian princess was regarded as insulting and at the same time alarming in that it suggested the reorientation of French policy from alliance with Russia to alliance with Austria. Feeling against Napoleon was further aggravated by his repudiation of the Russian convention on Poland which the French ambassador had signed in St. Petersburg and which Alexander had ratified.

Meanwhile Russia's participation in the Continental System was bearing heavily on the Russian economy. Merchants and landowners whose estates provided the goods and materials for export depended almost entirely on the English trade, and all felt the loss acutely. The cost of maintaining the army and of the war generally had added to the strain on the economy which was in the grip of severe inflation. All of these factors had intensified the anti-French feeling among the Russians. Toward the end of 1810 Alexander issued a series of ukazi which relaxed the embargo on English trade with Russia. Napoleon protested that this was a violation of the Tilsit treaties. Alexander refused to rescind his ukazi. Napoleon insisted, convinced that in the end Alexander would yield and, when he remained firm, he began to talk of the inevitability of war with Russia. Alexander was not seeking war. For all his feelings of mission he was an extremely cautious man. But he, too, recognized that war with France was inevitable, and he had faith in the power of Russia and her people to survive the assault of the French army.[10]

During 1811 Russo-French relations deteriorated steadily. Napoleon sought to make the Continental System more effective. He had annexed Holland in July 1810 and in December he seized the Hanseatic towns of Hamburg, Bremen, and Lubeck. But Alexander was most incensed by his seizure of the Duchy of Oldenburg, the heir apparent of which was his brother-in-law. The security of the duchy had been guaranteed in the Tilsit treaties. His protests to Paris were, however, brusquely rejected. Meanwhile, he pressed ahead with the reorganization of the army. The armaments factories at Tver, in St. Petersburg, and in the Urals, worked under pressure to provide equipment. He was concentrating troops on his western frontier. French forces were massing in Prussia and the Duchy of Warsaw.

Freed by the Tilsit treaties from the immediate pressures of war, Alexander had turned again to domestic reforms. In this he was prompted by his own lofty liberal ideals and by Mikhail Speransky, rather than by the angry discontent among his people. He came under the influence of several people during his reign. But he did not submit himself wholly to any one person. He was always aloof in some degree so that even his favorites never knew exactly where they stood with him. Alexei Arakcheev and Mikhail Speransky were very close to him at this period in his reign. They represented the extremes of his nature. Speransky was a champion of liberal ideas: Arakcheev was a reactionary, a parade-ground tyrant, a sadistic disciplinarian, whose period of greatest dominance was known as the *Arakcheevshchina*. Of the two men Arakcheev was closer to him and for a longer period.

Alexei Arakcheev came from the minor gentry. He was trained at the St. Petersburg Military Academy and in 1792 was posted to the garrison at Gatchina. He made an impression on the Grand Duke, as an expert in drilling troops and in gunnery, and after Paul's accession his rise was rapid. He was a major-general at the age of twenty-seven, created a count in 1799, and held many high offices. At Gatchina Alexander had met Arakcheev who, on occasion, had sheltered him from his father's furies, and the two young men had become friends. Not even Arakcheev, however, was immune from Paul's insane outbursts, and he was suddenly exiled to his estate at Gruzino in the Novgorod province. In 1803 Alexander, then Emperor, recalled him and appointed him Inspector-General of Artillery, a sound appointment, for Arakcheev was the outstanding artillery expert in Russia at this time. Five years later he became minister for war. No one was closer to Alexander during the campaigns of 1805–7.

Arakcheev's long dark face with piercing hooded eyes and small tight mouth always inspired fear both at court and in the army. All looked upon him as a monster and a sinister influence on the Emperor. He was, in fact, a strange mixture. He was devout, but also given to debauchery; he was arrogant, vengeful, ambitious, and reactionary, but occasionally also generous and charitable. His serfs at Gruzino, who lived harshly regimented lives, hated him. Driven beyond endurance by him and his mistress, Anastasia Minkina, they murdered her, and he lashed out savagely and indiscriminately in punishing them. The "Gatchina sergeant-major," as he was called, was also an administrator of great ability. He carried to extremes his obsession with order and discipline, but protected the finances of the state and reorganized the Russian artillery after Austerlitz. He even made efforts to protect serfs against excessive demands by their landowners and to provide for the poor and destitute. On occasions in later years he prevailed on Alexander to show clemency and to reduce sentences which were unduly severe. His evil reputation has survived, but he was a devoted and effective servant of the Emperor and the nation. In his concern for discipline, order, his devoutness, his severity and practical ability, he revealed the qualities which Alexander respected and in some degree shared.

By contrast Mikhail Speransky was a gentle, modest man of towering ability and industry. The son of a village priest, he was born in 1772 and educated in the Kiev Seminary. He showed such striking promise that at the age of eighteen he was teaching in the St. Petersburg Theological Academy. By a stroke of fortune he came to the notice of Princes Alexander and Alexei Kurakin, who persuaded Empress Catherine to have him released from the obligation to enter the priesthood. He became secretary to the Kurakins and later to Count Victor Kochubey, who was then minister of the interior. At every stage he had distinguished himself and further promotion awaited him.

Alexander had been attracted to Speransky and had taken him on his visit to Erfurt. He had appointed him to be assistant minister of justice in 1808 and secretary of state two years later. After Tilsit, when concerned again with internal reforms, Alexander treated him as his closest and most trusted adviser; strangely, it was during this period that he was also advancing Arakcheev.

In 1808 Alexander instructed him to prepare an over-all plan of constitutional reform. Speransky worked with intense dedication and in October 1809 he submitted his plan to Alexander. "An Introduction to the Code of State Laws," as it was called, was a comprehensive and systematic project, the first part containing a critical examination of the existing order, the second proposing major reforms. The opening review was devastatingly critical.

"Of what good are civil laws when their tablets can be smashed every day upon the first rock of autocracy?" he wrote in a typical passage, "People complain of the confused finances. But how can finances be organized in a state which lacks public confidence, where there are no national laws or order which could protect them? Of what use is education? Only to enable the public to observe more clearly its miserable condition . . . In the legal chaos there are laws not only vague and insufficient, but contradictory to each other . . . I do not mention here subjects of a more important character, namely, the relation of the peasants to their owners, that is, the relation between millions of people, composing the most useful part of the population and a handful of parasites who acquired, God knows why and how, all rights and privileges."[11]

Speransky's main recommendation was that, while retaining the autocracy, the state should be ordered by law with strict separation of legislative, administrative, and judicial powers. Many more people were to have political rights, but this was subject to property qualification. He envisaged the eventual emancipation of the serfs, but believed that this could only be achieved gradually, and at this stage he excluded them from his plan. Government was thus to be organized like a pyramid with the Autocrat at the apex and beneath him a State Council, responsible for coordinating the legislative, executive, and judicial powers, and extending to county level. Although the plan had many shortcomings, it represented a distinct advance on the existing conditions.

Alexander studied Speransky's proposals, but it is not known what he thought of them; presumably he approved for they furthered the liberal ideals which he cherished. He nevertheless shrank from implementing them. The draft plan was not published, and kept in the Emperor's private archives. Speransky managed, however, to obtain approval for setting up the State Council, but as an appointed, not an elective, body. More important, he succeeded in introducing basic reforms of the central administration and in financial organization.

In his efforts to modernize the bureaucratic system, Speransky gave special attention to raising the standard of civil servants. An ukaz of April 3, 1809, laid down that court appointments would no longer bestow a status in the Table of Ranks, allowing the holder to acquire a higher position on transfer to the civil service. A further ukaz on August 6 required that promotion beyond a certain grade would depend on passing examinations or holding a university degree.

At court and in the bureaucracy these ukazi aroused an uproar. Speransky's financial policies also met with bitter criticism, although they were clearly directed toward curing the inflationary chaos of the economy. Apart from such obvious measures as cutting back expenditure and increasing taxes, his most striking innovation was the imposition of a progressive tax on the revenue, as distinct from the number of serfs, on the estates of landowners. This was seen as a direct assault on the time-honored exemption of the nobility.

Hostility toward Speransky mounted. He had never been popular. At court and among civil servants the dramatic rise of this man of humble origin had aroused furious resentment. His reforms had intensified feeling against him. A campaign was begun to oust him from office. He probably knew nothing about it. He lived quietly with his English wife in a modest apartment, and such spare time as he had after long hours of work he devoted to the study of history and political economy. He had no time or inclination for court life. He cultivated no friends or supporters, and showed no interest in acquiring riches or honors. He worked in a closed secret world of his own, reporting directly and privately to the Emperor. His very secrecy aggravated the suspicion and antagonism of the court and the nobility against him.

Alexander's mother, the Dowager Empress, his sister, Grand Duchess Catherine, and Grand Duke Constantine, condemned him as a Jacobin. They mistrusted his influence. Arakcheev, to whom his liberal ideas were anathema, was also jealous of his primacy among those close to the throne. At first, Alexander himself appeared unmoved by the complaints and hostility directed against his chief adviser. In 1811, however, his sister gave him *A Note on Ancient and Modern Russia* by Nicholas Karamzin, the leading literary figure of the day, whom Alexander had virtually appointed official historian. Karamzin was a fervent champion of the autocracy, and he idealized ancient Russia. He had written this note as an indictment of Speransky's reforms. Alexander was probably impressed by Karamzin's note, for he held him in high regard. He was also influenced by the mounting hostility at court and among the landowning nobility. On the evening of March 17, 1812, Speransky was summoned to the palace. He was closeted with the Emperor for two hours. What was said during this long audience is not known, but the result was the exile of Speransky first to Nizhni-Novgorod and a few months later to Perm.[12] He had fallen because in his single-minded devotion to the national interest and in his liberal policies he had appeared as the enemy of the landowning nobility against whom Alexander was too weak to stand.[13]

On June 24, 1812 (NS), Napoleon ordered his army to cross the Niemen River and to advance into Russia. It was the beginning of an epic chapter in Europe's history. For Alexander it was a time of greatness. Never were the Russian Emperor and his people more completely united. He epitomized their will to resist and their deep faith that Mother Russia could never be conquered. Only a few months earlier the Austrian ambassador, Count Saint Julien, had reported to Metternich in Vienna that "the Emperor has little confidence in the talents of his generals . . . he puts his trust in the courage of his troops, their discipline and their passive obedience, but even more so in the obstacles which in his dominions are offered by the terrain—wooded, swampy, primitive, and sparsely populated. His Majesty greatly relies on the difficulty of supplies and the rigor of the climate. The Emperor also depends on public spirit, the sacrifices which are promised him in the name of the nation, and the justice of his cause which he considers sacred." To the French ambassador he had said earlier that "I shall withdraw to Kamchatka rather than cede any of my provinces or sign in my capital, occupied by the enemy, a peace that would be merely an armistice."[14] Several people expected him to capitulate, but even those closest to him, including his own sister, did not appreciate the strength of his resolve to resist so long as one French soldier remained on Russian soil.

Alexander was attending a grand ball in Vilna when General Balashev, his minister of police, drew him aside to report on the French invasion. He received the news calmly and, having made excuses to his hostess, returned at once to headquarters. There, after discussion with Admiral Shishkov and General Prince Peter Volkonsky, he wrote a strong but dignified appeal to Napoleon to halt his aggression. At dawn Balashev set out bearing the Emperor's note. He was brusquely received by Napoleon at Rykonti, not far from the Niemen. Napoleon maintained angrily that Alexander had provoked aggression by his alliances with England and Sweden. He was boastful and arrogant, and he bluntly refused to halt his army.[15]

In spite of their preparations the Russians were far from ready to meet the French onslaught. The Treaty of Bucharest, concluded with Turkey on May 28, 1812 (NS), had ended the war in the south. Russia had gained Bessarabia, but had had to yield Moldavia and Wallachia. The treaty had, however, ensured that Russia would not be engaged against two enemies on two fronts. But against the French army, some 575,000 strong, Alexander could muster only 220,000 troops and his effective forces were probably no greater than 180,000. Barclay de Tolly, the commander-in-chief, was in an unenviable position, for he had no choice but to retreat before the superior French forces. Napoleon took Vilna on June 28 (NS), but the Russians expected him to be halted at Smolensk, where the armies of Barclay and Bagration had come together. Meanwhile Alexander himself had made a difficult decision which showed him to be capable of listening to advice and of subjugating himself and his feelings to the national interest. Arakcheev, Balashev, and Shishkov wrote him a letter, proposing that he should leave the army and return to the capital. As head of the nation this was his proper place, whereas by remaining with the army he would be responsible for failures, the high command would be hampered by his presence, and troops would have to be detached especially to guard his person. Alexander had always wanted to lead his armies in the field. He was deeply hurt by this proposal, but he recognized the problems that his presence caused. In July he set out for Moscow, where he was welcomed with patriotic fervor.[16] His firmness of purpose aroused demonstrations of loyalty which moved him deeply. He traveled on to St. Petersburg, where he met with a less ardent welcome. He drove to the small palace on Kamenny Island and there he stayed throughout the French invasion.

Expecting that Napoleon would be halted at Smolensk, Russians were appalled when Barclay surrendered the city and fell back toward Moscow. All united in condemning him. Grand Duke Constantine accused him of treason and of "leading the enemy to Moscow." Barclay's position became impossible. In St. Petersburg Alexander found that everyone clamored for Kutuzov to be made commander-in-chief. From Moscow reports reached him that only the appointment of Kutuzov would restore confidence. Again Alexander was faced with an unpalatable decision. He personally disliked Kutuzov and had no faith in his leadership. But again he subordinated his personal wishes and on August 20 (NS) Kutuzov became commander-in-chief.

Field-Marshal Prince Mikhail Kutuzov was sixty-seven. He had only one eye and was so fat that he had difficulty in moving about. His father had served under Peter the Great and he himself was the last of the great generals of Catherine's reign. He was long past his best as a commander in the field, but he possessed the magic quality of leadership. The troops loved him for his homely language, his bluntness, and his devotion to the army and Russia. He inspired confidence, and he was not afraid to make unpopular decisions. Barclay's tactics of retreat had brought upon him the hostility of all Russians. But on assuming command, Kutuzov at once ordered further retreat. Reluctantly he decided to face the enemy in open battle at Borodino, but this was a concession to the general Russian feeling that it was unthinkable that Napoleon should be allowed to advance to Moscow unchallenged.

The battle of Borodino, fought on September 7 (NS), was a savage engagement. The Russians lost fifty-eight thousand men and the French fifty thousand. Napoleon considered it the most terrible battle that he had ever fought. Both sides claimed victory. The significant factors were, however, that Napoleon lost forty-seven of his best generals and that the Russian army fell back in good order.

Kutuzov now made the decision which stunned all Russians. They were deeply committed to the emotional conception of Moscow as the heart of the nation. But he saw that the choice was between saving

Moscow or saving his army, and he chose the latter without hesitation. On September 13 he ordered the army to evacuate the city and fall back to the southeast toward Ryazan. On the following day Napoleon entered Moscow. He was amazed to find the city almost deserted and fires, which broke out on the same evening, raged for four days, destroying whole districts.[17] Napoleon had believed that, on the fall of Moscow, Alexander would capitulate, and now he learned his mistake. He made three peace offers during his thirty-three days in the city and all were ignored.

Although bewildered by the surrender of Moscow, Alexander was even more determined not to make peace. In St. Petersburg he fretted over his uselessness. He was also hurt by the unjust criticisms directed against him for having brought disasters upon the nation. But he discovered in himself a stubborn strength which reflected the mood of his people. To his sister, who thought that his resolve might weaken, he wrote: "Rest assured that my determination to fight on is firmer than ever."[18]

On October 19 (NS), Napoleon began his retreat from Moscow. He had been acutely uneasy ever since he had entered the empty city and it had become a burned ruin. His army was far from its bases and surrounded by a hostile people who fought with a ferocity that surprised him and his men. Moreover, winter was approaching. The Grand Army, encumbered by booty and by the sick and wounded, could make only slow progress and was harried incessantly by partisan groups. Kutuzov followed at a distance, still unwilling to engage the enemy. He saw no need to sacrifice his men in battle when the winter and the partisan bands were slowly destroying the French army. Criticism mounted against him. Popular hatred of the French was so great that Russians could not understand why he did not attack. When finally he was committed to a plan, drawn up in St. Petersburg, to operate with two other forces in preventing the French from crossing the Berezina River, the plan failed. Napoleon, although outnumbered and with an army decimated by cold and hunger, extricated his forces brilliantly. But the invasion and great retreat had in effect destroyed the magnificent Grand Army. Of 575,000 men who had invaded Russia five months earlier, only some thirty thousand ragged and frostbitten survivors struggled across the Niemen River on December 14 (NS).

Russia had been freed from the invader, but vast areas had been ravaged and conditions were desperate throughout the country. The people now longed for peace and the chance to rebuild and to cultivate the land again. The army was exhausted and, as Kutuzov urged upon the Emperor, the men needed rest. Against the advice of everyone, even those closest to him like Arakcheev, Grand Duke Constantine, and Shishkov, Alexander resolved to advance westward. He had rejoined his army in Vilna in December and was determined now to remain with it until Napoleon had been overthrown and peace had been signed in Paris. The influence of certain foreigners close to him was strongly resented by Russians who believed that this had encouraged him in this desperate venture. But the real explanation of his new purpose and determination to advance westward into Europe was to be found in the transformation which had taken place in the man and in his outlook.

The events of 1812 had a tremendous impact on Alexander. From this time he began to display a religious ardor, touched with mysticism and messianism, which grew stronger with the passing years. He had never been noted for his piety. He had attended to the formalities of religious observance required of the Emperor, and no more. But latent in his many-sided nature was evidently a strong religious bent, which developed into a mania.

Two members of his intimate circle, Prince Alexander Golitsyn and Rodion Koshelev, had undergone a similar conversion and undoubtedly influenced him. Golitsyn had led a wild life as a young man, but about 1803, when he was appointed procurator of the Holy Synod, he began to take an interest in religion and became exceedingly devout. Instead of embracing Orthodoxy, however, he evolved a faith of his own, containing a strong mystical element.

Koshelev had served in the Horse Guards and had been ambassador for a time in Copenhagen. He had made contact with various esoteric groups in Western Europe and was also an enthusiastic freemason. He became more and more immersed in mystic cults. He had an apartment in the Winter Palace which he retained after he had resigned his various appointments in order to devote himself to the study of various arcane doctrines. Foreign ambassadors in St. Petersburg reported skeptically on both Golisyn and Koshelev but, as worldly men, they were probably not sympathetic toward mystical fervor. Alexander himself felt deeply indebted to the two men. He wrote to Koshelev on December 13, 1815: "You have powerfully contributed to make me adopt the course I am now following by conviction and which alone has brought me success in the most difficult task the Very High One has assigned me."[19]

With Golitsyn he was constantly exchanging notes on religious matters. Golitsyn attributed his own conversion primarily to reading the Bible, which is not usually read or studied in the Orthodox Church. Alexander, too, began reading the Bible and it became the mainstay of his faith. In December 1812 the Russian Bible Society was formed in St. Petersburg. It drew on the British and Foreign Bible Society in London for its aims and rules, except that it was financed liberally by the Russian government and had the ardent support of the Emperor who was one of its founder members. It recruited Roman Catholics and Protestants as well as the Orthodox. Alexander believed that through this Bible

Society he would achieve "one Christian faith which will unite all Christian denominations."[20]

The fervor of Alexander and his religious advisers, their unorthodox worship, and their spreading influence, disturbed the Russian hierarchy and also the Holy See. From Rome came directions that Catholics must not support the Bible Society. Among leaders of the Orthodox Church strong opposition was developing against the Emperor's religious activities. But Alexander was not deterred. He believed himself to be committed to a desperate struggle against the "reign of Satan" and that, in his own words, "I am the depository of a sacred, holy mission."[21] The messianic purpose, which had long been an element in the Russian religious outlook, appeared in Alexander in an extremely personal, mystical form.

In Vilna, Alexander fussed about the lack of smartness and discipline of his troops. The fact that they had marched from Ryazan in winter and had engaged the French at the Berezina was for him no excuse. He ignored Kutuzov's pleas that the men should be allowed to rest, and insisted that they must be drilled into smartness. He wanted to be rid of "old Kutuzov" as he called him, but could not do so because the Field-Marshal was a national hero.

Early in January 1813 the Russian army of 110,000 troops crossed the Niemen River to carry out their Emperor's mission of liberating Europe. Kutuzov was in command and, like his men, he had no enthusiasm for this expedition. But he was old and tired and, reaching Silesia, he died. The nation mourned him. Alexander was relieved, however, because he felt that now he could press forward more rapidly. The advance of the Russians had given courage to the Austrians and Prussians, who sent troops to reinforce them. But soon after leaving Dresden the allied army was engaged by Napoleon who had raised a new army, and at Lutzen it suffered defeat. The allies fought a further battle at Bautzen on May 20 (NS) which was indecisive. At Dresden, on August 26–27 (NS), Napoleon was again victorious, but then was defeated at Kulm three days later.

The allied commanders mistrusted and disliked each other, but Alexander was able to encourage and coordinate them. The battles of the past months had been leading to the decisive engagement at Leipzig and, thanks to his efforts, the allies gained a resounding victory. On October 16, when the French cavalry were driving all before them and the Austrian and Prussian monarchs were expecting defeat, Alexander galloped to his Cossack regiments and ordered them to halt the enemy. They made a furious attack and put the French cavalry to flight. On the following day Napoleon sent peace proposals and they were ignored. On the third day of fighting the Allies forced the French to flee beyond the Rhine.

Emperor Francis of Austria and King Frederick William of Prussia were anxious to make peace, now that Germany had been liberated. Alexander argued that Napoleon would arise afresh and plunge Europe into new disasters, unless he was removed and peace was signed in Paris. His obstinate faith and determination carried them with him. But his was a blind purpose. The arrival of Castlereagh, the English minister of foreign affairs, brought the Allies together on the rational basis of the Quadruple Alliance, established by the Treaty of Chaumont, signed on March 9, 1814, and binding Britain, Russia, Prussia, and Austria not to make separate peace with France.

On March 31, 1814 (NS), Alexander made his entry into Paris at the head of the allied army. The French welcomed him with wild enthusiasm; they were weary of war, and they were greatly impressed by the noble bearing and the benevolent attitude of the Russian Emperor toward them. Alexander was deeply moved by his reception. He wrote to Golitsyn that his soul "was almost dissolved in gratitude to God . . . I was hungry for solitude so that I could pour out my heart before Him." The liberal terms of the Treaty of Fontainebleau, April 11, 1814 (NS) under which Napoleon abdicated and was held in Elba, and of the first Treaty of Paris, May 30, 1814 (NS), justified the faith of the French in his benevolence. But he had to yield to his Allies on certain matters. They insisted on the restoration of the Bourbons in the person of Louis XVIII. Alexander would have preferred someone else on the throne or, even better, the creation of a republic. He was reconciled, however, by the provisions that Louis XVIII was to reign not as an absolute but as a constitutional monarch.

In June 1814 Alexander visited England and was received with popular acclaim all the way from Dover to London. But during his visit he, and even more his sister Catherine, behaved badly and caused offense. They showed discourtesy towards the Prince Regent, later George IV, and blatantly took sides in domestic politics by cultivating the Whigs and so far as possible ignoring the Tory government. Catherine was evidently the main offender, but it is remarkable that he did not restrain her. Anglo-Russian relations were beset by discords, and Alexander's visit aggravated English mistrust of him and his policies, at the time when the allies were about to assemble to establish a new and stable order in Europe.

The Congress of Vienna, convened for this purpose, met from September 1814 until June 1815. It brought crowding into the Austrian capital the monarchs or ministers, delegates and special agents from every country of Europe. The city provided a brilliant succession of receptions, parades, grand balls, and banquets. The Congress itself did not meet, and the negotiations were carried on informally by the main powers: Austria, Russia, England, Prussia and, at a later stage, France.

Emperor Francis was host, but took little part in its work, preferring to leave the negotiations to Metternich, who had originally proposed the Congress. Alexander himself led the Russian delegation and was active throughout the proceedings. Castlereagh, later succeeded by the Duke of Wellington, led the English delegation. Talleyrand represented Louis XVIII in its later stages.

The complexity of the issues and the conflicts of interest were formidable, but the future of the Grand Duchy of Warsaw and of Saxony presented the most serious problems. Russia, Austria, and Prussia had agreed in 1813 to partition Poland between them. In Vienna, however, Alexander claimed the whole duchy and proposed that Prussia should have Saxony as compensation for her losses of Polish territory. Most of the German states directly concerned in the fate of Saxony objected. Austria was deeply disturbed by the proposed annexation of the whole of the Duchy of Warsaw by Russia. When, in November 1814, Prince Nicholas Repnin, commanding the Russian army in Saxony, transferred the supreme command there to Prussia, the German states and France protested furiously.

On December 11 Alexander's brother, Grand Duke Constantine, issued a manifesto in Warsaw, calling on all Poles to unite as an independent nation under the Russian Emperor. This manifesto brought into the open the clear rift between the allies. On January 3, 1815 (NS), Castlereagh, Metternich, and Talleyrand formed a secret military alliance, directed against Russia and Prussia. Castlereagh in particular was concerned with the need to unite Europe against Russia. Austrian troops moved up to the Polish frontier; France ordered partial mobilization; only eight months after Napoleon's abdication Europe was again moving toward war. Realization of this danger had the effect of making Alexander more ready to compromise. In the Final Act of the Congress most of the Grand Duchy of Warsaw became a constitutional kingdom of which the Russian Emperor was King, but Prussia gained certain Polish territory. Austria regained Galicia, and Cracow became a free city. The Saxon King, Frederick Augustus, was restored to his throne, but had to cede more than a third of his kingdom to Prussia.

Alexander's stubborn efforts to procure the whole of the Duchy of Warsaw had demonstrated that, where Russian interests were involved, his lofty principles were laid aside. The escape of Napoleon from Elba and his return to Europe in March 1815 helped diminish Alexander's authority, for it was generally believed that his lenient treatment of the French had made this possible. When Alexander requested that he should be nominated commander-in-chief of the allied army in the west, Wellington curtly refused. After the battle of Waterloo, June 18, 1815 (NS), Wellington dominated the allied negotiations. Alexander, who arrived in Paris almost a month later than Wellington, had little say in the drafting of the second Peace of Paris, November 20, 1815 (NS) which imposed more severe terms on France.

Alexander liked to play the leading role. He saw himself as the noble Christian Emperor to whom the whole world looked for moral leadership. His vanity was hurt by the markedly less warm welcome that he received on his return to Paris. At the same time his religious mania and his sense of special mission had become more intense. He never tired of meeting and talking for hours with people who claimed to have a religious vocation or mystic knowledge. Some of them were sincere and devout men, like the two Quakers, William Allen and Etienne de Grellet, whom he had met in London in 1814 and who introduced him to the simple peace of silent prayer. Most of them were, however, cranks and imposters, readily accepted by the gullible Emperor. Among the latter was Baroness von Krudener, who was to exercise considerable influence over him for some twelve months until he became bored with her.

Julie Krudener was the young and handsome widow of a Baltic diplomat in the Emperor's service. She had a striking personality, and was both wildly extravagant and ambitious. She cultivated the leading people of the day, and in every city of Europe where she stayed she formed her own salon. Suddenly, through a shoemaker who belonged to the Moravian Brethren, she found her mission: She would convert the world into the Kingdom of God and soon she was claiming to be in direct communication with God and to have prophetic vision. At this stage in her career she saw that the Russian Emperor would be a wonderful prize, which would raise her renown to celestial heights. She achieved her conquest in a dramatic midnight meeting.

Alexander had heard of her through Mlle. Sturdza, his wife's lady-in-waiting, with whom he corresponded on religious matters. Leaving Vienna after Napoleon's escape from Elba, Alexander stopped at Heilbronn. He was feeling depressed. He was unable to find his usual comfort in the Bible. He found himself thinking of the Baroness, wondering where she was and what she was like. At this moment his aide knocked at his door and, apologizing for the late hour, explained that a lady was below, asking urgently to see him. It was Julie Krudener, and for three hours she sat with him, talking of sin and forgiveness. The dramatic coincidence of her appearance while he was thinking of her and then their long conversation made him attribute the meeting to divine providence. He saw her often and when apart they corresponded. She followed him to Paris and there he visited her daily. He gave her presents of money, for she was always in debt. But she took care that her role as spiritual adviser to the Emperor was widely known and she exaggerated greatly.

Out of his mixed emotions and such influences as Julie Krudener's teachings, was born Alexander's Holy Alliance, dramatically proclaimed to the world on September 26, 1815 (NS). It was, in fact, not an alliance, but a grandiloquent manifesto, prepared by Alexander himself and reluctantly signed by the Emperor of Austria and the King of Prussia. Subsequently all the monarchs of Europe endorsed it, except the King of England, the Pope, and the Turkish Sultan. The President of the United States also refused to subscribe to it.

The Holy Alliance was an extraordinary document, lofty in ideals but vague in application. The monarchs who signed it pledged themselves to regulate their conduct among themselves and toward their subjects in accordance with the principles of Christianity. To Alexander it was a declaration of faith which would commit signatories to a "universal union." Castlereagh dismissed it as "a piece of sublime mysticism and nonsense," and Metternich called it "a loud-sounding nothing."[22] In fact the Holy Alliance was forgotten in all but name as soon as it was signed. In subsequent congresses Alexander tried "to give the soul of the Holy Alliance a body" by transforming the Quadruple Alliance into a "universal union" in which the powers guaranteed the frontiers and regimes then existing in the countries of Europe. Castlereagh would not agree, however, and his attempts failed.

The real basis of cooperation between the allies was the Quadruple Alliance of November 20, 1815 (NS), agreed on the initiative of Castlereagh who sought to give the alliance some permanence. Alexander had readily accepted Castlereagh's proposals. Certain provisions of the new treaty appealed strongly to him. Clause 6, for example, provided that the four allied sovereigns or their respective delegates should meet at regular intervals, and he welcomed this arrangement. Most important to him, however, was the underlying principle established during the Congress of Vienna, that the great powers had the special duty of maintaining peace and internal order throughout Europe and the world. He always saw himself as the moral arbiter in world affairs.

The four allies soon found themselves divided on fundamental issues, however, and the Quadruple Alliance was reduced to a nominal existence. Alexander was wedded to the principle of great power intervention in support of legitimate governments. England held firmly to the policy of non-intervention in the internal affairs of foreign states. No fewer than five revolutions broke out in the years 1820–21, and Alexander sought in each case to rally his allies to join him in putting down the revolution and re-establishing the existing regimes. He was supported by Prussia and, after hesitations, by Austria and France. Castlereagh and, after his death in August 1822, Canning strenuously opposed such action, which amounted to the defense of reactionary regimes. In the case of the revolt in Greece in March 1821, Alexander was tempted to abandon his policy in order to support the Orthodox Greeks in their rebellion against their legitimate monarch. In the event Castlereagh and Metternich persuaded him to take no action.

At the beginning of his reign Alexander had cherished liberal ideas and had even talked of republicanism. Liberals throughout Europe had looked to him to launch great reforms. His noble appearance and Christian sentiments at the time of his triumphal entry into Paris in 1814 had won him the name of "Alexander the Blessed," and this reflected the public estimate of him. But his ideals, embodied in the Holy Alliance, had proved no more than lofty formulae without practical significance. Russia had gained vast areas of Poland, the whole of Finland and Bessarabia, and parts of the Caucasus; the rest of Europe had found him to be in the end only the champion of Russian interests and of reactionary regimes.

Within Russia the great hopes of reform were even more cruelly disappointed. Serfdom, which was increasingly recognized as an evil system and which Alexander himself knew must be abolished, remained virtually unchanged. Indeed, the military colonies which he established on a large scale in 1816 in an attempt to effect economies and train and maintain regular troops resulted in greater hardships for many peasants.

The sudden death in January 1819 of his sister, Catherine, of erysipelas stunned him and had the effect of intensifying his religious mania. But, although distracted from affairs of state, he continued to nurse vague ideas of reform. In October 1820, however, a mutiny in the Semenovsky Guards Regiment of which he was colonel convinced him that dangerous revolutionary ideas were spreading. The mutiny alarmed and distressed him. He disbanded the regiment, and from this time became openly reactionary, abandoning even his lip-service to liberal reform of any kind.

Alexander's obscurantism and religious obsessions in the last years of his reign coincided with the birth of a national Russian literature and the growth of a restless political movement which proved irrepressible. Nicholas Karamzin had been the dominant writer during the first part of his reign. He was a staunch conservative, but he contributed toward the forging of the modern Russian literary language, especially in his notable twelve-volume *History of the Russian State.* The ferment of ideas and the striving for literary expression were promoted by large numbers of translations, ranging from political studies to contemporary novels and verse, but this range was greatly restricted when Arakcheev's censorship became more severe. The national literature was brought to birth, however, by three writers of genius, Krylov, Griboedov, and above all by Pushkin, who remains the greatest of Russian poets.

The ferment of political ideas had had its beginnings in the long reign of Catherine II. She had encouraged the influx of the radical doctrines of the day, but when they had erupted in revolution in the West she had become reactionary. Her cruel persecution of Radishchev for his comparatively innocuous book, *A Journey from St. Petersburg to Moscow*, had epitomized the harsh repression of her last years. But in small liberal circles among the nobility and the gentry the radical ideas had not perished, and during Alexander's reign the political ferment had spread and developed in intensity until at his death it erupted in revolution.

Young nobles and especially guards officers were keenly aware of the need for reform and attracted by the liberal ideas of the West. They were also disappointed and thwarted by Alexander's rule. His reign had opened with such high promise that their disillusion was all the more bitter. He had declared his interest in republicanism and the rights of men. On annexing Finland and Poland he had granted both countries liberal constitutions with representative government. But he had never been prepared to allow similar rights to his own people. Indeed, he showed on many occasions that he had a low opinion of their ability and political maturity, and he depended mainly on foreigners as advisers. His attitude was all the more unpalatable to Russians at this time when they saw themselves as the saviors of Europe.

Army officers who had taken part in the campaigns in Western Europe, many of whom had been in France as part of the army of occupation for as long as three years, were incensed by the conditions they found on their return to Russia. Their own people led harsh lives with even the most rudimentary freedoms denied to them. They were burdened by heavy taxation; the courts were corrupt and they could look nowhere for justice; corruption was widespread in the bureaucracy. The peasantry, making up the great majority of the population, were no more than slaves at the mercy of their landowners.

The emancipation of the serfs was the fundamental problem which troubled all thinking Russians. Among them a festering feeling of anger and revolt was growing; their hopes of change and improvement had been disappointed too often. They felt that Alexander had betrayed them and the nation, for under cover of the Holy Alliance he had pursued reactionary policies abroad and at home nothing was changed. The young liberals and army officers, nevertheless, had to discuss their discontent and their ideas with great care. Alexander had at the outset of his reign made great play of abolishing the security police, organized by Catherine II: at the close of his reign a far larger secret police service was operating under Arakcheev. His agents were everywhere. A special branch was insinuated into the guards regiments and later more widely in the army. Its agents reported promptly on officers and men suspected of holding radical ideas, and thousands were imprisoned or exiled to Siberia. But repression and spying gave rise to secret societies.

The first secret political societies in Russia were influenced by the practices of the Masonic lodges. The first society was the Union of Salvation (*Soyuz Spaseniya*), founded in St. Petersburg in 1816. It was followed in 1818 by the Union of Public Good (*Soyuz Blagodenstviya*) which had the basic political aims of abolishing serfdom and introducing representative government. The union was composed of local organs under a central executive board. Among its members, never more than two hundred and often less, Colonel Paul Pestel was most radical. He procured a decision of the central executive board, meeting in Moscow in 1820, in favor of a republic. This new political aim alarmed the more conservative members and in January of the following year the union was dissolved. Pestel was with his regiment in the south at this time and he refused to accept the dissolution. He gathered together a few supporters and established the Southern Society. At the end of 1822 the union was re-formed in St. Petersburg as the Northern Society. This was an act of great courage, for earlier in the year many officers guilty of subversive activities, which often amounted to no more than taking an active interest in Western political ideas, had been reported to the Emperor and several had been arrested. Alexander had issued an ukaz on August 1, banning all secret societies and Masonic lodges, and calling on all army officers and government officials who had been associated with such bodies to swear that they would in future abstain from political activites.

The Northern Society was far more moderate than the Southern Society. The draft constitution, prepared by Nikita Muraviev, one of the leaders of the Northern Society, provided for representative government, a federal system, and a constitutional monarch. Pestel, the leader of the Southern Society, called for a revolutionary dictatorship and the assassination of the imperial family, followed by the setting up of an egalitarian republic. Cooperation betweeen the two societies was further complicated by conflicts of personalities. But Pestel's passionate faith in the need for revolution and his eloquence made a strong impression. In November 1825 Prince Serge Trubetskoy, one of the Northern Society leaders, returned from the south and reported that Pestel's army was ready to rise. He and his fellow conspirators in the north knew that the St. Petersburg garrison was unprepared, but they agreed provisionally that the revolution should take place in spring 1826.

Alexander had no legitimate children, his two daughters by his wife, Elizabeth, having died in infancy. He was concerned less, however, about the succession than about his dream of abdicating. In Kiev in 1817 he had spoken openly to his aides about his intention to abdicate. But no one knew how to take such remarks; he was always an enigma. It was clear, however, that, whether on his abdication or his death, his successor would not be his brother, Constantine. In 1801, at the time of his father's assassination, Constantine had said: "After what has happened my brother may reign if he likes, but if the throne ever comes to me I shall certainly not accept it."[23] He had consistently refused to take any interest in the succession, but it was his morganatic marriage that led to his formally renouncing his title to the throne. His first wife, a daughter of the Prince of Saxe-Coburg, had left him. He had had several mistresses, but his request for permission to marry a commoner was not granted by Alexander until March 1820. He then promptly married Countess Jean Grudzinska, a Pole and a Roman Catholic. But he was allowed to marry her only on condition that he formally renounced the succession. He confirmed his decision in a letter dated January 14, 1822, to Alexander, who wrote on February 2 approving his renunciation.

Alexander had long intended that his younger brother, Nicholas, should succeed him. This intention was strengthened when on April 17, 1818, the succession was secured by the birth of Nicholas's son, who was to become Alexander II. According to the diary of Grand Duchess Alexandra, the wife of Nicholas, Alexander dined with them on July 5, 1819, and later in the evening he told them that Nicholas was to be his heir. This statement apparently took them by surprise and husband and wife both burst into tears, a reaction which astonished Alexander.[24] Four years later Alexander signed a manifesto, drafted by Philaret, Archbishop of Moscow, making Nicholas heir to the throne.

The desperate confusion that subsequently arose was due to the secrecy surrounding these arrangements. The manifesto and Constantine's letter of renunciation together with Alexander's letter of approval were never made public. They were deposited in a sealed envelope in the Uspensky Cathedral in Moscow. Under vows of strictest secrecy Prince Alexander Golitsyn had made three copies of each document and deposited them in sealed envolopes in the offices of the State Council, the Senate, and the Holy Synod. The envelopes were to be opened "before any other action" was taken on receiving news of Alexander's death. Nicholas and Constantine knew their own positions, but not the provisions made to give them legal effect. This was known only to the Archbishop, Golitsyn, and Alexander himself. The nation continued to look upon Constantine as the heir apparent and indeed he was so described in official documents and in prayers in all churches for the imperial family.

Alexander had always surrounded his private thoughts and actions with secrecy. The habit had developed in boyhood when he had had to dissemble before his grandmother, Empress Catherine, and his father, then Grand Duke Paul. The practice had come to meet some need in his nature for mystery. His religious mania had also taken on the character of a private mystic rite. For such a man, it was strangely appropriate that death should come to him in a small sea town, hundreds of miles from St. Petersburg and Moscow, where he was always surrounded by the magnificence and ceremonial attaching to the imperial throne.

In the last years of his life Alexander had been reunited with Elizabeth. She had been waiting patiently for him to tire of Maria Naryshkina. It happened finally in 1816, after the affair had lasted some thirteen years. She had returned to St. Petersburg after a long sojourn in France. When she was alone with Alexander, however, he "talked to her of nothing else except the Cross and divine love, a language rather novel to this lady who, complaining that her lover had turned into a father confessor, had but one wish—to return at once to Paris." So the Comte de la Ferronays reported her conversation with him on the eve of her departure from St. Petersburg.[25]

Empress Elizabeth rejoiced. She could bear with his casual affairs, but the arrogant Polish woman had been like a rival wife. Now that he had broken with her and his bonds with his family had loosened, after the death of his sister, Catherine, he again sought Elizabeth's companionship. She was a religious woman, although not obsessed with mystic doctrines as he was, and with her quiet patience she shared his domestic life again.

In the autumn of 1825 they set out together for the warm south. Her doctors had advised her to avoid the savage cold of St. Petersburg's winter, and had recommended Taganrog, a small town on the shores of the Sea of Azov. The imperial couple arrived there as though on a long-delayed honeymoon. But they had only a few weeks together. Suddenly on November 19, 1825, after a brief illness, Alexander died. Elizabeth wrote in her simple piety to her mother that "Our angel is in heaven." And in death he gave rise to a mysterious legend.[26]

XVI
Nicholas I

1825–1855

The death of Alexander gave rise to a dynastic crisis which lasted for three weeks and had serious repercussions. The news from Taganrog reached St. Petersburg only on November 27. Nicholas was then in the capital, but his brother, Constantine, was in Warsaw. On first learning of Alexander's illness Nicholas had conferred with the leading advisers at court; all had confirmed that, since the Emperor had no children and had not proclaimed a successor, the throne must pass to Constantine, the oldest surviving brother. Nicholas knew that Alexander had intended him to succeed, and he himself wanted to be Tsar. But he also knew that the guards regiments would not stand for his accession, unless Constantine had publicly renounced the throne. Officers and men of the St. Petersburg garrison detested him as a cruel drill master. Constantine was, in fact, an equally ruthless disciplinarian, but he had been away in Warsaw for some ten years. Memories of him had softened; legends had grown that he was benevolent and liberal; it was even said that he would abolish serfdom and reduce the term of military service from twenty-five to eight years, as in the Polish army. Impelled by his strong sense of duty and anxious to avoid an interregnum, Nicholas at once swore the oath of allegiance to his brother and ordered the nation to follow suit.

In the State Council the sealed envelope, desposited by Alexander and containing the manifesto naming Nicholas as his successor, had been opened. The councilors had nevertheless sworn allegiance to Constantine. The Archbishop of Moscow and the Senate did not even open their sealed envelopes, but took the oath. The army, government officials, and the people did likewise. Constantine had become Emperor of Russia.

Constantine had no intention, however, of withdrawing his renunciation of the throne. In fact, on receiving the news of Alexander's death he had at once sworn allegiance to Nicholas. Couriers raced between St. Petersburg and Warsaw, bearing from each brother assurances of loyalty to the other. Nicholas and their mother, the Dowager Empress, frantically urged Constantine to make a public statement and to come post-haste to St. Petersburg. He flatly refused. "I am not able to accept your proposal to hasten my departure for St. Petersburg," he wrote on December 6, "and I warn you that I shall leave Warsaw only to retire to some greater distance if everything is not arranged according to the will of our deceased Emperor."[1]

Constantine's blunt letter reached St. Petersburg at the same time as a report from Baron Ivan Dibich in Taganrog, giving information of a conspiracy among officers of the guards and of the southern army. Nicholas received on the same day a personal report from a young officer, Yakov Rostovtsev, whom Prince Evgenie Obolensky had tried in vain to enlist into the conspiracy. Nicholas was desperately afraid that the guards would mutiny. He decided to proclaim his own accession and appointed December 14 as the day on which all would swear the new oath of allegiance.

During the days leading up to the fateful December 14, the modest apartment of Konrad Ryleev was the scene of furious activity as young officers came and went. Although only a retired junior lieutenant, he had emerged as a strong force within the conspiracy. He was an unprepossessing young man, "but when he touched on his favorite theme —love of his country—his face lit up, his black glowing eyes shone with an unearthly light and his words flowed like a stream of lava. Never have I seen him so beautiful as on that evening." So wrote Count Bestuzhev, one of the conspirators, in his memoirs.[2] The other leading members of the conspiracy were Colonel Prince Sergei Trubetskoy, Prince Evgenie Obolensky, and a certain Kakhovsky, a former officer of the Guards, who had the same passionate devotion to the revolutionary cause as Ryleev.

The conspirators were unprepared for their rebellion. In the Northern Society they had talked vaguely of action in the spring of 1826. But the confusion after Alexander's death provided an opportunity not to be missed. They were, however, few in number and all were idealists, not practical men, capable of planning and carrying out such a daring venture. They themselves recognized the shortcomings of their plans. But in their frenzy and exaltation they accepted that they would probably be no more than sacrifices in the cause of freedom. Ryleev had written that "A cruel fate awaits the one who first rises against the oppressors of the people. But liberty has never been gained without victims."[3] Prince Odoevsky, a twenty-year-old lieutenant of the Horse Guards, declared: "Death is waiting for us, but what a glorious death!"[4] They were all young men, the elite of the nation, with rich and privileged careers before them, but they were prepared to cast aside the future and to perish in the cause of the ideals which they had embraced. Their fervor and capacity for self-sacrifice were to make them the heroes of generations to come. Their insurrection, ineptly planned and doomed to tragedy from the start, was to mark the beginning of the revolutionary movement in Russia.

The Decembrists, as they were to be known in history, had planned a military uprising, without civilians taking part. Success depended on the conspirators winning to their cause officers and men of the guards and the garrison in sufficient numbers. During the confused weeks of the interregnum, members of the Northern Society had actively promoted rumors that Nicholas was holding Constantine and Mikhail, his younger brother, under arrest, that Nicholas had destroyed Alexander's "testament" which had provided for a reduction in the military term of service, and that his accession was illegal. Playing on the general dislike of Nicholas, they gained many supporters, but not enough.

The morning of December 14 was gray and leaden, bitterly cold with temperatures far below freezing. Icy winds blew across the Neva and heavy winter mists lay over the city, as the insurgents prepared to assemble in the Senate Square. Their immediate purpose was to prevent the State Council and the Senate from swearing the oath of allegiance to Nicholas. They would then prevail on the Senate to issue a manifesto, convening a constituent assembly which would serve as the first step to a constitutional monarchy. Such at least was Trubetskoy's plan: Ryleev's idea was to seize the Winter Palace and arrest the imperial family; Captain Yakubovich had talked of popular rebellion with mass murder and arson. All were agreed, however, that the first step was to prevent the swearing of the oath to Nicholas.

The insurgents were, however, too late. The State Council had taken the oath on the previous evening, and the Senate had sworn at 7 A.M. on December 14 before the rebels had arrived. Moreover, the majority of the St. Petersburg garrison had also sworn allegiance to Nicholas early in the morning. At 8 A.M. Grand Duke Mikhail arrived in the city, thus disproving the rumor that he was under arrest, and this strengthened Nicholas's cause.

At about 10 AM. the insurgents reached the Senate Square. They were joined soon afterward by some seven hundred men of the Moscow regiment who had refused to swear the oath to Nicholas; they were shouting for "Constantine and Constitution" and many of the simple soldiers were said to be under the impression that Constitution—*Konstitutsia* in Russian—was the wife of Constantine. Rebels from other regiments also joined them until thirty officers and some three thousand men were demonstrating in the Senate Square against Nicholas.

The cold was intense and standing in their parade uniforms of white breeches and dark green uniforms with gold piping, the rebel troops were hungry and impatient. Their leaders—Trubetskoy, Bulatov, and Yakubovich—were away on some errands of their own. Obolensky was in command, but seemed at a loss. Crowds of civilians were mingling with the rebels, urging them to attack the government troops which were beginning to arrive in force. Many people pelted these troops with stones. The mood of angry defiance was spreading through the square. At this juncture the Governor-General of St. Petersburg, Count Miloradovich, resplendent in full dress uniform, an old warrior whom the troops revered, rushed to the scene in a sleigh drawn by two galloping horses. He quickly mounted his aide's horse and, approaching the rebel troops, spoke as a father to them. "I myself would rather Constantine became our Emperor," he said. "I am his friend; this sword was given to me by him. But if he refuses the throne, what can we do? I have seen his abdication with my own eyes."[5] His words made a strong impression on the troops, and they appeared to waver. Obolensky then approached the Governor-General and asked him to go, but he took no notice. Then Kakhovsky fired his pistol at him point blank, and the old Count fell from his horse.

In the palace reports of the insurrection were growing more alarming. Fear and panic seemed to be mounting throughout the city. Nicholas, having made sure that the palace and his family were fully guarded, went himself to take command. He placed himself at the head of the first battalion of the Preobrazhensky Guards, who were renowned as the tallest and best troops in Russia. He also ordered troops to block the roads leading out of the square, for he was anxious to avoid dispersed fighting through the city.

The rebel crowds were increasingly unruly, but Nicholas did not lack courage, as he calmly lined up his troops opposite them and the Horse Guards on his right. The distance between Nicholas and the rebels was only thirty paces, but no rebel attempted to fire on him. Indeed, he hoped that this confrontation with their Emperor, backed by this display of force, would quell the uprising. But the rebels stood firm and they refused to heed the harangues of the Archbishop and of the Metropolitan of St. Petersburg who called on them to retire obediently. Finally Nicholas ordered the Horse Guards to charge the rebel lines. But this proved a fiasco. The ground was covered with ice and the horses slid and fell. When they attempted to charge again the rebels jeered and threw snowballs at them.

The early darkness of the St. Petersburg winter was gathering. Disaffection was spreading. Nicholas recognized the danger that under cover of night more troops and civilians would join the rebels and that the mutiny would become a popular uprising. He maintained an icy composure while his generals and aides became more and more anxious. But he ordered a battery of four guns to be brought to the square. He was clearly reluctant to fire and twice gave the order only to cancel it immediately. But he did not retract his order the third time. The shots went over the heads of the rebels, who reacted at once by preparing to attack with bayonets. The guns fired next into the midst of the rebels, and continued firing. Panic spread among the rebels; they broke ranks and suddenly fled. Within minutes the square had cleared except for seventy or eighty bodies sprawled in the snow where they had fallen. The insurrection had ended. It had failed, the Resident British Minister, E. C. Disbrowe, reported to London, "from want of management and want of head to direct it, and was too premature to answer any good purpose, but I think the seeds are sown which one day must produce important consequences."[6]

Nicholas did not go to bed that night. The palace was like an army headquarters in the midst of a great battle, as generals and couriers came and went. All the rebel leaders were rounded up and brought to him for interrogation. He was calm and precise in his questioning. But beneath his composure he was both exhilarated and anguished. He was distressed because so many officers and troops had betrayed the throne and the nation and because he had shed Russian blood. At the same time he was exhilarated because he had himself led the guards in suppressing the rebellion and had fulfilled his strong sense of duty. In the early hours of the morning he wrote hurriedly to his brother: "Dear, dear Constantine! Your will has been done. I am Emperor, but great God! At what a price—at the price of my subjects' blood!"[7]

The uprising planned in the south was also abortive. Baron Dibich, on uncovering evidence in Taganrog of the conspiracy, had on December 13 arrested Pestel and other members of the Southern Society. A leading member of the Society, Lieutenant Colonel Sergei Muravev-Apostol, escaped and made a desperate effort to arouse the Chernigov regiment to rebel, hoping that other regiments would then respond. But he found little support and his small force was crushed by government troops on January 3, 1826.

Nicholas at once appointed a commission of enquiry to investigate under his personal supervision all who had been involved. Some 570 people were interrogated and 121 were put on trial before a special court. More than a hundred of the accused were sentenced to penal servitude and deportation to Siberia. Five—Pestel, Ryleev, Kakhovsky, Bestuzhev-Ryumin and Muravev-Apostol—were sentenced to death.[8] The sentences, especially the death sentence, which had been formally abolished by Empress Elizabeth, shocked all Russians, but none so much as Nicholas himself, although he himself had confirmed them. He shut himself in his chapel and spent hours in prayer. To his mother he wrote: "It is difficult to express what I am feeling: it is as if I were shaken by fever . . . Added to this I feel extreme anguish and at the same time gratitude to God who has allowed us to bring this horrible case to an end . . . Only the idea of a terrible duty permits me to endure such martydom."[9]

The Decembrist uprising made a deep impression on Nicholas and it remained alive in his memory. On his work desk in the Winter Palace stood a richly bound volume, kept in a locked casket, and also a notebook. The first contained the full list of the 570 persons implicated in the uprising; the notebook was a precise record of the reforms proposed by the Decembrists. He kept both volumes on his desk throughout the thirty years of his reign.

Nicholas was twenty-nine at the time of his accession. He was very tall, handsome, and military in bearing. Like his brother, he had great presence and stood out in any crowd as Emperor. Alexander Herzen, the brilliant writer and revolutionary, saw him for the first time shortly after the execution of the Decembrists. "He was handsome," Herzen wrote, "but there was a coldness about his looks; no face could have more mercilessly betrayed the character of the man than his. The sharply retreating forehead and the lower jaw, developed at the expense of the skull, were expressive of iron will and feeble intelligence, rather of cruelty than of sensuality; but the chief point in the face was the eyes, which were entirely without warmth, without a trace of mercy, wintry eyes." In 1830, seeing him for the second time, Herzen noted his "pewtery eyes in which one could read distinctly the fate of Poland."[10]

Eighteen years later, when Nicholas was in England Queen Victoria, who was then only twenty-five, also observed him closely. "The expression of his eyes is terrible," she wrote. "I have never seen anything like them; he is severe and gloomy, imbued with principles nothing on earth could change; I don't think he is very intelligent; his mind is without refinement; his education is very inadequate; politics and the army—those are the only subjects that interest him."[11] The acute observations of the young Queen confirmed Herzen's earlier description: the Emperor was both formidable and forbidding.

Nicholas's childhood and early years were uneventful. His chief tutor was General de Lambsdorff, a German pedant, who caned him often. He and his staff, nevertheless, taught the boy something of universal and Russian history, geography, cosmography, French, German, English, and Latin. He was not interested in lessons, however, for his heart was already in the army. At the age of eighteen he traveled in Western Europe where his charm of manner and tall, handsome presence delighted all who met him. But the highlight of his tour was for him the meeting in Berlin with Princess Charlotte, daughter of the Prussian King, Frederick William III. Their marriage was already tentatively arranged by their parents, but they fell in love on sight. Nicholas wrote later that "It was here in Berlin that Providence decided the happiness of my whole life; it is here that I saw (in 1814) her who from the first glance and of my own free choice, awoke in me the desire to belong to her all my life."[12] She returned his love with equal ardor. She was received into the Russian Orthodox Church and rebaptized with the name of Alexandra Feodorovna. On July 13, 1817, they were married with great ceremony in St. Petersburg and during the next eight years they lived happily together. Their first child, the future Alexander II, was born on April 29, 1818, and was followed by three daughters. His wife adored him for his tenderness, his simple manners, and his gaiety. But in the intimacy of the family circle, he was quite unlike the man who occupied the Russian throne.[13]

A few days after the execution of the Decembrist leaders, Nicholas traveled to Moscow for his coronation. His entry into the ancient city and then the coronation and celebrations, which lasted a week, were all events of incredible magnificence. Descriptions of the parades and balls were soon circulating in the capitals of Europe. Then Nicholas settled to a routine; he was orderly and austere in his personal habits, and he had an immense capacity for work. He was determined to bring order, discipline and efficiency into Russian life. He approached his task as a military disciplinarian and, since he was Autocrat and absolute in his power, the whole nation suffered. "I cannot permit," he wrote at this time, "that a single person should dare to defy my wishes the moment he had been made exactly aware of them."[14] He began a detailed review of the law and the administration. But most important of all for him were army regulations and the training and uniforms of his troops. The grenadiers and gunners had worn breeches, but he now required them to wear trousers. The number and position of their buttons were also varied. Military men only were allowed to wear moustaches, which had to be black, although for many this meant dyeing them. Soon he was issuing regulations on the dress of civilians. He abhorred dress-coats, gray hats and beards, and in 1837 he banned them. His concern about uniforms and dress had already become an obsession.

"The principal occupation of the Emperor," the Austrian Ambassador reported in Vienna, "is always the army and this absorbs more than three quarters of his day."[15] He was as much absorbed by matters of important military policy as by trifling details, and it was typical of his unimaginative approach to everything that he could not order priorities. Thousands of recruits came annually to the St. Petersburg barracks and he would spend hours personally assigning them to the various guards regiments, according to the height and coloring of each man. He liked to take command of a parade and on maneuvers. His voice was deep and resonant and his orders could be clearly heard over the largest parade ground. Being at the head of his "beloved soldiers," as he called them, was for him always a stirring experience. In his emotion "He jerks at his horse's mouth until the jagged lips of the poor beast spurt blood, the fine animal's flanks whiten with foam, and it trembles with pain without losing for one moment its statuesque immobility." So one of his pages wrote subsequently.[16] But Nicholas was seldom aware of the suffering of his horses or his people; his sole concern was that they did their duty.

Russia was soon being governed as though it was a vast army camp. Nicholas granted each of his ministers an audience once a week, but his specially chosen Household Guards were constantly at his side. Any important mission, whether to put down a peasant revolt, to handle delicate diplomatic negotiations, to command the army, was sure to be entrusted to one of these officers. There were few not belonging to this military circle who ever really gained his confidence. To be outside the army and to a lesser extent the navy, which he revived, was to belong to an inferior class of citizens.

To be one of Nicholas's "beloved soldiers" was, however, a fate that filled every Russian peasant with dread. Recruits were supplied by landowners and administrators of state lands on the basis of so many recruits for every one thousand male serfs. The village communes usually kept a roll of recruits and decided by lot who should go. But the owner or his steward often intervened and domestic serfs were entirely at their disposal. A landowner could send an unsatisfactory or disobedient serf to the recruiting office, even when there was no levy. He then received a recruiting receipt which could be sold to another landowner who did not want to lose any of his serfs.

Domestic serfs were often given as recruits. Prince Peter Kropotkin in his *Memoirs of a Revolutionist* has described the gloom that descended upon a household when it was known that one of their number was to become a recruit. The unfortunate was placed under close guard so that he would not escape. On his departure all fellow serfs came to bid him farewell. He would make a deep bow to them and ask forgiveness for any offense that he might have caused. He would bow to the ground before his family and they would intone lamentations, using the same words as for a burial. He was taken from his own family and village. His male children were sent away to a military orphanage to be brought up as soldiers. His wife, bereft of husband and children, was allowed to remarry after three years. Her husband, having been taken for twenty-five years' service, was dead to her, his family, and his village.

Conditions in the army were inhuman and sadistic.

Blows from the officers, flogging with birch rods and with sticks for the slightest fault were normal affairs. The cruelty that was displayed surpasses all imagination. Even in the Cadet School, where only sons of the aristocracy were educated, a thousand blows with birch rods were sometimes administered, in the presence of the whole school, for a cigarette—the doctor standing by the tortured boy, ordering the punishment to end only when he ascertained that the pulse was about to stop beating. Whereupon the bleeding victim was carried away unconscious to the hospital.

The troops suffered far worse punishments.

When one of them appeared before a Court Martial, the sentence was that a thousand men should be placed in two ranks facing each other, every soldier armed with a stick of the thickness of a little finger . . . that the condemned man should be dragged three, four, five, and even seven times between these two rows, each soldier administering a blow. Sergeants followed to see that full force was used. After one or two thousand blows the victim, spitting blood, was taken to hospital and attended to, in order that the punishment might be completed when he had more or less recovered from the first part of it. If he died under the torture the execution of the sentence was complete upon the corpse.

Nicholas introduced no real changes in Russia's government and administration, but he carried to greater extremes the absolutism, centralization, and bureaucratic rule which held the nation in the thrall of backwardness. He sought to impose his direct personal rule over all aspects of government. He appointed many secret committees to report to him on matters of importance, but the most notable means by which he tried to exercise this personal rule was His Majesty's Own Chancery. Section I of the Chancery was concerned with matters requiring the Emperor's personal attention and with the carrying out of imperial commands; it later became responsible for supervision of the civil service. Section II was concerned with the codification of the Laws of Russia, a project which had been attempted without success many times in the past and which Nicholas achieved in two great compilations: *The Complete Collection of the Laws of the Russian Empire* in 51 volumes, and *The Code of the Laws of the Russian Empire,* bringing together in fifteen volumes the laws then in force.

The dread Section III of His Majesty's Own Chancery was in charge of the state and security police, and Nicholas made it in effect the instrument of his personal rule. Previous Autocrats had relied on special police, but he reorganized and expanded this force, virtually creating a police regime. He believed that by this means he could ensure public security, check corruption and inefficiency in the administration. But foremost in his mind when setting up Section III was the need to ensure that the events of December 14, 1825, were never repeated.

The Third Section operated through a uniformed military force, known as the gendarmery, and through secret informers. Russia was divided into five, later eight, gendarmery districts, each commanded by specially appointed officers. Secret agents were enlisted from all walks of life, including even schoolchildren. The Third Section was in effect "outside and above the law", as Herzen observed. The main reasons for its ascendancy were Nicholas's direct participation in its work and also the position of the director. Count Benckendorff, who held the office from 1826 until his death in 1844 and who had originally proposed the setting-up of the Chancery, was exceptionally close to Nicholas, as was his successor, Prince A. F. Orlov. Holding his complete confidence and sharing his outlook, they stood immediately below him in authority. Indeed, the director of the Third Section was not only a member of the committee of Ministers but also, according to A. P. Butenev, the Russian ambassador in Constantinople, he was "actually a kind of prime minister."[17]

In the field of social reform, too, Nicholas made few changes, although aware of the urgent need for reform. He feared that reform would open the gates to rebellion among the people and he would do nothing that might endanger absolutism or undermine the landowning nobility as a class. In fact, his relations with the nobility were uneasy. He could never forget that members of this class had provided the leadership for the Decembrist uprising. At the same time he recognized that the two main pillars of the regime were the Autocrat and the nobility, and that they had to stand firmly together. He curtailed some of the privileges of the nobility as set out in their Charter for, like his father, Emperor Paul, he maintained that their first duty was to serve the nation in the army or the civil service. He was careful, however, to do nothing that would affect their basic position, and his caution showed especially in his handling of the problem of serfdom.

"There is no doubt that serfdom, in its present form, is a flagrant evil which everyone recognizes," Nicholas declared in the State Council on March 20, 1842, "yet to attempt to remedy it now would be, of course, an evil even more disastrous."[18] This remained his attitude, but he was uneasy about the conditions of the peasantry and did not suppress discussion of the problem. A secret committee, appointed to consider the possibility of emancipation, reported on December 6, 1826, that the obstacles were insuperable and that reform should be limited to improving the conditions of the serfs. Nine further secret committees met to consider improvements. They produced a number of proposals, some of which were implemented, but they made little difference to the lives of the unfortunate peasants. The only noteworthy proposal was put forward by Count Kiselev, one of the few men in Nicholas's close circle who believed that emancipation with land grants was the inescapable solution. But he met with such strenuous opposition from the nobility and especially from Nicholas's brothers, Constantine and Mikhail, that his major proposals were abandoned. He was able, nevertheless, to introduce a law in 1842, allowing landowners to transfer land to serfs on payment of an agreed amount, and the serfs then became "bound peasants" and in effect independent. But as with the "free farmers" of the previous reign the number able to take advantage of the law (24,708 male serfs) was insignificant.

Surveillance by the army and the police of every aspect of national life was the chief method employed by Nicholas in his efforts to ensure the loyalty of his people. But the intellectual ferment in the West continued undiminished, as the outbreaks of 1830 and 1848 demonstrated, and his fear was that Western influence might inspire liberal groups in Russia to rebel. To counter such influence the guiding principles of autocracy, Orthodoxy and nationality were proclaimed like a slogan. At the same time every effort was made to regiment the intellectual life of the country and to restrict education.

Count S. S. Uvarov was the main author of this repressive policy. He was an educated man of wide interests and great ability who had discarded the liberal ideals of his youth. In a report to the Emperor, dated December 4, 1832, he maintained that dangerous liberal ideas could be countered only by an educational system rooted in "the truly Russian conservative principles of Orthodoxy, autocracy, and nationality, our last anchor of salvation and the best guarantees of Russia's strength and greatness."[19] This kind of argument appealed to Nicholas. In 1833 Uvarov was appointed minister of education. He approached his task with two practical objectives: the first was that students should receive the education appropriate to the social class from which they came; the second was, in his own words, "to collect and consolidate in the hands of the government the control of all intellectual resources."[20]

In Alexander I's reign the law of 1803 had marked an important advance in education. It had divided the country into six regions, each of which was to contain parish, county, and regional schools or gymnasiums, and a university. The curricula of the schools was so arranged that every student had the opportunity to progress to a university. The plan was only partially achieved, but it was a bold conception in Russia where education was lamentably backward and all but a small minority of the people were illiterate. But now Uvarov's laws of 1828 and 1835 broke up this educational structure, narrowed school and university teaching, and limited university autonomy. These changes and the restraints imposed by the security police and censorship might have retarded education yet further for decades. They were, however, far from effective. The general intellectual ferment and the demand for education could not be suppressed. The number of university students rose from 1700 in 1825 to 3600 in 1854. Primary church schools increased from 100 in 1837 to 4830 in 1853. By the early 1850s the number of school pupils was probably in the region of 300,000, but in a population of over seventy million the number of those privileged to gain education of any kind was pitifully small. If Nicholas had sought to develop the law of 1803 more rapidly, the results would have been spectacular, but as in every other field of national life he pursued narrow reactionary policies and sought to suppress all change.

It is one of the paradoxes of Russian history that the oppressive reign of Nicholas was also a time of remarkable intellectual activity and the golden age of Russian literature. The Decembrist uprising and then the repression stimulated the growth of the intelligentsia, a new and restless element in Russian society, which was to play a significant role in later decades. This new class was made up of "repentant nobles" and of the children of impoverished nobles, of the clergy and of townspeople, who had managed to obtain some education. They were the *paznochintsi*, people of no specific class who shared with a few others a "profound feeling of alienation from official Russia."[21] In St. Petersburg and Moscow and some provincial towns they met in small informal groups to talk about philosophy and social and political questions. They were few in number, but were soon wielding a profound influence on Russian life. In the 1820s and 1830s they tended to be concerned with the work of the German philosophers. Grappling with the problems of man's existence provided some escape from the stagnant society in which they lived. But they could not close their minds to the poverty, corruption and injustice surrounding them. The need for social justice led them to study the writings of the French socialists. Foremost among these intellectuals was Alexander Herzen, the son of an impoverished nobleman, who was remotely connected with the Romanovs, by his common-law German wife. At the age of fourteen Herzen pledged himself to the cause of revolutionary liberty and at Moscow University he became committed to Utopian socialism and political action. In 1834 he was accused of being involved with "unreliable" political elements and banished to a provincial town. But Herzen and his circle gave a momentum to the concept of Russian socialism which was to bear revolutionary fruits in the next century.[22]

From the passionate discussions of the Russian intellectuals, two broad currents of thought emerged in the 1840s. The intelligentsia became split into two opposed camps of the Slavophiles and the Westernizers, reflecting the basic division in outlook which is notable throughout Russia's history and has persisted into the present century. The Slavophiles were deeply religious and conservative. They believed that Holy Russia with its unique culture and traditional institutions, like the peasant commune, had the great mission of giving to the world a new civilization or of cleansing and revitalizing Western civilization, which had been corrupted by materialism and individualism. Within Russia they held that the first need was to purge the nation of the innovations made by Peter the Great and to return to the old Muscovite customs and outlook. For them Peter was the Antichrist who had turned Russia from her true heritage. St. Petersburg was the symbol of his abhorrent policies; Moscow was the true capital of Russia.

Although the Slavophile cause contained much to attract Nicholas and his circle, it also antagonized them. The Slavophiles were critical of the goverment and in particular they opposed the primacy of the state over the church. Uvarov expressed the fear that Slavophilism might lead to "the excitement of minds and the spreading of dangerous propaganda, criminal and obnoxious."[23] The Slavophile journal *Moskovsky Sbornik* (*Moscow Magazine*) was allowed to appear once, but then was closed down and the editor was punished.

The goverment had even less sympathy with the Westernizers. They argued that Russia was stagnating and that her past and traditions were without value. The future must depend upon the revival of the policies of Peter the Great, whose memory they venerated. Only by learning from the West and adopting up-to-date methods could the nation hope to survive. Peter Chaadayev, a guards officer and a man of the world who enjoyed great popularity in Russian high society, but was at the same time a religious thinker of sincere and profound views, was one of the most outspoken of the Westernizers. He criticised Orthodoxy as a sterile faith and held that Russia would have fared better as a Roman Catholic or Protestant country. "During our entire existence as a society we have done nothing for the common good of man; not one useful thought has been born on our arid soil . . . Led by a malevolent fate we have borrowed the first seeds of our moral and spiritual enlightenment from decadent, generally despised, Byzantium," he wrote, and this was typical of his forthright comment.[24] His philosophical letters, propounding the need to unify the Christian churches and much else, circulated freely in the salons of St. Petersburg and Moscow. But in September one of his letters, published in *The Telescope*, a Moscow journal, caused an uproar. This letter described in some detail the backwardness and stagnation of Russia compared with conditions in Western countries.

Nicholas was astonished by such apostasy. He was at a loss to understand how a guards officer, highly respected in responsible circles, could entertain, let alone propagate, such heretical ideas. He could only conclude that Chaadayev was mad. *The Telescope* was closed down, its editor exiled, and the censor who approved the article was dismissed. Chaadayev was publicly declared to be insane, but was not confined to an asylum. For a year he had to receive the daily visit of a doctor, a punishment of Nicholas's own devising. Chaadayev suffered only inconvenience, however, for he was feted everywhere and even those who did not share his views warmed to him as an opponent of the repression.

Many intellectuals of this period, however, suffered worse fates. Kostomarov, professor of history in the University of Kiev, had organized an informal group to study the socialism of Saint-Simon and Fourier. This group developed into a secret society, known as the Kiev Brotherhood of Cyril and Methodius, to work for the emancipation of the serfs and for autonomy in the Ukraine. In April 1847 all members of the brotherhood were arrested. Kostomarov and others received only light sentences, but Taras Shevchenko, the outstanding Ukrainian poet and painter, was condemned to serve for ten years as a private in a distant garrison and, worst of all for a man of his temperament and abilities, he was forbidden to write or paint during the whole period.

The Petrashevsky group merits special attention because it involved the novelist, Fedor Dostoevsky. An official in the ministry of foreign affairs, named M. V. Butashevich-Petrashevsky, who was interested in the socialistic theories of Fourier, held Friday literary receptions which became so well known that they attracted the attention of the security police. The revolutions of 1848 had awakened new hopes among liberals, but had led also to more intensive repression. On April 7, 1849, Petrashevsky and his circle attended a dinner in honor of Fourier. Two weeks later the police arrested thirty-nine members of the group. It was found after investigation that their only crime was "a conspiracy of ideas." A special military court, nevertheless, sentenced fifteen of them to be shot and six to hard labor in Siberia. The condemned men were prepared for death with the usual harrowing ceremonial, but at the last moment as the drums rolled and they awaited the order to

the firing squad, a courier dashed into the Semenov Square and proclaimed the Tsar's clemency, commuting the death sentence to banishment to Siberia. Dostoevsky and his comrades never forgot this experience, which was intended as a warning to all liberals.

The Decembrists had been a small group of young men, dedicated
to liberal ideals, but their example had inspired the new generations.
In the twenty years that had passed since their uprising, the ferment
of political ideas and the interest in reform had spread in spite of
censorship and police repression. The intelligentsia began drawing its
members from among the middle and lower classes and even from
among the peasantry. But the Autocrat, the goverment, and the massive
bureaucratic machine continued to take refuge in repression and became
increasingly isolated from the intelligentsia and the people.

At this time, too, literature began to flower in Russia, giving expression
to the discontent which so many felt. Of the writers who emerged,
three were men of outstanding genius—Pushkin, Lermontov, and Gogol.
Alexander Pushkin, one of the great figures of world literature, was
descended from an old noble family, which included on the maternal
side General A. Gannibal, an Ethiopian. He had been friendly with
the Decembrists and sympathetic to their ideas, and twice had been
banished from St. Petersburg. Expecting to be arrested after the uprising of December 1825 he had burned his papers. A few months later,
however, he had audience with Nicholas, was evidently won over by
his charm, and accepted his personal patronage. Pushkin, who had
always proclaimed the poet's need for freedom, found himself in a hate-
ful position, but he was indebted to the Emperor for recalling him
from banishment, for giving him money and providing him with a
sinecure so that he could write. Not only as a writer but also in his
personal life he was deeply troubled. He loved passionately the society
beauty whom he had married and was tormented by jealousy over her
flirtations which finally involved him in a duel in which he was killed.

During the years from 1825 until 1837 when Pushkin died, Nicholas
showed a genuine solicitude for the poet. He tried to protect him,
while also exercising his pernicious personal censorship. He prohibited
the printing of *Boris Godunov*, Pushkin's tragic drama, for three years,
and hampered the poet in other ways. He seemed to realize nevertheless that he was dealing with a writer of genius and within his limits
he sought to help him.

Mikhail Lermontov, an officer of the Hussars and of Scottish ancestry,
was fiery and uncontrollable, Byronic in character and in his work. He
was twice exiled to the Caucasus. He had fought in a duel, had insulted
Grand Duchess Maria, Nicholas's daughter, and in his verses on the
death of Pushkin he had written an impassioned indictment of "the
greedy crowd about the throne, the executioners of freedom, genius

and fame." Nicholas received a copy of this poem, and after reading it intently, commented that "these verses are beautiful and true; for them alone one could pardon the author all his folly."[25] Indeed he had acted mildly in sending him to a frontier garrison, and there Lermontov, the violent romantic and poet of genius, met his death in a duel.

Pushkin and Lermontov were of the nobility, highly educated and cultured, but Nicholas Gogol, an Ukrainian, was of comparatively humble origin. Moreover, he wrote as a realist of everyday life in Russia. He knew the lives of the poor, oppressed, and humble people, and was the founder of the realistic school of writers in Russia. In his great comedy *The Inspector-General* and his masterpiece, *Dead Souls*, he portrayed the life of provincial Russia in all its snobbery, corruption, ignorance, and humanity. His writings were hailed by liberal opinion and criticized by conservatives. But then he himself revealed his own deeply religious nature and his obscurantist outlook in his *Correspondence with Friends*, published in 1847, which was savagely denounced by liberals for its defense of the autocracy and of serfdom. From these three writers, the forerunners, was to develop a literature which defied the reactionary policies of the autocracy. They were to exercise an influence which Nicholas and many others understood only dimly.

On his accession Nicholas had issued the usual proclamation that he would follow the foreign policies of his predecessor. This meant endorsing the Holy Alliance and in particular the principle of legitimacy which involved supporting established regimes against nationalist and revolutionary challenges. He honored these principles, except when Russian interests involved departing from them. But his own personal conduct was soon to make him mistrusted in the West.

The once-mighty Ottoman Porte was stumbling toward collapse. The possible disintegration of "the sick man of Europe" raised critical problems, which were known in the chancelleries of Europe as "the Eastern Question." The control of Constantinople and of the Bosphorus and the Dardanelles, and the protection of the Christian minorities in Turkey were aspects of the Eastern Question. Britain, in particular, was disturbed by the danger that Russia would dominate the whole region and would press eastward in an attempt to conquer India. France shared the fear of Russian dominance in the Eastern Mediterranean. For his part Nicholas was hostile towards France as the home of liberalism and revolution. He had no such feelings toward Britain and tried strenuously for a close alliance, but he was incapable of understanding the people and in particular the constitutional monarchy. Initially, however, he appeared to succeed in his foreign policy.

The insurrections of the Greeks and Serbs against their Turkish masters had aroused no enthusiasm in him. He disliked rebellion, even when the minorities were co-religionists fighting against infidel Muslims. When, however, Sultan Mahmud II called in the help of his vassal, Mehemet Ali, the Pasha of Egypt, and the Greeks were threatened with extermination, he hurriedly reached an agreement with Britain on the handling of the Greek question. This agreement was negotiated by the Duke of Wellington, who paid a goodwill visit to St. Petersburg in spring 1826. It provided that Britain would mediate with Turkey to secure an autonomous Greek state under Turkish suzerainty. Austria and Prussia were appalled; support for the Greek rebels against their legitimate Turkish master was in their view absolutely contrary to the Holy Alliance. Nicholas was not concerned on this score, but he did not really want British mediation and was determined to safeguard Russian interests. Without reference to the British government, he made a series of demands on the Sultan in what amounted to an ultimatum. The Turks met his demands in the Treaty of Akkerman, signed on October 7. Turkish troops were withdrawn from Moldavia and Wallachia; the Serbs recovered their rights, as granted in the Treaty of Bucharest (1812); Russian sovereignty over certain disputed territory on the Caucasian shores was recognized; Russian merchant ships gained the right of free passage through to straits and sailing in Turkish waters.

Canning, then British Prime Minister, was shaken by Nicholas's action. But since the Sultan had rejected offers of mediation, it was now a matter of saving the Greek insurgents from mass destruction. On July 6, 1827 (NS), Britain, Russia, and France signed the Treaty of London with the purpose of bringing pressure to bear on Turkey. The situation was complicated, however, when through misunderstanding in October 1827 British, French, and Russian naval squadrons in the Aegean Sea engaged and destroyed the Turkish fleet. The Sultan protested vehemently. He closed down the allied missions in Constantinople, denounced the Christian powers, revoked the Treaty of Akkerman, and called on his people to wage a holy war.

Nicholas at once called for allied action against Turkey. Britain refused still to declare war on Turkey. Indeed, after the death of Canning, Wellington, who became Prime Minister in January 1828, adopted a more neutral policy toward Turkey. He was content to let Russia and Turkey fight by themselves. Nicholas was in a belligerent mood and impatient to order a campaign against the Turks. He delayed for several months, because Russia was already involved in war against Persia.

The Persians had invaded the Caucasus at the time of Nicholas's coronation. They had long resented and feared the growth of Russian power which now extended over most of the Caucasus and had been confirmed in 1813 by the Treaty of Gulistan. The British, too, disliked this southward extension of Russian might, and British agents were influential in persuading the Shah to declare war. At first the Persians had some success, but soon the Russians were pushing them back. By the end of 1827 the Russian army had captured Erivan and was advancing toward Teheran. The Persians capitulated and by the Treaty of Turkmanchay (February 22, 1828 NS) Russia gained the provinces of Erivan and Nakhitchevan, the exclusive right to maintain a fleet in the Caspian Sea and a contribution of twenty million rubles.

Encouraged by this proof of Russian military might, Nicholas declared war on Turkey in April 1828. His troops occupied Moldavia and Wallachia, but met with sturdy resistance elsewhere. In the following year the Russians inflicted severe defeats on the Turks and were soon advancing on Constantinople. Sultan Mahmud was under many pressures and threatened by an uprising of his own people. On September 14, 1829 (NS), he accepted the Russian terms, which were set out in the Treaty of Adrianople. Nicholas could well take pride in the gains he had secured from Russia's traditional enemy. They included the mouth of the Danube and certain Caucasian territories and the virtual annexation of Moldavia and Wallachia, although they remained nominally under Turkish suzerainty.

Britain and France were alarmed by this further growth of Russian power in the Eastern Mediterranean. They were slightly mollified, however, to learn at the St. Petersburg conference, held in September 1829, that Russia shared the view that it would be a mistake to dismember the Ottoman Empire. They noted at the same time that Nicholas was doing everything to entrench Russian influence over Turkey. Meanwhile he accepted the proposal that Greece should become an independent state. Prince Otto, second son of the King of Bavaria, was chosen to occupy the Greek throne. But, determined to have no further interference from Russia, the new Greek regime turned to the Western powers.

The events of the second half of 1830 horrified Nicholas. The French Revolution in July, followed by revolutions in Belgium and unrest in Germany and Italy threatened the old European order. Metternich and Count Nesselrode, the Russian foreign minister, promptly signed an agreement in Karlsbad, to which Prussia later subscribed, to defend "the internal peace of European states." Nicholas urged that the three powers should mount an armed crusade for this purpose. But suddenly he found himself faced with a major uprising in Poland.

Russo-Polish relations had become embittered. The constitution of 1815, granted to the Poles by Alexander I, had provided for autonomy under a hereditary monarch who was to be the Emperor of Russia. The bicameral legislature had extensive powers, including control over the executive and exclusive power to raise taxes. Freedom of the individual and a Polish army independent of the Russians army were important clauses of the constitution. But Alexander himself and Grand Duke Constantine, who was commander-in-chief of the Polish army, had often violated the constitution. The Russian attitude was one of arrogant superiority which the Poles resented, and strong nationalist and revolutionary movements had developed among them.

Nicholas had no love for the Poles, and he positively disliked the Polish constitution. He had sworn, nevertheless, the oath to uphold it when, in May 1828, he had made a state visit to Warsaw to be crowned King of Poland. Discontent continued to grow among the Poles and the revolutions in France and then Belgium carried them forward toward insurrection. The news that Nicholas, then eagerly preparing for a military crusade to suppress the revolutionaries in both countries, planned to include the Polish army in the crusading force, touched off the explosion. On the night of November 29, 1830 (NS), groups of cadets and students tried to capture Constantine and the Russian cavalry barracks. They failed, but the spirit of rebellion spread like a steppe-fire through the country. The Polish executive council called on the people to uphold order. The council represented conservative Poles who stood by the constitution and were anxious to avoid war with Russia. But the radicals, organized in the Patriotic Society, were soon in charge. Constantine himself had shown forebearance toward the insurgents, but Nicholas was uncompromising and refused to negotiate with their leaders. Amnesty in return for unconditional surrender was his final offer.

On December 18 (NS) an extraordinary Polish diet proclaimed the insurrection as a national movement. In January 1831 the diet voted to dethrone Nicholas and end the rule of the Romanov dynasty in Poland. Divided among themselves and ill-prepared to fight the overwhelming superiority of the Russian army, the Poles nevertheless struggled bravely. Only in September was Warsaw captured and the insurrection finally crushed. The Poles then suffered the full weight of Nicholas's retribution. He revoked the constitution of 1815 and imposed the Organic Statute (February 26, 1832 NS) by which Poland became "an indivisible part of the Russian Empire." The Statute provided for civil liberties, local government, and the use of the Polish language, but such rights were soon ignored. In the course of the next fifteen years Poland was brought under direct Russian administration and a crushing policy of Russification was enforced.

No sooner had the Polish insurrection been suppressed than the Eastern Question again became critical. The Pasha of Egypt, Mehemet Ali, had marched against his suzerain, Sultan Mahmud II, and had advanced so rapidly that he was threatening Constantinople. The Sultan appealed to the Western powers for support, but received little response. Nicholas was, however, eager to aid him, partly because of his hatred of rebels, but mainly because he wanted to strengthen Russia's grip on Turkey. In December 1832 his emissary, General N. N. Muravev, arrived in Constantinople. He assured the Sultan of the Emperor's friendship and counseled him to make peace with the Pasha. But he also informed him that he could call on a Russian naval squadron to defend Constantinople. The Sultan waited and only in February 1833, when his position was in even greater danger, did he request Russian aid.

The British and French were again disturbed by the further consolidation of Russian influence in Turkey. They brought pressure to bear on the Sultan who then asked the Russian ambassador to delay the despatch of armed support. But the Russian squadron had already sailed and by the end of April 1833 some ten thousand Russian troops had been convoyed into the Bosphorus and landed on the Asiatic shore. At this point the Sultan and the Pasha made peace. But hostility toward Russia was on the increase and the arrival of British and French naval squadrons at the Dardanelles seemed to threaten war with Russia. In July, however, the Russian troops embarked in their ships and the naval squadron escorted them from the Bosphorus.

The Russians had, in fact, gained a notable diplomatic victory. On the day before their withdrawal General Orlov, who was close to Nicholas and had been negotiating for some weeks with the Turks, had signed the Treaty of Unkiar Skelessi (July 8, 1833 NS). The treaty provided for alliance between Russia and Turkey and, according to Nesselrode, gave a basis of legality to Russian intervention in Turkish affairs. A secret article dealt with the closing of the Dardanelles to foreign ships of war. This provision, which became known to the British, was interpreted as meaning that Russian ships of war would have free passage, while the Straits remained closed to the ships of other powers.

The treaty provoked a storm of protest from Britain and France. Palmerston considered that it gave Russia "a kind of protectorate over Turkey." His alarm was increased by the meeting in September 1833 of the Emperors of Russia and Austria and the Crown Prince of Prussia in Bohemia at which they revived the Holy Alliance for the defense of the established order in Europe. Russia and Austria signed a special convention in which they agreed "to maintain the existence of the Ottoman Empire under its present dynasty."[26]

The Treaty of Unkiar Skelessi which Nicholas and his foreign minister, Nesselrode, regarded as a resounding diplomatic success, was to have dire consequences. In particular it earned for Nicholas and his regime the implacable hostility of Palmerston and the British Parliament. Latent suspicion of Russian intentions flared into angry conviction that Russia would threaten India and British interests in Persia, Afghanistan, and elsewhere. A fever of Russophobia swept through Britain and every move by Nicholas, his ministers, and ambassadors was interpreted as evidence of further Russian aggrandizement.

At this time Nicholas was intent on bringing about a rapprochement with Britain. The revived Holy Alliance was not satisfactory, since neither Austria nor Prussia was a dependable ally. The Treaty of Unkiar Skelessi had not ensured Russian ascendancy in Constantinople, where Britain in fact wielded greater influence. Moreover, the Treaty was due for renewal in 1841. Nicholas's chief motive was, however, to revive the Quadruple Alliance of 1814, which had included Britain, and had defeated Napoleon. By this means he would isolate France, the nation which he hated as the home of revolution. On the vexed Eastern Question he favored an international agreement on 'closing the Straits to warships and the maintenance of the Ottoman Empire. On these terms Russia and Britain might easily have found agreement, but Palmerston and others in power in Britain remained suspicious of Nicholas's good faith and of his intentions.

The struggle between Turkey and Egypt continued, but by June 1839 the Turks had suffered disastrous defeats in which they had lost their navy and their army. The Sultan died and was succeeded by his sixteen-year-old son. Turkey was on the point of collapse. A spate of frantic negotiations by the powers followed, resulting in an agreed note being presented in Constantinople by the ambassadors of Russia, Britain, Austria, France, and Prussia. The note announced that the five powers had agreed on a solution of the Eastern Question and requested the Turks to make no further move, pending their joint action. The powers then mediated between Turkey and Egypt and a treaty between them was agreed. Finally on July 13, 1841 (NS) the powers signed the Straits Convention, pledging themselves to honor the rule that the Sultan would not allow passage to any warships through the Straits. Thus the integrity of Turkey was guaranteed and the problem of the Straits appeared to have been settled. Both British and Russian governments welcomed the Convention. But it had created a dangerous situation: Russia began building up her naval strength inside the Black Sea; Britain and France built up their fleets outside. A decade later the Eastern Question was to provoke a major war.

Nicholas's antagonism toward France remained undiminished. He redoubled his efforts to bring Britain into the Holy Alliance and to exclude France. In 1839 he sent his son, the future Alexander II, to England on a goodwill visit. In 1844 he himself paid an official visit and was received with every courtesy. He had great faith in his own personal diplomacy. By his handsome, imposing presence, his exquisite courtesy and charm he believed that he would conquer English suspicions. In London he made a delightful impression in the drawing rooms of the leading hostesses and, mixing with the public in the enclosure at Ascot, he received an ovation. At Windsor he was assiduous in his attentions to the Queen.[27] But his visit was far from being the success that he had hoped. His open manner and frank speech only intensified English mistrust. He overstated his protestations of good faith. To the Prince Consort, Palmerston, Peel, and other leading men of the day he said: "I have not come here for political ends. I want to gain your confidence. I want to persuade you to believe that I am an honest and sincere man . . . I know I am considered an imposter . . . But it is not true; I say what I think and I keep my word."[28] But this was precisely what the British statesmen would not believe. Palmerston was convinced, and often said, that "Russia is a great humbug."[29] No matter how often Nicholas assured the British that he did not want another inch of Turkish territory, he could not allay their deep suspicion.

Revolutions convulsed Europe in 1848. National liberation movements erupted in France, where the eighteen-year-old monarchy of Louis Philippe was toppled, and spread through Italy, Austria, and Prussia. The whole continent was in turmoil. Nicholas was not perturbed by the fall of Louis Philippe, whom he had never liked, but the demands of so many people for liberation and for constitutional government alarmed him. They challenged the autocratic regimes which he saw as God's will. Impelled by his "terrible duty," he prepared to resist.

On March 14, 1848 a manifesto, which he himself had written, was proclaimed to the Russian people. It referred to the "lawlessness and rebellion" in Austria and Prussia which were threatening "our Holy Russia," and rallied them to stand fast "for faith, Tsar, and country." It closed with the words: "God is with us! Understand, ye people and submit, for God is with us!"[30] Meanwhile, having reluctantly cancelled his plans for military intervention in France, he gave all his attention to holding Russia's position in Turkey, putting down the uprising in Poland, and supporting the regimes in Austria and Prussia. In July 1848 his troops occupied Moldavia and Wallachia. But the progress of the revolutionaries in Austria disturbed him. The suppression of the Italian and Czech revolts was some satisfaction, but the Hungarians, led by Louis Kossuth, continued to resist stubbornly. In March 1849 the Austrian government asked Nicholas for military aid. He responded eagerly. The Hungarians were a real threat to the Austrian monarchy and an independent Hungary would menace Russia's Polish provinces. In June a Russian army 170,000 strong with 576 field guns invaded Hungary, joining there with the Austrian forces of similar strength. The Hungarian insurgents fought gallantly, but were overwhelmed by this massive force opposing them. On August 13, 1848 (NS) they surrendered.

In Britain and France the struggle of the Hungarians had fired the popular imagination. Accounts of atrocities inflicted on Hungarian patriots aroused furious indignation. Neither government, however, had given any support to the insurgents. Palmerston considered the maintenance of the Austrian Empire essential to the balance of power in Europe. But he could not stand against public opinion when a major crisis broke out over the fate of the Hungarians who had sought refuge in Turkey. Nicholas and Francis Joseph, the Austrian Emperor, had peremptorily demanded the surrender of these Hungarians, but the Sultan on the advice of Britain and France refused. The two Emperors then suspended relations with Turkey. Tension between the powers mounted, but Britain and France stood firm, believing that the sovereignty of Turkey was involved and suspecting that Russia and Austria were moving towards subjugating the Porte to their joint rule. Finally Nicholas yielded to this pressure and resumed relations with the Sultan.

The movement of the German states toward unity also disturbed Nicholas. He was anxious to maintain the Austrian Empire intact, and was opposed to the proposals for unification of the German states under the Prussian crown. He disapproved of his brother-in-law, Frederick William IV of Prussia, who, notwithstanding his devotion to the principles of monarchy and his dislike of constitutional government, stood for German nationalism and unification. In Nicholas's eyes both were dangerous and undesirable. He gave strong support to Austria and when the Prussians finally capitulated to Austria at Olmütz (November 29, 1850 NS) their anger was directed more against Russia than Austria.

Nicholas had little conception, however, of the hostility that had been mounting over these years in Europe toward him personally and toward Russia. It was not limited to liberal circles which in the words of De Tocqueville saw him as "the cornerstone of despotism in the world." They would never forgive him for crushing the Poles and the Hungarians. In Britain waves of Russophobia gripped the people, who saw in Nicholas a cruel despot who repressed all freedom-loving people, and who considered him a threat to British interests. Tennyson's references to the "o'ergrown Barbarian of the East" and to the "icy Muscovite" reflected the picture of the Russian Emperor which the British and the peoples of Western Europe held.

Nicholas had antagonized not only the peoples of Europe but also his brother monarchs in the West. Emperor Francis Joseph was weary of his clumsy protective friendship. Frederick William of Prussia wanted no more of his bullying and interference and would never forgive him for Olmütz. Napoleon III and the Kings of Sardinia and Belgium all held rankling memories of affronts suffered from him. All Europe, monarchs and people, shared in this general hostility towards this interfering despot and self-appointed "policeman."

As the tide of revolution receded in the early 1850s, Nicholas began to hope again that he could forge a close understanding with Britain. He was still anxious to isolate France and he wanted a firm agreement with Britain on the future of Turkey. But just as he did not realize how deep were the mistrust and the hostility toward Russia, so he did not recognize the dangers of the outbreak of a European war. The sudden realignment of the powers took him completely by surprise and the outbreak of the Crimean War had a devastating impact upon him.

The Crimean War arose out of the claims of the Greek and the Roman churches to custody of the Holy Places in Jerusalem, but its roots lay deep in fear of Russia and concern over Russia's growing strength and the balance of power. The dispute over the Holy Places was a minor matter; Palmerston called it "the churchwardens' quarrel." But it developed into a Franco-Russian conflict because the French championed the Roman and the Russians the Greek claims. Bitter and protracted diplomatic wrangling ended in a decision by the Turks in December 1852, awarding custody to the Roman Church. The French were pleased, but Nicholas resented it deeply. He mobilized troops on the Pruth and in February 1853 sent Prince Alexander Menshikov as his special envoy to the Sultan. His instructions were to demand satisfaction in Jerusalem and much else, including a secret alliance and rights which would give to Russia direct protection over the twelve million Christians who were Turkish subjects. The Sultan, believing that he had British and French support and resenting this attempt to encroach on his sovereignty, rejected Menshikov's demands. On July 1, 1853 (NS) the Russian army crossed the Pruth and invaded the Danubian principalities.

Britain and France and, to the immense surprise of Nicholas, Austria, and Prussia promptly protested against this military action. The four powers agreed to the terms for negotiating a settlement of the Russo-Turkish dispute, which were set out in the "Vienna Note." Nicholas accepted these terms as a basis for talks, but the Sultan proposed amendments which amounted to rejecting the note. The Turks were in a belligerent mood. They were emboldened, too, by the reinforcements of the Egyptian army and navy and by the proximity of the British and French naval squadrons on which they felt they could count.

On October 4 (NS) Turkey declared war on Russia. It seemed at first that this would be merely another war in the Russo-Turkish struggle which had extended over centuries. The event which proved the turning point was the battle of Sinope in the Black Sea in which Admiral Nakhimov's squadron destroyed part of the Turkish fleet. This battle inflamed public opinion in Britain and in France. The conflict between Russia and the Western powers had been developing with an inevitability which certain Western statesmen had observed but which Nicholas had never suspected, and now it erupted. On February 27, 1854 (NS) an Anglo-French ultimatum demanding the withdrawal of Russian troops from the Danubian principalities was presented in St. Petersburg. On March 12 (NS) Britain, France, and Turkey formed a defensive and offensive alliance.

In January 1854 when this growth of the war had become a real threat Nicholas had sent his trusted general, Count Orlov, to Vienna. His purpose was to ensure that Austria would maintain an "armed neutrality" favorable to Russia. He was confident that in crushing the Hungarian rebellion and in other ways he had earned the gratitude and support of Emperor Francis Joseph. But the Austrians rejected the proposal. Moreover, Francis Joseph and Frederick William of Prussia joined with Britain and France in a declaration of support for maintaining the Ottoman Empire and in demanding the withdrawal of Russian troops from the Danubian principalities. Francis Joseph went further by giving the Sultan an undertaking to secure this Russian withdrawal, if necessary, by force of arms. He moved troops into Transylvania and in the face of this threat of war with Austria the Russian troops withdrew over the Pruth. The Austrians then occupied both principalities. In the meantime representatives of Britain, France and Austria had met in Vienna and on August 8, 1854 (NS) had agreed on four conditions for peace negotiations. The conditions were, first, a European guarantee of the integrity of Moldavia and Wallachia and Serbia in place of the Russian protectorate; second, free navigation of the Danube; third, revision of the 1841 Straits Convention; fourth, the collective guarantee by the five powers of all Christians in Turkey and the abandonment of Russia's claims. Finally, on December 2, 1854 (NS), Francis Joseph had concluded a treaty of alliance with the Western powers.

Nicholas had thus in the course of one year seen his foreign policy collapse in ruins. At a time of crisis he could count on no allies; Russia had only enemies. He was bewildered by these events. He felt that he had been betrayed by his brother monarchs. The betrayal of his brother-in-law, Frederick William, in withholding support and insisting on Prussian neutrality, was hard to bear. The Austrian Emperor's betrayal and threat of war against him was far worse. Nicholas was a shattered man. On the day that he received the Austrian demand for the withdrawal of Russian troops from the Danubian principalities, an eyewitness reported that Nicholas "was unrecognizable, his face had a greenish pallor, his profile had lengthened, and his eyes had a fixed expression; only his step was firm. Half a century has passed since that day, but I can still see him, broken by suffering."[31]

The course of the war brought him further bitter disappointments. The Danubian campaign had been an ignominious failure. His army had been unable to take the Turkish fortress of Silistria by siege or by assault and had finally withdrawn. In the Crimea, which was the chief military objective of the allies, the Russians fought gallantly, but without success. Ninety British and French warships had escorted transports with some sixty-two thousand troops to the peninsula where the capture of the great naval port of Sevastopol was their objective. Sevastopol was defended by Totleben, a military engineer of genius, and by a small but courageous and determined garrison. It held out for nearly a year before it was taken by storm. But the Russians had suffered disaster at Balaklava (October 25, NS) and at Inkerman (November 5 NS).

Distressed by these reverses, Nicholas had finally accepted as the basis of negotiations the four points agreed by the allied powers in Vienna in August. To him this was an act of final capitulation and he was already a completely broken man. The final blow had been the realization that his army, the love and prize of his life, had failed against the armies of the West and was inferior to them in equipment, transport, and organization. Of the peacetime strength of one and a quarter men under arms, only 350,000 could be concentrated against the allied forces. He had believed the Russian army to be invincible. He began to see all around him the collapse of the work of the thirty years of his reign.

In January 1855 Nicholas attended a wedding and, wearing only the red full dress uniform of the Horse Guards, he caught a severe chill. He was forced to rest, but forbad the publication of health bulletins. The chill grew worse, especially after his insistence on going out into the bitter cold to bid farewell to troops leaving for the war. He was confined to his bed and his breathing became labored. He had regarded his illness as a minor ailment, but now he realized that he was dying. He took affectionate leave of each member of his family and of his suite. He awaited the end with dignity and fortitude.

A courier arrived from Sevastopol with despatches, which he always read eagerly. But already the war was beyond him. "These things no longer concern me," he said. "Let him give the despatches to my son."

On March 5, 1855 (NS), he took the last sacraments. To the priest who blessed him, he said: "I believe I have never done evil knowingly . . ."[32] In these dying words he expressed something of the bleak tragedy of his life: he had worked devotedly to carry out his "terrible duty," believing that he was doing God's will, but he had inflicted on the whole Russian nation a sinister and cruel tyranny.[33]

XVII

Alexander II

1855–1881

The reign of Alexander II, the eldest son of Nicholas I, began a new era in Russian history It was a time of great reforms and it witnessed the beginnings of a capitalist economy and of an industrial revolution in the backward agricultural society of Russia. Moreover, the nation was able to break out of the straitjacket of the militant personal autocracy which Nicholas I had imposed during the thirty years of his reign. The writer A. I. Koshelev commented that "it seemed as if out of a depressing dark dungeon we were emerging, if not into God's light, at least into an antechamber where we could sense refreshing air."[1] But this access of reform and freedom released forces beyond the control of Tsar and government. Alexander II began his reign as the Tsar-Liberator and ended it as the Tsar-Martyr.

By training, character and ability, Alexander was ill-equipped for either role and indeed, like his uncle, Alexander, he remains something of an enigma. He was thirty-six years old at the time of his accession and he had had a broader training for the throne than any of his predecessors. When he was only six, his father had appointed as his military tutor Captain Merder. He had then begun learning the rudiments of drill and parade ground maneuvers. He made his first visit to his grandparents in Berlin when eleven years old. He was proud of his Cossack dress, but when the King made him Colonel of the 3rd Uhlan Regiment he changed into Prussian uniform and could not be parted from it. The obsession with parades and military paraphernalia and love of Prussia appeared as strong in him at this early age as they had been in each of the previous five Emperors of Russia.

The civilian tutor, appointed in 1828, probably as a result of his mother's influence, was the renowned poet, Vasily Zhukovsky, who did something to counteract the military education on which Nicholas insisted.[2] "Passion for military occupation will narrow his soul," Zhukovsky wrote to the Empress. "He will be accustomed to see in the people only a regiment, in his fatherland only the barracks."[3] It was a bold comment to make in the reign of Nicholas I, but Zhukovsky was allowed to pursue his program, which aimed to make of the Tsarevich a man of virtue and a law-giver.

Both tutors found, however, that Alexander, while intelligent, was inattentive, vague, and hesitant whenever faced with problems. He disliked lessons and preferred to wander dreamily in the gardens of the palace. His father was disturbed by his son's lack of diligence. He himself prepared a detailed syllabus of military studies for him, but Alexander's approach to work remained dilatory. Unlike his father, however, he often displayed warmth and humanity. When in autumn 1832 Merder suffered a heart attack, attributed at least in part to worry over his student, Alexander at once mended his ways and became attentive. Merder was sent to Italy for his health and for over a year Alexander wrote to him every Saturday. When, in the spring of 1834, Merder died in Rome, he was reduced to tears.

At the age of nineteen Alexander's formal education was considered complete. For all his lack of diligence, he spoke Russian, English, German, Polish and French. He had had a six-month course on the laws of the Russian Empire, conducted by Speransky, and the appropriate ministers had tutored him in diplomacy, finance, and military matters. In fact, he had learned a great deal. In 1837 he made a tour of Russia, lasting seven months. He visited thirty provinces and traveled as far east as Tobolsk, being the first Romanov to set foot in Siberia. Although hurried and crowded with official engagements, the tour made a deep impression on him, awakening in him a fervent love of his country, "our mother Russia," as he usually called it.

Traveling with him, Zhukovsky took every opportunity to show him how his people lived. He took him to peasant huts and ensured that he met some of the Decembrists, surviving after more than twenty years of banishment. Alexander was moved by their plight. He sent a special courier to his father with a request that their lives might be made easier, and he was delighted when Nicholas sanctioned improvements in their conditions. The surviving Decembrists had to wait, however, until Alexander's coronation before they, and later political prisoners including Dostoevsky, were allowed to return to the cities.

In Vyatka, deep in the forests to the northeast of Moscow, Alexander met Herzen, who charmed him. Again he wrote to his father, asking him to allow Herzen to return to St. Petersburg. Nicholas considered that he could not single out one political exile for favorable treatment, but he gave permission for him to move to Vladimir, which was much nearer to Moscow. In his memoirs Herzen described Alexander as he appeared in Vyatka: "The Tsarevich's expression had none of that narrow severity, that cold merciless cruelty which was characteristic of his father; his features were more suggestive of good nature and listlessness. He was about twenty, but was already beginning to grow stout."[4]

In the following year Alexander set out on a tour of Western Europe which lasted sixteen months and included nearly every country except France and Spain. He made a good impression at the courts he visited. He had a gentle dignity, modesty, and charm which were attractive, but he was also reserved and timid at times. For Alexander the highlight of his grand tour was his meeting in Darmstadt with Princess Mary of Hesse-Darmstadt, a beautiful girl of fifteen with whom he fell in love. "She is the woman of my dreams," he told his suite. "I will never marry anyone but her."[5] His passion was deepened by the fear that his parents might not sanction the marriage. The father of Princess Mary, the Grand Duke Louis II of Hesse-Darmstadt, was not in fact her father. He had separated from her mother after two years of marriage. The Duchess had many lovers and some fourteen years after the separation from her husband had given birth to a son and then a daughter, Princess Mary. The Grand Duke had accepted paternity, but the true father, a man of humble birth, was known to everyone.

Alexander had written to his parents, asking permission to marry his Princess. In reply they had instructed him to return to St. Petersburg at once to discuss the matter. But face to face with them he displayed determination, declaring that he would renounce the throne rather than give her up. The scandal surrounding her birth did not affect his feelings. Faced by such resolution, surprising in a son who had always seemed weak in character, Nicholas yielded. In 1840 Alexander and his Princess were formally betrothed and Mary was rebaptized in the Orthodox Church with the name of Maria Alexandrovna. They were married in the following year. Nicholas and the Empress were soon won over by their beautiful daughter-in-law who was not only pious and devoted to charitable works, but who also gave birth to four sons and a daughter.

Nicholas had had misgivings about his eldest son. He was gratified now to find that Alexander sincerely revered him and held sacred the same autocratic principles. He entrusted him with far greater responsibilities. Attendance at meetings of the Council of Ministers was followed in 1846 and 1848 by chairmanship of the secret committees, appointed to study the problems of serfdom. Soon Alexander was acting as regent during the frequent absences of his father from the capital. On his deathbed Nicholas could feel that he had done all possible to prepare his son for the throne. "I hand over to you my command," he said, adding, "but unfortunately not in such order as I should wish. I am leaving you many labors and anxieties."[6] Alexander reassured him. He was awed by the responsibilities of the throne and had in the past expressed reluctance to succeed his father. But now he was Emperor and, although he believed that he was carrying on his father's policies, he had the sense and courage to promote fundamental reforms.

On Alexander's accession hopes were widespread that a new era was beginning. His conservative outlook and support for the autocratic system were known. Many believed nevertheless that he would recognize the inevitability of change, especially after the calamities of the Crimean War which had proved the bankruptcy of Nicholas I's policies.

Alexander's first task was to put an end to the Crimean War. Russia desperately needed peace. But as an ardent patriot he rejected the request of Prince Mikhail Gorchakov to be allowed to evacuate Sevastopol, and the allied capture of the fortress in September 1855, after the loss of one hundred thousand Russian troops, was a terrible blow to him. He sought to rally his forces, even sending to his army the banner of St. Sergei which had accompanied Peter the Great at Poltava. He himself traveled to Nikolaev, Russia's second naval stronghold on the Black Sea, to supervise the defense preparations. But allied pressure was mounting. The King of Prussia warned that he might have to join the allies. In December 1855 the terms, concerted by Austria with Britain and France, were presented in St. Petersburg. Alexander found that all members of his Council of Ministers favored peace. The nation was isolated, had exhausted its resources, and, after total losses of some six hundred thousand men, was hard pressed to raise more troops. With deep reluctance he agreed to negotiate and on March 30, 1856 (NS) the Treaty of Paris was signed. All that Nicholas had gained and sought to make permanent, especially Russian occupation of Wallachia and Moldavia, and rights amounting to domination of the Black Sea, was lost. The treaty was a terrible rebuff, but it was received with relief throughout Russia.

In a manifesto, proclaiming the peace to his people, Alexander gave the first promises of reforms. He had already relaxed the severity of his father's reign. Censorship had been eased; restrictions on foreign travel were raised; regulations which severely limited entrance to universities were amended, and other measures gave promise of a more enlightened reign. The Emperor's coronation was customarily an occasion of benevolent gestures, but Alexander's coronation manifesto, proclaimed in September 1856, was notably generous. It suspended all recruiting for three years and abolished the evil institution of cantonists, whereby the sons of men enlisted for military service, were held in military orphanages and brought up as soldiers. Amnesties were extended to political prisoners. Arrears of taxes owed by the poorest people were canceled and tax concessions made in many regions. All Russians could feel that their prayers for a new era in the life of their country were being granted.

At the heart of all such hopes lay the problem of the serfs. Rumors had begun circulating at the time of his accession that Alexander intended to abolish serfdom. Landowners were alarmed, but the mass of the people excitedly awaited this great reform. Like his father, Alexander recognized that serfdom was an evil and also that the landowning nobility was, in his own words, "the mainstay of the throne." From his chairmanship of the two secret committees, he was aware of the obstacles to abolition. He decided first to invite the proposals and cooperation of the landowning nobles themselves.

In an address to an assembly of the nobility in Moscow on March 30, 1856, Alexander spoke of the rumors that he would emancipate the serfs. "I consider it necessary to inform you that I have no intention to do this now," he declared. "But, of course, you yourselves understand that the existing order of serfdom cannot remain unchanged. It is better to abolish bondage from above than to wait for the time when it will begin to abolish itself spontaneously from below. I request, gentlemen, that you think over how this could be accomplished. Convey my words to the nobility for their consideration."[7]

This address caused astonishment, but the landowning nobility, with their incredible and suicidal concern only for their own selfish interests, did nothing to meet the Emperor's request. Alexander appointed a secret committee late in 1856, but its conclusion was merely that serfdom must be reformed "gradually and with great caution." Since the committee was composed of landowners who, except for S. S. Lanskoi, the Minister of the Interior, were reluctant to consider any solution affecting their possession of the land, this conclusion was not unexpected. At this time Alexander himself was thinking of emancipation spread over a lengthy period, but already he was beginning to move to the view that the resolution of the problem must be swift.

In October 1857, V. I. Nazimov, Governor-General of Lithuania, arrived in St. Petersburg with a petition from the nobles of his region, requesting that the Tsar should permit them to free their serfs without land. Most members of the secret committee recommended that the petition should be granted, hoping to establish a precedent for emancipating the serfs without losing their land. But Alexander now took a decisive stand. He firmly rejected the petition and directed that the committee should draft legislation implementing Lanskoi's scheme. This scheme provided that serfs should gain their personal freedom and also their homesteads, paying for the latter over a period of ten to fifteen years, while land allocated for their use would be paid for in money or labor on terms to be negotiated with their masters. Landowners would thus retain full title to their lands and no question of compensation would arise. On November 20, 1857 Alexander signed his rescript to Nazimov and the nobility of Lithuania, directing them to prepare a plan, enacting these principles. The rescript and an instruction from Lanskoi were circulated to all governers and marshals of the nobility in European Russia, inviting them to take a similar initiative.

Alexander had now made up his mind. At a ball in St. Petersburg he addressed the Governor-General and the nobility of the capital and ended with the words: "I hope that you will show a sincere interest in this matter and will turn your attention to a class of people who deserve that their situation should be justly assured. Further delay is impossible. The matter must be dealt with now . . . that is my unshakeable resolution."[8]

On January 8, 1858, the secret committee was renamed the Main Committee, and by the end of the year special committees were at work in every province, preparing their reports. In February 1859 two editorial commissions were appointed to formulate the emancipation statutes. The commissions met together under the chairmanship of General Yakov Rostovtsev, who as a young officer had refused to join the Decembrist conspiracy and had informed Emperor Nicholas of the plot. He was to serve now as a leading champion of the abolition of serfdom.

Alexander had taken a stand against the massed landowning class from which there was no turning back. He had the support of the intelligentsia and of the small but influential merchant class as well as the support of the peasant mass. Within the government Lanskoi and his department were the moving forces behind the reform. At court his wife, Empress Mary, and his mistress, Princess Alexandrina Dolgorukaya, and others, including in particular his brother, Constantine, strongly supported emancipation. Alexander toured the northern provinces to appeal personally to the nobility for their support. He took the chair in the Main Committee. While reports from the provincial committees were being studied, the basic elements of the reform took shape as the liberation of the peasants with land, redemption payments assisted by the government, and the effective completion of liberation within a minimum time.

Opposition inside the Main Committee became increasingly bitter. Alexander stood firm. He would not allow the request of Count P. A. Shuvalov, Marshal of the Nobility of St. Petersburg, and Prince Paskievich, that they should be permitted to record a ·minority report. Ownership of the land was the crucial problem. Paskievich questioned whether it was really the government's intention to make the serfs landowners and asked whether force would be used to ensure such a revolutionary change. Alexander replied that nothing would weaken his resolve that the peasants should own the land and he added that force would be used "if the nobility persist in their obstinacy."[9]

The conflict raged now between Rostovtsev's editing commission and the Main Committee under the chairmanship of Prince Alexei Orlov, an obdurate conservative. The pressure and the slanders spread by his opponents began to tell on Rostovtsev's health, although Alexander tried to reassure him. Finally he succumbed to an illness which proved fatal. Alexander visited him frequently and prayed by his bedside as he died. With other members of the imperial family he carried the coffin in the funeral procession. He was deeply grieved by the death of this dedicated servant of Russia.

Count V. N. Panin, the Minister of Justice, and an ardent opponent of emancipation, was appointed chairman of the editing commission. It was an extraordinary appointment, strongly criticized as a betrayal of Rostovtsev and of the reform. But Alexander did not intend that it should be a betrayal; he kept a close watch on Panin and on the commission to ensure that they did not depart from his policy. He had given directions that the commission must finish its work by October 10, 1860 and on that day he disbanded it. The next task was to ensure that the Main Commitee adopted the statutes drafted by the commission. This was in fact facilitated by the illness of Orlov and the appointment of Grand Duke Constantine in his place. The statute was adopted after strong opposition by the conservatives. The final stage was approval by the Imperial Council and again Alexander had to use all his authority. But on February 19, 1861, six years to the day since his accession, he signed the statute and a manifesto, read from the pulpits of all churches and carried to all provinces by special couriers, proclaimed freedom.

The emancipation statute was an enactment of tremendous significance. It abolished a system, akin to slavery, which had provided the basis of the feudal social order in Russia. The serfs had become free men; they were free to marry, to own property, to take part in commerce and to enjoy other rights of ordinary citizens. Alexander could claim that "an end had been put to centuries of injustice,"[10] and the great reform had been enacted as a result of his stubborn effort.

The general elation which gripped the nation was soon followed, however, by disillusionment. The emancipation statutes, containing more than a thousand sections and making a volume of three hundred sixty pages, were not understood by most people and least of all by the peasants themselves. To them the great reform meant freedom and possession of the land which they had always considered their own because they worked it. But now they believed that they had been cheated of both freedom and land. The allotments of land which they received were far from adequate and they were now burdened with redemption payments. Landowners used every means to retain as much of their land as possible, especially in the south where the black soil was exceptionally fertile. Seventeen years after emancipation official figures revealed that some thirteen percent of former private serfs were well-endowed with land; some forty percent were adequately endowed; the remaining forty-seven percent did not possess enough land to maintain themselves and their families. Household serfs were in the desperate position of receiving no land and on gaining their personal freedom they had to find work or starve.

Freedom also eluded the peasants. They were no longer dependent upon their masters, but their lives were dominated by the commune. This was the assembly of the householders of a village or town, who held all property in common and elected as their spokesman an elder and sometimes an executive board. Every peasant had to belong to a commune and was actually in bondage to it. The emancipation statutes strengthened this bondage. Land was allotted not to individual peasants but to the commune. It was responsible for paying taxes and enforcing the other obligations of its members. No peasant could leave the commune district without a passport and to withdraw from the commune was virtually impossible. Rumors began to spread that the true liberation was yet to come and many predicted that it would happen at the end of the first phase of the emancipation process, lasting two years. In many districts, however, the peasants rebelled, and troops had to restore order. At Bezdna in the province of Pensa the peasants, although unarmed, attacked the troops, who fired, killing fifty and wounding over three hundred. The Bezdna incident shocked opinion throughout the country.

The nobility, who had lost about one third of their land, felt that they had been robbed. As a class the nobles were improvident; they had soon spent the compensation received from the government and by 1870 they were heavily in debt. The liberals and radicals who had welcomed the emancipation with great enthusiasm were deeply disappointed with its application. The general disillusionment, intensified by the spreading unrest, fed the fires of revolution.

Alexander had devoted all his energies to ensuring that emancipation was enacted. Inevitably he had had to compromise, but he had not sacrificed the basic principle of freedom with land for the peasants. Now

fra lib ref

he found that all classes of his people were dissatisfied and that the spirit of rebellion was gathering strength. He felt compelled to act more severely, but he did not revert to his father's policy of repression. He reccognized that further major reforms were essential to the dismantling of the feudal system and the modernizing of the nation.

Alexander took the initiative and supervised the drafting and enactment of each of these reforms. He leaned heavily on his brother, Grand Duke Constantine, who had given enthusiastic support to the liberation of the serfs and worked with similar zest for further reform. As Minister of Marine he encouraged criticism of the navy and proposals for improvements. The *Naval Almanack*, the official publication of his ministry, was one of the most outspoken publications in Russia. He attracted into his circle a number of the most able radicals of the time, several of whom became ministers in 1861 and were able to promote important reforms.

Already in March 1859 Alexander had given instructions for the reform of local government. Nicholas Milyutin, then assistant minister of the interior, was chairman of the commission responsible for drafting appropriate legislation. He favored the participation of all classes in the Zemstvos, as the new elective councils were called. In April 1861, however, Alexander dismissed both Lanskoi and Milyutin on the ground that they were too liberal in outlook. In fact, he was seeking to make some gesture to the landowning nobility who were distressed because they had lost land to the peasants and had not been compensated by any increase in political power. It was indeed in such compromises between liberal reforms and the need to retain the support of the nobility that Alexander disappointed so many of his people. Now he appointed as the new minister of the interior Count P. A. Valuev, whose policy was to ensure that the nobility were dominant in local government. Strenuous attempts were made by liberals to gain greater autonomy and powers for the Zemstvos, but their efforts had very limited success. *use as quote*

The Zemstvo statute, which Alexander signed on January 1, 1864, provided for local government at district and provincial levels. Electors were grouped into three categories, according to property qualifications, and peasants elected their representatives indirectly. By carefully defining the membership of every Zemstvo, the law ensured that no single social class could dominate. Members of the district Zemstvos, elected for a three-year term, chose from among themselves the members of the provincial Zemstvos. The new system was hampered in many ways. The election of the Zemstvo chairman had to be approved by the provincial governor and the provincial Zemstvo chairman had to be confirmed in office by the minister of the interior. The Zemstvos had no executive powers and had to rely on the cooperation of the police and other officials who were under the control of the governor or the ministry.

Notwithstanding these disabilities the Zemstvos were soon achieving remarkable results. They brought about striking improvements in hospitals and other institutions, such as orphanages and lunatic asylums, entrusted to their care. They organized medical and veterinary services in rural districts, but their most outstanding achievement was in the field of elementary education. Some eight thousand elementary schools existed throughout Russia in 1856. The number had increased to twenty-three thousand in European Russia alone by 1880. Toward the end of the reign Zemstvo or Zemstvo-assisted schools were increasing at the rate of one thousand annually.

In 1870 a statute established Dumas or elective town and city councils with powers similar to those of the Zemstvos. The Dumas acted with energy, providing public services, long taken for granted in Western Europe but lacking in Russia. Water supplies, the paving and lighting of streets, upkeep of bridges, the better organization of benevolent institutions were some of the new amenities provided. But, as with the Zemstvos, the most spectacular achievement of the Dumas was in the provision of schools. In St. Petersburg alone between 1873 and 1880 the number of schools increased from sixteen to eighty-eight. In Moscow and other cities and towns the achievement was on the same scale.

In cities, towns, and villages Russians were awakening to the need for education. From the time of his accession when he had facilitated entrance to universities, Alexander had sought to expand educational facilities, and after 1861 the movement gathered momentum. In place of the obscurantist Admiral Putyatin, Alexander appointed as Minister of Education, A. V. Golovnin, a close associate of Grand Duke Constantine, and he applied himself with energy to liberalizing education. He had opposed the claim of the church to exclusive responsibility for primary education and had thus made it possible for the Zemstvos and Dumas to attain their striking results. He encouraged secondary education and by a statute of 1864 all who passed the entrance examinations could attend such schools, a right which had in the past belonged exclusively to children of the nobility. The number of secondary schools was increased; teaching methods were revised; new text books were commissioned.

Golovnin's outstanding achievement was, however, the university statute of June 1863. He had sent a team of professors to study Western universities and to make recommendations for Russian universities. The statute that resulted restored to universities their autonomy, first granted in 1804. It provided them with an independent administrative system, including tribunals responsible for student discipline. In the academic field full freedom was granted. He also provided for special training for future professors and by scholarships and other means gave strong encouragement to higher education. Indeed, the fact that the universities entered into a brilliant and fruitful period during the second half of Alexander's reign was largely due to his work.

Another reform of great and enduring importance was the reorganization of the judicial system. This reform was close to the heart of Alexander, for he knew that the courts were corrupt, savage in their sentences, arbitrary, and dilatory. On his accession he had expressed the wish to establish in Russia "expeditious, just, merciful, and impartial courts for all our subjects; to raise the judicial authority by giving it proper independence and in general to increase in the people that respect for the law which national well-being requires and which must be the constant guide of all and everyone from the highest to the lowest."[11] Nicholas I had been aware of the need for reform of the courts and had set up a commission to prepare draft laws. At the end of 1861 Alexander enlarged this commission by appointing several eminent jurists to serve on it.

The basic principles of the reform, submitted by the commission and approved by Alexander on September 29, 1862, included the complete separation of the judiciary from all other branches of the administration, the fullest publicity for court proceedings, trial by jury in criminal cases, the institution of summary courts, presided over by Justices of the Peace, and the simplifying of legal procedures.

The proposals were widely publicized and were finally enacted on November 20, 1864. The new system of courts was simple. Minor civil and criminal cases were tried by justices of the peace from whom appeal lay to the district session of justices of the peace. More important cases were tried by district courts and higher courts which had judges appointed by the Crown from lists of experienced jurists, compiled by the judiciary. The Senate was reorganized to serve as the supreme court. But more significant than the structure of the courts was the new spirit of justice, impartiality, and courtesy which began to permeate the administration of justice. The liberation of the peasants, formerly at the mercy of their landowners, and independence from the bureaucracy introduced a sense of pride and fairness which had never been part of the administration of Russian law in the past.[12]

The armed forces were another field of spectacular reforms. Defeat in the Crimean War had demonstrated the inefficiency, corruption, and inadequacies of the Russian army. With few exceptions commanders of ability had been lacking; transport and supplies had failed; medical services had been so deplorable that more men had died from sickness than from enemy action.

Alexander was keenly aware of the need for reform in the army and he heeded his brother, Constantine, who as Minister of Marine introduced sweeping changes in the navy and was instrumental in securing the appointment of Dmitri Milyutin as Minister of War. Milyutin, a liberal possessed by great reforming zeal, had been wounded in action when serving as an officer in the Guards Artillery in 1840. He had written extensively on military subjects and was for fifteen years a professor in the Military Academy. But his interests were wide. Bismarck described him in 1861 as "the most daring and radical spirit among the reformers . . . the bitterest enemy of the nobility."[13] For twenty years he was Minister of War and with the steady support of Alexander against frantic opposition he transformed the army.

Milyutin first eliminated the harshest forms of punishment and discipline. He had opponents even in this most humanitarian reform. The Minister of Justice, Panin, and the Orthodox Metropolitan, Philaret, strongly defended branding and flogging, which often ended in death, as necessary instruments of discipline. But on April 17, 1863, Alexander signed the ukaz, prohibiting the more barbarous forms of punishment not only in the army and the navy but also for civil offenses.

Milyutin then set about introducing methods and efficiency into every branch of the armed forces. He greatly improved the conditions of the ordinary troops. He introduced the most modern weapons in place of the obsolescent equipment which had been one of the reasons for Russian defeats in the Crimean War. For the training of officers he established army gymnasia in place of the aristocratic Cadet Corps. He even made provisions for teaching recruits to read and write, a development that would have astonished Nicholas I.

The institution of conscription was, however, Milyutin's greatest achievement. He maintained that all men, irrespective of birth or wealth, should be liable for service. The uproar against this egalitarian proposal was so strident that, although a commission was set up to draft the new statute on military service in 1863, more than a decade passed before it was enacted.

In signing this statute on January 1, 1874, Alexander stated the principles underlying it.

Under present legislation the duty of military service falls exclusively on the lower class of town dwellers and on the peasants, he said. A significant section of the Russian people is exempt from a duty which should be equally sacred to all. Such an order of things, which came into being in different circumstances, no longer accords with the changed conditions of national life; nor does it satisfy our military needs. Recent events have shown that the strength of armies is based not only on the number of soldiers but on their moral and intellectual qualities. These attain their highest development where the defense of the fatherland has become the common concern of the whole people and where all, without exception and without distinction of calling or estate, combine in this sacred task.[14]

The statute provided that all men would be liable for military service on attaining the age of twenty. The conscripts to be taken from each military district annually would be chosen by ballot. They had to serve for six years and then were on the reserve for nine years after which they were liable for service until the age of forty. Educational qualifications shortened the period of service, but exemption could be obtained only on three clearly defined compassionate grounds. The introduction of the principle of social equality was a striking innovation, as was the encouragement given to education.

In the economic field, too, Alexander gave his support to policies of reform and expansion. His Minister of Finance, Count Mikhail Reutern, brought all the accounts of the various departments under the control of his ministry. He established effective methods of audit, made the national budget public, and abolished the pernicious system of farming out the sale of spirits. These and other reforms in financial administration were directed toward eliminating the corruption and inefficiency which crippled the nation, still recovering from the cost of the war and of maintaining as many as two million men under arms in the previous reign.

Reutern's contribution to Russian economic expansion was even more striking. He was especially active in developing railways. Communications in Russia were primitive and not only hampered trade but had contributed directly to the defeat in the Crimean War. Proposals to build a network of railways in 1835 had met with strong opposition. The then Minister of Finance, Count Igor Kankrin, had considered the project an extravagance and a threat to "public morals"; he maintained that railways would "encourage frequent purposeless travel, thus fostering the restless spirit of our age."[15] It was mainly Reutern's achievement that the railways, covering less than 660 miles in 1855, had been extended to some 14,000 miles by 1881. Indeed, the development of the railways was part of the general economic expansion of Alexander II's reign. Banks and other credit institutions were established. Trade flourished and exports trebled giving the country a surplus on balance of payments. Socially and economically Russia was in a state of revolution as it began transforming from a feudal into a capitalist nation.

The reign of Alexander II was also a time when the arts flourished. In music "the Five" (*Kuchka*) brilliant composers—Balakirev, Cui, Musorgsky, Borodin, and Rimsky-Korsakov—were active, and Tchaikovsky began producing some of his operas and other compositions. But it was in the field of literature that the remarkable eruption of works of genius took place. His father's reign had been a golden age of poetry and Alexander II's reign was notable as the age of the Russian novel. Turgenev, Dostoevsky, and Tolstoy all wrote and published their greatest works during this period. They were all so outstanding as writers that they overshadowed others, like Aksakov, Goncharov, Saltykov-Shchedrin, and Alexei Tolstoy, who also produced works of merit.

Alexander had begun his reign under the cloud of Russia's humiliating defeat in the Crimean War. It had lowered her prestige as a military power and her authority in international affairs. At the same time Russia was watched suspiciously by most of Western Europe. England in particular remained in the grip of strong anti-Russian feelings. The English attitude as expressed by one statesman was that Russia was a "great grim shadowy power which sits brooding over Europe and Asia, and of which no man knows whether it be strong or weak."[16]

The immediate purpose of Alexander's foreign policy was to find allies, especially against Russia's chief enemies, England and Austria, and to recover the losses confirmed by the Treaty of Paris. Prince Alexander Gorchakov, who succeeded Count Nesselrode as Minister of Foreign Affairs in April 1856 and held this office throughout Alexander's reign, was responsible for the conduct of foreign policy. He was an impressively loquacious man whose command of diplomatic French obscured his lack of real ability. Alexander listened to his advice, but also the advice of others, and he himself decided on the policy to be followed. Prussia seemed to be Russia's sole reliable ally at this time, although the policy she had followed during the Crimean War had not been helpful. Alexander counted on Prussia looking to him for support against Austria. Gorchakov also hoped for closer understanding with France. Napoleon III was keen to gain Russia's friendship and was ready to support Russian efforts to have the more unpalatable terms of the Treaty of Paris moderated. But Alexander's mistrust of Napoleon was not abated by their three-day meeting in Stuttgart in September 1857. It was clear that Napoleon would do nothing to jeopardize the Anglo-French alliance. Although there was strong support for a pro-French policy in St. Petersburg, all hopes of alliance were destroyed when Napoleon espoused the Polish cause at the time of the insurrection in 1863.

Alexander was counting on Prussia's help to further his policies in the south. In June 1870 King William I and Bismarck conferred with Alexander and Gorchakov at Ems. Alexander gave assurances that Russia would prevent Austrian intervention on the side of France in the Franco-Prussian War and in return William undertook to support Russian demands for revision of the Treaty of Paris. The Franco-Prussian war ended in the defeat of France, the fall of the third empire, and the final unification of Germany, King William of Prussia being proclaimed Emperor of Germany at Versailles on January 18, 1871 (NS).

Meanwhile on October 31, 1870 (NS) Gorchakov sent notes to all signatories of the Treaty of Paris, repudiating the Black Sea provisions of the Treaty. This unilateral act provoked a major crisis. England made furious protests. But the Russian note was well timed. France was at war with Prussia, and Austria was isolated diplomatically. England was not prepared to go to war alone against Russia. When Bismarck proposed a conference of interested countries, all agreed. The seven-power conference met in London in January 1871 and, thanks to German support, resulted in a diplomatic victory for Russia.

Alexander was, however, uneasy about the emergence of the German Empire. Bismarck was eager to strengthen German friendship with Russia and also with Austria in order to isolate France. Alliance with France as a counterweight to German power would have been a logical policy for Russia at this time, but Alexander had no love for republican France and was afraid that French influence would promote revolutionary ideas inside Russia. He was therefore ready to accept Bismarck's proposals, which resulted in the formation of the League of the Three Emperors in 1873. The Emperors of Russia, Germany and Austria mutually guaranteed the frontiers of their respective countries; they agreed to consult on all problems arising from the Eastern Question; they agreed also to concert action against threats of revolution. The League appealed strongly to Alexander as a revival of the Holy Alliance which his uncle, Alexander I, had conceived and his father, Nicholas I, had endorsed. But, like the Holy Alliance, the League was to prove ineffective.

The Eastern Question had not been resolved by the Treaty of Paris, as the signatories had hoped, and was in fact entering upon a more complex phase. Ottoman power was declining rapidly and the subject peoples were clamoring for independence. The Bulgars and the Serbs in Bosnia and Herzegovina were demanding freedom; Serbia and Rumania, although already autonomous, wanted full independence. Many in Russia began to champion the cause of the Orthodox Slavs in the Balkans. They argued that Russia, as the greatest of the Slav nations, should free brother Slavs from the yoke of the Muslim Turks. Nicholas Danilevsky and General Rostislav Fadeev, whose book *Opinion on the Eastern Question* was especially influential, enunciated the doctrine of Panslavism. Alexander and Gorchakov did not support this emotional nationalistic concept and tolerated it only because of its strong appeal to many Russians. But the policies advocated by the adherents of Panslavism were, in fact, to prove an embarrassment to the government, and they alarmed Western powers who interpreted the doctrine as a form of aggressive pan-Russianism.

The Eastern Question erupted in 1875 with revolts in Bosnia and Herzegovina, followed by a Bulgarian insurrection. The Sultan suppressed these uprisings savagely, and again public opinion throughout Europe was incensed. Under the Treaty of Paris the great powers had undertaken to intervene jointly in such a situation, but now they were divided in their policies. The British government under Disraeli was concerned primarily to halt any extension of Russian power. Austria and Germany were anxious to avoid another European war. Russia alone was prepared to intervene, but Alexander was cautious and tried to resist strong pan-slavist pressure for action. The situation developed rapidly, however, and he found himself committed.

In July 1876, Serbia and Montenegro declared war on Turkey and their small armies were soon in danger of annihilation. Russia proposed an armistice, which the Turks rejected. The new Sultan, Abdul Hamid III, was warlike and, believing that he could depend on English support, he was not inclined to bow to Russian demands. In Russia secret preparations for war with Turkey were put in hand. But Alexander was uneasy, mindful of the disastrous escalation which had led to the Crimean War. Neither the economy nor the army, then in the midst of reform, was ready for a war on a broad scale. But he was emboldened by a secret treaty signed in January 1877 with Austria who promised to take up a position of benevolent neutrality in the event of war; in return Russia gave undertakings not to annex Serbia, Montenegro, or Constantinople and to allow Austria a free hand with Bosnia and Herzegovina.

In April 1877 war was declared and on the Balkan and the Transcaucasian fronts the Russians pressed forward, until early in 1878 they were poised to advance on Constantinople. At this point Disraeli, having declared that England would never permit Russian occupation of the city, sent an English fleet to guard the straits. But the Turks had already agreed an armistice and on March 3, 1878 (NS) they signed the Treaty of San Stefano, conceding extensive gains to Russia.

Alexander now found himself faced with the threat of the European war which he had been so anxious to avoid. He grasped at the alternative course, which had resulted from frantic diplomatic exchanges in London, Berlin, and Vienna, that a congress of representatives of the powers should meet to reconsider the Treaty of San Stefano. This congress, held during June and July 1878 in Berlin, produced the Treaty of Berlin which drastically revised the earlier treaty. The independence of Serbia, Montenegro, and Rumania was confirmed, as was the cession to Russia of Ardahan, Kars, Batum, and southern Bessarabia. But Bosnia and Herzegovina were placed under the supervision of Austria, and Bulgaria was divided into two provinces and deprived of direct access to the Aegean Sea.

The Treaty of Berlin provided no permanent solution of the Eastern Question. For Russia, despite her considerable gains, it was a humiliation. Twice in Alexander's reign Russia had been compelled to submit to the European powers and had been thwarted, particularly by England. Alexander himself felt isolated and he welcomed the opportunity to re-establish friendship with the German Emperor, William I, and on Bismarck's instigation the Austrian Emperor was included so that the League of the Three Emperors was restored in 1881 on the eve of Alexander's death.

Russian expansion in Central Asia and the Far East also revived during the reign of Alexander II. It began as a more or less spontaneous movement. Governors and frontier garrisons, remote from the central government, were eager for conquest, booty, and fame. A contemporary remarked that "it was indeed impossible that such desires should be resisted when by gratifying them it was possible for a Lieutenant in four years to become a General."[17] Close on the heels of the conquering forces followed the Russian merchants, impatient to share in the enormous and quick profits. Alexander was involved in spite of his caution. He tried to exert restraint, fearing conflicts with other powers, but he was also an ardent Russian patriot, who rejoiced over any extension of Russia's territory or power. In effect, he encouraged the expansionist movement.

In Central Asia the conflict between the nomad Kazakh, Kalmyk, and other tribes and the Russians had been delayed for many years. Russians had reached down the Volga to the Caspian Sea and also eastwards beyond the Urals in the reign of Ivan the Terrible in the sixteenth century. Peter the Great and other Tsars had shown interest in conquering Central Asia, but had been distracted by other commitments. Now in the nineteenth century the conquest of this vast region was suddenly completed. Count Vasily Perovsky, the dynamic governor-general of Orenburg, built a network of strongholds into the Kazakh lands as the first stage in his conquest of the rich valleys of the Syr-Darya and the Amu-Darya, belonging to the rulers of Khiva, Bokhara and Kokand. By 1854 he had established positions along the Syr-Darya from which the Russian forces were able to subdue the nomads and to capture Tashkent. Three years later they had taken Samarkand.

The new territory was incorporated into the province of Turkestan with Tashkent as its capital. General Constantine von Kaufmann, the efficient but brutal governor-general of Turkestan, firmly established Russian control over the region. The Emir of Bokhara and then the Khan of Khiva acknowledged Russian suzerainty. Next came the conquest of the Amu-Darya Valley. Russia was soon on the frontiers of Afghanistan, Persia, and China, a development disturbing to several powers.

In Eastern Siberia the Treaty of Nerchinsk, signed with China in 1689, and limiting Russia's further expansion southward, had remained in force until 1858. The Russians had, however, moved northward along the Pacific coast of Siberia and into the Kamchatka Peninsula in search of furs and tribute from the native tribes. They had taken possession of many of the Kurile Islands, but only in 1855 under the Treaty of Shimoda were they able to establish trade relations with Japan.

Meanwhile Russian hunters and traders had moved into the Aleutian Islands and Alaska and down the Pacific coast of North America. They behaved with such greed and brutality, however, that the native peoples rebelled. The Russian government was forced to take action to establish order and the chartered Russian-American Company was set up with a monopoly of the fur trade in Alaska, the Aleutians, the Kuriles, and other North Pacific islands.

Russian activities in the North Pacific alarmed the Spanish and also the Americans and the British. Alexander I's decree in 1821, claiming the Pacific coast of North America south to the 51st parallel and his insistence on Russia's monopoly of trade in the North Pacific was attacked by the Secretary of State, John Quincy Adams. Then in December 1823 President James Monroe, in his message to Congress, declared the opposition of the United States to further colonization of the Americas by European powers. Alexander I had heeded the strong stand taken by the United States, which was supported by Britain. In 1824 he had agreed that the southern limit of Russian claims should be 54 degrees 40 minutes, and that the United States and Russia should both be free to trade and fish in the North Pacific.

Meanwhile the Russian-American Company had declined in importance, its finances becoming chaotic through corruption and inefficiency. Mainly for this reason Alaska had become an economic liability and, when a Franco-British naval squadron attacked the port of Petropavlovsk during the Crimean War, it became clear that Alaska was also a strategic liability. In 1854 informal discussions were begun between St. Petersburg and Washington on the sale of Alaska. The discussions dragged on until March 1867 when all the properties of the Russian-American Company, including Alaska, were transferred to the United States at the price of $7,200,000.

Interest in Russo-Chinese relations had also reawakened at the beginning of the nineteenth century. Nicholas I had been impressed by the successful war waged by England against China from 1839 to 1842 and in 1847, to protect Russian interests, he had appointed Count Nicholas Muraviev, later known as Muraviev-Amursky, one of his most able and energetic advisers, to be governor-general of Eastern Siberia.

Muraviev-Amursky had promptly extended Russian settlements of Cossacks and freed convicts through the vast area north of the Amur River. In 1851 he established the town of Nikolaevsk at the mouth of the river. After China had become involved in war with France and England, Alexander decreed the creation of a new province, including the north Amur region. This was a blatant annexation of Chinese territory, but China was in no position to resist. Indeed, Muraviev-

Amursky on his own initiative proceeded to negotiate with the Chinese commander of the region the Treaty of Aigun, providing for joint Russo-Chinese occupation of the lands from the Amur and the Ussuri Rivers to the Pacific coast.

Meanwhile Admiral Putyatin had opened negotiations with the Chinese government, resulting in the Treaty of Tientsin, signed in June 1858, which conceded to the Russians the right to trade in certain Chinese ports and to maintain a legation in Peking. England and France had just wrested similar rights from China. But then the Chinese government repudiated these agreements and renewed hostilities against France and England. Alexander sent General Nicholas Ignatiev to take over from Putyatin and to obtain confirmation of the Treaties of Aigun and Tientsin. In November 1860 China, weakened by the war against England and France, signed the Treaty of Peking, ceding to Russia the lands between the Amur and Ussuri and the Pacific. The vast region was divided into two provinces: the Amur with its administrative center at Blagoveshchensk, and Maritime Province with its center at Vladivostok, founded in 1860.

Alexander had deserved the gratitude and support of his people: he was staggered to find himself the object of their bitter criticism and hostility. He had eased the shackles of his father's rule, but this had been interpreted as weakness. The people demanded greater freedom and he rejected their demands as encroaching on his autocratic power. The landowners were for the most part sullen opponents of the changes which destroyed their traditional privileges and which they considered politically dangerous. People of other classes were reproachful because the reforms, the emancipation of the serfs in particular, had fallen so far short of their expectations. The reforms suffered, too, from many defects in operation, especially as they were administered by the old bureaucracy, which was not only grossly inefficient and corrupt but also unsympathetic to them.

The liberals seemed to have expected the reforms to effect an overnight transformation of their country, and their disillusionment was all the greater for this reason. They were, however, moderate in their demands. But among the intelligentsia the ferment was greatest and advocates of revolutionary and socialist programs became more vehement. Unrest broke out in the universities. Students demonstrated against regulations in Kiev in 1857 and more violently in St. Petersburg and Moscow. Socialist policies gathered greater support among them, encouraged in particular by Herzen's publication *Kolokol* (*The Bell*), published by the Free Russian Press in London, which had a wide clandestine circulation in Russia. In autumn 1861 new regulations introduced by Admiral Putyatin, a severe disciplinarian who had been recalled from the Far East and appointed Minister of Education, led to a massive student demonstration in St. Petersburg. Police and troops suppressed the rioters; the university was closed, and some three hundred students were held in the St. Peter and St. Paul Fortress.

Alexander had been away from the city at the time, but, angered by the brutality of the police and the imprisonment of the students, he had hurried back and had intervened personally. The students were released and both the Governor-General of the city and the Minister of Education were replaced. But his moderation did not quiet the unrest, which erupted afresh in the following year. A leaflet, called *Young Russia*, demanding radical policies which included elective national and provincial assemblies, dissolution of monasteries, and abolition of marriage, aggravated the ferment. A few weeks later serious fires broke out in various parts of the country, and in St. Petersburg fires destroyed some two thousand shops and warehouses. Arson was strongly suspected and, although no one was ever charged, public opinion blamed the Poles and the socialists. But the fires intensified the general uneasiness and insecurity throughout the country.

Alexander reacted angrily to these disorders and the government turned its attention to the press, closing some publications and prosecuting writers believed to be fomenting the troubles. Mikhailov, a poet responsible for producing radical leaflets, was arrested in September 1861 and sentenced to penal servitude in Siberia, where he died four years later. The police next arrested Nicholas Dobrolyubov and Nicholas Chernyshevsky, who had displaced Herzen as spokesmen of the young Russian radicals. Both were sons of priests, highly intelligent and well educated. They believed in the socialist transformation of society and in *The Contemporary*, then the leading journal of the intelligentsia, they attacked the slowness and the inadequacy of the reforms. While in prison Chernyshevsky wrote, in the form of a novel under the title of *What Is to Be Done?* (*Chto delat'*), his vision of the future in Russia. The book was published despite the censorship regulations and became one of the basic documents of the intelligentsia.

Opinion throughout Russia had generally favored the struggle of the liberal intelligentsia against the Emperor and the government. But the outbreak of the fires and the Polish insurrection in January 1863 had hardened feeling against all radicals. A strong body of opinion was, however, pressing for a national assembly. The constitutionalists, as they were called, were gaining wide support. Thirteen nobles of Tver went so far as to submit an address to the Emperor, having printed and circulated it at the same time, calling for the convening of a national assembly, representing all classes of the Russian people. Alexander was furious. He had the thirteen nobles imprisoned in the St. Peter and St. Paul Fortress and then they were sentenced by a special court to be detained in a lunatic asylum and to lose all civil rights. They spent only four days in the asylum, but their civil rights were never restored.

Alexander was not opposed to the principles of constitutional government and was prepared to concede that participation in government by popular representatives might have advantages. But he did not accept that this could ever apply to Russia. Like his father, Nicholas I, he believed fervently that he had been appointed by God and that he held his power in trust to be administered for the good of the nation. His special relationship with his people could never be shared. In 1865 and again in 1866 the Zemstvo of St. Petersburg demanded that a central Zemstvo office, akin to a national assembly, should be established. Alexander firmly rejected the proposal. To one of the constitutionalists he said:

> I suppose you consider that I refuse to give up any of my powers from motives of petty ambition. I give you my imperial word that this very minute, at this very table, I would sign any constitution you like, if I felt that this would be·for the good of Russia. But I know that, were I to do so today, tomorrow Russia would fall to pieces.[18]

Alexander was also disturbed at this time by the ferment in the Polish provinces of Russia. The Poles were restless under Russia's tutelage and eager to regain their freedom. The Polish landowners who represented moderate opinion were encouraged when in 1861 Alexander began extending a degree of autonomy to Poland. This did not, however, satisfy nationalist Poles who could think only of a free Poland, restored to her boundaries of 1772. Tempers mounted, and in January 1863 rebellion broke out against Russian garrisons in Poland, Lithuania, and White Russia. The Poles were disappointed in the help they had expected from France, and the insurgents were finally suppressed in 1864.

Alexander had tried to extend greater freedom to the Poles while maintaining Poland as part of the Russian Empire. He had dealt leniently with the nationalists, but had been forced to revert to repression. The ten provinces of the Kingdom of Poland were renamed the Vistula Provinces and were placed under a Russian governor-general. Stern measures were enforced to stamp out all signs of Polish nationality. Russian was the compulsory language of administration and education; even in the University of Warsaw, which reopened in 1869, Russian was the sole language of instruction.

By contrast the Finns, always more adept in managing their relations with Russia, accepted Alexander's concessions and quietly but stubbornly pressed for a Diet and for autonomy. In 1863 they were able to hold elections and, on opening the Diet in September, Alexander declared that "in the hands of a wise nation . . . liberal institutions not only are not dangerous but are a guarantee of order and well-being."[19] Indeed Alexander provided the foundations upon which Finnish independence was built and to Finns he had remained the Tsar-Liberator.[20]

The unrest in Russia, insurrection in Poland, struggles over the emancipation statutes and other reforms, and the hostility directed against him personally oppressed Alexander. The gains in Central Asia and the Far East and also against Turkey were no compensation. When he returned to St. Petersburg from Warsaw in 1860, he was so exhausted and drawn that certain ambassadors thought that he was seriously ill. He lived in a state of tension and was readily provoked to anger. In his private life, too, he was beset by troubles. He had retained in their privileged positions the small clique of his father's favorites and had made his friends among them. Their many opponents at court were disappointed when they were not displaced on Alexander's accession. Allegations of corruption among members of the clique and countermovements against certain of those close to Alexander poisoned the atmosphere at court.

Empress Mary was active in trying to offset the influence of those whom she felt were harmful to her husband. She also began to interest herself in state affairs. On retiring for the evening she would read state papers and discuss proposed measures with him. Alexander respected her advice and often acted on it. But the clique of favorites, fearing her influence upon him, spread rumors that she was seeking to Germanize Russia. Her position became more difficult in spring 1857 when she was pregnant and Alexander became involved in an affair with one of her maids of honor, Princess Alexandrina Dolgorukaya. Members of the clique were quick to build up the position of the Princess into that of an official mistress. The Empress, distressed by her husband's infidelity, went so far as to upbraid him, and for a time they were estranged.

Avoiding his wife and the palace, Alexander now sought refuge in the company of members of the clique. He had always been a keen hunter and he was often away from the capital hunting bears or wolves. His wife, languishing in the palace, evidently recognized that she would have to overlook his frequent affairs if her marriage was to endure and she was to have any influence. She cultivated her friendships with other members of the imperial family, especially the Dowager Empress. With their help she was able to effect a reconciliation. The imperial couple lived again as husband and wife. She was able, moreover, to influence and encourage him in his reforms.

In 1865, however, Alexander, then aged forty-seven, fell desperately in love with Princess Catherine Dolgorukaya, an attractive girl of eighteen. In the following year she became his mistress. He vowed that "at the first opportunity I will marry you: from now onward and forever I regard you as my wife before God."[21] Several times a week the young Princess would drive to the Winter Palace and, letting herself in by a hidden door to which she had the key, she would meet secretly with her lover. But soon their affair was the talk of the court and of the city. Catherine's family took her to Italy in the hope that the infatuation would wither away. But they wrote to each other daily and in May 1867, when Alexander visited Paris, they met again. Soon afterward she returned to St. Petersburg where he installed her in a luxurious apartment.

Most of the Tsars had had several mistresses. Catherine II had had a series of young men as official favorites. The private life of the Tsar had always been accepted without causing scandal or harming the prestige of the throne. But Alexander lacked the imperious self-confidence of so many of his predecessors, and he so mishandled this affair that it aroused indignation at court, split the imperial family, and damaged his authority. The Empress was respected and all felt sympathy for her predicament. The difference in the ages of Alexander and his mistress were the subject of harsh comment. The imperial family and especially Alexander's sons, Nicholas and Alexander, later to be Alexander III, were bitterly antagonistic toward Catherine Dolgorukaya.

The affair took a more serious turn in May 1872 when Catherine gave birth to a son, christened Yury, and she bore Alexander three more children. The health of the Empress was failing. The possibility that on her death Alexander would marry his mistress and nominate her son as heir to the throne was anxiously discussed. The imperial family and nearly all at court rallied in support of Alexander as heir and this increased the isolation of the Emperor from his family and his people.

The double life that Alexander was forced to lead created special problems for those responsible for protecting him. It was clear now that he needed close protection. One morning in April 1866 when walking in the Winter Garden in St. Petersburg, he was nearly assassinated. He was saved only by the timely intervention of a bystander. The assassin, a young revolutionary named Dmitri Karakozov, who had been a student at Kazan and Moscow universities, was arrested. His associates were rounded up and all were connected with the universities. Thirty-five of them were banished. Karakozov was hanged.

Alexander was shaken by this attempt on his life. He was readily persuaded that the universities, as the forcing ground of revolutionary ideas, should be more strictly controlled. He summarily dismissed Golovnin, who had achieved so much as Minister of Education, and appointed in his place Count D. A. Tolstoy, a strong reactionary and an enemy of academic freedom in any form. Tolstoy at once applied police methods to suppress all liberal and revolutionary ideas in the universities and to curtail the new programs in secondary education. He met with strong opposition from students and others, but his repressive policies were enforced.

The conservatives and nationalists were now firmly in power. In M. N. Katkov, moreover, they had an able journalist who had cast aside his early faith in liberal policies and constitutional government to dedicate himself to promoting conservative policies and militant Russian nationalism. The liberals became passive. The radicals went underground to work for political and social revolution.

At this time the intelligentsia began to produce a number of remarkable men, of whom Mikhail Bakunin, Sergei Nechaev, and Peter Lavrov were outstanding. Bakunin, a nobleman of striking presence and personality, was the father of revolutionary anarchism. Among his disciples was Sergei Nechaev, a young fanatic who believed in complete dedication to the revolutionary ideal,[22] and who first enunciated political terror as an essential tactic of revolution. At this stage Peter Lavrov was most influential. A professor of mathematics who had embraced the theories of Marx, Lavrov argued that, since Russia had no proletariat, the revolution must stem from the peasantry and the natural socialism of the commune. From the teaching of Lavrov and others the Populists (*Narodniki*) emerged as the foremost socialist group in the 1870s. Young radicals, their numbers swollen by the return on government orders of all Russian students in Switzerland, eagerly embraced their mission of "going to the people" to educate them politicially. Starting in 1873, the movement developed into a crusade by the summer of 1874 when some two thousand young radicals dressed as peasants flocked into the villages, expecting the peasants to embrace them as brothers. But they met only with suspicion and hostility. Peasants even attacked them and handed them over to the police. Many were arrested and imprisoned or banished to Siberia.

Disillusioned by this experience, many Populists assembled in St. Petersburg in 1876 when they formed the first Russian revolutionary party or secret society, which later became known as Land and Liberty (*Zemlya i Volya*). They planned a more realistic movement to the people, but the significant development was the adoption of terrorism as a weapon against the regime. The spectacular trial of Vera Zasulich encouraged the use of terrorist methods. In January 1878, she fired at the military governor of St. Petersburg, General F. F. Trepov, severely wounding him.[23] The evidence against her was conclusive, but the jury returned a verdict of not guilty. The whole city wildly celebrated the verdict.

Terrorists became more active, concentrating on the high officials

312

whom they saw as special enemies. In August 1878 General N. V. Mezentsov, head of the security police, and in the following February the governor-general of Kharkov, were assassinated. On April 2, 1879, Alexander Solovyev, a member of Land and Liberty, fired five shots at the Emperor, but missed him. At a secret conference in Lipetsk in June 1879 the policy of terror was endorsed and the immediate objective was laid down as the assassination of the Emperor himself. Land and Liberty now divided into two independent groups of which the Peoples' Will (*Narodnaya Volya*) stood for immediate violent action.

Led by fanatical revolutionaries, the party planned at least seven attempts on the life of Alexander. In November 1879 they blew up the imperial train near Moscow. In February 1880 terrorists, posing as workmen, managed to place a charge of dynamite in the banquet hall of the Winter Palace. The guest of honor, Prince Alexander of Bulgaria, was late, however, and the Emperor and his family had not yet entered the hall when the dynamite exploded.

The daring and the increasing activity of the terrorists, against whom the police seemed powerless, aggravated the uneasiness in the capital and elsewhere in the country. Alexander himself became more indecisive and unsure of himself, as though feeling himself to be hounded and doomed. He had, moreover, become cynical and mistrustful. He remarked, when told that someone had spoken ill of him, "Strange, I don't remember ever having done him a favor; why then should he hate me?" In his loneliness he turned for comfort to Catherine and her children, for only among them could he find the love which he craved. His great concern was to give her and their children a secure status. Two months after the death of the Empress in May 1880 he married Catherine morganatically, conferring on her the title of Princess Yurevskaya.

Meanwhile the bold ventures of the terrorists in gaining entry to the Winter Palace and blowing up the Banquet Hall called for urgent action. Alexander himself presided over a conference of high officials lasting three days. The heir-apparent urged that all government activities should be coordinated under one person to fight the terrorists. This proposal led to the creation on February 12 of the Supreme Executive Commission. Count M. T. Loris-Melikov, a former governor-general of Kharkov, who was generally popular, was president of the commission with quasi-dictatorial powers. He considered that it was essential to revive support for the government, especially among the liberals. Many Russians had resented the fact that the liberal constitution granted in Bulgaria had not been permitted in Russia. Several Zemstvo assemblies requested powers and privileges like those bestowed on the Bulgarians. All Russians had been antagonized by the repressive policies of Dmitri Tolstoy.

The new policy which Loris-Melikov and his commission proposed and which he called "a dictatorship of the heart" sought to relax tension. Tolstoy was dismissed and Section III of His Majesty's Own Chancery was dissolved, and a new department of the police under the Ministry of the Interior took its place.

Loris-Melikov announced further, with the approval of the Emperor, that the reforms enacted earlier in the reign would be continued as originally enacted. Another proposal was that an assembly of elected representatives of the Zemstvos and the city Dumas should be convened to advise and assist the government in preparing new legislation. The new proposals did not amount to constitutional reforms but they were important in seeking earnestly to bridge the gulf which had been growing between the government and the people. In August 1880, satisfied that the Supreme Executive Commission had fulfilled its function, Loris-Melikov had it dissolved.

Liberals welcomed these proposals, seeing in them a step toward the constitutional reform which they considered essential. The revolutionaries, who had halted many of their activities pending the announcement of the Commission's proposals, decided to renew their opposition and confirmed their policy of terror. They were now convinced that only by the assassination of the Emperor could they hope to provoke a revolution.

On the morning of March 1, 1881, Alexander gave his formal approval to the statutes, embodying Loris-Melikov's proposals. He then left the palace to attend the Sunday parade, which he had not attended for three weeks in response to the pleas of his wife, Princess Yurevskaya. Now she asked him to avoid two streets which, it was discovered later, had been mined by terrorists. On his return journey, the route for which, as had become the practice, was revealed only at the last minute, he drove in his sledge along Catherine Street which, due to a police error, had not been closed to the public. As the imperial sledge passed along this street a student, named Rysakov, threw a bomb. It exploded near the escort, wounding several Cossacks, but Alexander was unscathed. He stepped from the sledge to help the injured men. At that moment a Polish student, Hriniewicki, threw a bomb at Alexander's feet. It exploded, shattering both his legs and caused fearful mutilation of his face and body. When his brother, Grand Duke Mikhail, came to his aid, he could only whisper: "'Home to the palace to die there." Held in his brother's arms he was driven back to the Winter Palace where Princess Yurevskaya, not knowing what had happened, was awaiting him, and there he died.

Alexander's reign had been a time of momentous reforms. He had emancipated some forty million serfs, established a new legal system and the principle of equality before the law; he had abolished barbarous punishments and had sought to eliminate the arbitrary bureaucratic rule to which the people were prey. Like Peter the Great in the previous century he had launched Russia on the road to modernization. But throughout the country the news of his death was heard with indifference. He had never been popular. He was too reserved to make any personal impact on his people and his love for Princess Yurevskaya had damaged his reputation irreparably. But, in the words of the French ambassador, "He was a great Tsar and deserved a kinder fate."

XVIII

Alexander III

1881–1894

Tall, heavily built and so strong that he could bend an iron bar in his bare hands, Alexander was an impressive figure of a man. He did not possess great intellect or outstanding abilities, but he knew his mind and he had common sense as well as the talent to choose competent ministers. More important, he was a natural Autocrat who expected to be and was obeyed. He was, in fact, the last of the Romanov Autocrats.

As the second son of Alexander II, he had not expected to become Tsar, and had had no special training. With his brother, Nicholas, he had been entrusted to tutors in charge of a Lieutenant General N. B. Zinoviev. One of these tutors was Constantine Pobedonostsev, a brilliant jurist and an extreme reactionary, who influenced him strongly and was to be a powerful force throughout his reign. Alexander was said to be a dull pupil, compared with his clever brother. But this was not considered important, for it was taken for granted that he would serve in the army, the usual function of the Grand Dukes.

In 1865, Nicholas died of consumption and Alexander was declared heir to the throne. Some attention was paid to his further education, at least to the extent of a course on Russian history, conducted by the great historian, S. M. Solovyev. But in 1866 at the age of twenty-one he was held to have completed his education and to be ready for marriage. His brother, Nicholas, had been betrothed to Princess Sophie Frederica Dagmar of Denmark and Alexander now became engaged to her. She was admitted to the Orthodox Church and rebaptized Maria Federovna, and they were married on October 28, 1866. Although arranged, the marriage was very happy. Alexander was sincerely devoted and faithful to his wife, who was a gay sympathetic companion. He had strict ideas on morality and his own private life was free from scandal. Avoiding the formal court life of St. Petersburg, he lived much of the time in the seclusion of the imperial residence at Gatchina. There he could relax with his family and close friends. With them he was good-natured and jovial. He was fond of the theater and of music and often during musical evenings he played the trombone. But he was also conscientious, with an enormous capacity for work, and never neglected his duties as Emperor.

The assassination of his father made a deep and enduring impression on Alexander. He had strongly disapproved of his father's long affair and subsequent marriage with Catherine, Princess Yurevskaya. But the liberal reforms had disturbed him most of all and he saw in the assassination a vivid demonstration of the evil of liberal and revolutionary ideas. He was not alone in this reaction. The murder of the Tsar had sent a wave of horror through the country. It had destroyed the sympathy and support which so many Russians had felt for the populists and for liberal and revolutionary policies, and had strengthened the position of the conservatives and reactionaries. The mood of the Russian people was conducive to the counterreforms, the chauvinism and bigotry which were to characterize the reign of Alexander III.

Like his father and grandfather, Alexander held sacred the principle of autocracy and the holy bond between the Autocrat and his people. He was devoutly Orthodox in his personal faith. As a young man he had come under the influence of the Panslavists, but then had reacted strongly against the obstinate demands of the Balkan Slavs for democratic institutions. By the time he came to the throne his outlook was narrowly and aggressively nationalistic. On a despatch from his ambassador in Berlin he minuted: "To exact from every situation all that is needed by or is useful to Russia, to disregard all other considerations, and to act in a straightforward and resolute manner. We can have no policy except one that is purely Russian and national; this is the only policy we can and must follow."[1]

Proclaiming that he would honor the example of his father, Alexander was at once faced with the statutes embodying Loris-Melikov's liberal proposals. His father had given them his formal approval on the morning of March 1 before going to his death. Filial piety made Alexander hesitate to renounce this last act. At a meeting of high officials on March 8, however, Pobedonostsev, the Chief Procurator of the Holy Synod and leader of reactionary opinion in Russia, attacked the proposals as an affront to the principle of autocracy. Alexander was fully in agreement with his strictures. The statutes were allowed to expire without further discussion.

Pobedonostsev confirmed his triumph in the imperial manifesto, which was customarily issued on the accession of a new sovereign. He himself had drafted the manifesto, which Alexander approved and the essence of which was contained in the declaration that:

> In the midst of our great grief God's voice commands us to stand courageously at the helm of the government, relying upon Divine Providence, with faith in the power and truth of the autocracy which for the benefit of the people we are called upon to strengthen and guard from any encroachments.[2]

Loris-Melikov and A. A. Abaza, the Minister of Finance, who had not been consulted and were taken aback by this reactionary declaration, resigned at once and were soon followed by Dmitri Milyutin and Grand Duke Constantine. The new appointments, made on the advice of Pobedonostsev, were not chosen from among the extreme reactionaries, but by May 1882 Dmitri Tolstoy, the hated Minister of Education whom Alexander II had dismissed, had become Minister of the Interior and Ivan Delyanov, a reactionary and friend of Tolstoy, had taken over the Ministry of Education.

Constantine Pobedonostsev was now the dominant influence behind the throne. He was close to Alexander and enjoyed his complete confidence. The publicist of the repressive policies of the new government was M. N. Katkov, the able journalist who had been active in the previous reign. His articles in the *Moscow News* (*Moskovskiya Vedomosti*) were widely read and admired. Alexander himself read them regularly. On occasion Katkov was carried away by his chauvinistic fervor and his articles embarrassed the government, as when he attacked the Russo-German alliance in 1887, but he could always count on the protection of Pobedonostsev.

One of the most urgent tasks of the new Emperor and his ministers was to crush the revolutionaries and all political opposition. The police had acted promptly in rounding up all concerned with the assassination of Alexander II. On April 3, 1881, five young terrorists of the People's Will were hanged publicly on the Semenovsky Square in the presence of a vast crowd of troops, clergy, officials and foreign diplomats. During the following months all members of the party still in Russia were hunted down and imprisoned. In August 1881 the powers of the police were extended by the Law on Exceptional Measures, enacted initially for three years, but regularly extended until 1917. This measure gave governors and police officials extraordinary powers in areas declared to need special attention. In effect, the authorities were empowered to declare a state of emergency in such areas, which were then placed under the equivalent of martial law.

Censorship, which Loris-Melikov had planned to relax, became more repressive. Pobedonostsev had written to Alexander before his accession: "I believe that the government should not allow the control of the press to slip from its hands, that it should not relieve itself of this responsibility. To entrust it to the courts would give the press unbridled licence; this would cause great injury to the state and the people."[3] Censorship remained one of Pobedonostsev's obsessions and as Chief Procurator of the Holy Synod he was a member of the committee, set up by the new regulations, which had power to close any offending publication and to ban an editor from future activity.

In education the restrictive policies, introduced by Dmitri Tolstoy under Alexander II, were revived by Count Delyanov. Tolstoy, Pobedonostsev, and Delyanov were in complete agreement in considering that liberal policies in the schools and universities were the source of revolutionary agitation. They urged, too, that all primary schools should be brought under the church. Delyanov was able, however, to have only a few of the existing schools transferred to the church and in the rural areas, where church schools competed with those maintained by the Zemstvos, the latter were acknowledged to be superior.

Golovnin's statute of 1864, opening the secondary schools to all who passed the entrance examinations, was amended. In March 1881 Pobedonostsev reported to Alexander that "Unfortunately our gymnasiums aim at leading the students further and further to universities; hence the fallacious trend towards higher education, and those half-educated students who fail are doomed, having lost contact with the social environment to which they belong."[4] Delyanov raised the tuition fees to ensure that "Children of coachmen, servants, cooks, laundresses, small shopkeepers and the like" would have difficulty in attending, and other restrictions were imposed to the same end. Education was once more a class privilege.

The restrictions which Tolstoy had tried to impose on the universities, and which Alexander II had vetoed, were now introduced. The new code of 1884 deprived university councils of all authority and universities came completely under the control of the Ministry of Education. All student organizations were suppressed. Fees were increased. The admission of women to universities was severely restricted and, in some cases, prohibited.

The autocratic regime depended, as Alexander recognized, on the support óf the landowning nobility, who had been weakened by the reforms of the 1860s. Active steps were now taken to strengthen their economic and political standing. In 1885 the Nobles' State Bank was established to provide mortgage credit on favorable terms as a "means of preserving for their posterity the estates in their possession."[5] They made full use of the bank's facilities, but even this aid failed to prevent the break-up of many large estates and their passing into the hands of merchants and the small class of wealthy peasants.

The Zemstvos, providing local government at district and provincial levels, were soon fighting for their existence. Tolstoy and Pobedonostsev disapproved of them, both because they were elective and because the 1864 statute prevented their domination by the nobility. The new statute, introduced in 1890, provided that the nobles would in future have a fifty-seven percent majority of the delegates elected to most of the Zemstvos. At the same time the electoral rights of the peasants were severely restricted. Further, the powers of the Zemstvos were subjected to the authority of the governor to veto any act which he considered harmful to the interest of the state or the region. The Zemstvos could appeal to the Senate against a governor's veto, but such appeals were usually thrown out.

At the same time the government brought the peasants more closely under the supervision of the nobility, partially reviving the patriarchal authority which landowners had wielded before the emancipation. This was achieved by appointment of a "land captain" (Zemsky Nachalnik) chosen from the nobility in each locality and confirmed by the Minister of the Interior. The land captains possessed extensive, almost dictatorial, powers over the communal life of the peasants. They even interfered in their private lives. In bondage to the commune and subject to the control of the land captains, the peasants were hardly better off than they had been as serfs.

The economic conditions of the mass of the peasants were certainly worse than under serfdom. The lands allocated in 1861 did not allow the majority to maintain themselves and their families and they were burdened now not only by taxes but also by redemption payments. Their hardships were further aggravated by the natural increase in population, resulting in the subdivision of holdings into smaller, even more uneconomic, lots. The communes imposed the old methods of cultivation and thwarted efforts to improve cultivation. Peasants had no capital and in most areas they could not rent extra lands, for landowners were finding the growth of markets for their produce at home and abroad so profitable that they would not part with land, preferring to hire cheap peasant labor. Migration remained difficult, but many peasants sought work in the towns, and many more moved eastward into Siberia where land was plentiful.

The mass of the peasants remained in their villages, where conditions deteriorated so seriously that the government was forced to act. By a law of December 28, 1881, the redemption of holdings of land, which had been optional, was made compulsory and at the same time redemption payments were reduced. Poll tax, introduced originally by Peter the Great, was abolished. But still peasants were required to pay taxes out of proportion to their earnings. The government recognized the need to make more land available to them. The renting of state lands to the communes was made easier and in 1882 the Peasant Land Bank was set up to help peasants to buy land. It made loans to the wealthier peasants, who could be counted on to repay. The poor peasants, who were the great majority, did not benefit. Against the opposition of the landowners, migration to Siberia was facilitated and even encouraged by new legislation, promoted by S. J. Witte, the active and far-sighted Finance Minister, appointed in August 1892.

Bolder, more extensive reforms were needed. The inadequacy of the measures taken by the government was demonstrated in the calamities which overtook the nation in 1891–92. Harvests had been poor during the 1880s and in 1891 there was a total failure of crops. Famine and disease overwhelmed twenty provinces. The government was slow to organize relief and the measures taken were too limited. But the liberals, and especially the students, worked devotedly to help the starving peasants. They came closer to the villages of rural Russia during this catastrophe than at any time during the Populists' mission to the people. Moreover, the Zemstvos proved their worth, gaining a new moral authority and attracting wider support.

Conditions of workers in the towns were no less deplorable. The minor industrial boom of the 1870s had given way to a recession. Workers were sacked; wages fell; strikes became frequent. In 1882 the government put a stop to certain of the worst abuses in the use of child labor in factories. Factory inspectors were appointed, but met with constant obstruction from the managers. Further legislation in 1884 brought considerable improvements in the working conditions. But, like the peasants, the workers were still condemned to live harsh, poverty-stricken lives.

In trade and finance the policies adopted towards the end of Alexander II's reign were continued. High tariffs protected Russian industry from foreign competition. This policy added to the burdens borne by the mass of the people, but industry was able to earn vast profits. Witte introduced currency reforms and in 1897 adopted the gold standard, which attracted investment from abroad. The coal and iron industries expanded rapidly. Railway construction boomed and in 1891 the Trans-

Siberian Railway was started. Exports mounted, especially of grains, with the result that there was often not sufficient for home consumption and the peasants suffered.

During these years Russia appeared to be a most prosperous nation, but the prosperity was on the surface and dependent on the people continuing to bear intolerable burdens of direct and indirect taxation and poverty. In this soil the seeds of revolution were to take root. But at this time the revolutionary movement was inactive inside Russia. The only notable revolutionary act was the attempt in March 1887 to assassinate Alexander III. The plot failed and five young university students were sentenced to death. One of the five was Alexander Ulyanov, the elder brother of Lenin.

The repressive policies which Alexander imposed on his own people were matched by the chauvinism and bigotry of his rule over the minorities peoples. Aggressive nationalism, called "official Russification," led to widespread persecution. Again Pobedonostsev exercised a sinister influence. He was bitterly hostile to Jews, Poles, Russian dissenters, Roman Catholics, and Protestants. Like many Russians he was obsessively suspicious of racial and religious minorities, whom he saw as active threats to the unity of the Orthodox Russian Empire.

The Russification policy was enforced with special severity in Congress Poland from the beginning of the reign. All teaching in Polish schools had to be carried on in Russian. Roman Catholic Poles could not hold official positions. In every field of Polish life this repressive policy made itself felt. The Finns and the Baltic Germans and the people of Central Asia and the Caucasus were subjected to similar regulations, enforced by governors-general with policy and, when necessary, troops.

All who were not members of the Russian Orthodox Church were liable to be persecuted. Old Believers, who in 1881 numbered as many as thirteen million, were more or less tolerated. Stundists, who were akin to Baptists, were banned and severely punished. The Dukhobors who rejected the Orthodox liturgy and sacraments and who refused to bear arms had been persecuted since the reign of Nicholas I and they were harassed even more savagely by the government of Alexander III.

Anti-Semitism, which had long been widespread, became an active policy under Alexander III. Many Russians blamed Jewish revolutionaries for the assassination of his father. In April 1881 the first pogrom took place and during the next few months it was followed by 215 pogroms in which Jews were murdered and their property destroyed. Alexander and his ministers officially condemned these excesses, but they condoned the pogroms in practice. Indeed, anti-Semitism was encouraged in what were known as "dry pogroms" which meant persecution without bloodshed. The rights of Jews, already limited, were further curtailed.

Quotas kept to a minimum the number of Jewish children who could obtain secondary and university education. All Jews were barred from government service, from practicing law, and they were persecuted in countless other ways.

In foreign affairs, Alexander was to depart from his father's policy. In June 1881 he endorsed the terms of the revived League of the Three Emperors. But it was an uneasy alliance. Russian and German interests conflicted in the Baltic and, unlike so many of his predecessors, Alexander actively disliked and mistrusted Germany. Gorchakov, the Minister of Foreign Affairs, who had never forgiven Bismarck for the part that Germany had played in the Congress of Berlin in 1878, shared this mistrust. He was, however, an old man and N. K. Giers, who was to succeed him in April 1882, was more flexible. As a personality he was less striking than Gorchakov, but he was a realist and, although Alexander maintained that he was his own foreign minister, Giers influenced policy and succeeded in restraining his master from chauvinistic ventures. Indeed, to Giers belongs much of the credit for the fact that the reign of Alexander III was a period of peace, although not without its crises.

The first crisis, erupting in 1885, brought Russia close to war with England. The Russian advance south of the Sea of Aral toward Afghanistan had aroused English concern for the security of India. The violent anti-Russian feeling of earlier decades had quieted, however, and there was general agreement that delimitation of the Russo-Afghan frontier should be carried out by a joint commission. The first commission, appointed for the purpose in July 1884, was suspended at Russia's request. Russian forces then advanced closer to Afghanistan and on March 30, 1885 (NS), were engaged by Afghans whom they defeated.

In England strong feeling was aroused by this incident which was regarded as proof of Russian bad faith. Queen Victoria had appealed personally to Alexander to prevent a conflict with the Afghans. In fact, the engagement had taken place in violation of his instructions. This was not known in London and a rupture between Russia and England was expected. Parliament voted eleven million pounds for war purposes and reserves were called up. But the storm passed. An Anglo-Russian commission was appointed and on September 10, 1885 (NS), reached agreement on the northwestern frontier of Afghanistan.

The crisis which developed over Bulgaria was more serious and led to the disruption of the alliance between Russia, Austria, and Germany. The Treaty of Berlin had provided for Russian occupation of Bulgaria for only nine months. But Alexander III looked upon the country as a vassal state and took for granted that its prince, Alexander of Battenberg, the nominee of his father, would obey his wishes. But neither the Prince nor his people were prepared to accept subordination to the Russian Emperor. Relations between Russia and Bulgaria became strained. Then, in September 1885, as the result of a coup, Eastern Rumelia was united with Bulgaria under Prince Alexander who became a national hero to the Bulgarian people.

Russia had not been consulted over these events and Alexander was furious. He struck the name of the Prince from the Russian army list and recalled all Russian officers from the Bulgarian army. In August 1886, against the advice of Giers, he gave support to a palace revolution as a result of which Prince Alexander was forced to abdicate. But Russian efforts to secure the election of a new Prince of Bulgaria, who would further Russian interests, failed completely. The arrogance and interference of the Russians had antagonized all Bulgarians and they rallied in support of the Austrian candidate, Prince Ferdinand of Saxe-Coburg, who became Prince of Bulgaria. Alexander III refused to recognize him and only after his death were relations between Russia and Bulgaria resumed.

Among all Russians anti-German and anti-Austrian feeling had become intense during the Bulgarian crisis. The Russian press, and Katkov in particular, had published violent attacks on both allies. Heatedly Alexander had informed Giers that there could be no renewal of Russia's alliance with either country. But then, recognizing the dangers of Russia's isolation, he agreed to the negotiation of a treaty with Germany. This was welcomed by Bismarck, who had been disturbed by the virulently anti-German stand of the Russian press and feared that Russia and France would become allies. The secret Russo-German treaty was signed on June 12, 1887 (NS). But despite mutual assurances of goodwill relations between the two nations were disturbed. While Bismarck remained in power, there was no fear of a complete rupture. But in March 1888 the aged Emperor William I died and his successor, William II, felt no emotional attachment to Russia. Moreover, when the new German Emperor paid a state visit to Russia and subsequently, with great reluctance, Alexander returned the visit, the two monarchs were wholly out of sympathy with each other. In March 1890 Bismarck was forced to resign. German policy was now to strengthen the alliance with Austria and to cultivate the friendship of England. When, later in 1890, the date for the renewal of the Russo-German alliance was approaching, the German ambassador politely informed Giers that it would not be extended.

Alexander was not greatly perturbed by the lapse of the alliance, but it took all of Giers' persuasion to overcome his antipathy to alliance with France, the home of revolution and republicanism. Giers had the same prejudice against France, but with the collapse of his policy of alliance with Germany, Russia was friendless and isolated, and alliance with France was the obvious alternative. Already, in 1888, France was providing Russia with military equipment and French bankers and industrialists were taking an active part in Russia's economic development. Commercial relations paved the way for closer political understanding. In July 1891 the French fleet called at Kronstadt and received a hearty welcome. Negotiations for an alliance began soon afterward. A military convention was signed in August 1892, but the terms of the alliance were not finally agreed until January 4, 1894 (NS). This alliance committed Russia to extend military aid to France if Germany or Italy with German support attacked her, and committed France to render similar aid to Russia in the event of Germany or Austria-Hungary with German support attacking her. The alliance, the terms of ness in the legs. Doctors prescribed rest in the warm climate of the division of Europe into two hostile camps and was the prelude to world war.

Alexander impressed everyone by his great strength, energy, and robust health. It seemed impossible that such a man could fall ill. In 1894, however, he began to suffer from insomnia, migraines, and weakness in the legs. Doctors prescribed rest in the warm climate of the Crimea. Alexander decided to go to his country residence at Spala in Poland. There he became worse and a specialist brought from Vienna diagnosed nephritis. This time Alexander agreed to retire to the Crimea.

At first the warmth and sunshine brought improvement in his health, but then he began to decline. He was surrounded by his family, including his son, Grand Duke Nicholas, who was joined by his fiancée, Alix, Princess of Hesse-Darmstadt. Alexander received her in his bedroom, sitting in a chair and wearing full-dress uniform. He had insisted that he should be properly attired to receive the future Empress of Russia. During the next ten days his strength slowly ebbed and on October 20, 1894 he died.

XIX

Nicholas II

1894–1917

Nicholas II, the last of the Romanovs, bore some resemblance to Tsar Mikhail who had begun the rule of the dynasty three centuries earlier. Both were gentle and devout men, and both had ascended the throne with deep reluctance. Their fates were, however, quite different.

Mikhail had had the active support of his father, Filaret, and the Russian people had rallied to him as the center around which they had to unite in order to survive as a nation. Nicholas had succeeded on the death of his father, who had not prepared him for the throne and had burdened him with a reactionary heritage. Also, while the people still needed their Tsar as the center of national unity, they were at this time straining desperately to break from the feudal institutions which shackled their lives. At his accession the tide carrying Russia into the twentieth century was flowing strongly, and he tried to resist it.

In his reign Tsar Mikhail had established the dynasty and had enabled it to take root. Tsar Nicholas allowed the autocratic regime to collapse about him and was responsible for the extinction of the dynasty.

Nicholas was born on May 6, 1868, the eldest of Alexander III's five children. He was a shy, gentle boy, devoted to his mother, who closely supervised the upbringing of her children. His father, immersed in affairs of state, was remote from his children. His great size, gruff voice, and autocratic manner made him seem like a forbidding Jehovah against whom their mother was their only defense. Nicholas stood in awe of his father and revered him as a god. It troubled him even as a small boy that one day he would have to succeed him. He felt that he would never be able to measure up to his father's standards and to rule with the same authority. He regretted that the first-born son of his parents, Alexander, had died in infancy, for he would have been heir to the throne.

Nicholas studied under private tutors. He was a diligent pupil and a good linguist, speaking Russian, English, French, German, and some Danish. But the dominant force in his education was Constantine Pobedonostsev, who had been his father's tutor and then Chief Procurator of the Holy Synod. Pobedonostsev had become even more bigoted and reactionary as he had aged, and he instilled in Nicholas the blind faith in autocracy and Orthodoxy which he never lost. This lesson had been further entrenched in the mind of Nicholas, as it had been in his father's mind, by the assassination of Alexander II. A boy of thirteen at the time, Nicholas never forgot this tragic event. The shattered body of the Emperor had been carried into the Winter Palace, and then he had been led with other members of the imperial family into the room to take his last leave of his grandfather. The grim drama of the occasion, intensified by the mutilation of the face and body of the dying man, had left an indelible impression. Pobedonostsev had stressed that this horror was the result of liberal and constitutional reforms.

Nicholas was nearly twenty-two when his formal education came to an end. He was short and slender in build, but handsome, and he had a gentle charm and goodness of heart which gained him friends. He enjoyed army life and attended summer maneuvers with the Imperial Guard. Although heir to the throne, he had few duties and, like other young officers, he went to theaters and balls, and lived gaily. In the spring of 1890 he was attracted by a young dancer in the Imperial Ballet, named Mathilde Kschessinska, and began to see her regularly. In October, however, he went with his brother, George, on a nine-month cruise, which included visits to Egypt, India, Southeast Asia, and Japan. He was nearly killed in Japan when for no apparent reason a Japanese suddenly attacked him with a sword, gashing his forehead. The wound proved superficial, but the incident may well have strengthened his strong prejudice against the country and its people whom he always called "monkeys." In Vladivostok he laid the first stone of the eastern terminus of the Trans-Siberian Railways.

On his return to St. Petersburg, Nicholas resumed his few functions at court and his attendance at meetings of the committee of ministers and the State Council in which he took little interest. His father did not bother to involve him further in government affairs. Count Witte, the Minister of Finance, related that, when he proposed that Nicholas should be appointed chairman of the Siberian Railways Company, Alexander III was astonished. "He's a mere boy," he said. "His judgements are truly childish: how can he be chairman of a committee?"[1]

Although twenty-four years old, Nicholas was young for his age. Alexander, no doubt believing that he would reign for many years, may have been waiting for him to mature. But he did not even keep him informed on subjects of major national interest. It was not until after his accession that Nicholas learned of the existence of the Franco-Russian alliance and other important matters.

Meanwhile Nicholas had resumed his friendship with Kschessinska, who had become very fond of him. But already he was attracted to Princess Alix of Hesse-Darmstadt, the younger sister of Grand Duchess Elizabeth, wife of Grand Duke Sergei, Nicholas's uncle. He met her when she visited Russia to stay with her sister and during her visit in 1889 his love for her was born. Early in 1894 Nicholas told Kschessinska that he intended to propose to this Princess, and they took leave of each other.

Alix was tall, fair haired, and intense. She had not made a favorable impression on the high society of St. Petersburg. She lacked elegance, danced poorly, spoke French indifferently, and was awkward in company. She had been a laughing spirited child until at the age of six she had lost her younger sister and then her mother from diphtheria. She became solemn and withdrawn, and she was always to be shy and ill at ease in company. Her mother, Princess Alice, had been the daughter of Queen Victoria, who had virtually adopted the grandchildren, of whom Alix was her favorite. The Queen took special interest in their welfare and education and was delighted by the rapid progress of Alix, who was intelligent and musical. Regarding the old Queen as a mother, and making frequent visits to England, it was natural that she should have become, as one contemporary described her, "in the deepest sense a Victorian gentlewoman."[2]

Nicholas's parents were both staunchly anti-German and were distressed when he asked permission to marry Princess Alix. They suggested as more suitable brides Princess Helene, daughter of the Comte de Paris, Pretender to the throne of France, or Princess Margaret of Prussia. Nicholas demurred and was relieved when both Princesses declared that they were unwilling to embrace Orthodoxy, for this meant that his parents could not press either proposal. Indeed, Alexander's illness early in 1894 made his parents more anxious to see Nicholas married and settled with his wife before he succeeded to the throne. With some reluctance they agreed therefore that he should be allowed to propose to Alix.

In spring 1894 the wedding of Ernst, Grand Duke of Hesse-Darmstadt, the elder brother of Alix, brought to Coburg most of the royalty of Europe. Queen Victoria herself attended and Nicholas, accompanied by three of his uncles, represented the Russian Emperor. Alix was at the railway station to greet him when he arrived, and on the following day he proposed. But she dissolved into tears, declaring that she could not renounce her Protestant faith to embrace Orthodoxy, as was necessary before she could marry the heir to the Russian throne. She was desperately earnest in everything she did and to change her religion faced her with a crisis of conscience. But the persuasions of Nicholas, supported by those of Queen Victoria and of her own sister who had voluntarily adopted the Orthodox faith, finally overcame her scruples. On the following day she accepted him. Deeply in love, the young couple radiated happiness during their remaining days together in Coburg. In June they were reunited in England where Granny, as they called Queen Victoria, lavished affection on them and gave every thought to their happiness. The six weeks spent together in England were among the happiest in their lives, and in the years to come they would cheer each other by recalling incidents from their carefree sojourn in the English countryside.

On his return to Russia, Nicholas found that his father's health was declining. He wanted to go to Germany to be with Alix, but dutifully he accompanied his father and the rest of the family to Livadia in the Crimea. When it became clear that the Emperor was seriously ill, Alix traveled to the Crimea so that she could meet him and be with Nicholas. For the young couple it was a harrowing experience, but they were able to comfort each other. Nicholas needed her support at this time. He had always lived in dread of his succession to the throne. On the day of his father's death he felt overwhelmed and inadequate. "What is going to happen to me, to you, to Xenia, to Alix, to all Russia?" he exclaimed to the brother of Alix, who had accompanied her. "I am not prepared to be the Tsar. I never wanted to become one. I know nothing of the business of ruling. I have no idea of even how to talk to ministers."[3]

On November 14, 1894, one week after the funeral of Alexander III with its long-drawn-out formalities, Nicholas married Alexandra Fedorovna, the name with which she had been rebaptized in the Orthodox Church. They loved each other passionately, and throughout the twenty-three years of their marriage they remained completely united. But this deep and harmonious union was to give rise to terrible tragedy.

Alexandra became the dominant influence in Nicholas's life and it was a dire influence. She was a dedicated wife and mother, but frantic and inflexible. When, after deep searching of heart and conscience, she had embraced Orthodoxy she had done so with the extreme fervor of the convert. She had no understanding of Russia or of the court, where her great reserve and unbending dignity, contrasting with the gaiety and easy charm of Nicholas's mother, the Dowager Empress, made her unpopular. But on marrying Nicholas she became a chauvinistic Russian nationalist, dedicated to the principle of autocracy. Ill at ease at court and jealous of her mother-in-law, who took precedence over her, she was lonely in St. Petersburg. But she was anxious, too, about Nicholas. "I weep and worry all day long," she wrote to a friend, "because I feel that my husband is so young and inexperienced."[4] A woman of great courage and will and inflexible prejudices, she saw it as her duty to give him strength and ensure that he ruled as Autocrat. She advised him and in later years she was to interfere more and more in matters of government. Devoted but misguided, she played the major role in the tragedy of his reign and the extinction of the dynasty.

On the accession of Nicholas many Russians hoped for some relaxation of the repressive rule of his father. Nicholas destroyed such hopes at the first opportunity. On January 17, 1895, when addressing an assembly of Zemstvo delegates, he said:

"I am happy to see the delegates of all social classes assembled here to express their feelings of loyalty. I believe in the sincerity of those sentiments which have always been characteristic of the Russians, but I am aware that lately there have been in certain Zemstvo assemblies raised voices of certain persons who have permitted themselves to be carried away by the senseless dream of participation by Zemstvo representatives in internal government. Let all know that, in devoting all my strength on behalf of the welfare of my people, I shall defend the principles of autocracy as unswervingly as my deceased father."[5]

He evidently believed that the nation would continue in the same obedient and loyal mood as under his father's rule. He had little inkling of the ferment seething beneath the surface of Russian life.

The liberals had grown in number and in authority since the famine years of 1891–92. Working together for the relief of the peasants and other poor they had found a sense of common purpose. They were no longer prepared to accept for themselves and for the nation the rule of the Autocrat and of the massive bureaucratic machine, which had proved so inadequate. Conditions on the land were growing worse and further crop failures occurred in 1897, 1898, and 1901, adding to the urgency of the problem. Unrest was increasing also in Russia's expanding industries, and strikes were frequent. The revolutionaries were organizing in the Social Democrat Party and the Socialist Revolutionary Party, but they were not yet active on any scale, and their influence was negligible.

Nicholas's declaration of autocracy antagonized many of his subjects. But also from the beginning of his reign ill-fortune hounded him with calamities, until this mild and kindly man was regarded as a cruel tyrant. The first calamity happened on May 18, 1896, the day after his coronation in Moscow. The traditional banquet for the people was arranged on the Khodynka Field outside Moscow. By dawn some five hundred thousand people had gathered to feast and drink the health of their new sovereign. Suddenly a rumor started that there would not be enough beer and food. A stampede began to get what there was. The squadron of Cossacks posted to keep order was pushed aside by the thousands of people pressing forward. Men, women, and children fell and were trampled into the muddy ground by the vast crowds rushing over them. Police and troops finally arrived, but already Khodynka Field was littered with thousands of bodies of people killed or injured.

Nicholas and Alexandra were shattered by this tragedy. At first he wanted to retreat to a monastery to pray. He said that he could not attend the ball at the French embassy on that evening. His uncles, all tall impressive men who towered over him, insisted that he must go. It was bad advice which he accepted. Among the people the word spread that the Emperor and Empress had danced while Russia was in mourning. Although during the following days they both visited the injured in hospitals and Nicholas did what he could to help the families of the dead, the people did not forget Khodynka Field and it was considered a bad omen.

During the early years of his reign, demonstrations against the Tsar and his government became so violent and widespread as to defy suppression. The universities became stormy centers of unrest, and police and troops acted with brutal severity. But Russians in increasing numbers everywhere took part in clandestine political gatherings and secretly worked for reforms. A small number were revolutionaries, but few even among the moderates would cooperate with the police or with government officials. The number of people charged with political crimes rose from 1580 in 1900 to 5590 in 1903, and these figures did not include the many cases of administrative arrest and exile. Workers came out on strike in waves. In 1903 strikes with violence which broke out in Rostov spread like a forest fire across southern Russia from Odessa to Baku. The peasants, unpredictable and at times like a destructive elemental force, set fire to the houses and barns of landowners and murdered all who came in their path.

Terrorism was soon on the increase. In February 1901 a Socialist

Revolutionary terrorist assassinated N. P. Bogolepov, the Minister of Education. It was the first political murder of Nicholas's reign. In the following month an attempt was made on the life of Pobedonostsev, the man most hated by liberals and revolutionaries alike. In April 1902 D. S. Sipyagin, Minister of the Interior, was killed. In other parts of the country the terrorists chose as their victims the governors and high officials who were known for their severity.

Nicholas reacted uncertainly. He wanted to appoint men who would exercise firmness. But he was haphazard and usually mistaken in his choice of ministers and, more and more under the influence of his wife, he chose the most reactionary. To succeed as Minister of the Interior he appointed Vyacheslav Plehve, a narrow police bureaucrat who had won recognition by bringing to justice all who had been involved in the murder of Alexander II. Plehve acted energetically. He was virulently anti-Semitic and in his ministry were forged the *Protocols of the Elders of Zion*, purporting to be the plans, prepared by the Zionist Congress of 1897, for the domination of the world by the Jews. He was mainly responsible for the increased persecution of the national minorities, especially the Finns, Poles, and Armenians. But he was most active in promoting police action. His agents infiltrated into every political group in Russia and among émigrés abroad; they provided detailed reports on Lenin and the Bolsheviks, then organizing in Western Europe. In July 1904 Plehve was killed by a terrorist's bomb, but during his short term in office he had wielded a sinister influence and had aggravated unrest throughout Russia.

Bewildered by the growing threat of revolution, Nicholas allowed himself to be drawn into a policy of aggrandizement which led to war against Japan. The prospect of annexing Manchuria would, he hoped, surely distract the people from the general malaise. He listened to the advice of Plehve, who argued that "a small victorious war" would dispose of his troubles. But this war was to prove a humiliating disaster.

After the Sino-Japanese War of 1894–95, revealing the weakness of China and the emergence of Japan as a new power, Russian ambitions in the Far East had quickened. China had agreed to cede the Liaotung Peninsula to Japan, but then had appealed to Russia, who, supported by France and Germany, brought pressure to bear on Japan to restore the Peninsula to China. In the following year Witte took advantage of the presence of the Chinese chief minister at the coronation of Nicholas to exact the price for Russia's intercession. This price was alliance with Russia against Japan and rights to continue the Trans-Siberian Railways across northern Manchuria to Vladivostok with a branch line from Harbin to Mukden and Dalny. In further negotiations two years later, Witte secured a twenty-five-year lease of the southern tip of the

Liaotung Peninsula with rights to establish a naval base at Port Arthur and a commercial port at Dalny.

The threat that Russia would now seize Manchuria and dominate the Far East alarmed other powers. Japan, convinced that Russia would attack her, formed an alliance with Britain. The United States made clear its dislike of Russian policy in the Far East. Such strong opposition disturbed Nicholas and his ministers. But Witte, the practical politician who recognized the dangers of the situation and urged caution, was suddenly dismissed. Nicholas chose to listen to Plehve, who discounted all the risks and held that a small emerging power like Japan would not dare to attack the greatest land-power in the world. His arguments emboldened Nicholas, who was eager to prove himself as a strong Tsar but had small understanding of world affairs. While many governments saw clearly that war between Russia and Japan was imminent, he was evidently blind to the danger.

On the night of February 8–9, 1904, the Japanese attacked without warning. They were counting on a quick victory while they had superior forces in the Far East. They virtually immobilized the Russian naval squadrons in Port Arthur and Vladivostok. In April the main Japanese army landed in Korea and gained a clear victory against the small Russian force holding the line of the Yalu River. At Nanshan in the following month they again defeated the Russians, whom they outnumbered by ten to one. The Russian garrison in Port Arthur was now cut off from Manchuria.

On August 25 the Japanese engaged the main Russian force at Liaoyang. They intended this to be the decisive battle of the war, but the Russians, although defeated, withdrew in good order. Indeed, Kuropatkin, realizing that the Japanese were nearing the end of their resources, took the offensive. But the battles fought in October and then in January 1905 were costly and indecisive. Meanwhile the small Russian garrison in Port Arthur had bravely fought off repeated Japanese attacks, but on the death of Kondratenko, its commander, Strossel, his successor, treacherously surrendered. The Russians were defeated in the battle of Mukden and retreated to the north. Russian prestige suffered a final devastating blow in the Straits of Tsushima on May 27. The Russian Baltic Fleet, commanded by Admiral Rozhestvensky, had sailed from Kronstadt to assert Russian naval superiority in the Far East. It had suffered numerous mishaps on the long voyage and then, reaching the China Sea, it was annihilated by the Japanese navy, commanded by Admiral Togo.

Japan had failed, however, to win a quick and decisive victory and now, her economy strained by the war, she faced the Russian forces massing in Manchuria which would crush her. But in Russia the war had been resented from the start as a costly, unnecessary venture for which the ineptitude of the Tsar and his ministers was responsible. The humiliating defeats had merely demonstrated their incompetence, and the demand for peace was becoming general.

Alarmed by the unrest and criticism, Nicholas grasped at the offer of mediation, made by President Theodore Roosevelt. He recalled Witte to conduct the negotiations with the Japanese, and he handled them with skill. By the Treaty of Portsmouth, signed on September 5, 1905, Russia had to surrender to Japan the Liaotung Peninsula, half of Sakhalin as well as to evacuate Manchuria and acknowledge Korea as a Japanese sphere of interest, but the Amur and the Maritime Provinces remained in Russian hands.

In January 1905, when public anger over the disasters in the Far East was mounting, a calamity in St. Petersburg irreparably damaged Nicholas's position and authority as Tsar. A strike in the turbulent Putilov works had spread until it involved all workers in the capital. They were not interested in the slogans of the Social Democrats or the socialist revolutionaries, and looked on Father Georgii Gapon, an Orthodox priest, as their leader. Gapon was a devious, excitable man who had organized the St. Petersburg Society of Russian Factory and Workshop Workers; he was also a police agent.

Addressing a mass meeting on January 20, Gapon declared that the workers must march in procession to the Winter Palace and present a petition to the Tsar, setting out their demands. He grew more excited as he spoke. He said that if they were kept outside the palace gates they would force their way through. "If the troops fire on us, we will defend ourselves. Part of the troops will then come over to us. We will then make a revolution. We will build barricades . . . The Socialist Revolutionaries have promised us bombs . . . We will win through!"[6]

Gapon notified the Minister of the Interior that the procession was planned and assured him that it would be a peaceful demonstration. He sent him, too, a note of the demands to be presented to the Tsar, which included full civil and political freedom and a constituent assembly. But the police agents who had heard his inflammatory speech had reported that, far from being peaceful, the procession would be a violent revolutionary demonstration. Nicholas and his family were at Tsarskoe Selo, not at the Winter Palace, but ministers and the police feared that Gapon's workers would take over the city, and they ordered military and police reinforcements.

On the morning of Sunday, January 22, "Bloody Sunday" as it was to be called, workers, many with wives and children, gathered from all parts of the city for the procession to the Winter Palace. Gapon, resplendent in Orthodox robes and with ikons carried on either side of him, led the great crowd. The workers were orderly and peaceful, and many carried ikons and portraits of the Tsar. But as the crowd surged forward, the authorities, believing them to be armed with bombs, took fright. In the approaches to the palace military and police detachments called on them to halt. But with the momentum of their numbers they moved forward inexorably. Then, in the square before the palace, troops and police lost their heads and began firing into the crowd. Many fell dead and hundreds were wounded. The cries of the injured and dying and the screams of the women and children echoed through the city, as the people scattered in their thousands.

The news of this massacre of innocent people sent a wave of horror through the country. It was widely believed that the Tsar had deliberately ordered his troops to shoot down helpless men, women and children, who had gathered to present a loyal and humble address. The Tsar had always been cherished as the "Little Father" of his people, and even in the midst of the violent unrest of the nineteenth century he had been revered by all except a few extremists as the protector of his people. The tragic events of Bloody Sunday damaged this traditional image of the Tsar. Gapon, who had made his escape unharmed, later told Lenin that "We have no Tsar any more. Rivers of blood separate the Tsar from the people."

Nicholas was bewildered, as he had been after the tragedy of Khodynka Field. But he was shaken now by reports of the hostility of his people toward him. He sincerely loved them as a father and protector and he found that many hated him as a monster.[7] He tried to make amends by ordering payments of compensation to families of the dead and wounded, and by appointing a commission to investigate the workers' complaints. It was too late to undo the damage. The change in the traditional attitude of the people toward their Tsar weakened one of the main foundations on which the regime rested.

After the assassination of Plehve in July 1904, Nicholas had intended appointing a successor who would pursue the same repressive policies. But he finally selected Prince Svyatopolk-Mirsky, a liberal and a man of integrity who was generally respected. This appointment opened a new period, known as the "Russian Spring," when the liberals organized themselves more effectively. A conference of Zemstvos in St. Petersburg in November 1904 approved a petition to the Tsar, requesting the grant of full civil liberties for all classes, including the national minorities, and the creation of a national assembly. Nicholas responded with a curt instruction that the Zemstvos were to desist from discussing political matters, but he declared his intention of granting some reforms. All progressive elements in Russia nevertheless confirmed their strong support for the proposals of the Zemstvo conference. Lawyers, teachers, doctors, authors, and other professions came together in unions, and in the following years they were all amalgamated in the Union of Unions under the chairmanship of P. N. Milyukov, an historian and an outstanding liberal. The pressure of the demands for constitutional government was becoming irresistible.

Meanwhile, following on the massacre of Bloody Sunday and the news of the shameful surrender of Port Arthur to the Japanese, violence and unrest erupted afresh. On February 17, 1905, a terrorists assassinated Grand Duke Sergei in the Kremlin in broad daylight. The Grand Duke had been a harsh reactionary of whom his own cousin had written: "Try as I will, I cannot find a single redeeming feature in his character."[8] But Nicholas felt now that firmer control had to be exerted. He dismissed Svyatopolk-Mirsky and appointed Alexander Bulygin as Minister of the Interior. He announced also his instruction to Bulygin to prepare a plan whereby "the most worthy persons should be elected to share in the drafting and discussion of laws."[9] But the imperial decree, proclaimed on August 17 enacting Bulygin's law, provided only for a consultative body with minimal powers.

Agitation for a constituent assembly with real powers mounted. Late in September spontaneous strikes spread from printers in Moscow and St. Petersburg to railway workers, teachers, and other professions until the whole country was at a standstill. In desperation, Nicholas turned for advice to Witte, who had just returned from negotiating the peace with Japan. Witte faced him bluntly with two alternatives: a military dictatorship, with which he would not be associated, or the grant of civil rights and of an elected Duma or council with the undertaking that no law could be enacted without its consent. Nicholas hesitated, but he knew that he had no choice, for a military dictatorship would lead inevitably to a bloody civil war.

On October 30 the imperial manifesto proclaimed the grant of civil rights, the institution of a Duma in the election of which all classes would participate, and the guarantee that all laws, including decrees of the Tsar himself, could be enacted only with the consent of the Duma. This October Manifesto amounted to a revolution and not only the liberals but all Russians welcomed it jubilantly, for it established the beginnings of a parliamentary democracy and of a constitutional monarchy.

On July 30, 1904, when harassed by the unrest which gripped the country and by the disasters of the war against Japan, Nicholas and Alexandra were overjoyed by the birth of Tsarevich Alexei. Between 1894 and 1901 four daughters had been born, but they had longed for a son, especially as it would ensure the continuity of the dynasty.

Nicholas and Alexandra were devoted parents. They lavished affection on their children without spoiling them and, in spite of the opulent surroundings of the palace and the innumerable servants and attendants, parents and children alike lived lives of ordered simplicity. With the birth of Alexei they felt themselves to be a complete and united family.

But ten weeks after his birth it was learned that he suffered from the fearful, incurable disease of hemophilia.[10]

The effect upon Alexandra of this discovery was devastating. She had prayed earnestly that she might produce an heir to the throne of her beloved Nicholas and now her thanksgiving had been cut short by this tragedy. But she adored the boy and dedicated herself to protecting him. Nicholas, too, loved the boy and at the same time, feeling her anguish, he gave his wife tender and patient support. But the illness of his son moved him profoundly and the sense of fatalism which had been growing in him since his accession became more marked. He believed with increasing sureness that his life would always be beset with trials and tragedy.

Alexandra had leanings toward the occult. When desperate for a son, she had turned to a certain "Dr. Philippe" from Lyons and, although he had been prosecuted in France for practicing medicine without being qualified, he had quickly gained her confidence. In 1902 he had persuaded her that she was again pregnant, and the customary announcements had been made. When it was found to be a false alarm, Dr. Philippe was forced to leave Russia. Alexandra nevertheless retained her faith in his powers. But now she was seeking a miracle to save the life of her son and, obsessively devout and given to superstition, she was a ready prey to cranks and charlatans.

On November 1, 1905, Nicholas made the fateful entry in his diary: "We have got to know a man of God, Grigori, from the Tobolsk region."[11] Like many Russian peasants he had no surname, but from an early age he had been known as Rasputin, meaning "the debauched." He had had to flee from Tobolsk as a young man and for some years had roamed through Russia as a penitent, one of the *stranniki*, who searched for truth and salvation. They were revered as holy men, lived on charity, and were accorded a certain freedom and authority, so that they spoke to all, even on occasions to Tsars, with simple bluntness. Rasputin had wandered as far afield as the Balkans and had twice made the pilgrimage to Jerusalem. Late in 1903 he appeared at the Theological Academy in St. Petersburg where he made a strong impression. He had learned to read and write during his wanderings and had also acquired some theological knowledge. He was reputed to have great powers of healing and prophecy. The Bishop of Saratov, Hermogen, and the Inspector of the Academy, Archimandrite Feofan, both eminent and saintly men, gave him their blessing and support.

Rasputin was sturdily built, of medium height with pale skin, long greasy hair and beard, bushy eyebrows overhanging steely gray eyes and, never washing, he had a pungent unpleasant smell. In appearance and in other ways he was a typical Russian peasant. He combined cruelty and kindness, cunning and innocence, viciousness and piety; he was a drunkard and a crude sensualist from whom few women were safe, but he also had a capacity for religious devotion and mystic feeling. He was a man of extremes and he seemed to have evolved the dangerous creed that, since repentance alone could secure salvation, it was needful to sin in order to repent. But he was not entirely a charlatan. He had powers of healing and witnesses attested to the fact that on several occasions when doctors were powerless, as the Tsarevich lay bleeding or writhing in agony from internal hemorrhage, Rasputin alone was able to give relief.

To Alexandra, who lived in fear of every cut and fall which might threaten her son with death, and who spent hours alone in her chapel, praying for a miracle, Rasputin was the man sent by God in answer to her prayers. With her fanaticism she believed in him completely. She revered him as a holy man, as a Christ. His drunken sexual orgies gave rise to terrible scandals. He had an extraordinary fascination for many women and took pleasure in degrading ladies of the nobility. But women put up with his gross sensuality and ill-treatment, amounting at times to rape. One of his victims turned on him, stabbing him in the abdomen, but he recovered quickly. Alexandra rejected such scandals angrily. She closed her mind to reports, no matter how irrefutable, that he was corrupt and evil.

Nicholas also accepted Rasputin as a holy man. He had witnessed his power to relieve the suffering of his son. But he was less fanatic than his wife and he was not blind to some of Rasputin's failings. At the same time he saw in him not only a man of God but also a true Russian peasant. This was important to him, for after the revolution of 1905, culminating in the October Manifesto, he had retired with his family from the Winter Palace and the magnificence of the court life of the capital to live quietly at Tsarskoe Selo, fourteen miles away. He was contented in his quiet family circle, but increasingly he felt isolated from his people. He welcomed Rasputin because he felt that through him he was in contact with the peasant masses.

Rasputin was soon wielding a powerful influence over Alexandra, and Nicholas condoned their relationship. Rasputin had convinced her that while he lived the Tsarevich could not die. His sinister power over her was soon so great that she felt that she had to be guided by him in everything, including the policies which she should press her husband to follow. Unwilling to distress his wife, Nicholas usually accepted the advice even when he was not convinced that it was right. The time soon came when the Empress and Rasputin were virtually ruling Russia.

The experiment in democracy under the new constitution, provided by the October Manifesto, gave rise to furious activity. Political parties were hurriedly formed. Elections were held and the first Duma opened on May 10, 1906. The constitution provided for an upper house, formed by enlarging the State Council, established by Alexander I in 1810, and an elected lower house, which was the Duma. It introduced the cabinet system in which the Prime Minister was responsible for his ministers who were appointed by the Tsar on his recommendation. The constitution had many faults. Article 87 in particular gave rise to conflict for it empowered the government to make laws to deal with any emergency when the Duma was not sitting, but such laws had to be submitted for the Duma's approval within two months after its reassembly. Also the Tsar retained wide powers. He could dismiss the government and dissolve the Duma at will. He could proclaim a state of emergency, thus suspending the constitution, and he held sole command over the armed forces. But for all its faults the constitution, which provided that all new legislation must have the approval of the Duma, laid the foundations of parliamentary government.

Five days before the first Duma met, Nicholas dismissed Witte from the office of Prime Minister or president of the Council of Ministers. He had come to hate Witte, who had opposed his Far Eastern policy, had drafted and pressed him to accept the October Manifesto, and who was the chief architect of the new constitution, which reduced him to the status of a constitutional monarch. Witte believed in autocracy and had served Alexander III wholeheartedly. But he was an astute and practical politician and he had promoted the new constitution because he recognized the inadequacy of Nicholas as Autocrat. An arrogant, crude, vindictive man, who had risen to power by his own abilities, he felt contempt for Nicholas and he did not hide it. The Empress was his most bitter enemy. She hated him particularly for the October Manifesto and because she believed that he was seeking to emulate the British Prime Minister and to relegate Nicholas to the impotence of a constitutional monarchy. Witte was, nevertheless, one of the few men in Russia with experience and political sense who might have saved the dynasty from the tidal wave of revolution which was to engulf it.

Aroused by Alexandra's blind faith in autocracy, Nicholas soon began to question the great constitutional concessions that he had granted. He had believed them to be inevitable at the time and had intended sincerely to implement them. But now on her instigation he sought to reassert his autocratic powers. He appointed as his Prime Minister I. L. Goremykin, a bureaucrat who hated change and did not conceal his belief that the Tsar was absolute and that his ministers were merely his servants. The Empress approved this appointment and spoke of him affectionately as "the old man." Certain other members of the cabinet, chosen earlier by Witte or Nicholas himself, were, however, men of caliber.

The Duma with its liberal majority at once came into conflict with the government. The Duma submitted an address to the throne, setting out its main legislative proposals, including compulsory appropriation of the land for distribution to the peasants. Goremykin came before the Duma, harangued the deputies, and dismissed their address as "inadmissible." There followed a debate in which the deputies vehemently condemned the government for incompetence.

Nicholas was impatient to dissolve the Duma, which he considered was far exceeding its powers and privileges. He was dissuaded from this step by fear of a public outcry and also because it might antagonize opinion in Britain and France. He considered a proposal that he should call on the liberals to form a government, for it was expected that such a government would fail so disastrously that he would be justified in establishing a military dictatorship. Informal approaches were made to Milyukov, leader of the Constitutional Democrats or Kadets, but he would accept office only on impossible conditions. Already the opportunity to establish a working parliamentary system was being cast aside through the doctrinaire attitude of the liberals and their lack of experience and moderation.

On July 20 Nicholas finally dissolved the Duma. The deputies were infuriated. Many rushed to Vyborg in Finland, where they had greater freedom from police interference, and from there they issued an appeal to the country to demand the recall of the Duma and to withhold taxes and recruits until this was done. It was a stupid and ineffectual action. Moreover, all deputies who had signed the appeal were charged under Russian law, which meant that they could not stand for re-election.

On dissolving the first Duma, Nicholas had appointed dates for new elections, for he had not dared to dissolve it permanently. But he approved a revision of the franchise, intended to ensure that a majority of conservative deputies were elected. In the event the new Duma was as strongly opposed to the government as its predecessor. But in appointing Peter Stolypin to be the Prime Minister in place of Goremykin, Nicholas had made one of the wisest decisions of his reign.

Stolypin was a big, impressive man whose ability, courage, and integrity commanded wide respect. He was a constitutionalist and he was eager to work with the Duma and "to show the country that it had parted company forever with the old police order of things."[12] During the period between the dissolution of the first and the election of the second Duma, Stolypin ruled the country, relying on the controversial Article 87 for authority. He held that the government must not delay any longer in tackling essential reforms. In a series of ukazi he transformed the conditions of the peasantry. He gave every peasant the right to leave his commune, claiming his share of the communal lands as his personal property which he could bequeath to his heirs. Between 1906 and 1915 more than two and a half million peasants withdrew from their communes. This and other land reforms brought a marked advance in agriculture. Landowners began to take a direct interest in improving their estates. The new prosperous class of yeomen farmers, known often as kulaks, increased the productivity of their lands. The problems of overpopulation and poverty remained, but the further encouragement of migration to Siberia gave some relief.

Stolypin's ministry lasted only five years, but it was a period of exceptional political, economic, agricultural, and industrial development. A series of good harvests brought widespread prosperity. Industry expanded with growing momentum. Indeed, it was the judgment of Bernard Pares, the leading British authority on Russia in this period, that the seven years from 1907 to 1914 were the most prosperous in Russia's history.[13]

The growth of political consciousness was of special importance during these years. Stolypin was keenly aware of it and deeply concerned that nothing should disrupt it. In July 1911 he wrote to Izvolsky, the Russian ambassador in Paris, that "every year of peace fortifies Russia not only from the military and naval point of view, but also from the economic and financial. Besides, and this is most important, Russia is growing from year to year: self-knowledge and public opinion are developing in our land. One must not scoff at parliamentary institutions. However imperfect, their influence has brought about a radical change in Russia . . ."[14]

Such vision was beyond the narrow fanatic mind of the Empress. She had become increasingly antagonistic toward Stolypin. In physique, personality, and ability he towered over Nicholas, and she resented his ascendancy. She arranged an interview between Stolypin and Rasputin so that the holy man could report to her. Stolypin felt only "an indescribable loathing for this vermin," as he described Rasputin, who reported unfavorably on him to the Empress. But then early in 1911 Stolypin became alarmed by accounts of the monstrous behavior of Rasputin. He ordered an investigation and submitted the results to Nicholas, who read the report but took no action. Stolypin then acted on his own initiative and ordered Rasputin to leave St. Petersburg. Alexandra was enraged and begged her husband to intervene. For once Nicholas stood firm, refusing to overrule his Prime Minister, and Rasputin set out on a pilgrimage to Jerusalem. But Alexandra was now intent on persuading her husband to dismiss Stolypin, losing no opportunity to poison his mind against him, but fate intervened.

In September 1911 Stolypin and V. I. Kokovtsov, the Finance Minister, attended the Tsar on a visit to Kiev to unveil a statue of Alexander III. In the opera house as the curtain was about to rise for the final act of the gala performance, Stolypin was shot at point-blank range. Hearing the noise the Tsar looked down from his box to see Stolypin in the stalls turn slowly, make the sign of the cross in the air toward him, and then slump in his seat. The assassin, a certain Bogrov, who was apparently active both as a revolutionary terrorist and a police agent, was saved from being torn to pieces by the crowd when he was hustled away by the police.

The murder of Stolypin caused an uproar. The police were strongly criticized for failing to protect him. An official inquiry recommended the public trial of all who had been negligent. But Nicholas, whose son had just come near to death but was now recovering, refused to sanction the trial. His gesture of forgiveness was doubtless genuine, but it encouraged the rumors that high officials had been implicated in the assassination and that the Tsar was anxious to avoid publicity.

Kokovtsov succeeded Stolypin and was at once plagued by the public outcry against Rasputin. Criticism of his influence and his scandalous conduct was voiced in the Duma early in 1912. The Russian press began a campaign, condemning "that cunning conspirator . . . that fornicator of human souls and bodies." Nicholas gave orders that references to Rasputin in the press were to be banned in future. But this was a violation of the law abolishing censorship, and it antagonized the liberals. In any case the press ignored the ban. Far worse than the press campaign were the rumors and gossip which alleged that Rasputin was the lover of Anna Vyrubova and the Empress.

The Dowager Empress, mother of Nicholas, invited Kokovtsov to call on her and they discussed Rasputin's influence over Alexandra. She promised to speak with the Tsar, but did not expect to achieve anything. "My poor daughter-in-law does not perceive that she is ruining both the dynasty and herself," she said.[15] Mikhail Rodzyanko, the President of the Duma, also spoke with the Dowager Empress and he agreed to seek audience with Nicholas to warn him of the harm that Rasputin was causing. A huge man, Rodzyanko, at the thanksgiving service in the Kazan Cathedral in June 1913, had lifted Rasputin out of his seat and ejected him from the cathedral. Granted audience, he spoke bluntly to Nicholas. He was authorized to make a detailed report, which he delivered, but again nothing was done. Alexandra's own brother, Duke Ernst of Hesse, was present when Nicholas read the report. He later commented sadly: "The Emperor is a saint and an angel, but he does not know how to deal with her."[16]

The third Duma, which met in November 1907 and continued for its full five-year term until June 1912, was dominated by the Octobrists, a moderate conservative party, and by nationalist and reactionary groups. Arbitrary revision of the franchise had procured this result. The third Duma, nevertheless, functioned effectively, due mainly to the leader of the Octobrists, Alexander Guchkov, and his cooperation with Stolypin. The fourth Duma, which continued until 1917, was similar in composition, but lacking such men as Stolypin and Guchkov, who was not re-elected as a result of police interference, it was far less effective.

During the period of the first three Dumas, unrest on the land and in industry had declined remarkably. The Social Democrats and the Socialist Revolutionaries were still a negligible force. Unrest had revived, however, in 1912 on a smaller scale and the revolutionary parties sought to take advantage of it. But the main threat to the constitution and the Duma came from the ultraconservatives.

The tercentenary of the Romanov dynasty had been celebrated in 1913. The Winter Palace came to life with its old splendor, when Nicholas and Alexandra received and entertained the notabilities of the land, and they were cheered by vast crowds as they rode in their carriage for the magnificent thanksgiving service in the Kazan Cathedral. In May they visited Kostroma where in 1613 Mikhail had received the delegation bearing the news from Moscow that he was the chosen Tsar. They had then traveled downriver to Moscow, the ancient capital. Every-where the people greeted them with demonstrations of loyalty. The culmination of the celebration was the entry of Nicholas ahead of his Cossack guard into Moscow. He dismounted in the Red Square and walked in procession into the Kremlin to give thanks in the hallowed Uspensky Cathedral.

This was the last of the great imperial occasions. It had moved Nicholas deeply, but the experience had also confirmed Alexandra's faith in the bond between the Autocrat and his people. Moreover, it had the effect of rallying the monarchists and reactionaries and, includ-ing the landowning nobility, many of whom had been incensed by Stoly-pin's land reforms, they were a powerful force. Alexandra now harassed the unfortunate Nicholas with demands that he dismiss the Duma and all who diminished his autocratic powers. She waged her tireless campaign especially against Kokovtsov, Guchkov, and others who were critical of Rasputin. Nicholas was also under pressure from certain people at court and in the government to dissolve the Duma and to abrogate the 1905 constitution. But the most that he ever considered was to reduce the Duma to a consultative body and, meeting strong opposition to this proposal from certain quarters, he did not press it. Indeed, had he not been unsettled by the restless zeal of his wife, he would have fulfilled the role of constitutional monarch with dignity and effect.

On August 1, 1914, the German declaration of war united the Rus-sian people suddenly and completely under their Tsar. They gathered before the Winter Palace in thousands from all parts of St. Petersburg and listened with patriotic fervor as Nicholas publicly swore word for word the oath, that Alexander I had sworn at the time of the French invasion, that he would never make peace while one enemy soldier remained on Russian soil. The vast crowd then knelt on the cobblestones and sang "God save the Tsar." Not for over a century had the nation been so united in this spirit of dedication and loyalty.

The war against Germany and Austro-Hungary had full popular support. The liberals welcomed it particularly, because it brought Russia into alliance with republican France and constitutional England against the reactionary monarchal Central Powers. The hostility of the Russians toward Germany, suppressed for so long, now erupted. St. Petersburg was promptly given its Slav name, Petrograd. All were convinced, moreover, that the war would be short and victorious.

Certain voices were raised in warning. Kokovtsov had advised Nicholas that, even with foreign loans, Russia could not afford a major war. He had repeated Stolypin's warning of July 1911 that "we need peace: a war during the coming year and especially in the name of a cause which the people would not understand would be fatal for Russia and the dynasty."[17] Rasputin, when in Pokrovskoe in 1914 recovering from the knife wound inflicted by a woman whom he had degraded, sent a cable to the Tsar: LET PAPA NOT PLAN WAR, FOR WITH WAR WILL COME THE END OF RUSSIA AND OF YOURSELVES.[18] Angrily Nicholas tore up the cable and brushed aside other warnings.

Nicholas was elated by the feeling of union with his people. He threw himself into the war preparations, and his family ties with Germany in no way affected his determination to fight to the end. The nation prepared feverishly. Full mobilization required three months. In spite of poor roads, inadequate railways, and vast distances, however, over four million men had answered the call-up by September 30. Morale and discipline were high, but in equipment and transport the Russian forces were at a terrible disadvantage against the Germans.

Within five days of the German ultimatum, the French government was demanding through its ambassador that the Russian armies should invade Germany to hinder the German advance on Paris. Nicholas, whom Bernard Pares described as "the simple, impressionable Tsar . . . conspicuous in his chivalry to his country's allies," responded promptly.[19] The Russians were far from ready for action, and the policy should have been to remain on the defensive, drawing the enemy deeper into the country so that, like the Swedes and the French in previous centuries, they would perish. But, ignoring this traditional strategy, Nicholas at once ordered three armies to march into East Prussia. Notwithstanding their inferiority in equipment, the Russians came near to victory, but were finally defeated in the battle of Tannenberg. Against the Austro-Hungarian army, which was one million strong, the Russians won a decisive victory.

Morale remained high among the troops, and throughout the country, and 1915 was expected to be a year of victories. It was to be a year of retreats, however, and the appalling casualties began to disturb the nation. By the end of the first ten months of the war 3,800,000 Russians had lost their lives. Equipment of every kind was in desperately short supply. Men were moved into the front lines without rifles and had to wait for comrades to fall to seize their equipment. Artillery was rationed to firing a limited number of shells a day. In part the shortages of essential supplies was due to the incompetence of the War Office and its minister, Sukhomlinov, who was later impeached. But in part the shortages were due to the backwardness of Russian industry.

Nicholas fretted over the casualties and hardships suffered by his troops. He appointed a new War Minister, General Alexei Polivanov, on the advice of Rodzyanko, and set up a special defense council to expedite supplies to the army. He recalled the Duma, which opened its new session on August 1, 1915. Although the majority of the deputies were conservatives, they strongly criticized the government, and especially Goremykin, for the mismanagement of the war. Milyukov and the leaders of certain other parties agreed to form a coalition under the name of the Progressive Block, with a moderate program which gained wide support, even among the conservatives. The majority of ministers were eager to negotiate with the coalition. But Goremykin refused to consider negotiations. Alexandra was furiously opposed to the Progressive Block and all that it proposed. Nicholas, while not unsympathetic to the coalition, insisted that it would not be considered until the war had been won. On September 16 he adjourned the Duma until November.

The deputies dispersed, deeply disturbed by the feeling that the nation was drifting without leadership. A mood of hopelessness and defeatism began for the first time to spread among the people and this mood was profoundly deepened at this time by Nicholas's decision to assume supreme command of the army. Since the beginning of the war he had wanted desperately to be with the army, sharing its fortunes and misfortunes, and demonstrating that he was personally committed to the war. It was a fateful decision. He knew nothing of military matters. Grand Duke Nicholas, who had been commander-in-chief from the outset, had impressed everyone, his own troops and the Allies alike, as a man of courage and ability. General Ludendorf acknowledged him to be "a really great soldier and strategist."[20] It was lunacy to displace him at this critical stage of the war.

Eight ministers protested in a letter to Nicholas that for him to assume the supreme command would "threaten with serious consequences Russia, your dynasty, and your person."[21] Goremykin and other reactionaries urged him to reverse his decision. On September 2 the whole cabinet met at Tsarskoe Selo and begged him to his face to reconsider.

Nicholas, pale and withdrawn, stood his ground, clutching all the time in his hands the small ikon which Alexandra had given him.

During the first year of the war Alexandra had not interfered in government matters. She tended the wounded in hospitals, accepting the most menial and harrowing tasks cheerfully. But she worried constantly about Nicholas and felt that he was being pushed aside by stronger men who should be serving him. She knew his goodness of character and his weakness and devoted herself to strengthening him with her firmness and courage. She exhorted him: "Be firm, remember you are Emperor", and she wrote repeatedly to him when he was away at the Stavka, the Supreme Headquarters at Mogilev.[22] She believed it to be her duty as his wife to work for the maintenance of the autocracy for him and their son and for Russia. Her motives were selfless and noble: her advice and activities were disastrously misguided.

Early in the war Alexandra's hostility became concentrated against Grand Duke Nicholas. As commander-in-chief he completely overshadowed Nicholas and she believed it to be deliberate on his part. The Grand Duke was, in fact, a loyal subject who showed respect and obedience to the Tsar. But Alexandra hated him also because he had rejected her man of God. Rasputin had proposed visiting the Stavka to present an ikon to the commander-in-chief, who was a deeply religious man. The Grand Duke's response to Rasputin's proposal was curt: he telegraphed the message, COME AND I'LL HANG (YOU).[23] Alexandra began to blame the Grand Duke for the bloodshed on all fronts. She readily believed and repeated any rumor against him. She urged tirelessly that he must be relieved of his command and that the Tsar himself must lead the nation to victory.

From the day that Nicholas departed for the Stavka at Mogilev, the government in the rear passed into the hands of the Empress and Rasputin. This had been the greatest fear of all who had urged Nicholas not to assume the supreme command and now it had come to pass. All who fell from favor with Alexandra or Rasputin were dismissed. Goremykin was removed from office and Boris Sturmer, a crude and incompetent reactionary, but one of Rasputin's associates, took his place. The government became more and more debased, and the people could only watch impotently. Rumors gained currency that the Empress and Rasputin were German agents, that she was Rasputin's mistress, and that the Tsar himself had lost all faith in victory. Rumors besmirched the imperial family and demonstrated how the throne as the great symbol of national unity had been degraded.

By frantic efforts, especially on the part of voluntary organizations and with military supplies from the Allies, the most critical shortages had been relieved by early 1916. But again the Russian armies were committed to action before they had properly prepared. The Austrians had opened an offensive against Italy which was so successful that the King of Italy had appealed to the Tsar to attack Austria from the east. This meant bringing forward the Russian offensive, planned to take place later in the summer. In June, General Alexei Brusilov advanced along a 300-mile front from Lutsk to the Carpathians. The Russian forces moved forward rapidly until the hurried transfer of fifteen German divisions reinforced the Austrians and slowed down the Russian advance. The campaign, which continued until September, was nevertheless highly successful for the Russians, but their casualties were more than 1,200,000 men killed. Also, Brusilov's offensive brought Rumania into the war on the side of the Allies and this was to prove a heavy liability to the Russian army, which had to go to their aid.

Russian morale remained high at the front. Hindenberg noted that, while the Austrian army was at breaking point, the Russians showed no signs of weakening. Indeed, a Russian offensive was being planned for the spring of 1917. But in the rear conditions had deteriorated seriously. The cost of living had risen by three hundred percent. Food shortages were acute. But the main cause of the breakdown of morale and order in Russia was the general feeling that the nation was drifting toward disaster for lack of leadership.

The Duma had begun its new session on November 1. Deputies of all parties denounced the government so violently that Sturmer was forced to resign. His place as Prime Minister was taken by Alexander Trepov, but he was powerless. He tried desperately to remove Alexander Protopopov, the Minister of the Interior, and the most hated and despised man in the government. But Protopopov was Rasputin's friend, and remained in office. On December 2 Vladimir Purishkevich, an extreme conservative, brought the proceedings of the Duma to a climax when he condemned Rasputin as a Judas and destroyer of the dynasty and the nation. Relations between the Duma and the government had reached crisis point, and on December 17 the Duma was prorogued.

On the same day Rasputin was murdered. The conspiracy had been organized by Purishkevich, Grand Duke Dmitri Pavlovich, a nephew of the Tsar, and Prince Felix Yusupov. Rasputin was invited to Yusupov's home where he was given cakes and wine, containing poison and, when this had no effect, Yusupov shot him. He was still alive when they pushed his body through a hole in the ice of the Malya Neva River, and he died finally by drowning. The body was found two days later and buried secretly in the grounds of the imperial residence in the presence of Nicholas and Alexandra, and their children. But the only action taken against the conspirators was that Yusupov was banished to his country estate and the young Grand Duke was posted to the Persian front.

The death of Rasputin was greeted with general relief, but it brought no dramatic changes. Yusupov had maintained that within two weeks of his death the Empress would become mentally unhinged and that Nicholas would then rule as a constitutional monarch with power being exercised by the Duma. But Alexandra did not collapse. The death of her holy man was for her a terrible tragedy, for she believed that he was the protector of the Tsar and her children and the savior of the Tsarevich. But she would never collapse while Nicholas and the children needed her. She drew strength from her faith and she had tremendous courage. She retired with Nicholas and the family into a closed world of their own. Anna Vyrubova wrote that "Never had the Emperor and the Empress . . . seemed so lonely or so helpless."[24]

In Petrograd and throughout the country, unrest, strikes and food riots increased. When Trepov resigned, Nicholas appointed Prince Nicholas Golitsyn, an old man, incapable of dealing with the explosive situation, but nominated by Alexandra. Antagonism between the government and the Duma mounted dangerously. The State Council, composed of ultraconservatives, joined with the Duma in demanding the appointment of a Prime Minister and a cabinet commanding the confidence of the nation. All senior members of the imperial family warned Nicholas urgently that he was leading Russia to disaster, but he seemed not to hear their warnings. Hatred of the Empress reached such a pitch that there was talk of removing or killing her. Sir George Buchanan, the British ambassador, was so distressed by the threatening revolution that, putting aside protocol, he earnestly warned Nicholas in a long audience of the terrible crisis that was imminent.[25] •

The most dramatic warning came from Mikhail Rodzyanko a few days later. In the past Nicholas had resented the respectful but forthright reports of this giant of a man, but this time he listened. Rodzyanko spoke of the "Indignation against and hatred of the Empress . . . growing throughout the country." He named the able and honest ministers who had been dismissed or replaced by creatures of Rasputin or nominees of the Empress, most of whom were despicable men like Protopopov.

"Your Majesty," Rodzyanko continued, "do not compel the people to choose between you and the good of the country. So far the ideas of the Tsar and the Motherland have been indissoluble, but lately they have begun to be separated."

The Tsar pressed his head between his hands and then said: "Is it possible that for twenty-two years I have tried to act for the best, and that for twenty-two years it was all a mistake?"

"It was a hard moment. With great effort at self-control I replied: 'Yes, Your Majesty, for twenty-two years you have followed a wrong course.' "[26]

In the first weeks of 1917 the unrest in Petrograd was nearing explosion point. But the gravity of the crisis was not apparent. Strikes and demonstrations had become commonplace in the city. The British ambassador telegraphed to London early in March that SOME DISORDERS OCCURRED TODAY BUT NOTHING SERIOUS.[27] No one realized that Russia was on the point of revolution and that the Romanov dynasty, like an imposing cathedral, grown frail with age, was about to collapse, the cupola falling and then the walls, leaving the people bewildered in the midst of all that had given order and stability to their lives.

Nicholas was at Mogilev at the beginning of March. He received reports regularly on the unrest in the capital. The troops at the fronts were loyal and disciplined, and the industrial unrest in the rear angered him as irresponsible sabotage of the war effort. He sent peremptory instructions to the commander of the Petrograd military district to suppress all disorders, using such force as was necessary. Proclamations and warnings to this effect were posted throughout the city and on March 11 troops fired on demonstrators. But a mutinous spirit was spreading among the regiments in the city.

At this point Mikhail Rodzyanko sent an appeal to the Tsar at the Stavka. It read: "THE SITUATION IS SERIOUS. THERE IS ANARCHY IN THE CAPITAL. THE GOVERNMENT IS PARALYZED. IT IS NECESSARY IMMEDIATELY TO ENTRUST A PERSON WHO ENJOYS THE CONFIDENCE OF THE COUNTRY WITH THE FORMATION OF A GOVERNMENT. ANY DELAY IS EQUIVALENT TO DEATH . . .

Receiving no reply, Rodzyanko sent a more urgent warning on the following morning. THE SITUATION IS GROWING WORSE. MEASURES MUST BE ADOPTED IMMEDIATELY, FOR TOMORROW WILL BE TOO LATE. THE LAST HOUR HAS COME WHEN THE FATE OF THE FATHERLAND AND THE DYNASTY IS BEING DECIDED.[28] Still Nicholas made no reply.

Conditions in the capital had, in fact, sharply deteriorated. On March 12, mutiny had broken out in the Preobrazhensky and other regiments. Troops made their way on foot across the frozen Neva River to the Vyborg district, where they joined with strikers. The mutiny of the troops was the turning point. While they obeyed their officers, order could be maintained. But now revolution swept through the city.

Late in the afternoon of March 13, Nicholas set out from Mogilev to return to Petrograd. His train was diverted westward to Pskov, the headquarters of General Ruzsky, commanding the northern front. On arriving, Nicholas told Ruzsky that he would accept the proposals of Rodzyanko and others. He would appoint a Prime Minister, commanding the confidence of the nation, and would give him full authority over the cabinet and general policy, excluding foreign policy and the armed forces, which would remain under his own control.

Ruzsky spoke at once with Rodzyanko by telephone. The city was already in the grip of revolution. The Soviet of Workers' and Soldiers' Deputies had been formed and a committee of the Duma was seeking desperately to avert the anarchy which threatened. Rodzyanko's blunt reply to Ruzsky was that the Tsar's concessions had come too late.

Rodzyanko then communicated with General Alekseev, the chief of staff, in Mogilev. Alekseev got in touch with the commanders on all fronts, including Grand Duke Nicholas, commanding in the Caucasus. They were unanimous that Nicholas must abdicate. Alekseev informed Ruzsky of this opinion on the morning of March 15 and he at once reported to the Tsar.

Nicholas was taken by surprise. He had never envisaged that he would have to face such a demand, least of all from his own generals whom he regarded as brother officers. But he made his decision promptly. To Alekseev he sent a telegram which read: IN THE NAME OF THE WELFARE, TRANQUILLITY, AND SALVATION OF MY DEARLY BELOVED RUSSIA I AM READY TO ABDICATE FROM THE THRONE IN FAVOR OF MY SON. I REQUEST ALL TO SERVE HIM TRULY AND FAITHFULLY.[29]

Meanwhile Ruzsky had received a message from Petrograd that two representatives of the Duma committee had already set out for Pskov to propose the Tsar's abdication. For this reason he did not send a copy of Nicholas's telegram to Rodzyanko.

The Duma spokesmen, Alexander Guchkov and Vasily Shulgin, reached Pskov by train on the evening of March 15. Both men were profoundly moved by their mission, but believed sincerely that this was the only way to save the country and the dynasty and, indeed, the life of the Tsar himself.

Nicholas received both men kindly. He knew their purpose and was at pains to put them at their ease and help them in their task. Guchkov, unaware of the decision already taken, explained why abdication was in the Duma's view unavoidable. Nicholas looked to the front during his speech, hidden behind an impenetrable reserve. All his life he had been overburdened by the responsibilities of the throne and of his Romanov heritage. He had tried, often mistakenly, but always sincerely, to honor his coronation oath and to preserve the autocratic principles, bequeathed to him by his father. But he had realized that the task was beyond him. He was always a humble, devout man and now he submitted quietly to the demand for his abdication. Some who knew him felt that he welcomed this release from intolerable burdens and that he looked forward fondly to days to be spent in freedom with the wife and children whom he loved deeply.[30]

Nicholas heard Guchkov to the end and then indicated his acceptance of the deed of abdication, subject to one amendment. The deed provided that he should abdicate in favor of the Tsarevich. But since sending his telegram to Alekseev he had come to a different decision. He knew now that his son would not live for long and he was anxious that Alexandra and he himself should care for the boy. He therefore appointed his brother, Mikhail, as his successor.[31] He signed the deed. Guchkov and Shulgin sadly took their leave of him.

In the imperial carriage, standing at the deserted railway station in Pskov, the Romanov dynasty, which had reigned for three centuries, quietly came to an end.

Epilogue

The dynasty of the Romanovs had not expired under the assaults of popular rebellion or revolution; it had collapsed feebly and undramatically. The vast majority of Russians were in 1917 still loyal to their Tsar, but Nicholas had made such slight impression upon them that in the confusion of the times the sudden news of his abdication made no great impact. It was as though the Romanovs had slipped away ignominiously from the throne. Indeed the failure of the last Tsar and the anticlimax of the regime's demise have tended to cast a shadow over the whole dynasty and its significance. It was, however, a dynasty which produced several remarkable Autocrats who ruled with dedication and purpose, and which, having forged the vast Russian Empire, held it united for nearly three centuries. The Romanovs belong, in fact, among the great dynasties in history.

Notes

Notes To Prologue:

1. B. A. Rybakov and others *Istoriya SSSR* 11 (Moscow 1966)
2. Klyuchevsky 111, 63
3. Solovyev V
4. *Ib*

Notes to Chapter I:

1. Adam Olearius *The Voyages and Travels of the Ambassadors sent by Frederick, Duke of Holstein . . .* (London 1662) 62, 71
2. N. H. Baynes and H. StL. B. Moss *Byzantium* (Oxford 1961) 384
3. Klyuchevsky 11, 125
4. Solovyev 111, vol. VI, 431–32
5. G. Vernadsky *Kievan Russia* (Yale 1948) 62
6. G. P. Fedotov *The Russian Religious Mind* (Harvard 1947)
7. 1 Corinthians IV, 10; 1, 25, 27
8. N. Zernov *The Russians and their Church* (London, 1945) 71; Ian Grey *Ivan the Terrible* 59–60
9. Adam Olearius *op. cit.* 42
10. John Perry *The State of Russia under the Present Tsar* (London 1716) 237
11. Adam Olearius *op. cit.* 43
12. Samuel Collins *The Present State of Russia* (London 1671) 22; J. G. Korb *Diary of an Austrian Secretary of Legation* (London 1863) 98–100
13. Adam Olearius *op. cit.* 62
14. Samuel Collins *op. cit.* 22
15. Adam Olearius *op. cit.* 61
16. *Ib* 60; Samuel Collins *op. cit.* 71–74
17. Adam Olearius *op. cit.* 63
18. *Ib* 81

19. John Perry *op. cit.* 217–19
20. C. H. Manstein *Memoirs of Russia 1727–44* (London 1773) 416
21. Adam Olearius *op. cit.* 86, 89, and *passim*

Notes to Chapter II:

1. Mikhail had every reason to fear for his safety. Learning of his election as Tsar, a band of Poles, or possibly Cossacks, set out to find him and murder him, since a new Tsar and the restoration of order in the country and safety would mean an end to their lawlessness. They searched for him in Kostroma itself. They captured a peasant, Ivan Susanin, whom they suspected of knowing the Tsar's hiding place. Under the most savage tortures he refused to divulge the place, which he knew. He was finally tortured to death.

    This incident provided the story for *A Life for the Tsar*, now known as *Ivan Susanin*, the opera of the great Russian composer, Mikhail Glinka. Solovyev V. 11
2. *Ib* 15
3. *Ib* 17
4. *Ib* IV, 281–82
5. *Ib*
6. *Ib* 169–71
7. *Ib* 254

Notes to Chapter III:

1. Samuel Collins *The Present State of Russia* (London 1671) 110
2. Klyuchevsky 111, 324
3. *Ib*
4. Samuel Collins *op. cit.* 113–15: Olearius *op. cit.* 21–3, 25
5. Guy Miege, Carlisle, Charles Earl of, *A relation of Three Embassies to the Great Duke of Muscovie* (London 1669); W. R. Morfill *Russia* (London 1897) 126–27
6. Ivan Zabelin *Domashnii Byt . . .* (Moscow 1862) 290–92
7. Grigori Kotoshikhin *O Rossii v Tsarstvovanie Alekseya Mikhailovicha* (St. Petersburg 1906) 4th ed 29
8. Ivan Zabelin *op. cit.* 291
9. Klyuchevsky 111, 270
10. V. V. Kallash (ed.) *History of the Russian Theatre* (Moscow 1914) I. 17–18
11. *Ib* 61
12. Klyuchevsky 111, 271
13. *Ib*
14. Solovyev V, 502–3
15. *Ib* VI, 266–67
16. Samuel Collins *op. cit.* 107–9
17. Klyuchevsky 111, 326–27
18. *Ib* 345

Notes to Chapter IV:

1. According to the accounts of foreigners, Matveev did not at once announce the death of Tsar Alexei and made use of the time to bribe the *streltsi* to declare their support for the immediate accession of Tsarevich Peter. But when finally late at night he informed the Patriarch and the boyars of Alexei's death and tried to persuade them to endorse Peter's accession he found them firmly supporting Fedor, as the late Tsar's proclaimed heir.
   Solovyev rejects this account as unsubstantiated and highly unlikely. Moreover Matveev was never charged with this plot after his fall when the Miloslavsky were grasping at every pretext to destroy him. Solovyev VII, 185–86

2. *Ib* 249–51

3. In the campaigns of 1677 and 1678 the Scot, Patrick Gordon, played an outstanding part and was as a result promoted to the rank of Major General. He also served with distinction later in the Crimean campaigns of 1687 and 1689, and was then promoted to the rank of full General. Patrick Gordon entered the Russian service in 1661 and served with distinction until his death in 1699. See *The Diaries of Patrick Gordon* (Aberdeen 1859) and "A Scot in the service of three Tsars: Patrick Gordon of Auchleuchries 1635–99" in *History Today* (London 1968) for accounts of his long career.

Notes to Chapter V:

1. Bogoslovsky I, 38–39
2. Descriptions of Sofia differ. The Englishman, Captain Perry, described her as "a handsome young lady," but he had apparently never seen her, and was speaking from hearsay. The Frenchman, La Neuville, who had seen her, described her as having "A shapeless body, monstrously fat, a head as big as a bushel measure, hair growing on her face." John Perry *The State of Russia under the Present Tsar* (London 1716) 143; La Neuville, quoted by Ustryalov I, 273.4
3. Bogoslovsky I, 40
4. This account of the *streltsi* rebellion is based on the eyewitness report of the Danish Resident, Butenant von Rosenbusch, printed in full as an appendix by Ustryalov (I, 330–46, Appendix vi)
5. *Ib*
6. Bogoslovsky I, 44
7. One report stated that Peter stood quietly at his mother's side throughout the terror, his expression unchanging and that his fearlessness impressed all who saw him, particularly the *streltsi*. But this report, based on hearsay evidence, was recorded some fifteen years after the event. Ustryalov I, 61.
8. Ivan Mazepa has often been portrayed as a romantic hero as in Byron's poem, but neither the man nor his career justify such portrayal. A Cos-

sack of humble origin, Mazepa obtained a good education in Kiev and served as a page at the court of John Casimir V where he learned Polish, German, and courtly manners. He was handsome, with a strong personality, and an eloquent tongue, but also unscrupulous, vain, and quarrelsome. His career in Poland ended when an angry husband had him seized on his way to a secret meeting with his wife. His servants stripped him naked and bound him to the back of a horse which they terrified by firing pistols and whipping it until it galloped away through bushes and thickets. Mazepa escaped alive, but was bruised and bleeding, and the disgrace was such that he had to flee from the Polish court. Fourteen years later he turned up among the Ukrainian Cossacks. He impressed Hetman Samoilovich who treated him as a son and advanced him rapidly, only to find himself betrayed and supplanted.

Mazepa lacks a biographer. Russians historians have scorned him as a traitor; Ukrainian nationalists have proclaimed him as a hero of the Ukrainian separatist movement. Melchior de Vogue in *The True Story of Mazepa* (London 1884) has written a lively essay on the romantic legend of Mazepa, created by Voltaire, Byron, and others, and has given a short account of his life. The most objective account of his career and fall is probably that of S. M. Soloviev in his *History of Russia*. W. E. D. Allen in *The Ukraine A History* gives valuable bibliographical notes on him.

9. Gordon *Passages from the Diary of Patrick Gordon* (Aberdeen 1859)
10. *Ib*

Notes to Chapter VI:

1. In his own autobiographical introduction to the Naval Code, published in 1720 and reprinted by Ustryalov (11, Appendix i). Peter gave this account of the birth of his love of ships and the sea. Bogoslovsky states (I, 66) that "the recollections of the Tsar, written thirty-two years after the events related, are fully accurate and confirmed by other documents." The English origin of the boat is disputed. One claim is that Dutch carpenters built it with the Orel in 1668. The author has been content with Peter's own version.
   The little boat was moved to St. Petersburg in 1723, where it was preserved. It is now in the Central Naval Museum on Vassilevsky Island. See also Klyuchevsky IV, 15.
2. P & B I, No. 7
3. Ustryalov II, 161
4. *Ib* Appendix i
5. P & B I, No. 140
6. Ustryalov III, Appendix xi.
7. Macaulay *History of England* Chapter 23
8. Blomberg, 295
9. *Ib*
10. Bogoslovsky II, 121
11. The Russian peasant drew comfort from being buried in a coffin hewn

from solid oak. English coffins were made from planks and were thus far less extravagant in consumption of timber. Peter was particularly anxious to conserve oak trees, for their timber was best for shipbuilding.

12. Peter himself is said to have ruined Evelyn's great holly hedge by trundling through it in a wheelbarrow. Holly bushes have such thick branches that the story can hardly be true. Without doubt, however, he played his part in damaging the bowling green, gravel walks, and other parts of the garden and the house. Wheelbarrows were almost unknown in Russia at this time and Peter was probably interested for this reason. The survey of damage included an item for "three wheelbarrows . . . broken and lost."

Diary of John Evelyn edited by Austin Dobson (London 1906) III, 334; W. G. Hiscock John Evelyn and his Family Circle (London 1955) 200

13. Dew History of Deptford (London 1884) 182

14. Gilbert Burnet History of His Own Times (London 1818) III, 244–46

15. A. N. Andreev (ed.) Peter I: A Symposium (Leningrad 1947) 88–89

16. J. G. Korb Diary of an Austrian Secretary of Legation at the Court of Tsar Peter the Great (London 1863) I, 179–80

17. Ustryalov III, 193–95

18. P & B I, Nos. 255–56

19. Ustryalov III, 346, 348

20. Diary of Patrick Gordon (Aberdeen 1859)

21. Bogoslovsky IV, 166–69

22. Ustryalov IV (i) 106–7; IV (ii) 106

23. Solovyev VIII, 274

24. P & B IX, No. 3259

25. Ib No. 3266

26. There are many conflicting accounts of Catherine's origins. Some have denied that she was of peasant stock and have claimed noble blood for her. A story so romantic as hers invites embroidery.

The account followed here is that of F. C. Weber, the Hanoverian resident in Moscow. He obtained it from Gottfried Wurm who, as tutor to Gluck's children, lived in the house at the same time as Catherine. F. C. Weber Das Veranderte Russland II, 24–25; III, 6–10; Ustryalov IV (i) Chapter 5; W. Coxe Travels into Poland, Russia, Sweden, and Denmark (London 1787, 3rd ed) II, 398–434

27. Alexander Gordon History of Peter the Great, Emperor of Russia (London 1755) II, 258–59

28. Four were sons, two named Peter and two named Paul, all of whom died in infancy. Of the eight daughters, only Anna and Elizabeth survived.

29. Sbornik I.R.I.O. XXXIV, 145–46

30. Ib 150–1; Solovyev IX, 67–69

31. Solovyev IX, 321

32. Klyuchevsky 139

33. Solovyev IX, 125

34. Ustryalov VI, 46–49, 346–48
35. *Ib* 50–51, 349–50
36. *Ib* 51
37. *Ib* 52
38. *Ib* 54, 56–57
39. *Ib* 116–17
40. John Bell *Travels from St. Petersburg in Russia to Diverse Parts of Asia* (Glasgow 1763) II, 359
41. N. A. Voskresensky (ed.) *Legislative Acts of Peter I* (Moscow 1945) 58–59, 67–68, 88, and *passim*
42. Solovyev IX, 184
43. Golikov X, 35–39
44. Golikov IX, 296
45. Rumors at court attributed the sudden disgrace of Mons and Matrena Balk to Peter's discovery that Mons was and had been for many years the lover of Catherine. Prince Pierre Dolgorukov in his *Mémoires* (Geneva 1867) even alleged that Peter had found them in the act of making love. In this age court gossip was uninhibited and vicious but taken seriously. There is however no real evidence to support these rumors and allegations.

Notes to Chapter VII:

1. Solovyev IX, 558
2. *Ib*
3. This story is supported by an incident that happened in later years, when he was a prince of great wealth and power. He had incurred the anger of the Tsar, who threatened to return him to his former trade. Menshikov rushed off to Catherine to beg her intercession. While she was soothing away the Tsar's anger, Menshikov found a pie-vendor and, putting on his tray, he returned to Peter's presence calling out his wares. Peter was highly amused and promptly forgave him. "But listen, Alexashka," he added, "stop your mischief or you'll be worse off than a pie-vendor." Menshikov went after the Empress, calling "Hot pies! Hot pies! Peter followed laughing, but he repeated, "Remember, Alexander!" "I will remember, Your Majesty," he answered. "I will not forget! Hot pies! Hot pies!" Ustryalov IV (i) 20708
4. Alexander Gordon *History of Peter the Great, Emperor of Russia* (London 1755) II, 277
5. Solovyev IX, 571
6. *Ib* X, 80

Notes to Chapter VIII:

1. Rybakov III, 258
2. Solovyev X, 112
3. Klyuchevsky IV, 303

Notes to Chapter IX:

1. Solovyev X, 199
2. *Ib* 202–3
3. Meanwhile Dmitri Golitsyn had drafted and discussed with the Privy Council a new constitution. This limited the authority of the Empress to her own court and reposed the supreme authority in a Privy Council of ten or twelve members, drawn from the most notable families. Under this Supreme Privy Council there were to be three institutions: 1. The Senate of thirty-six members, which would give preliminary consideration to all matters which would then be decided by the Council; 2. The Chamber of the Nobility, comprising two hundred chosen members with the main purpose of defending the rights of the classes against encroachment by the Supreme Privy Council; 3. The Chamber of Townsmen, concerned with matters of trade and manufacture and serving the interests of the ordinary people. It was a most interesting plan which, with modification, might have proved practical and would certainly have put an end to absolutism. But the plan, like its author, was ahead of the times.
   Klyuchevsky IV, 284–85
4. Solovyev X, 219–20
5. Manstein 35–36
6. Solovyev X, 220
7. *Ib* 22–23
8. *Loc. cit.*
9. Manstein 250–51; Solovyev X, 529–31
10. Manstein 246–47
11. *Loc. cit.*
12. Manstein 37
13. *Ib* 38–41

Notes to Chapter X:

1. Ivan Antonovich was the third Tsar Ivan, counting from Ivan the Terrible who was the first crowned Tsar. He was, however, the sixth Ivan to occupy the Russian throne, starting from Ivan Kalita (1328–41). He is thus known both as Ivan III and Ivan VI.
2. Biron was sentenced to death, but this sentence was commuted to banishment in Siberia. In 1742 he was permitted by Empress Elizabeth, who was indebted to him for dissuading Anna from sending her to a nunnery, to reside in Yaroslavl on the Volga. Twenty years later Peter III, an ardent Germanophile, recalled him to St. Petersburg, and in 1763 Catherine II restored him to the Duchy of Courland.
3. In his despatches from St. Petersburg, de la Chetardie often gives an exaggerated account of his influence and participation in the affairs of

the Russian court and the preparation for the revolution. His account of the rising itself, as set out in his personal report to the King, is however generally endorsed by other accounts.

Sbornik I.R.I.O. Vol. 96 (St. Petersburg 1896) 641–51

4. Ian Grey *Catherine the Great* (New York 1962) 128–32

Notes to Chapter XI:

1. Dashkova *Memoirs* (London 1958) 30.

2. *Ib*

3. Seeing the theater as a means of popular education, Peter wanted a wider audience than the court performances provided. In 1702 a German, Johann Kunst, had arrived in Moscow with a troupe of seven players. Peter directed him to train twenty Russian clerks as actors. To the horror of old Muscovites, a theater was erected on the Red Square so that the people could witness special performances, which were mainly allegorical. Kunst produced several plays, but in 1703 he died and his successor, Otto Furst, was ineffective. This brief experiment in presenting drama made little impression on the Russians who preferred their own *skomorokhi* or wandering minstrels.

   The theater on the Red Square was closed down in 1706 and demolished in the following year. Tsarevna Natalya, Peter's sister, had the properties and costumes taken to Preobrazhenskoe where she established her own court theater which she later moved to St. Petersburg.

   S. S. Ignatov "The Theatre of the Petrine Epoch" in *The History of the Russian Theatre*, edited by V. V. Kallash and others (Moscow 1914) I, 69, 75–76

4. Catherine *Memoirs* 78

5. Klyuchevsky IV, 341

6. Count Bartolomeo Francesco Rastrelli (1700–71) was the son of the Italian sculptor, Count Carlo Bartolomeo Rastrelli, who went to Russia in 1715 and executed bronze busts of Peter and Menshikov. The son early showed distinctive ability as an architect and was sent abroad in 1719–21 and again about 1725 to study architecture. Empress Anna recognized his talent and commissioned him in 1732 to reconstruct the existing Winter Palace and other work, including a palace for Biron in Mittau.

   G. H. Hamilton *The Art and Architecture of Russia* (London 1954) 177–78

7. This was in effect the fourth Summer Palace. The Regent Anna Leopoldovna had in 1740 ordered the enlargement of the small house, erected in the Summer Garden by Catherine I for Peter. Elizabeth had requested a complete reconstruction. *Ib*

8. Solovyev XI, p. 99; Nisbet Bain *The Daughter of Peter the Great* (London 1899) 143

9. Catherine *Memoirs* 178–79

Notes to Chapter XII:

1. Dashkova, *Memoirs* 45
2. Bilbasov I, 459
3. Elizabeth regarded the Holstein-Gottorps as almost part of her own family. Her elder sister, Tsarevna Anna Petrovna, had married the Duke of Holstein. Catherine's mother, Princess Johanna, was the youngest sister of Prince Karl Augustus of Holstein-Gottorp, to whom Elizabeth herself, when Tsarevna, had been betrothed. He had died from smallpox in St. Petersburg on the eve of their marriage, and Elizabeth cherished a fond memory of him and an affection for the whole family.
4. Catherine *Memoirs* 96
5. *Ib* 99
6. Bilbasov I, 220
7. *Loc. cit.*
8. According to Catherine (*Memoirs* 205, 208) Choglokova proposed at the end of December 1752 that she should have an affair either with Lev Naryshkin or with Sergei Saltykov in order to have a child and heir to the throne. A few weeks earlier Choglokova had been intriguing to bring the Grand Duke together with a pretty young widow, named Madame Groot. From Catherine's account it would seem that Choglokova was acting with the knowledge of the Empress, presumably with the purpose of demonstrating that he was impotent.
9. There is strong evidence for believing that Sergei Saltykov, not Peter, was the father of Paul. Peter was incapable of consummating the marriage in August 1752, and there is no reason to doubt Catherine's statement (*Memoirs* 23) that her marriage was still unconsummated seven years later. The cause of his impotence is not known; it may well have been psychological, although Castera (I, 74) states that he suffered from a physical defect which any rabbi or surgeon could readily have corrected with a small operation, but Peter would not consider it. None of Peter's affairs, so far as is known, resulted in any of his mistresses falling pregnant by him. Elizabeth Vorontsova, his mistress for several years, bore him no children but, marrying a year after his death, she promptly bore a son and a daughter. It is in fact an unavoidable assumption that Peter remained impotent all his life.
   While the Tsars occupied the throne, Russian historians avoided discussing the legitimacy of Paul, since it involved questioning whether Paul himself and his successors were of the Romanov blood.
   Ian Grey, *Catherine the Great* 53–54
10. Dashkova, *Memoirs* 92
11. The grandfather of the Orlovs had been a ranker in the *streltsi*, the unruly palace guards whom Peter the Great had put down and finally disbanded. The grandfather escaped death at the execution block through the clemency of Peter, who posted him to an infantry regiment in which, through brave service, he became an officer.

12. Bilbasov I, 471
13. *Russky Arkhiv* (1766) III, 13, quoted by Bilbasov I, 464
14. Bilbasov II, 21

Notes to Chapter XIII:

1. Bilbasov I, 186; Sbornik XLVIII, 137
2. Three days after Catherine's death, Grand Duke Alexander and Count Bezborodko were instructed to go through her personal papers. It was then that Alexei Orlov's note was found. It was taken at once to the new Emperor, Paul I, who read it and handed it back to Bezborodko. For a few minutes it passed into the hands of Count F. V. Rostopchin, who identified the writing as Alexei Orlov's and quickly made a copy of it. On the following day the Emperor read through it carefully, and then threw it into the fire, thus destroying the sole evidence of Catherine's innocence of any complicity in the murder of Peter III. The hurried copy taken by Rostopchin is the only record to survive, but its authenticity has never been doubted.
   Vorontsov Archives, XXI, 430–32
   For the text of the note see Ian Grey *Catherine the Great* 116
3. Ian Grey *op. cit.* 131
4. Dashkova, *Memoirs* 77–78
5. Vorontsov Archives V, 105–8; Solovyev XXV, ii 1380
6. Goethe *Conversations with Eckermann* (London 1850) II, 209
7. Ian Grey *op. cit.* 145, 152
8. *Ib* 146, 152
9. Klyuchevsky
10. W. F. Reddaway *op. cit.* 216–17, 258, 231
11. *Ib* 114
12. Some landlords who had treated their serfs humanely received protection from this fury. The family estate near Saratov of Radishchev, who was later to suffer the full blast of Catherine's anger for championing the peasant cause, was an example. Radishchev's father had always been good to his serfs and they hid him and his wife and disguised his children as peasant children, until the danger had passed. But such cases of happy relationships between landowners and their peasants were rare, and few landowners, found with their families on their estates, were spared.
13. W. F. Reddaway *op. cit.* 192, 194, 196, 199
14. D. M. Lang *The First Russian Radical: Alexander Radishchev 1749–1802* (London 1959) 87
15. Bilbasov II, 428
16. In her letters to Voltaire Catherine attributed the victory wholly to the leadership of Alexei Orlov, and was enthusiastic in her praises of him. "Was I wrong," she wrote, "when I said that these Orlovs were forged for great things?" Intent on making it a Russian victory, she did not mention Elphinston, Greig, or Lieutenant Dugdale, the officer who

led the fireships into Chesme Bay. The British officers were, neverthe-less, decorated and rewarded.

Sbornik I, 166; W. F. Reddaway *op. cit.* 74–77

17. Countess Bruce, a sister of Field-Marshal Rumyantsev, was married to Count James Alexandrovich Bruce, a descendant of the Scottish officer who arrived in Russia in the time of Tsar Alexei (1645–76) and gained the rank of major-general in the Russian army.

The Countess was an intimate friend of Catherine. But she evidently delighted in her duties as L'Eprouveuse, and in her excessive ardour she forgot that she was entrusted with the task of testing the sexual prowess of a lover before, and not continuing to test it after, his ap-pointment to the Empress. One young officer, Ivan Rimsky-Korsakov, was so much to her liking that she carried on an affair with him after he had become the imperial lover and, caught in the act of love with him by Catherine, she was angrily dismissed.

The office of L'Eprouveuse at the Russian court was the talk of Europe at this time. Byron in *Don Juan* actually named Madame Protassov, Countess Bruce's successor, and refers to her "mystic office."

Lord Byron *Works* (London 1904) VI, 3990

18. It was rumored that the Orlovs, resenting the warmth of Potemkin's relations with Catherine, set upon him and beat him so severely that he lost one eye. The more probable explanation, however, was that having caught some infection, Potemkin refused to be treated by court doctors and went to some village charlatan who applied fermentations con-taining poisonous ingredients. These brought up the swelling on the eye which Potemkin with typical impatience lanced with a rusty needle, with the result that he became completely blind in this eye.

Alexander Polovtsoff *Les Favouris de Catherine la Grande* (Paris 1939) 75

19. Ian Grey *op. cit.* for the full text of this letter.

20. Soloveychik *op. cit.* 73

21. Sbornik XXIII, 4

22. G. Oudard (ed.) *Lettres d'Amour de Catherine II a Potemkine* (Paris 1934) 168; Soloveychik *op. cit.* 95

23. In an outburst of jealousy early in their union, Potemkin evidently accused her of having had fifteen lovers before him. Catherine replied with "A Sincere Confession" in which she listed her lovers and closed with the following paragraph:

"Well, Sir Hero, after this confession may I hope to be forgiven my sins? You must see that it was not fifteen, but one third of that number. Of them the first happened from compulsion and the fourth from despair, which cannot be put down to indulgence. As for the other three, God knows that it was not due to debauchery, for which I have no inclination. If as a young woman I had got a husband whom I could have loved I would have remained forever faithful to him . . ."

Catherine *Memoirs* 356; Soloveychik *op. cit.* 81–82

While Catherine asserted that she was not inclined to debauchery, the number of lovers and the promiscuity and opulence of her court gave rise to all manner of licentious gossip throughout Europe.

In his *Secret Memoirs of the Court of St. Petersburg* (London 1801) 117–18, C. F. Masson stated that later in her reign Catherine formed an intimate society, comprising her favorites and most trusty ladies and courtiers, who met once or twice a week in parties in which they were often masqued and the greatest secrecy prevailed for there was nothing that was not permitted.

24. The evidence of their marriage is circumstantial and unsatisfactory. See Ian Grey *op. cit.* 184–85; Castera *op. cit.* III, 90; Soloveychik *op. cit.* 100–6.

25. James Harris, First Earl of Malmesbury *Diaries and Correspondence* (London 1844) I, 179

26. Sbornik XXIII, 412

27. *Mémoires par Le Comte de Segur* (Paris 1826) III, 182

28. *Les Lettres de Catherine II au Prince de Ligne* (Brussels and Paris 1924) 77

29. Quai d'Orsay Archives as quoted by D. M. Lang *Op. cit.* 127

30. Sir James Harris *op. cit.* I, 181

Notes to Chapter XIV:

1. A contemporary wrote that "It would require a volume to describe the ceremonies and honors with which this crown was conveyed from Duval's, the jeweler, to the Emperor's palace: never was the Ark of the Covenant, in the processions of the people of God, surrounded with so much awe and pomp. The jeweler, like another Pygmalion, was obliged to fall on his knees and adore the work of his own hands".
C. F. Masson *Secret Memoirs of the Court of St. Petersburg*. London 1801–2 III, 79

2. Another example of Paul's concern for utility was the fate of Count Bezborodko's mansion in Moscow. Paul had lodged there during his coronation visit to the old city. He was impressed by the immense gardens. "What a capital place for exercising a regiment!" he exclaimed. Taking the hint, Bezborodko arranged that "during the night, trees, alcoves, parterres, fountains, all were removed or destroyed. The next morning this beautiful garden no longer presented anything but a naked sandy soil just fit for a place of exercise. Bezborodko carried his attention still further. Mademoiselle Nelidov, then the favorite, lodged in a neighboring house; he took care to have a gallery of communication made, leading to the apartment of his master. The Emperor, delighted, purchased his house at its weight in gold, and made him Prince and Highness." *Ib* 79–80

3. Waliszewski *Paul the First of Russia* (London 1913) 106

4. Florinksy I, 622–23

Notes to Chapter XV:

1. Florinksy II, 651
2. *Ib* 693
3. *Ib* 694
4. Serfs were sold like cattle and indeed changed hands at public auctions. The *Moskovskie Vedomosti* (*Moscow News*) regularly published advertisements like the following:

   "For sale: domestics and skilled craftsmen of good behavior, viz. two tailors, a shoemaker, a wheelwright, an engraver, a watchmaker, a coachmaker, a gilder, and two coachmen, who may be inspected and their price ascertained in the 4th District, Section 3, at the proprietor's own house, No. 15. Also for sale are three young race-horses, one colt and two geldings, and a pack of hounds, fifty in number, which will be a year old in January and February next."
   "In District 12, a maid of sixteen for sale, able to weave lace, sew linen, do ironing, and starching, and to dress her mistress; further-more, has a pleasing face and figure."

   Prices of serfs were not high, but a sturdy young man or a comely and talented girl would fetch the highest prices. Sometimes a serf would be bartered against a horse or a dog or even gambled away at cards. Ian Grey, *Catherine the Great* (New York) 122
5. Nicholas Mikhailovich, *Perepiska Imperatora Aleksandra I s sestroi Velikoi Knyaginei Ekaterinoi Pavlovnoi* (St. Petersburg 1910)

   An English edition was published in 1917 under the title *Scenes of Russian Court Life: Being the Correspondence of Alexander I with his Sister Catherine.*
6. Florinsky II, 661
7. *Ib* 664
8. *Ib*
9. *Ib* 668
10. Alexander's outlook was succinctly expressed in a letter addressed to him by Count Rostopchin, the Governor of Moscow, who wrote: "I am not afraid of military reverses; your Empire has two powerful defenders in its vastness and its climate. The Emperor of Russia will always be formidable in Moscow, terrible in Kazan, and invincible in Tobolsk." Florinsky II, 675
11. Anatole G. Mazour, *The First Russian Revolution* (California 1937) 25
12. Calling on the Emperor next morning, Prince Alexander Golitsyn found him in a mood of deep depression. "Would it not hurt you if someone cut off your right hand?" he said to the Prince. "Last night they made me part with Speransky and he was my right hand." But this dismissal was received with widespread relief and also as a defeat for the pro-French party in St. Petersburg. A contemporary commented that "I do not know whether the death of a ferocious tyrant would have created such general elation" as the exile of Speransky. A. G. Mazour *op. cit.* 27

13. Speransky made several appeals directly to Alexander to be allowed to return to the capital and the imperial service. His appeals were ignored. Finally he humbled himself and begged Arakcheev, his great enemy, who was now close to the Emperor, to intercede for him. It is of interest in view of Arakcheev's sinister reputation that he used his good office with success. In 1816 Speransky was appointed Governor of Penza and in 1819 Governor-General of Siberia. In 1821 he was allowed to return to the capital where he was appointed a member of the State Council and of the Commission on Codification.

    Alexander himself took no further interest in Speransky after sending him into exile in 1812 and did not receive him after his return to St. Petersburg. Meanwhile Speransky himself had become increasingly conservative.

14. Florinsky II, 637–38

15. Although his mission had failed, Balashev acquitted himself well. Napoleon, learning of the great number of churches in Moscow, commented that in no other country would one find such piety. Balashev then remarked that in Spain churches were to be found in even greater profusion. It was a pointed reminder that in Spain the French had met with savage resistance from the people. Breaking the silence that followed this remark, Marshal Ney asked which was the best road leading to Moscow. Balashev rose to the occasion. "Is it not said that all roads lead to Rome?" he answered. "In Russia we think that all roads lead to Moscow—including the road from Poltava, taken by Charles XII!" The French invasion recalled to many the Swedish invasion which had ended with Peter the Great's crushing defeat of Charles XII at Poltava in 1709. Napoleon himself was keenly interested in the Swedish campaign. He usually kept on his night table a copy of Voltaire's *History of Charles XII*. Later as he penetrated farther into Russia and found the Russian army steadily falling back before him, he was heard to remark that "My brother Alexander wants me to play the role of Charles XII." Had he taken heed of the lessons of the Swedish campaign he would have saved his army and the humiliation of defeat.

    Comtesse de Choiseul-Gouffier *Historical Memoirs of the Emperor Alexander I and the Court of Russia,* translated from the French (London 1904) 115

16. Alexander was deeply hurt by this proposal that he must leave the army and the strong implication that his presence inspired no confidence and actively hindered the prosecution of the war. See his letter to his sister in Nicholas Mikhailovich *Scenes of Russian Court Life: Being the Correspondence of Alexander I with his Sister Catherine* 111–14

17. The burning of Moscow soon after the entry of the French has never been explained satisfactorily. At first Napoleon and Russians everywhere believed that the French troops were to blame. But then it came to be believed that Count Rostopchin had fired the city rather than leave it to the occupation of the French. In November 1816 the Count went to live in France where he was fêted as a hero who had played an

important part in bringing about the downfall of Napoleon. In 1823, however, he published a pamphlet, *La Vérité sur l'Incendie de Moscou* in which he denied that he was responsible. His denial was not generally accepted, even by his own family. His son wrote:

"My father never gave a direct order to anyone to set fire to Moscow, but he took all kinds of measures to see that it did burn. When they came to tell him that the French were entering the town by one gate, he left on horseback by another and, a hundred paces from the gate, he turned around, raised his hat, and said to my brother, who was accompanying him: 'Salute Moscow for the last time. In an hour, it will be in flames.'

"To begin with, the Muscovites applauded the destruction of their homes, but once they had returned to the capital they began a chorus of complaints and bitter recriminations against the author of this disaster. It was under pressure of these that my father wrote his pamphlet . . ."

The most probable answer is that Rostopchin was the principle, but not the sole, author of the great fires.

See Daria Olivier *The Burning of Moscow 1812* translated from the French (London 1966) 186–97

18. Nicholas Mikhailovich *op. cit.* p. 109
19. Florinsky II, 640
20. *Ib* 641
21. *Ib* 645
22. *Ib* 686
23. Constantin de Grunwald *Tsar Nicholas I* translated from the French (London 1954) 34
24. *Ib*
25. Florinsky II, 632
26. The legend may best be described in the words of Leo Tolstoy who, in 1905, was working on a story which he did not complete, but which had the tentative title: *The posthumous writings of the Elder Fedor Kuzmich who died on 20 January 1864 in Siberia near the town of Tomsk in a village of the merchant Khromov.* Tolstoy had studied the facts of the legend which he set down in his preface, as follows:

"While the Elder Fedor Kuzmich, who had appeared in Siberia in 1836, and had lived in various places for twenty-seven years, was still alive, strange rumors about him circulated to the effect that he concealed his name and rank, that he was none other than the Emperor Alexander I; after his death the rumors spread more widely and grew in strength. And the belief that he was really Alexander I was held not only among the people, but also in the highest circles and even in the Tsar's family during the reign of Alexander III. The learned Schilder, the historian of the reign of Alexander I, also believed it.

"The reason for these rumors were, first, the fact that Alexander had died quite unexpectedly, without having suffered any serious illness beforehand; second, the fact that he died far away from everyone in a fairly deserted place, in Taganrog; third, the fact that when he was laid in his coffin those who saw him said that he had so changed that it was impossible to recognize him, and that his coffin was closed and he was not shown to anyone; four, the fact that Alexander had repeatedly said and written, and with special frequency in his last years, that he wanted only one thing—to be freed from his position and to retreat from the world . . .

"With regard to the fact that Kuzmich was taken as the disguised Alexander, the reasons for this were, first, the fact that the Elder was in height, build, and appearance so like the Emperor that people who had seen Alexander and his portraits found the resemblance between them striking; second, the fact that Kuzmich gave himself out to be a person of forgotten parentage and a wanderer, and knew foreign languages and by his manners of great and easy friendliness he was distinguished as a person accustomed to the most elevated position; three, the fact that the Elder never revealed his name or rank to anyone, but at the same time involuntarily by expressions which broke through he revealed himself as a man who at some time stood higher than all other people; and four, the fact that before his death he destroyed papers of which only one sheet remained with strange signs in code . . . five, the fact that despite his entire piety, the Elder never fasted . . ."

In February 1912 V. G. Korolenko, editor of the periodical *Russkoe Bogatstvo*, published the preface and unfinished story of Tolstoy. He was at once charged with "showing gross disrespect towards the supreme power and denial of the form of government established by the fundamental laws." He was acquitted, thanks mainly to the defense of his counsel, O. O. Gruzenberg who, notwithstanding the circumstantial evidence which grew up in support of the legend, expressed most effectively the reason for the legend:

Emperor Alexander I, Alexander the Blessed, the absolute monarch, the spoilt child of fate, the saviour of Europe . . . and alongside him and he himself in him . . . the wanderer Fedor Kuzmich, thrashed with rods for vagrancy . . . The great, essentially Russian legend—the legend which both the highest and the very lowest of Russia alike fondly believed . . . for many decades soldiers and artisans and simple peasants have revered and cherished it. The people wanted to believe and passionately believed that in this one person were combined the most powerful of the Tsars and the most deprived of his humblest subjects. For the intelligentsia and for the highest circles Fedor Kuzmich embodied the idea of expiation by the sovereign of the great sin which may not be forgiven to anyone, the sin of murder or participation in murder. And this legend of humility, of expiation, is so close, so natural to the sensitive Russian soul! . . ."

See L. Lyubimov "The Secret of the Elder Fedor Kuzmich" in *Voprosy Istorii* No. I January 1966 209–15

Notes to Chapter XVI:

1. Warren B. Walsh *Editor Readings in Russian History* 3rd edition (Syracuse 1959) 257–61

2. Constantin de Grunwald *Tsar Nicholas I* translated from the French (London 1954) 4
   N. A. Bestuzhev *Vospominaniya* (Moscow 1919)

3. de Grunwald *op. cit.* 5

4. *Ib*

5. *Ib* 7

6. David M. Lang *The Decembrist Conspiracy through British Eyes* in *The American Slavic and East European Review* Vol VIII No. 4

7. de Grunwald *op. cit.* 18

8. Empress Elizabeth had abolished the death penalty by an ukaz, proclaimed on September 30, 1754, and Catherine II had confirmed the ukaz. Elizabeth's ukaz was always interpreted as not applying to state crimes. Herzen commented that "the Russian people had become unaccustomed to the death penalty . . . men had died under the knout, soldiers had run the gauntlet (contrary to the law) until they fell dead, but the death penalty *de jure* did not exist." Alexander Herzen *My Past and Thoughts*, translated by Constance Garnet, revised by Humphrey Higgens (London 1968) I, 50, 123
   Nicholas reintroduced the death penalty into the Russian criminal code. The impact of the execution of the Decembrists was increased when the way they had died was known. On the morning of July 25, 1825, all of those who had been found guilty were assembled on the parade ground of the St. Peter and St. Paul Fortress. There, kneeling, one by one each man heard his sentence read aloud; his epaulettes were then torn off and the executioner broke his sword over his head; he was then clad in a penitential shirt, before being led off to serve his sentence. Still wearing plumed helmets and high boots, some burst out laughing.
   Finally only five men remained on the parade ground, standing before the five gibbets. An executioner had been brought from Sweden. But at the moment of execution three of the ropes broke and the unfortunate victims fell to the ground. The operation had to be carried out again. "Unhappy country, where they don't even know how to hang you!" was Ryleev's last comment.
   de Grunwald *op. cit.* 68–69

9. *Ib*

10. A. Herzen *op. cit.* I, 50, 123

11. *Letters of Queen Victoria* (London 1907)

13. Notwithstanding his adoration of his wife, Nicholas had mistresses, foremost among whom was Barbara Nelidova, a lady in waiting to his wife. This affair lasted for many years, and a number of children were born of their union. When Nicholas was dying Barabara Nelidova came to the court and the Empress asked him if she could take her leave of him. "No, my dear," he replied, "I must not see her again; you will say that

I beg her to pardon me, that I have prayed for her and hope that she will pray for me." Barbara Nelidova was respected and it was said that she never tried to exploit her influence on Nicholas for personal ends or to interfere in political matters. After his death she continued to reside in the imperial palace at the request of Alexander II and of Alexandra Feodorovna, Nicholas's widow; indeed, she became a member of her intimate circle. de Grunwald *op. cit.* 285; Florinsky *op. cit.* II, 756

14. de Grunwald *op. cit.* 79
15. *Ib* 81
16. *Ib* 82
17. Florinsky *op. cit.* II, 772
18. *Ib* 755
19. *Ib* 797
20. *Ib* 800
21. A. Herzen *op. cit.* I, 139; Florinsky *op. cit.* II, 807
22. In 1847 after the death of his father, Herzen decided to emigrate "to be and do something in the world". In Paris he joined with the extreme left wing of the revolutionary socialists. The Russian government, learning of his activities, ordered him to return to Russia. He refused and resigned himself to living abroad all his life. He became a Swiss citizen and then settled in London. Here he began editing and publishing *Kolokol* (*The Bell*) which was immensely successful and the most outstanding of all Russian periodicals published abroad.
23. Florinsky *op. cit.* II, 810
24. *Ib* 814
25. de Grunwald *op. cit.* 840
26. Florinsky *op. cit.* II, 840
27. Nicholas's austere personal habits caused surprise at Windsor Castle, especially when fresh straw had to be collected daily to stuff the mattress of his camp stretcher. de Grunwald *op. cit.* 197
28. *Ib* 198
29. *Ib* 199
30. Florinsky *op. cit.* II, 851
31. de Grunwald *op. cit.* 273
32. *Ib* 285–86
33. Depressed by the collapse of his policies and the failures in the Crimean War, Nicholas became more and more morose. Rumors began to spread even before he had actually died that his death was not due to illness, but to suicide by poisoning. The fact that Nicholas had forbidden the publication of the usual health bulletins during his last illness added to the general belief that Dr. Mandt, his personal physician, had helped him to suicide by poison. The theory is certainly plausible. Nicholas was broken in heart and spirit and may have been tempted to take his own life. Evidence in support of this theory is, however, completely lacking.

Notes to Chapter XVII:

1. Sidney Harcave *Russia: A History*, 5th edition (Philadelphia 1964) 278
2. Vasily Zhukovsky as a poet led the Russian Romantic School, but he deserves special mention as a sensitive translator of English and German verse. The publication of his translation of Gray's *Elegy in a Country Churchyard* in 1802, which is in no way inferior to the original, is sometimes called the dawn of modern Russian poetry.
3. A. G. Mazour *The Rise and Fall of the Romanovs* (New York 1960) 102
4. Alexander Herzen *op. cit.* I, 281
5. W. E. Mosse *Alexander II and the Modernization of Russia* (London 1958) 34
6. *Ib* 37
7. Florinsky II, 883
8. Mosse *op. cit.* 53
9. *Ib* 66
10. *Ib* 77
11. *Ib* 87
12. D. Mackenzie Wallace spent the years 1870 to 1875 in Russia, studying the life and institutions. He was a patient, perceptive and sympathetic observer whose two volumes, entitled *Russia*, published soon after his return to England, contain remarkable descriptions of the lives of the peasantry, the commune, the legal system, and other aspects of Russian life in the reign of Alexander II.
13. Mosse *op. cit.* 98
14. *Ib* 102
15. Florinsky II, 789
16. *Ib* 949
17. B. H. Sumner *Russia and the Balkans* (Oxford 1937) 48
18. Mosse *op. cit.* 133
19. *Ib* 122
20. W. E. Mosse records that "To the Finns, his assassination in 1881 was an occasion of sincere regret and grief. To this day, while other relics of Russian rule have long since vanished from Finland, the statue of the 'Tsar-Liberator' dominates the Senate Square in the heart of official Helsinki". *Op. cit.* 123
21. *Ib* 138
22. Sergei Nechaev accepted no limits to the fanatical dedication to the cause. When he doubted the complete obedience of his fellow student and comrade, Ivan Ivanov, he judged and executed him with his own hands. Dostoevsky in *The Possessed* (*Besy*) has described this world of revolutionary activity vividly, including in one of the leading characters, Peter Verhovensky, a nihilist, a portrait recalling Nechaev.
23. General Trepov had visited the prison where accused populists were being held for a mass trial. One young prisoner angered him and he

ordered him to be flogged. The flogging was so savage that the young man went mad and some years later died as a result. The cruelty and injustice of the flogging incensed revolutionaries and several planned revenge. Vera Zasulich went with a crowd of petitioners before the governor, and when her turn came to speak she drew a revolver and fired point blank.

Vera Zasulich had been a revolutionary since the age of seventeen and had experienced both imprisonment and exile. Her trial and acquittal sent a current of excitement throughout Europe, and she became a heroine both there and in Russia.

Notes to Chapter XVIII:

1. Florinsky II, 1088
2. Harcave *op. cit.* 310
3. Florinsky II, 1111–12
4. *Ib* 1114
5. Harcave *op. cit.* 316

Notes to Chapter XIX:

1. Florinsky II, 1142
2. Bernard Pares *The Fall of the Russian Monarchy* (London 1939) 33
3. Robert K. Massie *Nicholas and Alexandra* (London 1968) 41
4. *Ib* 47
5. Sidney Harcave *Russia: A History* (Philadelphia 1964) 5th edition. 309
6. F. A. Golder *Documents of Russian History 1914–17* (New York 1927) 29–37
7. Twelve years later a simple soldier, serving as one of the guards of the ex-Tsar, remarked how the popular idea of Nicholas as a terrible tyrant had vanished from his mind on personal contact with him. "His eyes were good and kind . . . the impression he made on me was of a man who was kind, simple, frank, and ready to talk." Bernard Pares *op. cit.* 495
   It was part of Nicholas's personal tragedy that he made no contact with or impact on his people. He was a little man, lost in the immensity of his realm and unknown to his people. By contrast, his father, Alexander III, who possessed nothing of his goodness, was a big man and a strong and confident Autocrat, who made an impact on his subjects.
8. Bernard Pares *op. cit.* 80
9. Bernard Pares *History of Russia* (London 1947) 488–89
10. Hemophilia was introduced by Alexandria into the Romanov family; she was a carrier of the affliction through her grandmother, Queen Victoria. Dr. Victor A. McKusick, Professor of Medicine, Johns Hopkins University, considered that the mutation in the X-chromosome occurred in Edward, Duke of Kent, father of Queen Victoria, who be-

came the first to transmit the mutation. Victoria's third child, Alice, married Louis IV, Grand Duke of Hesse. Of her seven children, three—two daughters and a son—received the mutant gene. The son died early from hemophilic hemorrhage. The elder daughter bore three sons of whom two were hemophilic; Alexandra, the younger daughter, had four daughters and the Tsarevich, who was hemophilic.
Victor A. McKusick *Human Genetics* (New Jersey 1964) 39–40. See also Robert K. Massie *op. cit.* 139–44

11. Bernard Pares *The Fall of the Russian Monarchy* (London 1939) 137
12. *Ib* 97
13. *Ib* 207
14. *Ib* 228
15. Robert K. Massie *op. cit.* 218
16. *Ib* 219
17. A. Kerensky *The Crucifixion of Liberty* (London 1934) 169
18. Anna Vyrubova *Memories of the Russian Court* (London 1923) 104
19. Bernard Pares *op. cit.* 190
20. *Ib* 201
21. *Ib* 207
22. *Ib* 251; see also *Imperatritsa Aleksandra Fedorovna, Pisma Imperatoru Nikolayu* II (Berlin 1922) I, 117–19, 133–41, and *passim*
23. Bernard Pares *op. cit.* 250
24. Anna Vyrubova *op. cit.* 186
25. Buchanan had cabled the foreign office in London for permission to speak openly to the Emperor either on behalf of the British government or in a personal capacity. In due course he was authorized to give a personal warning. The audience took place at Tsarskoe Selo on January 12, 1917. Buchanan said: "Your Majesty, if I may be permitted to say so, has but one safe course open to you—namely, to break down the barrier that separates you from your people and to regain their confidence."
Drawing himself up and looking hard at Buchanan, the Emperor said: "Do you mean that I am to regain the confidence of my people or that they are to regain my confidence?"
"Both, sir," Buchanan replied, "for without such mutual confidence, Russia will never win this war . . ."
Buchanan also referred to the fact that the Empress was discredited and believed to be using her influence in the interests of Germany, and that Protopopov was bringing Russia "to the verge of ruin. So long as he remains Minister of the Interior, there cannot be that collaboration between the Government and the Duma which is an essential condition of victory."
G. Buchanan *My Mission to Russia* (London 1923) 42–49
26. M. V. Rodzyanko *The Reign of Rasputin* (London 1927) 252–54
27. W. H. Chamberlan *The Russian Revolution 1917–1921*
28. *Ib* 78
29. *Ib* 91
30. *The Murder of Nicholas and his family*
Nicholas was not destined to enjoy the companionship of his wife and

children for long. They were held under arrest in Tsarskoe Selo until the summer when the possibility of a German advance on Petrograd and the menacing attitude of the extreme revolutionaries at Kronstadt made it necessary to move them. They were taken to Tobolsk in Siberia and in the spring of 1918 they were moved to Ekaterinburg, where they were lodged in the house of a merchant named Ipatyev, which was now ominously named the House of Special Purpose.

Until the Bolshevik Revolution they were treated with a certain courtesy and consideration, although kept under close guard. But in Ekaterinburg they were handled with crude hostility. Their new guards took pleasure in humiliating not only Nicholas and Alexandra but also the children. Their daughters were made to sleep on the floor and they were denied every privacy, even when going to the lavatory. Nicholas and each member of the family endured the hardships and humiliations with saintly patience. All were devout and in their faith they found courage. Alexandra was as always completely devoted to Nicholas, having accepted his abdication in a spirit of quiet resignation without recrimination. They were comforted, too, by Dr. Botkin, the Tsar's personal physician, by Trupp, the valet, Kharitonov, the cook and Demidova, the maid, all of whom had refused to be parted from the family. Meanwhile their fate was being decided. The Ural Soviet had decided unanimously soon after their arrival in Ekaterinburg, that they must be executed. Unwilling to take the responsibility wholly upon themselves, the Soviet sent a representative, Goloshchekin, to Moscow to obtain the ruling of the central government. Yakov Sverdlov, chairman of the All-Russian Central Executive Committee and Lenin's closest comrade at this time, gave Goloshchekin his instructions. On July 12, Goloshchekin returned to Ekaterinburg, which had been outflanked by White troops and by detachments of the Czech brigade who in fact captured the town on July 25. Nicholas had indeed received two messages that friends expected to rescue them all. But the threat to Ekaterinburg made the Ural Soviet hasten the execution.

Yuvorsky, the leader of the local Bolshevik guard, made careful plans to keep the decision secret from the family. On the night of July 16 they all went to bed at 10:30 P.M. as usual. Near midnight he told them that they must dress quickly and go downstairs as the Czechs and the White army were approaching.

Nicholas went down first, carrying his sick son in his arms. The others followed with Anastasia carrying their spaniel, Jimmy. Yuvorsky led them down to a semi-basement room with heavy bars on the window. Here he told them to wait. Yuvorsky went out and returned with his Cheka guard, all carrying revolvers. He announced that they had been condemned to death and at once shot Nicholas through the head. The guards then began shooting down the rest of the family and servants. Alexandra had time only to make the sign of the cross before she died. The girls, Olga, Tatiana, and Marie all died quickly as did Dr. Botkin, Trupp, and Kharitonov. The maid, Demidova, was missed by the shots.

The guards pursued her with bayonets. She tried to parry them with a cushion, but she had been pierced more than thirty times when she fell dead. It was then discovered that the boy, Alexei, was still alive in his father's arms, for he moaned and tried to clutch his coat. Yuvorsky fired two shots into his head. The dog too was killed, its head crushed by a rifle butt. Anastasia who had only fainted regained consciousness at this point and screamed, and she was promptly killed with bayonets and blows with the butts of rifles.

The bodies were wrapped in sheets and taken by lorry to an abandoned mine near the village of Koptyaki. There the bodies were cut into pieces with saws and axes and so far as possible destroyed with acids and fire, and the remains thrown down the mine shaft.

N. A. Sokolov *Ubiistvo Tsarskoi Semi* (Berlin 1925); P. M. Bykov, *The Last Days of the Tsardom* (London 1937); Paul Bulygin *The Murder of the Romanovs* (London 1935); Pierre Gilliart *Thirteen Years at the Russian Court: Last Years* (London 1921)

31. Grand Duke Mikhail and most of the members of the Duma committee met a few days later in his house on the Millionnaya in Petrograd. Milyukov begged him to accept the throne. Kerensky made an impassioned appeal to him to reject the throne.

Rodzyanko and Lvov, although both strong monarchists, recognized that already the Russian monarchy belonged to the past. Finally Mikhail announced that he would not accept the throne unless requested to do so by the constituent assembly when elected. The second deed of abdication was then typed and signed. F. A. Golder *op. cit.* 298–99; Bernard Pares *op. cit.* 469–70

Grand Duke Mikhail was killed by the Bolsheviks in Perm on July 10, 1918, six days before his elder brother, the ex-Tsar.

Bibliography

The following are the main primary and secondary sources on which I have relied. Specific references to these and other works will be found in the notes to each chapter.

An asterisk indicates that the work is available only in Russian.

ALEKSEEV, E. N. *Alexander I: His Personality and Government.* London 1908
——*Scenes of Russian Court Life,* London 1917

ALLEN, W. E. D. *The Ukraine: A History.* Cambridge 1940

*ANDREEV, A. N. [editor] *Peter I: A symposium.* Leningrad 1947

AVVAKUM, *The Life of Archpriest Avvakum* Translated by Jane Harrison and Hope Mirrlees. London 1924

BAIN, NISBET R. *The First Romanovs 1613–1725.* London 1905
——*Peter the Great and His Pupils.* London 1897
——*Daughter of Peter the Great.* London 1899
——*Charles XII and the Great Northern War* in "The Cambridge Modern History" Vol. V. Cambridge 1907
——*Slavonic Europe.* Cambridge 1908

BELL, J. *Travels from St. Petersburg in Russia to Diverse Parts of Asia.* Glasgow 1763

*BILBASOV, V. A. *History of Catherine the Second.* Berlin 1900
——*Diderot in St. Petersburg.* St. Petersburg 1884

BLUM, JEROME, *Lord and Peasant in Russia from the Ninth to the Nineteenth Century.* New York 1964

*BOGOSLOVSKY, M. M. *Peter the First: Materials for a Biography* 5 volumes. Leningrad 1940–48
——*Peter the Great and his Reform.* Moscow 1920

BULYGIN, PAUL, *The Murder of the Romanovs: the Authentic Account*. London 1935

CASTERA, J. H. *Life of Catherine II* Translated and enlarged by W. Tooke. 4th edition. London 1800

CATHERINE II, the Works of Empress, Edited by A. N. Pypin. St. Petersburg 1901–7
——*Memoirs* Edited by Dominique Maroger. Translated by Moura Budberg. London 1955

CHANCE, J. F. *George I and the Northern War*. London 1909

CHARQUES, RICHARD, *The Twilight of Imperial Russia*. London 1958

CHOISEUL-GOUFFIER, COMTESSE DE, *Historical Memoirs of the Emperor Alexander I and the Court of Russia* Translated from the French. London 1904

COLLINS, SAMUEL, *The Present State of Russia*. London 1671

COXE, W. *Travels into Poland, Russia, Sweden, and Denmark* 3rd edition. London 1797

DASHKOVA, PRINCESS E. R. *Memoirs* Translated and edited by Kyril Fitzlyon. London 1958

FEDOTOV, G. P. *The Russian Religious Mind*. Cambridge (Mass.) 1947

FLORINSKY, M. T. *Russia: A History and an Interpretation* New York 1947
——*The End of the Russian Empire*. New York 1961

GERHARDI, WILLIAM, *The Romanovs: Evocation of the Past as a Mirror of the Present*. London 1940

*GERSHENZON, M. O. [Editor] *The Epoch of Nicholas I*. Moscow 1910

*GOLIKOV, I. I. *The Works of Peter the Great*. Moscow 1788–97

GOOCH, G. P. *Catherine the Great and other Studies*. London 1954

GORDON, ALEXANDER, *History of Peter the Great, Emperor of Russia*. London 1755

GORDON, GENERAL PATRICK, *Passages from the Diary of*. Aberdeen 1859

GREY, IAN, *Peter the Great*. New York 1960
——*Catherine the Great*. New York 1962
——*Ivan the Terrible*. New York 1964
——*The First Fifty Years: Soviet Russia 1917–1967*. New York 1967

GRUNWALD, CONSTANTIN DE, *Tsar Nicholas I* Translated from the French. London 1954

HERZEN, A. I. *My Past and Thoughts: The Memoirs of Alexander Herzen*.

Translated by Constance Garnett. Revised by Humphrey Higgens. London 1968

HYDE, H. MONTGOMERY, *The Empress Catherine and Princess Dashkov.* London 1935

*KAFENGAUS, B. B. *The Foreign Policy of Russia in the Reign of Peter I.* Moscow 1942

*KARAMZIN, N. M. *History of the Russian State* 5th. edition. St. Petersburg 1842–43

KEEP, J. H. L. *The Regime of Filaret 1619–33* in the *Slavonic and East European Review* Vol. 38, 1960

KLYUCHEVSKY, V. O. *A Course of Russian History.* Soviet edition. Moscow 1956–59

*KNYAZKOV, S. *Sketches from the History of Peter the Great and his Time.* Moscow 1709

KORB, J. G. *Diary of an Austrian Secretary of Legation at the Court of Tsar Peter the Great.* Translated from the Latin. London 1863

*KORNILOV, A. *A Course of the History of Russia in the 19th Century.* Moscow 1918

*KOTOSHIKHIN, G. *On Russia in the Reign of Alexei Mikhailovich,* St. Petersburg 1840

KROPOTKIN, PETER, *Memoirs of a Revolutionist.* London 1899

LANG, D. M. *The First Russian Radical: Alexander Radishchev 1749–1802.* London 1959

LODGE, R. *The Extinction of Poland 1788–97* in "The Cambridge Modern History" Vol. VIII. Cambridge 1934

LOEWENSON, L. *The Moscow Rising of 1648* in the "Slavonic and East European Review." Vol. 27, 1948

MACKENZIE, WALLACE D. *Russia* 3rd. edition. London 1877

MANSTEIN, BARON DE, *Memoirs of Russia from the year 1727 to the year 1744* 2nd edition. London 1773

MARSDEN, CHRISTOPHER, *Palmyra of the North: The First Days of St. Petersburg.* London 1942

MASSIE, ROBERT K. *Nicholas and Alexandra.* London 1968

MASSON, C. F. *Secret Memoirs of the Court of St. Petersburg.* Translated from the French. London 1801–2

MAZOUR, A. G. *The First Russian Revolution, 1825: The Decembrist Movement.* Berkeley 1937

——*Rise and Fall of the Romanovs.* New York 1960
——*Russia: Tsarist and Communist.* Princeton 1962

MONAS, S. *The Third Section: Police and Society in Russia under Nicholas I.* Cambridge, Mass. 1961

MOSSE, W. E. *Alexander II and the Modernization of Russia.* London 1958

MOTTLEY, J. *The History of the Life of Peter I, Emperor of Russia.* London 1739

NICHOLAS, GRAND DUKE, [Editor] *Scenes of Russian Court Life: Being the Correspondence of Alexander I with his Sister Catherine.* Translated from the Russian. London 1917

NICHOLAS II, EMPEROR. *Journal intime de, 1890–1917* Translated into French. Paris 1925
——*Letters of the Tsar to the Tsaritsa 1914–17* Translated from the Russian. London 1929
——*Letters of Tsar Nicholas and Empress Marie* [Edited by E. J. Bing]. London 1937

*NIKIFOROV, L. A. *Russian-English Relations in the Reign of Peter I.* Moscow 1950

O'BRIEN, C. B. *Russia under two Tsars 1682–89: The Regency of Sophia Alexeevna.* Berkeley 1952

OLEARIUS, ADAM, *The Voyages and Travels of the Ambassadors sent by Frederick, Duke of Holstein to the Great Duke of Muscovy* . . . Translated from the Latin. London 1662

OLIVIER, DARIA, *The Burning of Moscow 1812.* London 1966.

PALÉOLOGUE, MAURICE, *The Enigmatic Tsar: Alexander I of Russia.* Translated from the French. London 1938
——*L'Empereur Alexander II et la Princesse Yurievskaya.* Paris 1922

PARES, B. *A History of Russia* Revised Edition. London 1955
——*The Fall of the Russian Monarchy.* London 1939

*PEKARSKY, P. *Science and Literature in Russia in the Reign of Peter the Great.* St. Petersburg 1862

PERRY, JOHN, *The State of Russia under the Present Tsar.* London 1716

*PETER THE GREAT, EMPEROR, *Letters and Papers of.* St. Petersburg-Leningrad 1887–1964. Cited as P & B in the notes to Chapter VI

*PLATONOV, S. F. *Peter the Great.* Leningrad 1926

POTEMKIN, PRINCE G. A. *Memoirs* Translated from the German, 2nd edition. London 1813

RADISHCHEV, A. N. *A Journey from St. Petersburg to Moscow* Edited by N. P. Silvansky. St. Petersburg 1905

REDDAWAY, W. F. [Editor] *Documents of Catherine the Great*. Cambridge 1931

RIASANOVSKY, N. V. *Nicholas I and Official Nationality in Russia 1825–55*. Berkeley 1959
——*A History of Russia*. New York 1963

ROBINSON, G. T. *Rural Russia under the old Regime*. New York 1949

SCHAKOVSKOY, ZINAIDA *Precursors of Peter the Great* Translated from the French. London 1964

SETON-WATSON, H. *The Decline of Imperial Russia 1855–1914*. London 1952
——*The Russian Empire 1801–1917*. Oxford 1967

*SHILDER, N. K. *Emperor Paul I*. St. Petersburg 1901
——*Emperor Alexander I: His life and reign*. St. Petersburg 1904–5
——*Emperor Nicholas I: His life and reign*. St. Petersburg 1903
*SHUMIGORSKY, E. S. *Emperor Paul: His life and reign*. St. Petersburg 1907

SCHUYLER, EUGENE *Peter the Great*. London 1884

SÉGUR, COMITE DE, *Mémoires*. Paris 1826

SOLOVEYTCHIK, G. *Potemkin: A picture of Catherine's Russia*. London 1938

*SOLOVYEV, S. M. *History of Russia from the Earliest Times*. [Soviet Edition] Moscow 1959–66

STANLEY, A. P. *Lectures on the History of the Eastern Church*. London 1861

SUMNER, B. H. *Survey of Russian History*. London 1944
——*Peter the Great and the Ottoman Empire*. Oxford 1949
——*Peter the Great and the Emergence of Russia*. London 1950

*TARLE, E. V. *The Russian Navy and the Foreign Policy of Peter I*. Moscow 1949

*TATISHCHEV, S. S. *Emperor Alexander II: his life and Reign*. St. Petersburg 1903
——*Emperor Nicholas I and the foreign courts*. St. Petersburg 1899

TOOKE, W. *View of the Russian Empire during the reign of Catherine II*. Dublin 1801

TOURNEUX, M. *Diderot et Catherine II*. Paris 1899

*USTRYALOV, N. *History of the Reign of Peter the Great*. St. Petersburg 1858

*VASENKO, P. G. AND OTHERS *The Beginning of the Romanov Dynasty*. St. Petersburg 1912

*Vorontsov, Prince M. L. *Archives*. Moscow 1870–95

Waliszewski, K. *La Dernière des Romanov: Elizabeth I-re Impératrice de Russie*. Paris 1902
——*La Russie du temps d'Elizabeth I-re, dernière des Romanov*. Paris 1933
——*Paul the First of Russia: Son of Catherine the Great*. Translated from the French London 1913
——*La Règne d'Alexandre I-er*. Paris 1923–25
——*Le Berceau d'une dynastie; Les premiers Romanov*. Paris 1909
——*Pierre le Grand: L'éducation, L'homme, L'oeuvre*. Paris 1914
——*L'Héritage de Pierre le Grand: Règne des femmes, gouvernement des favoris 1725–41*. Paris 1900

*Zabelin, I. E. *History of the City of Moscow*. Moscow 1905
——*The Domestic Life of the Russian Tsars and Tsaritsas*. Moscow 1862–69

*Zaozersky, A. I. *Tsar Alexei Mikhailovich in his reign*. Petrograd 1917

*Zaozerskaya, E. I. *Manufacture in the Reign of Peter I*. Moscow 1947

Zernov, N. *The Russians and their Church*. London 1945

*Zhitkov, K. G. *History of the Russian Navy: Petrine Period 1762–1725*. St. Petersburg 1912

Index